The New Politics of Nort

❖ The New Politics of North Carolina

edited by Christopher A. Cooper & H. Gibbs Knotts

THE UNIVERSITY OF NORTH CAROLINA PRESS ❖ CHAPEL HILL

Manufactured in the United States of America

Designed by Heidi Perov

Set in Minion and TheSans

The paper in this book meets the guidelines for
permanence and durability of the Committee on
Production Guidelines for Book Longevity of the
Council on Library Resources.

Library of Congress Cataloging-in-Publication Data

The new politics of North Carolina / edited by
Christopher A. Cooper and H. Gibbs Knotts.

   p. cm.

   Includes bibliographical references and index.

ISBN 978-0-8078-3191-5 (cloth: alk. paper)
ISBN 978-0-8078-5876-9 (pbk.: alk. paper)

1. North Carolina—Politics and government—1951–

I. Cooper, Christopher Alan, 1975–

II. Knotts, H. Gibbs.

JK4116.N49 2008

320.9756—dc22   2007047099

*Title page illustration: Senate Chamber, North
Carolina State Capitol. Photo by Tim Buchman.*

cloth   12 11 10 09 08   5 4 3 2 1
paper   12 11 10 09 08   5 4 3 2 1

❖ Contents

Part IV. Public Policy

❖ Tables and Figures

Tables

Figures

❖ Preface

The creation of this book was motivated by an interest in state politics. As political junkies, we find states to be full of interesting politics and compelling characters. As political scientists, we are increasingly convinced that the study of state politics is the best way to answer enduring questions about institutional design and democratic processes. As Tar Heel State residents, we firmly believe that North Carolina offers fertile ground for understanding politics and society in the New South.

This book brings together leading thinkers to explain recent developments in North Carolina politics and state politics more generally. This approach provides multiple perspectives in the same volume, giving readers a rich and diverse understanding of the Tar Heel State. We asked all of our authors to place North Carolina in the context of other states to determine where it fits and how its institutions and culture shape political outcomes.

Of course, this book would not have been possible without the hard work of our contributors. We also thank our colleagues at Western Carolina University, including Claudia Bryant, Todd Collins, Scott Higgins, Don Livingston, Alex Macauley, Elizabeth McRae, Gordon Mercer, Niall Michelsen, and Richard Starnes. We also thank Alan Abramowitz, Jay Barth, Merle Black, Ferrel Guillory, Moshe Haspel, Martin Johnson, Tony Nownes, John Shelton Reed, and Lilliard Richardson for helpful discussions about politics, political science, and the South. Emily Cooper, Jennifer Cooper, Wiley Cooper, Lynn Kaufman, Heyward Knotts, Robert Knotts, Stacy Knotts, Michel Kozuch, and Karen Nicholson all gave helpful comments on drafts of selected chapters. In addition, Jason Coggins and Jill Ingram provided excellent research assistance. Our reviewers, Thad Beyle and Bill Moore, gave important feedback on the entire manuscript. The staff at the University of North Carolina Press, particularly Ellen Goldlust-Gingrich, Chuck Grench, Katy O'Brien, and Paula Wald, have been extremely helpful and supportive throughout this process. Of course our greatest debts are to our families: Emily Cooper, Jennifer Cooper, Peter Cooper, Wiley Cooper, Chesnee Knotts, Craig Knotts, Heyward Knotts, Robert Knotts, Stacy Knotts, Whitney Knotts, Alan Nix, Karen Nix, Al Smuzynski, and Pam Smuzynski.

The New Politics of North Carolina

❖ Introduction

Traditionalism and Progressivism in North Carolina

CHRISTOPHER A. COOPER AND H. GIBBS KNOTTS

Political observers treat North Carolina more favorably than other states in the American South. In his classic work on southern politics, V. O. Key Jr. labeled North Carolina a progressive plutocracy, praising the state's "progressive outlook and action in many phases of life" (1984, 205). Although Key recognized the power of North Carolina's business and financial elite, he described the state as "far more presentable than its southern neighbors" (1984, 205). More recently, Jack D. Fleer (1994, 1) wrote that North Carolina's citizens "demonstrated a progressive spirit as leaders of the region," and Paul Luebke (1998, 23) highlighted the strength of the "modernizer" philosophy in the major cities of the North Carolina Piedmont.

Considerable evidence supports the progressive view of North Carolina politics. North Carolinians elected several progressive governors, most notably Charles Aycock (1901–5), Terry Sanford (1961–65), and Jim Hunt (1977–85, 1993–2001). These governors were known for their enlightened policies, particularly when compared to leaders of other states in the region. For example, Sanford gained a reputation as the education governor during the same time George Wallace stood at the schoolhouse door denying African Americans entry to the University of Alabama. Similarly, Hunt's time in the governor's mansion "supplied voters' cravings for a competent, largely scandal free state government that has helped keep North Carolina in the forefront of Sunbelt growth" (Christensen and Fleer 1999, 82).

North Carolina is also known for its political competitiveness (Christensen and Fleer 1999; Prysby 2003). In contrast to many other southern states, two-party competition has long flourished in North Carolina (Key 1949). North Carolinians elected a Republican governor, James Holshouser (1973–77), before many other southern states supported state-level GOP candidates. During a period of racial demagoguery, North Carolina voters were also less willing to support racially charged presidential campaigns. When other southern states backed the presidential candidacies of Barry Goldwater in 1964 and George Wallace in 1968, North Carolinians supported Lyndon Johnson and Richard Nixon.

Does North Carolina deserve this progressive reputation? Although the state's residents have elected many progressive politicians, Tar Heel voters have also supported traditionalists such as Sam Ervin, Everett Jordan, and Jesse Helms. Helms, "the unreconstructed foe of civil rights and the chief tormentor of Tar Heel liberals" (Christensen and Fleer 1999, 81), employed racially charged tactics in his re-election bids, tactics that should have backfired in a progressive state. Moreover, white males have always dominated statewide political offices, and despite a few exceptions, Tar Heel voters have most often supported national candidates with traditional rather than progressive policy positions. There are also reasons to question the true beneficiaries of the state's progressive economic policies (Key 1949; Luebke 1998).

The most notable challenge to North Carolina's progressive reputation was levied by Jack Bass and Walter DeVries (1995 [1976], 218), who referred to the "progressive myth" of North Carolina. After analyzing a host of factors, the authors noted that "migrants to the state who are familiar with the progressive reputation tend to be struck by the reality they find" and that "in terms of social and economic development, North Carolina—like Alabama under George Wallace—has not kept pace with the rest of the South" (1995 [1976], 218, 247). Questions about North Carolina's progressive spirit were perhaps most succinctly stated by veteran journalist Ferrel Guillory, who quipped that "the farther you get from North Carolina, the more progressive it looks" (Bass and DeVries 1995 [1976], 218–19).

The New Politics of North Carolina revisits this progressive legacy through a systematic analysis of North Carolina's citizens and context, governmental institutions, linkage institutions, and public policies. This introduction begins by making the case for the importance of state politics and the value of the comparative method. Following this section, the introduction utilizes the comparative method to examine basic demographic and political characteristics in the North Carolina. Next, the introduction revisits North Carolina's progressive reputation by updating Key's measures and comparing North Carolina to its southern neighbors. The introduction concludes with a brief overview of the remainder of the book.

❖ The Importance of State Politics and the Comparative Method

Some readers may question the utility of examining the politics of the American states. After all, the federal government garners more headlines in America's newspapers and greater saliency in most people's minds. Despite this lack of attention, states have become increasingly important in American politics. Beginning with Nixon's "new federalism," political power has shifted from the national to the state level. Issues of national importance such as gay marriage, abortion rights, and tax policies are settled in statehouses and state courts across the county. Many citizens see Washington as mired in gridlock and polarization and consequently believe that states are well equipped to help solve problems. Moreover, survey data reveal that citizens trust and place more faith in state and local governments than in government in Washington (Hetherington 2005).

In addition to these substantive reasons, there are also theoretical reasons for studying state politics. Political scientists are primarily interested in explaining variation—why some legislators engage in more casework than others, why some executives are more popular than others, why some citizens turn out to vote year after year while others abstain. Studying states provides political scientists with tremendous variation in political structures and outcomes. For this reason, political scientist Christopher Z. Mooney (2001, 1) recently remarked that "the American states provide, arguably, the world's most advantageous venue in which to test general propositions about political behavior and policymaking."

For example, a legislative specialist who wants to explain why some legislators perform more casework than others could study the U.S. Congress and estimate the effects of individual-level factors such as partisanship, time in office, and the gender of the legislator. However, the same legislative scholar will not be able to determine how institutional factors such as district structure, term limits, or district size affect casework because the federal government has only one legislative institution. By studying states, the same scholar could see whether legislative bodies with different structures and institutional arrangements produce different political outcomes. For these reasons, the study of state politics has been transformed from a "neglected world" (Jewell 1982) to a burgeoning field within political science (Morehouse and Jewell 2004).

This volume evaluates the new politics of North Carolina in the context of other states, frequently relying on the literature on comparative state politics. Although we often compare North Carolina to the forty-nine other states in the union, some questions lend themselves to comparison with the eleven states of the American South (Alabama, Arkansas, Florida, Georgia, Louisiana, Mississippi, North Carolina, South Carolina, Tennessee, Texas, and Virginia). At times, we also make comparisons between North Carolina and the peripheral South (Arkansas, Florida, North Carolina, Tennessee, Texas, and Virginia) as well as the Deep South (Alabama, Georgia, Louisiana, Mississippi, and South Carolina). By looking at North Carolina in comparison to other states, we will learn more about the politics and government of the North Carolina as well as gain a greater understanding of state politics more generally.

❖ North Carolina in Comparative Perspective

How does North Carolina compare demographically and politically to other U.S. states as well as other states in the American South? North Carolina is the nation's

TABLE I.1. Comparing Basic Demographics in the South, 2000–2005

State	Total Population (2005)	% Population Change (1990–2000)	% Born in State of Current Residence (2000)	% Black Population (2004)
Alabama	4,557,808	10.1	73.4	26.4
Arkansas	2,779,154	13.7	63.9	15.8
Florida	17,789,864	23.5	32.7	15.7
Georgia	9,072,576	26.4	57.8	29.6
Louisiana	4,523,628	5.9	79.4	33.0
Mississippi	2,921,088	10.5	74.3	36.8
North Carolina	8,683,242	21.4	63.0	21.8
South Carolina	4,255,083	15.1	64.0	29.4
Tennessee	5,962,959	16.7	64.7	16.8
Texas	22,859,968	22.8	62.2	11.7
Virginia	7,567,465	14.4	51.9	19.9
United States	296,410,404	13.1	60.0	12.8

Source: U.S. Census Bureau (2000, 2003, 2004a, 2005).

eleventh-most-populous state, with 8.6 million residents (see table I.1). Among southern states, North Carolina ranks fourth behind Texas, Florida, and Georgia in total population. The Tar Heel State is also a national leader in population change, growing by 21 percent between 1990 and 2000, considerably higher than the national growth rate, 13 percent. Within the South, North Carolina trailed only Georgia and the megastates of Florida and Texas in population growth. Finally, many of the state's residents were not born in North Carolina. Within the South, North Carolina has the fifth-fewest percentage of people born in their current state of residence, surpassing only Florida, Virginia, Georgia, and Texas in the percentage of nonnative citizens.

While North Carolina has never been a haven for ethnic diversity, it does have a sizable African American population. The state's black population is almost 22 percent, compared to 13 percent nationally. In the South, North Carolina ranks sixth in percentage black population, trailing the Deep South states of Mississippi, Louisiana, Georgia, South Carolina, and Alabama. North Carolina's Hispanic population has grown considerably, reaching 6 percent by 2004. Among southern states, North Carolina ranks fourth in the percentage of the population that considers itself Hispanic, trailing only Texas, Florida, and Georgia.

North Carolina's median household income is $39,438, nearly $4,000 below the national average. However, in the South, North Carolina ranks fourth, behind Virginia, Georgia, and Texas. The homeownership rate in North Carolina is 69.4 percent, higher than the national average of 66.2 percent. Regionally, North Caro-

% Hispanic Population (2004)	Median Household Income (2003)	Homeownership Rate (2000)	% in Poverty (2003)
2.2	36,131	72.5	15.2
4.4	33,445	69.4	16.0
19	38,985	70.1	13.0
6.8	42,421	67.5	13.3
2.8	33,792	67.9	18.1
1.7	32,397	72.3	18.3
6.1	39,438	69.4	13.4
3.1	38,003	72.2	13.8
2.8	37,925	69.9	13.5
34.6	39,967	63.8	16.2
5.7	50,028	68.1	9.9
14.1	43,318	66.2	12.5

lina ranks sixth in homeownership, tied with Arkansas. The poverty rate in North Carolina is the fourth-lowest in the South.

North Carolinians often split their votes between national-level Republicans and state-level Democrats, typically supporting Republican presidential candidates but electing Democratic governors and state legislators. Not surprisingly, the state's partisan identification is divided evenly between Democrats and Republicans (see table 1.2). When comparing southern states' partisan identification, North Carolina ranks as the third-most Democratic. This stands in stark contrast to South Carolina, its staunchly Republican neighbor. Although 56 percent of North Carolinians who voted supported George W. Bush in 2004, North Carolina ranked eighth out of the eleven southern states.

North Carolina Democrats differ from Democrats in other regions of the country. In North Carolina, 40 percent of residents identify as conservative, compared to 34 percent nationally. In the South, North Carolina has the seventh-highest percentage of conservative residents, tied with Louisiana.

❖ Revisiting the Progressive Reputation

In *Southern Politics in State and Nation*, Key identified three areas—industrial development, public education, and race relations—where North Carolina appeared progressive compared to other southern states. Key praised North Carolina's industrial development, highlighting the state's diverse and productive economy.

TABLE I.2. Comparing Political Basics in the South, 2004

State	% Democrats	% Republicans	% Independents	% Bush	% Conservative
Alabama	34	48	18	63	44
Arkansas	41	31	29	54	42
Florida	37	41	23	52	34
Georgia	34	42	24	58	41
Louisiana	42	40	18	57	40
Mississippi	38	47	15	60	46
North Carolina	39	40	21	56	40
South Carolina	33	44	23	58	39
Tennessee	32	40	28	57	46
Texas	32	43	24	61	45
Virginia	35	39	26	54	38
United States	37	37	26	51	34

Source: CNN.com (2004).

According to Key's figures, North Carolina ranked second in both value of farm products and growth in the value of farm products. Key presented a similar picture when it came to manufacturing. North Carolina was second behind Texas in the value of manufactured products in 1939 and first in percentage increase in manufacturing (1949, 210).

How does North Carolina's industrial development compare nearly six decades after Key? As detailed in table 1.3, North Carolina's manufacturing strength continues. The state currently stands second to Texas in manufacturing among the southern states. On a per capita basis, North Carolina ranks fourth behind Louisiana, South Carolina, and Tennessee. However, farming and manufacturing are no longer the sole measures of economic development. Healthy state economies are now expected to diversify. On the positive side, the state has become a center for banking, and, as table 1.3 shows, North Carolina is third overall in the South in the annual payroll for the finance and insurance sector. On a per-capita basis, North Carolina ranks second behind Virginia. However, in the increasingly important technology area, the North Carolina fares worse, ranking fifth in overall receipts from professional, scientific, and technical services, trailing Texas, Florida, Virginia, and Georgia. Per capita, Virginia stands far ahead, followed by Georgia, Texas, and Florida.

In addition to North Carolina's industrial development, Key lauded the state's educational progress. He highlighted Aycock, the "education governor," who led the fight in support of the principle that "the best investment a state can make is in

TABLE I.3. Comparing Industrial Development in the South

State	Value of Manufacturing Shipments ($1,000)	Annual Payroll from Finance and Insurance Sector ($1,000)	Receipts from Professional, Scientific, and Technical Services ($1,000)
Alabama	66,686,220	3,255,448	8,757,629
Arkansas	46,721,413	1,285,696	2,599,015
Florida	78,474,770	15,993,236	42,457,665
Georgia	126,156,636	8,555,209	25,165,914
Louisiana	89,540,799	2,554,625	8,243,267
Mississippi	38,276,054	1,163,724	2,922,664
North Carolina	156,821,943	9,140,171	17,622,547
South Carolina	81,132,781	2,514,131	7,494,425
Tennessee	109,293,454	5,078,547	11,022,883
Texas	310,815,965	19,703,380	62,549,237
Virginia	83,952,547	8,175,722	40,683,149
United States	78,322,734	7,555,803	17,736,020

Source: U.S. Census Bureau (2002).

the education of its children" (1984, 208). Key does not provide empirical evidence on educational spending or achievement, but this reputation has been perpetuated over time. For example, Rob Christensen and Jack D. Fleer (1999, 83) note that North Carolina's state university system has been "long considered one of the best in the South."

By most contemporary measures, North Carolina ranks in the top third of southern states in education (see table I.4). The state ranks fourth in percentage of high school graduates, behind Virginia, Florida, and Georgia, and fourth in the percentage of college graduates, trailing Virginia, Texas, and Georgia. Based on twenty-one factors, only Virginia tops North Carolina in rankings of the region's "smartest states" (Morgan and Morgan 2006).

Key also trumpeted North Carolina's progressive race relations, noting that although the state "has been no picnic ground for its Negro citizens, the spirit of Aycock has persisted in a consistently sensitive appreciation of Negro rights" (1984, 209). As with education, however, Key provided scant empirical evidence of North Carolina's progressive policies on race relations. Following the publication of Key's book, North Carolina experienced several racially polarized political campaigns, most notably the 1950 race for the U.S. Senate that pitted Willis Smith against Frank Porter Graham and the 1990 U.S. Senate contest between Helms and Harvey Gantt.

TABLE 1.4. Comparing Educational Achievement in the South

State	% High School Graduates (2000)	% College Graduates (2000)	National Ranking of Smartest States (2005)
Alabama	75.3	19.0	44
Arkansas	75.3	16.7	36
Florida	79.9	22.3	39
Georgia	78.6	24.3	38
Louisiana	74.8	18.7	46
Mississippi	72.9	16.9	47
North Carolina	78.1	22.5	25
South Carolina	76.3	20.4	32
Tennessee	75.9	19.6	41
Texas	75.7	23.2	33
Virginia	81.5	29.5	12
United States	80.4	24.4	—

Source: U.S. Census Bureau (2000); Morgan and Morgan (2006).

According to one index of public opinion, North Carolina is currently the South's ninth-most-progressive state on race relations, in front of only Arkansas and Alabama (Brace et al. 2002). Table 1.5 also shows the percentage of black elected officials in the South: North Carolina ranks sixth, behind Mississippi, Alabama, Louisiana, South Carolina, and Georgia. Only 8.5 percent of North Carolina's elected officials are African American, far below the state's 22 percent black population. North Carolina ranks fifth in the percentage of blacks registered to vote, lagging Mississippi, Alabama, Louisiana, and South Carolina.

Based on this snapshot, North Carolina is not as progressive as the state described by Key during the first half of the twentieth century and is perhaps closer to the "progressive myth" posited by Bass and DeVries in the 1970s. North Carolina's manufacturing prowess continues, but the state has fallen behind according to other economic development measures. Educationally, North Carolina continues to do well, ranking in the top third in the region. However, on several measures of racial progress, the empirical evidence places North Carolina near the bottom of southern states. When reevaluating Key's measures of progressivism, North Carolina is not a laggard, but it is no longer at the forefront of progressive politics in the region.

TABLE I.5. Comparing Race in the South

State	Racial Integration Ranking (1974–98)	% Black Elected Officials (2000)	% Blacks Registered to Vote (2004)
Alabama	.50	16.7	72.9
Arkansas	.52	6.0	63.7
Florida	.69	4.0	52.6
Georgia	.65	8.9	64.2
Louisiana	.72	13.9	71.1
Mississippi	.73	18.9	76.1
North Carolina	.55	8.5	70.4
South Carolina	.77	13.7	71.1
Tennessee	.60	2.5	63.9
Texas	.71	1.7	68.4
Virginia	.71	8.1	57.4
United States	.73	1.8	64.4

Source: Bositis (2000); Brace et al. (2002); U.S. Census Bureau (2004b).

❖ Outline of the Book

The New Politics of North Carolina is divided into four parts and eleven essays. Although the book provides a comprehensive analysis of North Carolina politics, we made hard choices about which essays to include. These choices meant that we had to exclude relevant institutions, like the state bureaucracy, and important policy areas, such as health care. Nevertheless, we believe that the resulting product provides a compelling if not exhaustive picture of modern North Carolina politics.

The first part, "Citizens and Context," introduces readers to political history and public opinion in North Carolina. In chapter 1, Thomas F. Eamon focuses on the state's unique political culture by examining political history, geography, institutional structure, and transformational leadership. Chapter 2, by Timothy Vercellotti, presents data from opinion polls comparing public opinion in North Carolina to political views in other states.

Part 2, "Linkage Institutions," examines the connections between citizens and government. Chapter 3, by Charles Prysby, addresses political parties, with particular attention to the development of the party system. In chapter 4, Adam J. Newmark focuses on interest groups and lobbying activities. In the final essay in this part, Ferrel Guillory argues that the media are important actors in North Carolina politics, but he also cites the increasingly soft bark of these watchdogs in North Carolina politics.

The third part evaluates the state's governmental institutions. Chapter 6, written by Jack D. Fleer, examines the governor, focusing on running for office, transitions to power, informal powers, and gubernatorial performance. Chapter 7, by Christopher A. Cooper, evaluates the legislature, focusing specifically on legislators' three primary goals: election, power, and good public policy. Chapter 8, written by Ruth Ann Strickland, considers judicial structure, judge selection, and court funding. In the last essay in this part, Sean Hildebrand and James H. Svara explore intergovernmental relations and federalism by considering governmental structure, tools of federalism, fiscal affairs, and the challenges faced by local governments.

The next part focuses on public policy. Although a variety of important policy areas exist, including economic development, health care, and law enforcement, we chose environmental and educational policies. These two policy areas are among the most important and provide vital lessons for policymakers operating in other areas. Chapter 10, by Dennis O. Grady and Jonathan Kanipe, considers the ambivalent legacy of environmental politics in North Carolina. In chapter 11, Hunter Bacot examines the role of public education. North Carolina has long benefited from a world-class higher education system, but state political leaders also focus considerable attention on other levels of education. Both essays in this part consider the state's approach to the policy area, the specific policies in place, their effectiveness, and what they teach us about policy in the Tar Heel state more generally.

The conclusion identifies trends, pulls together common themes, and highlights what the volume has taught us about North Carolina government, politics, and policy. The conclusion also revisits the state's progressive reputation in light of the dramatic changes in North Carolina politics over the past half century.

❖ References

Bass, Jack, and Walter DeVries. 1995 [1976]. *The Transformation of Southern Politics: Social Change and Political Consequence since 1945*. Athens: University of Georgia Press.

Bositis, David A. 2000. *Black Elected Officials: A Statistical Summary 2000*. Washington, D.C.: Joint Center for Political and Economic Studies.

Brace, Paul, Kellie Sims-Butler, Kevin Arceneaux, and Martin Johnson. 2002. "Public Opinion in the American States: New Perspectives Using National Data." *American Journal of Political Science* 46:173–89.

Christensen, Rob, and Jack D. Fleer. 1999. "North Carolina: Between Helms and Hunt No Majority Emerges." In *Southern Politics in the 1990s*, edited by Alexander P. Lamis, 81–106. Baton Rouge: Louisiana State University Press.

CNN.com. 2004. Election and Exit Poll Results. <http://www.cnn.com/ELECTION/2004/>. Accessed November 1, 2006.

Fleer, Jack D. 1994. *North Carolina Government and Politics*. Lincoln: University of Nebraska Press.

Hetherington, Marc J. 2005. *Why Trust Matters: Declining Political Trust and the Demise of American Liberalism*. Princeton: Princeton University Press.

Jewell, Malcolm E. 1982. "The Neglected World of State Politics." *Journal of Politics* 44:638–57.

Key, V. O., Jr. 1949. *Southern Politics in State and Nation*. New York: Knopf.

———. 1984. *Southern Politics in State and Nation: A New Edition*. Knoxville: University of Tennessee Press.

Luebke, Paul. 1998. *Tar Heel Politics 2000*. Chapel Hill: University of North Carolina Press.

Mooney, Christopher Z. 2001. "State Politics and Policy Quarterly and the Study of State Politics: The Editor's Introduction." *State Politics and Policy Quarterly* 1:1–4.

Morehouse, Sarah M., and Malcolm E. Jewell. 2004. "States as Laboratories: A Reprise." *Annual Review of Political Science* 7:177–203.

Morgan, Kathleen O'Leary, and Scott Morgan, eds. 2006. *Education State Rankings 2006–2007*. Lawrence, Kans.: Morgan Quitno.

Prysby, Charles. 2003. "North Carolina: The Development of Two-Party Competition." In *The New Politics of the Old South: An Introduction to Southern Politics*, 2nd ed., edited by Charles S. Bullock III and Mark J. Rozell, 153–75. Lanham, Md.: Rowman and Littlefield.

U.S. Census Bureau. 2000, 2003, 2004a, 2005. *Census of Population and Housing*. Washington, D.C.

———. 2002. *Economic Census*. Washington, D.C.

———. 2004b. *Current Population Survey*. Washington, D.C.

❖ Part I. Citizens and Context

❖ 1. The Seeds of Modern North Carolina Politics

THOMAS F. EAMON

A blend of conservative and progressive ideas shaped the evolution of North Carolina politics from the end of the nineteenth century to the beginning of the twenty-first. The Democratic Party, which dominated the state for the first seventy-two years of the twentieth century, grew out of a consolidation of white supremacy and conservative economic interests.

The dominant figure in this transformation, Governor Charles Aycock (1901–5) ruled more by spirit and force of personality than tactical skills. Aycock supported the fundamental conservatism of the North Carolina Democratic Party but also held a passionate belief in education as the means of human fulfillment. Aycock's legacy resulted in a state creed promoting economic advancement and education while protecting the privileged status of major corporations.

Later, as the national Democratic Party moved leftward in the aftermath of the Great Depression and Franklin Roosevelt's New Deal, leading North Carolina Democrats embraced some of the New Deal's liberalism as well as an agenda for greater racial equality. But with rare exceptions, they also maintained close ties to the state's business leadership, ties that served state-level Democrats well even after the emergence of a strong two-party system. In the twentieth and early twenty-first centuries, North Carolina's political culture reflected a powerful strand of the traditionalism of the Old South along with a moralistic element, the latter leading in both reformist and conservative directions. Also, an entrepreneurial spirit was especially associated with burgeoning urban areas. The result was a state quite different from any other in the American South, even as it remained distinctively southern. The most successful politicians incorporated all these strands into their campaigns and administrations.

This essay focuses on North Carolina's unique political culture through the perspectives of history, geography, institutional structure, and transformational leadership. It begins with a closer look at the state's political history through a discussion of the post-Reconstruction period between the late 1870s and the end of the nineteenth century. Next, the essay examines the historical claim that North Carolina is one of the most enlightened and progressive southern states before moving on to discuss the state's varied geographic landscape and the ways political geography has shaped Tar Heel politics. Next, the essay examines the institutional environment created by the rise of direct primaries in the early twentieth century and the subsequent political tensions within the Democratic Party. Of course, politics is more than just a collection of institutions; individual politicians and personalities exert important influences. The penultimate section focuses on the most important figures in the state's politics, while the essay concludes by outlining the continuation of the progressive conservative heritage at the dawn of the twenty-first century.

❖ North Carolina Politics in the Post-Reconstruction Era

In the early 1900s, the shadow of Reconstruction remained ever present. The state's would-be rescuers saw Reconstruction as a time of rape, pillage, government theft, and general decadence. They attributed that curse to a takeover by northern conquerors, southern opportunists, and newly enfranchised but manipulated blacks. White conservatives had in fact narrowly controlled state government from the 1870s until the early 1890s, but blacks remained a significant force in parts of North Carolina. From the 1860s through the 1930s, most African Americans were Republicans, assuring that the party threatened the Democrats in North Carolina's heavily black eastern counties. White Republicans were numerous in the state's western half and dominant in a few mountain and foothill Piedmont counties. But white Republican adherents were more common in lowland eastern North Carolina than is sometimes supposed. The Populist Party, which supported small farmers and fought big business, surged in the mid-1890s and received much of its backing from economically insecure white Democrats. The combination of Populists, black Republicans, and white Republicans alarmed white conservative Democrats. The Fusionists, the term used for the Republican-Populist coalition, gained control of the state legislature in 1894. They consolidated their gains in 1896 when Republican standard-bearer Dan Russell (1897–1901) of Wilmington won the governorship. The Fusionists—one Populist and one Republican—occupied both of North Carolina's seats in the U.S. Senate, and the alliance controlled the state legislature (Powell 1989).[1]

A dynamic and jolting period in Tar Heel politics resulted, if only for a short while. Reports alleged corruption, and some of the rookie officeholders clumsily approached their duties. However, corruption was much less rampant than in the Reconstruction era. Nor were the state's new keepers a violent bunch when compared to activists of three decades earlier or two years later.

In 1898, white conservative Democrats came back with a vengeance. Organization, intimidation, and thuggery led the party to make big gains in ballot boxes across the state. Having won on the basis of official voting returns in Wilmington, then the state's largest city, the conservatives staged a military style coup d'état and seized control of local government immediately rather than waiting for incumbents' terms to end. Two years later, the Red Shirts (white conservative activists noted for their bright attire) finished the mission. Attorney Furnifold Simmons of New Bern, the leading conservative strategist, began a long career in the U.S. Senate (1901–31). Aycock, an articulate advocate of white supremacy and universal public education, won the governorship. Aycock was in many respects the spiritual father of twentieth-century North Carolina politics, embodying its prejudices as well as the promise for a better life. A state constitutional amendment passed in the name of securing a literate electorate in effect barred most blacks from voting, a goal that already had largely been accomplished (Cecelski and Tyson 1998).[2]

From 1900 to the 1960s, North Carolina was a quasi-democracy, a place where many citizens lacked basic political rights. A U.S. constitutional amendment adopted in 1920 but not ratified by North Carolina until 1971 gave white women basic voting rights. For African Americans, however, these rights came later and more slowly, in a long struggle from the 1930s through the 1960s.

❖ The Enlightened Southern State?

Despite North Carolina's history of racism and white male dominance, many scholars have argued that by the early twentieth century, the state was actually quite enlightened. Five points have buttressed this claim: Republicans could always count on a significant vote, Democratic primaries had two well-identified factions, captains of industry and bankers made up the progressive Tar Heel elite, the state was more flexible on racial issues than most other southern states, and the state had a relatively honest political leadership and bureaucracy.

Even at the height of Democratic supremacy, North Carolina's Republican Party could count on a significant vote, usually 30 percent or more in statewide general elections. Furthermore, North Carolina had a continuing state Republican organization and many county-level organizations. Among southern states, only Tennessee and Virginia could make similar claims (Key 1949).

During the first half of the twentieth century, North Carolina's Democratic primaries often saw competition between a conservative faction and another regarded as more critical of the status quo. The in faction pushed for probusiness policies on taxes and regulation, though to a point they were also enthusiastic about economic modernization, promoting education, and road building. The rival faction accused the establishment of not doing enough to better the lot of the average North Carolinian. Its leaders criticized machine rule, referring to the dominant group led first by Senator Simmons and later by Governor Max Gardner (1929–33). Thus, a semblance of two-party competition existed within the Democratic Party. In many southern states, such factions were fleeting, changing from election to election, but more than in other southern states, North Carolina's two-party system and the competition within the state's Democratic Party offered some hope for those out of power as well as more potential for democracy (Key 1949).[3]

In addition, the captains of industry and their banker allies constituted the elite, both in the state and in its Democratic Party. These elites were urban based in a state that was heavily agricultural—even more rural than most other southern states. In much of the South until the 1960s, rural-based landholders and their banker-merchant kindred wielded strong influence and dominated Democratic affairs. This is not to say that the rural landholder class was a weak element, but industrial elites were more powerful in North Carolina. Among nonsouthern states, Pennsylvania stood out as a place where an urban-based industrial leadership wielded vast influence, using the Republican Party as its vehicle. However, in the first half of the twentieth century, big industry and related businesses were a much larger part of the economy there than in North Carolina. North Carolina's captains of industry worked for internal improvements such as roads and more modern state services, but they were hardly enthusiastic about a participatory democracy harkening back to the old Populist era. While wanting the state to be regarded as progressive, its elites were often just as opposed to major political and social reforms as were the planter classes of Mississippi and South Carolina (Key 1949).[4]

The state was ostensibly more liberal on racial matters than all other southern states with the possible exception of Tennessee. North Carolina's governors (see table 1.1) spoke out against lynching at a time when other southern governors often winked and turned in the other direction. North Carolina and Virginia, hardly a democracy in most respects, had much lower lynching rates than the other southern states. Governors Cameron Morrison (1921–25), himself a former Red Shirt; Gardner; and J. Melville Broughton (1941–45) prided themselves on being racial progressives, although their stance was symbolic and largely constituted tokenism and they strongly supported the basic social order of segregation. North Carolina equalized the salaries of black and white schoolteachers before other southern states did so, paying on the basis of highest degree earned rather than maintaining dual pay scales based on race. Political scientist V. O. Key Jr. (1949) and the great American travel writer John Gunther (1946) lauded North Carolina for its racial progress in the mid–twentieth century. The shadow of the Wilmington race cataclysm of 1898 was a bit of an embarrassment, something to be dismissed as an event of the distant past.[5] Schoolchildren learned of Governor Aycock's great progressive ideas on education but heard nothing of the bloodshed that preceded it.

Finally, North Carolina and Virginia were unusual among southern states in

TABLE 1.1. North Carolina Governors, 1865–2006

Governor	Party	Term
Jonathan Worth	Democrat	1865–68
William Woods Holden	Republican	1868–70
Tod Robinson Caldwell	Republican	1870–74
Curtis Hooks Brogden	Republican	1874–77
Zebulon Baird Vance	Democrat	1877–79
Thomas Jordan Jarvis	Democrat	1879–85
Alfred Moore Scales	Democrat	1885–89
Daniel Gould Fowle	Democrat	1889–91
Thomas Michael Holt	Democrat	1891–93
Elias Carr	Democrat	1893–97
Daniel Lindsay Russell	Republican	1897–1901
Charles Brantley Aycock	Democrat	1901–5
Robert Broadnax Glenn	Democrat	1905–9
William Walton Kitchin	Democrat	1909–13
Locke Craig	Democrat	1913–17
Thomas Walter Bickett	Democrat	1917–21
Cameron Morrison	Democrat	1921–25
Angus Wilton McLean	Democrat	1925–29
Oliver Max Gardner	Democrat	1929–33
John C. B. Ehringhaus	Democrat	1933–37
Clyde R. Hoey	Democrat	1937–41
J. Melville Broughton	Democrat	1941–45
R. Gregg Cherry	Democrat	1945–49
W. Kerr Scott	Democrat	1949–53
William B. Umstead	Democrat	1953–54
Luther H. Hodges	Democrat	1954–61
Terry Sanford	Democrat	1961–65
Daniel Killian Moore	Democrat	1965–69
Robert W. Scott	Democrat	1969–73
James E. Holshouser Jr.	Republican	1973–77
James B. Hunt Jr.	Democrat	1977–85
James G. Martin	Republican	1985–93
James B. Hunt Jr.	Democrat	1993–2001
Michael F. Easley	Democrat	2001–6

Source: State Library (2004).

that top officials and continuing state bureaucracies strived to meet high ethical standards. Leaders and their subordinates were not constantly on the take.

Historians and political scientists offer two conflicting interpretations relating to the controlling forces in North Carolina politics from the early twentieth century to the 1960s. The first view—until the early 1970s, the dominant one—saw North Carolina as the most progressive of southern states. Key's North Carolina chapter in *Southern Politics in State and Nation*, one strongly influenced by his research associate, Alexander Heard, argued that North Carolina was special, a southern state that avoided major scandals and white racist demagoguery and pursued economic development and educational improvements. While aware of the bitter racial campaign of 1900, Key and Heard accepted the North Carolina image of Aycock as one of the most progressive of southern governors and believed that his legacy had made North Carolina unique among southern states. In many respects, Key and Heard saw North Carolina as a model for other states despite its many imperfections.

Key and Heard never confused the terms "progressive" and "liberal." They recognized that the state's controlling elites, the "progressive plutocracy," defended privilege and the status quo on matters of labor relations, taxation, and the distribution of wealth in the society. *Southern Politics* examined factionalism in the state's Democratic Party and looked in some detail at challenges, usually not successful, to the conservative progressives. This version of mild economic populism stressed opposition to sales taxes yet also sought to move rapidly forward on public education. Whatever the state's flaws, the Key-Heard view and that of many North Carolinians was that the state political system had produced good works.

Today, the prevailing current among academics is much more skeptical, even hostile. J. Morgan Kousser's *The Shaping of Southern Politics: Suffrage Restrictions and the Establishment of the One-Party South* (1974) was a pioneering work in this debate. Most concerned with the period from 1880 to 1910, Kousser sought to demolish the image of Aycock as a forward-thinking savior, highlighting Aycock's racist rhetoric and the techniques used by white supremacists to wrest the state from Republican-Populist control. In the 1990s, political sociologist Paul Luebke, while recognizing some progressive instincts among the state's elites, saw the dominant Democratic establishment as fundamentally out to protect the interests of big business during the first sixty years of the twentieth century. At the end of the century, historians David S. Cecelski and Timothy B. Tyson (1998) and Glenda Gilmore (1996) also ripped into the North Carolina establishment. They saw Aycock as a sinister figure whose sometimes progressive rhetoric masked evil intentions in race relations. In their view, the conservative Democratic counterrevolution of the 1898–1900 period cast an evil shadow on state politics for the next one hundred years.[6] Their arguments might have been still more persuasive if they had dealt in more depth with the reasons for Aycock's reputation as a progressive innovator.

❖ A Varied Land

Another important political factor in North Carolina is the state's geography. No state east of the Mississippi River offers greater geographic and climate contrast than North Carolina. With its alligator-inhabited waters, palmetto trees, and giant live oaks and cypresses bearded with Spanish moss, Wilmington, in the southeast section of the state, is indistinguishable from North Florida or the Mississippi Gulf Coast. In Boone, in North Carolina's northwest, the dogwoods bloom in mid-May and howling winds accompany sudden snowstorms from late autumn to early spring. Boone's January mean temperature is below that of many cities of the Atlantic Northeast and the Lower Midwest.

North Carolina is divided into three regions: eastern, Piedmont, and western. Some geographers point to the sand hills as a fourth region. The Atlantic coastal plain, or east, was long synonymous with agriculture. Until recently, it produced more tobacco than anywhere else in the world. Late in the twentieth century, cotton revived and in some cases thrived on former tobacco fields. What cotton could not provide was the generous revenue of tobacco. However, hogs, chickens, and turkeys, often raised on a huge scale, have enhanced farm income if not air and stream quality. The coastal plain is changing as some towns and resort communities prosper, but outside observers still see it as North Carolina's version of the Third World.

The Piedmont, characterized by red clay hills, loblolly pines, decaying mill towns, and sprawling metropolitan areas, is the state's economic engine and population center. Charlotte and the Raleigh-Durham–Chapel Hill area are dynamic business and education centers, places possessing considerable charisma. Greensboro and Winston-Salem may lack glamour, but their roles in the national and state economy are also substantial. Formerly, they were among the world's leading nerve centers for textiles and tobacco. The bustling urban belt, roughly a crescent extending from Raleigh to Charlotte and Gastonia, masks the fact that parts of the Piedmont are bleeding as a consequence of declines in the traditional mainstay industries of furniture and textiles.

The west, or Appalachian Mountain region, was long an economic stepchild, much like parts of the coastal plain. It was also a vacation haven, with terrain ranging from temperate rain forests near the South Carolina and Georgia borders to subtundra conditions in the higher mountain slopes. Poverty remains, but well-heeled migrants including retirees attracted by the beauty and distinct four seasons are flocking to several of the region's counties. The mountain city of Asheville is a mecca for intellectuals, aging hippies, artsy types, and the rich.

Some geographers point to the sand hills straddling the coastal plain and Piedmont in the state's south as a fourth region. While the soil is of marginal quality for big agriculture, fruit production, horses, and golf do quite nicely here. The eastern sand hills have much in common, both socially and in appearance, with the coastal plain. To the west, the resorts of Pinehurst and Southern Pines identify with the Piedmont. Conventional political discussions treat the eastern sand hill region as part of the coastal plain and the western sand hills as part of the Piedmont.[7]

The rural counties of the northern coastal plain and northeastern Piedmont historically have had African American populations exceeding 30 percent. In a few counties, African Americans have surpassed 50 percent of the population. Whites here were Deep South Democrats and strong party loyalists until the George Wallace revolt of 1968. The southern coastal plain and southern Piedmont also had substantial minority populations, usually between 20 and 40 percent. Here, too, whites leaned Democratic, but more pockets of support existed for Republicans and the ill-fated Populist Party than in other sections of the state. Throughout the coastal plain, the spirit of economic populism, if not always the party, was stronger than elsewhere in North Carolina, suggesting a certain independence from the big planter class, which dominated the politics of similar areas in much of the American South.

Aside from the counties with high minority populations near the Virginia and South Carolina borders, the Piedmont had black populations ranging from near 10 to 30 percent, with some of the big-city counties seeing their minority populations rise at the end of the twentieth century. Most of the Piedmont voted Democratic until the early 1950s, but a Republican presence did exist. Even during the heyday of Democratic strength, a few Piedmont counties regularly reported Republican majorities.[8]

Conventional wisdom holds that counties of the Appalachians are Republican, reflecting a seething resentment at being forced into the Civil War, about which the independent mountain folk cared little. They felt isolated from their far-off state capital, where the councils of war held sway. Indeed, Appalachian North Carolina long had a few Republican bastions. But many more of its counties were closely divided, places where neither party could be sure of victory. Bitter partisanship was rampant, and blacks had only a small presence (typically 1 to 10 percent), placing the race issue on the back burner. Many whites might have been racist, but few were preoccupied with the subject.

❖ A Step toward Democracy?

The move toward direct primaries influenced North Carolina politics. In fact, scholars have debated the motives that led southern Democratic parties to adopt the direct primary. Nationally, the adoption of primaries was associated with Theodore Roosevelt–style Progressivism. The political elites of the South, including North Carolina, strongly intended to promote white supremacy and saw the Democratic Party as a means to that end. Soon after the Civil War, southern conservatives promoted the idea of the primary as a way to maintain electoral "purity." In 1892, Louisiana held a preelection white Democratic vote on whether to have a lottery. The stated purpose was to eliminate largely black Republican and Populist influence in the general election, when the issue would be officially decided. In the 1898–99 period, *Raleigh News and Observer* owner Josephus Daniels met with white supremacy Democrats in Louisiana, Mississippi, and South Carolina. Following these discussions, he argued in an editorial that a white primary was necessary "to keep the white man united" (Kousser 1974, 76). Alluding to his meetings with out-of-state Democrats, Daniels said that "the fear was expressed that divisions among white men might result in bringing about a return to the deplorable conditions when one faction of white men call upon the Negroes to help defeat another faction" (Kousser 1974, 76).

North Carolina's Democratic Party experimented with internal statewide primaries in 1900 and 1912. In both cases, the primaries served to nominate candidates for the U.S. Senate (or, more technically, to make recommendations, which party leaders were bound to accept because the state legislature rather than voters made the official decisions). The 1900 primary launched the thirty-year Senate career of Simmons, the Democratic Party's mastermind. Simmons easily prevailed in 1912, after Aycock's death prevented him from challenging Simmons.

Not until 1916 did North Carolina officially implement a direct primary, after most southern states and some Midwest and West Coast states. If voters rather than party activists at state conventions were to have a direct voice in choosing nominees, the primary was essential. Many of the old Populists had now joined the Democratic ranks. Significant numbers of longtime Democrats also wanted to vote on Democratic nominees (and thus, in effect, the state officials). The Progressive movement, which had many adherents in the first quarter of the twentieth century, promoted direct primaries. Although North Carolinians were likely influenced by national trends, the fact remains that the idea originated with people with racist agendas. In 1915, when the primary legislation was passed, North Carolinians and other southerners saw the Democratic Party as a vehicle for white supremacy. Furthermore, despite the trappings of democracy, the conservative faction, with strong support from big business and the big landholder class, most often prevailed in North Carolina Democratic primaries. Yet the primary situation offered greater possibilities for change and for a power shift than did the establishment-dominated conventions.[9]

❖ Political Tensions Erupt

The creation of primaries led to substantial political tensions in politics. From 1932 to 1948, four of five North Carolina primaries featured at least one leftist insurgent. In these cases, "left" refers to antiestablishment candidates with economic populist platforms. The establishment took seriously the challenges in 1932, 1936, 1944, and 1948. In the first three elections, establishment forces were sufficient to beat the insurgents. In 1948, however, a man from the left aligned with someone with links to the establishment and prevailed. The Democratic victor, W. Kerr Scott (1949–53), might not have revolutionized state politics but nevertheless left a firm imprint. His victory over establishment-backed state treasurer Charles Johnson represented a major upset.

The outcome produced a governor reviled by sophisticates for his gruff manner. Not surprisingly, state legislative leaders detested Scott. He had less success in getting proposals through the legislature than any other post–World War II governor. Yet Scott prevailed in the areas he cared most about, roads and schools. A state bond issue referendum, an idea Scott had opposed before becoming governor, made possible much of this progress.[10] However, Scott had failures outside the legislative arena. The most notable came in the aftermath of the interim appointment of liberal historian and University of North Carolina president Frank Porter Graham to fill a vacant seat in the U.S. Senate. Scott worked tirelessly for Graham in the special 1950 Democratic primary, only to see him defeated by conservative Willis Smith.[11] However, three years later Smith suffered a fatal heart attack. William Umstead (1953–54) had become governor by this time and named conservative Democrat Alton Lennon (1953–54) to serve out Smith's term. Then Scott ousted Lennon in the 1954 Democratic primary and held the Senate seat until he died in 1958. Of all North Carolina's governors, Scott came closest to the old economic Populists. While no integrationist, his racial views were moderate for his time. His appointment of Graham hinted that his social instincts were liberal. Unlike future Democratic governors of a progressive bent, Scott rarely bowed to the establishment that had historically run North Carolina.

Both of Scott's immediate successors, Umstead and Luther Hodges (1954–61), were men of vision who wanted North Carolina to move ahead in education and economic development. But they were progressive conservatives generally well regarded by the state's business and political elites. Politically, at least, a return to normalcy occurred, although that normalcy was strained by the impending challenge to the longtime racial order.

In the aftermath of *Brown v. Board of Education of Topeka* (1954), the U.S. Supreme Court decision that declared school segregation unconstitutional, North

Carolina's chief executives adopted a moderate course. In this case, moderate meant expressing vigorous opposition to the ruling while calling for calm and respect for the law. At the same time, Virginia and the Deep South states adopted positions of massive resistance and threatened to close their public schools if necessary to prevent racial integration. North Carolina adopted the Pearsall Plan in 1956, transferring authority from the state board of education to local school boards. The plan was touted as both maintaining segregation and keeping public schools open. In fact, a key provision of the plan outlined a means through which the public schools could be closed if a federal court ordered them integrated. The decision was to be left to the local boards of education, and this provision was never invoked. In 1957, without a direct court order, the school boards in the cities of Charlotte, Greensboro, and Winston-Salem admitted a few African American students to formerly all-white schools. Although the action was mere tokenism, it set a major precedent, and over the years, other school systems reluctantly followed. Many advocates of the Pearsall Plan, including Governor Hodges and his successor, Terry Sanford (1961–65), later explained the plan as one designed to smooth the way for racial change. Support for the plan hardly represented an act of bravery by such politicians as Hodges and Sanford, but the plan might have calmed the waters.[12]

❖ Terry Sanford and the "Progressive Spirit"

Sanford was a crucial figure in the shaping of North Carolina politics. The innovative Sanford wanted the state to be a national leader, and a Harvard survey placed him as one of the ten top American governors of the twentieth century.[13] In one legislative session, teachers and other educators received a 21 percent salary increase, universities expanded, and a school specializing in the arts was established. Gingerly but steadfastly, Sanford pursued racial equality even while initially employing some of the rhetoric of a segregationist. Before his term ended, Sanford spoke out forcefully for the concept of racial equality and worked quietly to integrate public and private facilities even before the passage of the Civil Rights Act of 1964. He moved to transform North Carolina into a modern industrial state and was hardly an old-school economic populist.[14] To finance his ambitious school programs, Sanford pushed through the state legislature a 3 percent tax on food, which had previously been exempt from the general sales tax. Some of his operatives justified the tax by saying, "It will catch everybody." "Everybody" in this case was a code word for poor minorities. It was the ultimate antipopulist tax, but even organized labor, reflecting its general fondness for Sanford, offered only halfhearted opposition. After the adoption of the tax, people on the right—social populists favoring segregation—were among the measure's most ardent critics. Left-leaning individuals consider a levy on food the most regressive of taxes, but Sanford believed in his mission and was unrepentant to the end. In the introduction to his book, *But What about the People?*, Sanford harkened back to the introduction of a state sales tax in the depression-scarred 1930s: "Governor J. C. B. Ehringhaus [1933–37], whose political courage I have always admired, insisted on a new tax structure, the first [sales tax] in the nation. 'If it is a choice between a sales tax on the one hand and a decent school, I stand for the school,' he told the General Assembly" (1966, 7). Sanford had voted for R. Mayne Albright, a fierce opponent of the sales tax, in the first gubernatorial primary of 1948. Following Albright's elimination, Sanford switched to the neopopulist Scott, who never seriously attempted to end the sales tax. But Sanford, North Carolina's most celebrated liberal politician, now associated the sales tax with courage. No captain of industry could have defended it with greater eloquence.

❖ Transition to New North Carolina Politics: A Reflection of the Old?

From 1900 through 1964, North Carolina gave its electoral votes to the Democratic presidential candidate every year except 1928. Even as conservative 1964 candidate Barry Goldwater made a strong showing in the Deep South, he lost North Carolina, failing to carry a single county in the eastern part of the state, which was most culturally akin to the Deep South.[15] Only Herbert Hoover, running against the Catholic and anti-Prohibitionist Al Smith, carried the state for the GOP. While the coming of the Great Depression shortly after Hoover took office scarred the Republican Party for years to come, Republican presidential contenders usually collected close to one-third of the state's popular votes. From the time of Dwight Eisenhower's first election in 1952, the Republican tickets were competitive in North Carolina and typically won much of the Piedmont plateau and mountain areas. In 1968, Richard Nixon took a plurality in North Carolina, winning 40 percent of the state's popular vote as part of his narrow national victory. George Wallace came in second in North Carolina, taking 31 percent of the total vote and the largest share of the votes in the Democratic stronghold of eastern North Carolina. Hubert Humphrey garnered only 29 percent of the state's ballots, running poorly everywhere except a few academic centers and majority black counties, where for the first time in decades African Americans voted in large numbers. In Nixon's landslide 1972 presidential victory, his culturally liberal opponent, George McGovern (termed an extremist by his antagonists), mustered just 29 percent of North Carolina's popular vote, about 10 percent below his national showing. In the state,

McGovern carried only Orange County (Chapel Hill) and Northampton, which was more than 60 percent African American. Democrat Jimmy Carter temporarily brought back happy days for the Democrats in 1976, when he won 55 percent of the state's vote and all its regions. Even when swamped nationally by Ronald Reagan in 1980 as the Iranian hostage crisis and economic stagflation raged, Carter just barely lost North Carolina. But from 1984 through 2004, Democratic fortunes sagged. Only in 1992, Bill Clinton's first national victory, did the Democrats even come close to winning the Tar Heel State.

From 1968 through 2004, the Republican ticket carried North Carolina in nine of ten elections while winning seven of ten nationally. The three elections from 1996 through 2004 best illustrate how North Carolina has become much more comfortably Republican than the United States as a whole. In none of these North Carolina elections were the Democrats close, yet in 1996, Clinton won a near landslide nationally. In 2000, Al Gore narrowly won the national popular vote yet lost the electoral vote; in North Carolina, however, he lost by 10 percent. In 2004, Democrat John Kerry was defeated in the national popular vote, 51 to 48 percent, but he and his vice presidential running mate, John Edwards, a North Carolinian, trailed by 10 percent in North Carolina. Democratic presidential candidates saw only two optimistic signs. First, the party's candidates did well in some formerly Republican big-city counties. Second, the party now seemed to have a hard-core base vote near 43 percent, a level considerably higher than in the electoral disasters of 1972 and 1984.[16]

As table 1.2 details, from the early 1900s until 1972, U.S. senators from North Carolina were Democrats. The table does not show, however, that most were conservative. Exceptions were Robert Rice "Our Bob" Reynolds (1932–45), an economic populist in rhetoric and often in voting, and Scott (1954–58). Reynolds's affinity with the commoner was overshadowed by his buffoonery and ethnocentrism (Pleasants 2000).[17] Senator Sam J. Ervin (1954–74) was something of an intellectual with a conservative bent on economic and racial matters. Yet he became an icon for liberals as he chaired the Senate investigation into the misdeeds of the Nixon administration in the early 1970s.[18] His Senate colleague, B. Everett Jordan (1958–72), had a conservative image but a moderate voting record. By far the most influential and probably most conservative was the venerable Simmons, the state's political kingpin for many years.

North Carolina's towering congressional figure of the late twentieth century was Senator Jesse Helms (1973–2003). Superficially, at least, his career resembled that of Simmons. Both were apostles of social conservatism. In Simmons's case, his stance was race driven. Helms, a television editorialist in the 1960s and early 1970s, was one of North Carolina's most hard-hitting foes of the civil rights movement. From the Senate in the 1980s, he worked assiduously to block a national holiday honoring slain civil rights leader Dr. Martin Luther King Jr. In later years, Helms was a defender of traditional moral standards and an opponent of leftist international movements. Adding to the symmetry, both Simmons and Helms spent thirty years in the Senate, one at the beginning of the twentieth century and the other at the end. The Simmons era ended on an inglorious note when he lost in the 1930 Democratic primary after having openly opposed his party's presidential ticket in 1928. Helms retired in 2002 as a series of heath problems took their toll.[19]

Simmons wielded greater influence within North Carolina, but Helms had the larger national impact, both as a patron saint of the conservative movement and as chair of the Senate Foreign Relations Committee. Simmons thrived on the art and science of politics. His grassroots political organization was perhaps the most effective ever seen in North Carolina. He knew the state's courthouses. Helms, though not his key supporters, sometimes seemed bored by the nuts and bolts of campaigning and strategy. He was a man of causes, sometimes heedless of the consequences for himself and his party. Both Helms and Simmons employed a take-no-prisoners approach when it suited their aims. Both left a trail of enemies, but Helms especially had many admirers.

North Carolina's other congressional representatives in the last third of the twentieth century were a diverse lot. The senators typically did not serve for long. The seat not occupied by Helms changed hands in every election from 1974 through 2004, with occupants ranging from intellectual conservative Republican John East to liberal Democrats Sanford and Edwards. Some House members, too, were very conservative, while others were very liberal. On the whole, the Democrats in the delegation were in greater harmony with the national party than North Carolina Democrats of the mid–twentieth century. Without exception, the Republicans were dependably conservative on a wide range of issues, though Howard Coble of Greensboro and Walter Jones of Farmville had independent streaks. The generally conservative Jones became a leading critic of the Bush administration's Iraq War agenda.

Partly reflecting the pattern of creating safe congressional seats for each party, the Democrats could now back the national party without fear of retribution. Conservative southern Democrats in Congress represented a dying breed. At one time, drawing districts that would reliably elect liberals would not have been easy, but the process was facilitated by the greatly increased African American vote and the growing cultural liberalism around several of the state's larger cities and academic centers, most notably Charlotte, Greensboro, and the Research Triangle area of Raleigh, Durham, and Chapel Hill.[20] Safe Republican seats were even easier to create and could now be found in all sections of North Carolina. In a reversal from

TABLE 1.2. North Carolina U.S. Senators, 1868–2006

Senator	Party	Term
Seat 1		
Joseph C. Abbott	Republican	1868–71
Matt W. Ransom	Democrat	1872–95
Marion Butler	Populist	1895–1901
Furnifold M. Simmons	Democrat	1901–31
Josiah W. Bailey	Democrat	1931–46
William B. Umstead	Democrat	1946–48
J. Melville Broughton	Democrat	1948–49
Frank P. Graham	Democrat	1949–50
Willis Smith	Democrat	1950–53
Alton A. Lennon	Democrat	1953–54
W. Kerr Scott	Democrat	1954–58
B. Everett Jordan	Democrat	1958–73
Jesse Helms	Republican	1973–2003
Elizabeth Dole	Republican	2003–6
Seat 2		
John Pool	Republican	1868–73
Augustus S. Merrimon	Democrat	1873–79
Zebulon B. Vance	Democrat	1879–94
Thomas J. Jarvis	Democrat	1894–95
Jeter C. Pritchard	Republican	1895–1903
Lee S. Overman	Democrat	1903–30
Cameron A. Morrison	Democrat	1930–32
Robert R. Reynolds	Democrat	1932–45
Clyde R. Hoey	Democrat	1945–54
Samuel J. Ervin Jr.	Democrat	1954–74
Robert B. Morgan	Democrat	1975–81
John P. East	Republican	1981–86
James T. Broyhill	Republican	1986
J. Terry Sanford	Democrat	1986–93
D. M. (Lauch) Faircloth	Republican	1993–99
John Edwards	Democrat	1999–2005
Richard Burr	Republican	2005–6

Source: U.S. Senate (n.d.).

earlier days, the Republican primary was the time for any meaningful contest in these districts, all of which contained overwhelming white majorities.[21]

Recent North Carolina governors have been in the mold of Aycock, Morrison, and Gardner, self-proclaimed progressives keenly aware of the state's corporate power structure and the popular streaks of social conservatism. This has been true of Democrats Jim Hunt (1977–85, 1993–2001) and Mike Easley (2001–present) (discussed further in the following section) and Republicans Jim Holshouser (1973–77) and Jim Martin (1985–93). While he considered himself a conservative, Holshouser enthusiastically backed groundbreaking environmental legislation and much of the program proposed by the liberal teachers' associations. Martin maintained a surface cordiality with the Helms wing of the party, but his key political operatives were most definitely not Helms people. As for policies, Martin continued Hunt's initiatives in economic development and education while pushing a Republican agenda on tax reduction. On the controversial issue of abortion, he walked a political tightrope, expressing opposition to abortion but not pushing hard on the subject.

If there was a last refuge for the more purely conservative Democrats, it was the North Carolina legislature. In fact, the Democratic caucuses featured a sometimes uneasy blend of conservatives, moderates, and liberals. Key leaders, the president pro tem of the Senate and speaker of the House of Representatives, were pragmatic conservatives or pragmatic moderates. Exceptions were Liston Ramsey, an economic populist whose fellow members sometimes resented his dictatorial ways, and Dan Blue, the first African American to lead the House. A coalition of Republicans and insurgent Democrats ousted Ramsey, with the insurgents coming from a wide variety of ideological backgrounds but united by a dislike for Ramsey. Blue's time as speaker ended when Republicans took control of the House in the 1994 elections. For a four-year period, tax cuts and a more conservative agenda took the stage, but Governor Hunt maintained a strong influence.

Political scientists have argued that states may be divided into three cultural spheres: moralistic, which embodies a certain moral puritanism along with a sense of government responsibility for improving public life; individualistic, which stresses a spirit of enterprise and freedom of the individual; and traditionalistic, which promotes elitist rule while discouraging popular movements to improve the lot of the masses. Political scientist Daniel Elazar (1984, 118–22), the leading advocate of this thesis, describes North Carolina as a traditional state with a pronounced moralistic streak (see also Fleer 1994, 15–20). The state's history in race relations and its corporate hierarchy reflect this strain. So did its paternalism when designed to keep the existing power structure in place. More recently, the moralistic streak was shown in Scott's sense of righteousness in promoting economic equality. But Helms, who some might call the personification of a traditional politician, embodied many of the ideas of a puritan. So does the North Carolina public. With economic growth and urbanism has come a more entrepreneurial spirit. In some people, this change enhances a libertarian streak with skepticism of government, while others see government programs in education and economic development as a means to promote general prosperity. As the twentieth century ended, successful politicians were those who satisfied the public's craving for prosperity and at the same time respected the state's strong religious traditions. It is no accident that many leading North Carolina politicians also served as Sunday school teachers. Today, unlike in the past, politicians profess a belief in racial equality even if they oppose specifics such as affirmative action. To be effective, they also need ties to business leaders.

❖ The Progressive Conservative Heritage Lives

By the early twenty-first century, North Carolina had become a tricky state politically, neither solidly Democratic nor solidly Republican. Nor was it an easy state to place along ideological lines. Over the long term, the state clearly had trended Republican.[22] Most observers label North Carolina conservative, but the state produces some decidedly nonconservative politicians. Mildly liberal candidates have a solid base in the state, as do Democrats. In presidential politics, North Carolina would seem to be decisively "red," having gone Republican in nine of ten presidential elections from 1968 through 2004. However, only in 1968, 1972, and 1984 did the Democratic candidates suffer devastating defeats. The overall pattern suggests a state mildly more Republican than America as a whole. Republicans won nine of thirteen U.S. Senate races during the same period. Excluding the five victories by Helms, however, each party won four. U.S. House voting outcomes depend heavily on reapportionment. The Republicans held a seven-to-six edge in 2002 and 2004, but the Democrats reversed the margin in 2006. These electoral outcomes offer a reasonable reflection of the state's sentiments in national politics.

On the state level, the story was different. From 1968 to 2004, Democrats won seven of ten gubernatorial elections, including all four in the 1992–2004 period. In the process, Democrats Hunt and Easley managed victories as impressive as those of Republican presidential candidates in North Carolina. Despite GOP inroads, Democrats had a clear advantage in electing other state executive officials and winning the state Senate. Beginning in 1994, the state House of Representatives was closely divided, the bright spot for the GOP in state-level politics. But here too, by hook or crook, the Democrats maintained a slight upper hand except for a four-year period after the 1994 elections.

North Carolina, like the rest of the South, is more Republican than it was in the middle of the twentieth century. But unlike in neighboring states such as South Carolina and Georgia, North Carolina's Democrats remain a powerful force. Despite Jesse Helms's towering shadow, the state was hardly an economic or social conservative's dream. Yet committed liberals also expressed serious discontent.

How did North Carolina reach its early-twenty-first-century position, giving considerable discomfort both to serious Democratic partisans and committed Republican ideologues? The situation reflects the state's progressive conservative heritage, produced partly by bloodshed and political shenanigans and partly by cautious politicians blending probusiness conservatism with a commitment to education, economic development, and internal improvements such as roads. Among latter-day politicians, attitudes toward African American equality have ranged from grudging acceptance to enthusiasm on the theory that such changes would make the state more prosperous. On the state level, those modern politicians—Democrats and Republicans—who have adapted to the state's heritage have met with the most success, but the Democrats have most often adapted.

Democrats have achieved success in North Carolina in a period when the party has run poorly in much of the South for three reasons. First, the Democratic Party has fielded strong candidates for governor in most elections since 1968 and all contests since 1992. When he was elected in 1992, Hunt was a North Carolina political legend, having blended moderation on social issues with the gospel of economic growth during his first two terms in the governor's mansion. Hunt was comfortable among party activists and in corporate boardrooms. He backed the 1977 constitutional amendment that permitted governors to succeed themselves and became the first beneficiary in 1980.[23] The second Hunt era offered more of the same, with just a slight tilt to the right. Easley's easy wins in 2000 and 2004 provided still more solid evidence of the state-level Democratic strength, occurring when Republican George W. Bush won presidential landslides of 12 percent in the Tar Heel State. Easley was not a political genius in the tradition of Hunt. Some of his actions—for example, skipping major political or civic events—seemed politically inept, yet he, even more than Hunt, connected with ordinary North Carolinians. Easley thrived on stock car racing as a spectator and occasional driver—he even wrecked at Lowe's Motor Speedway in Charlotte. The NASCAR crowd saw him as one of their own. A former prosecutor, Easley supported capital punishment out of more than political expediency: he really seemed to like the death penalty. Sounding a progressive note, Easley ardently supported education, pressing even in lean budgetary times for early childhood education and teacher salary increases. His rhetoric was halting but somehow conveyed what many citizens perceived as a commonsense message. Easley had a sensitive ear to the needs of the business community. In style, Easley combined some of Scott's common touch with an agenda stressing North Carolinians' historic blend of progressive and conservative themes.

Second, the Democrats' path to victory has been cleared in part by growing

Republican factionalism. By the time of the second Hunt era and Easley's ascent, Republican primaries had become mean-spirited affairs. In 2000, Easley's opponent, former Charlotte mayor Richard Vinroot, was scarred in a bitter runoff with state house Republican leader Leo Daughtry. Four years later, Senator Patrick Ballantine of Wilmington prevailed over Vinroot in a late primary, but in the process, Ballantine exhausted his funds. The GOP splits were partly personal and partly ideological. Moderate conservatives and those further to the right disagreed about government's role in society. Some of those on the right expressed strong libertarian views, while others stressed moral conservatism.

Third, the Democratic Party suffered few high-profile defections. Exceptions were Helms in the early 1970s and Walter Jones in the mid-1990s. Both men saw the GOP as more receptive to their conservative philosophies and political ambitions. But most leading Democrats stuck with the party, as did many corporate and civic leaders, even if they might sometimes have backed specific Republicans for president and other offices. North Carolina's Democrats often have prestige and money provided by big business.[24] All the while, the Democratic Party has maintained the support of its core groups, including blacks, feminists, public employees, academics, and lawyers, a powerful coalition at election time.

Near the beginning of twenty-first century, North Carolina is poised to move into megastate status. While some of its localities languish, the overall pattern has been one of economic and population growth. New residents have come from the Northeast, Midwest, and California as well as other parts of the South. Though not yet voting in large numbers, many Hispanics have also arrived in the state. The political culture remains quite traditional in some rural areas, but the large black vote has liberalized the political climate. In the cities, a spirit of entrepreneurship and experimentation prevails. However, conservative churches (including rapidly growing megachurches) exert a strong pull even in places such as Charlotte that seem to be abandoning their traditional roots. North Carolina faces new challenges relating to government accountability, taxation, urban and resort growth, and the environment. It has come a long way from its past, but the political system remains a product of the state's sometimes flawed history.

❖ Notes

1. For a detailed picture of the politics of this period, see Hunt (2003).

2. Essays in this volume focusing especially on Wilmington are Cecelski and Tyson's introduction, Cecelski (1998), and Prather (1998). However, the entire volume presents interesting perspectives on the South and North Carolina in this era. See also Kousser (1974). The

investigation by the Research Branch of the Office of Archives and History in Raleigh offers much information, documentation, and objectivity. For the preliminary draft, which I read, see Umfleet (2005). Umfleet was the principal researcher. The report was released for comment on December 15, 2005.

3. My collection of election statistics in North Carolina shows considerable insurgent strength, especially during the 1930s and 1940s.

4. Some governors—notably Morrison and Gardner—were genuine reformers, but only to a point. Gardner in particular had arguments with the more conservative forces in the state's business and political establishments, but he never wanted to overturn the fundamental societal order.

5. Growing up in North Carolina and keenly interested in history, I recall Aycock's portrayal as our man of enlightenment. Never was any mention made of his racial views except for his belief that children of all races were entitled to public education. Such an education, according to the story line, would qualify everyone to vote.

6. For a broad argument that elitist control promoted conservative values along with some growth, see Luebke (1990).

7. In appearance as well as history and culture, the western sand hills around Southern Pines resemble the Piedmont. The eastern sand hill region is flatter, has more African Americans, and is much like the coastal plain.

8. Specifically, the counties of Davie and Yadkin, entirely within the Piedmont, consistently voted Republican throughout the twentieth century in national state and local elections. Randolph was closely divided. Other Piedmont counties were typically 40 percent or more Republican.

9. Then as now, activists dominated conventions. The Democratic establishment had tremendous institutional advantages in determining convention schedules and agendas.

10. For an excellent account of Scott's political and governing strategy, see Coon (1968). Scott had ridiculed the idea of a bond issue during the 1948 campaign. The legislature was skeptical about Scott's plans for road building and education and thought the state's voters would not approve a bond issue. After his election, Scott saw a popular vote as the only chance to enact his programs. Despite his earlier opposition, he persuaded the legislature to authorize a popular referendum. Scott's gamble paid off, and voters approved the measures, much to the chagrin of Scott's legislative enemies.

11. See Pleasants and Burns (1990).

12. Covington and Ellis (1999) provide a thorough explanation that still leaves the reader in doubt about Sanford's true motives. Overall, this book provides a comprehensive, sympathetic, but penetrating picture of Sanford the man and the governor. For good background on Sanford and race, see Drescher (2000).

13. Critics called Sanford's campaign promises on education pie in the sky. Delivering on them required all the negotiating skills Sanford could muster and some manipulation, but deliver he did.

14. Sanford's personal instincts seemed to be for the underdog. He was of the Great Depression–New Deal generation. He was also pragmatic. Sanford may never have read Key's *Southern Politics*, but he knew the influence of the state's corporate leadership and cultivated it in his 1960 gubernatorial campaign. He also understood that many legislators were probusiness and deeply conservative on social issues, an understanding that influenced his strategy on policy.

15. Goldwater's weakness in the strongly segregationist lowland areas of North Carolina was unique in the South. In the 1960 and 1964 Democratic primaries, segregationist Beverly Lake had turned in strong showings in eastern North Carolina. Voters in the region failed to support Goldwater in part because of fear that he would advocate ending a federal tobacco price support program. Another factor was a strong state Democratic Party push to vote the straight party ticket. Most officials worked hard for the ticket. Lyndon Johnson's southern roots also seemed to help.

16. The official general election returns and primary returns are available in the *North Carolina Manual*, published every two years by the Office of the Secretary of State. I have developed an election profile with an emphasis on partisan trends and racial voting.

17. Pleasants (2000) portrayed Reynolds as a paradoxical figure, not a classic southern demagogue. Pleasants deals skillfully with the manner in which Reynolds blended elements of economic populism and ethnocentrism.

18. Ervin's role in Watergate initially was not especially popular back home in North Carolina. In the spring of 1974, he might have been vulnerable to a challenge from Attorney General Robert Morgan in a primary. As it turned out, Ervin retired, and Morgan won both the primary and general election. By the general election, Nixon had resigned.

19. Had Helms run again, a serious health crisis might have arisen during the campaign. This would have weakened him against a strong Democratic challenger, much as Terry Sanford lost his bid for reelection after having open-heart surgery in October 1992.

20. Illustrating the liberal trend in urban areas, the counties of Durham and Orange (Chapel Hill) supported Democrat John Kerry by a two-to-one ratio in 2004. Mecklenburg (Charlotte) and Guilford (Greensboro) gave Kerry narrower edges, bucking the trend whereby both counties had voted Republican in the great majority of presidential elections from the 1950s through the 1980s.

21. Moderate to liberal white Democratic politicians were privately very upset over the creation of majority black districts, fearing that they would elect either black Democrats or white Republicans. Likewise, Republican strategists indicated off the record that they were pleased with the new districts, which created new opportunities for the GOP. While the Supreme Court ruled that race could not be the primary motive in drawing district lines (*Shaw v. Reno*, 1993), North Carolina's boundaries were not drastically altered. For an excellent account of the legal and political arguments over reapportionment, see Yarbrough (2002).

22. Republican strength in presidential elections reached peaks in 1972 and 1984, levels to which it has not come close to returning. The trend in congressional races has been Repub-

lican, but this trend has been subject to twists and turns. For U.S. House seats and the state legislature, a major shift in partisan balance is likely only if and when Republicans control both houses of the state legislature as well as the governorship in a reapportionment year.

23. Though members of both parties may not have anticipated this outcome, the succession amendment might well have paved the way for a Democratic edge in gubernatorial races over the next quarter century. Hunt in 1980 and 1996 and Easley in 2004 won reelection as powerful incumbents in election seasons when less seasoned Democratic candidates might have been vulnerable. Martin, a Republican, easily won reelection in 1988, but the GOP's presidential candidate, George H. W. Bush, also ran strongly in North Carolina.

24. Partly because of close personal relationships and partly because they like being with winners, North Carolina's business elites have often been highly generous with Democratic candidates. Businesses such as banks and utilities benefit from growth and general prosperity, agendas strongly promoted by Democrats such as Hunt and Easley. Business interests dependent on growth could well see more benefits form Democratic spending on public education and infrastructure than from Republican tax reduction.

❖ References

Brown v. Board of Education of Topeka. 1954. 347 U.S. 483.

Burns, Augustus M., and Julian M. Pleasants. 1990. *Frank Graham and the 1950 Senate Race in North Carolina.* Chapel Hill: University of North Carolina Press.

Cecelski, David S. 1998. "Abraham H. Galloway: Wilmington's Lost Prophet and the Rise of Black Radicalism in the American South." In *Democracy Betrayed: The Wilmington Race Riot of 1898 and Its Legacy*, edited by David S. Cecelski and Timothy B. Tyson, 43–73. Chapel Hill: University of North Carolina Press.

Cecelski, David S., and Timothy B. Tyson, eds. 1998. *Democracy Betrayed: The Wilmington Race Riot of 1898 and Its Legacy.* Chapel Hill: University of North Carolina Press.

Coon, William John. 1968. "Kerr Scott, the 'Go Forward' Governor: His Origins, His Program, and the North Carolina General Assembly."

Covington, Howard E., Jr., and Marion A. Ellis. 1999. *Terry Sanford: Politics, Progress, and Outrageous Ambitions.* Durham: Duke University Press.

Drescher, John. 2000. *Triumph of Good Will.* Oxford: University of Mississippi Press.

Elazar, Daniel J. 1984. *American Federalism: A View from the States.* New York: Harper and Row.

Fleer, Jack D. 1994. *North Carolina Government and Politics.* Lincoln: University of Nebraska Press.

Gilmore, Glenda Elizabeth. 1996. *Gender and Jim Crow: Women and the Politics of White Supremacy in North Carolina, 1986–1920.* Chapel Hill: University of North Carolina Press.

Gunther, John. 1946. *Inside U.S.A.* Philadelphia: Curtis.

Hunt, James L. 2003. *Marion Butler and American Populism.* Chapel Hill: University of North Carolina Press.

Key, V. O., Jr. 1949. *Southern Politics in State and Nation*. New York: Knopf.

Kousser, J. Morgan. 1974. *The Shaping of Southern Politics: Suffrage Restrictions and the Establishment of the One-Party South*. New Haven: Yale University Press.

Luebke, Paul. 1990. *Tar Heel Politics: Myths and Realities*. Chapel Hill: University of North Carolina Press.

Pleasants, Julian M. 2000. *Buncombe Bob: The Life and Times of Robert Rice Reynolds*. Chapel Hill: University of North Carolina Press.

Pleasants, Julian M., and Augustus M. Burns. 1990. *Frank Graham and the 1950 Senate Race in North Carolina*. Chapel Hill: University of North Carolina Press.

Powell, William. 1989. *North Carolina: Through Four Centuries*. Chapel Hill: University of North Carolina Press.

Prather, H. Leon, Sr. "We Have Taken A City: A Centennial Essay." In *Democracy Betrayed: The Wilmington Race Riot of 1898 and Its Legacy*, edited by David S. Cecelski and Timothy B. Tyson, 15–41. Chapel Hill: University of North Carolina Press.

Sanford, Terry. 1966. *But What about the People?* New York: Harper and Row.

Shaw v. Reno. 1993. 509 U.S. 630.

State Library of North Carolina. Information Services Branch. 2004. "North Carolina Governors." <http://statelibrary.dcr.state.nc.us/nc/stgovt/governor.htm>. Accessed September 14, 2007.

Umfleet, LeRae. 2005. "1898 Wilmington Race Riot Report" (draft). <www.ah.dcr.state.nc.us/1898-wrrc/>. Accessed September 15, 2007.

U.S. Senate. N.d. "U.S. Senators from North Carolina." <http://www.senate.gov/pagelayout/senators/one_item_and_teasers/north_carolina.htm>. Accessed September 14, 2007.

Yarbrough, Tinsley E. 2002. *Race and Redistricting: The Shaw-Cromartie Cases*. Lawrence: University Press of Kansas.

❖ 2. How Southern Is the Old North State?

Public Opinion in North Carolina

TIMOTHY VERCELLOTTI

Social scientists typically treat the South as a region unique unto itself in terms of political behavior and opinion. The general perception of the South has been that its residents are more ideologically conservative than the rest of the nation, are less trusting of national government, and eschew active government and embrace the self-reliance of individualism as core political values (Black and Black 1987; Glaser 2005; Reed 1986). While evidence exists to support these broad assertions, treating the South as a monolith overlooks the potentially varying effects of historical, cultural, and social forces in different parts of the region.

In the case of public opinion in North Carolina, there is reason to believe that while the state shares some characteristics with the rest of the South, clear differences also exist. V. O. Key Jr., in his landmark 1949 study, *Southern Politics in State and Nation*, argued that North Carolina was distinct from the rest of the South and more like the rest of the nation because the state's residents were relatively progressive regarding education, industrial development, and race relations. Key traced the roots of the differences to a coalition of Republican and Populist rule at the turn of the twentieth century. Nearly five decades after the publication of Key's study, Paul Luebke (1998) also argued that North Carolinians were distinct from other southerners, but for different reasons. Luebke pointed to the recent in-migration of nonsoutherners as a motivating force behind North Carolina's more moderate brand of politics, which stood in contrast to what had been observed in Deep South states such as Alabama, Mississippi, and South Carolina.

In this essay, I will explore the dynamics of public opinion in North Carolina, with an emphasis on how the state compares to the rest of the South and to the nation as a whole. National poll data permit comparisons of attitudes in the South to those of the rest of the country. But there is also the potential for variation in opinion within the state, with differences among native North Carolinians, those who have migrated to North Carolina from other parts of the South, and those who have moved there from outside the South. Several statewide public opinion surveys in which respondents were asked to state their places of birth permit testing for variation by comparing the views of natives and newcomers from within and outside the South. The data provide an opportunity to examine whether those who have moved to North Carolina from other parts of the South and from areas outside of the South differ in systematic ways from native North Carolinians.

The essay will pay special attention to variation in political ideology, one of the key characteristics that shapes public opinion about politics and policy. I will also examine variation in public opinion concerning trust in government, political values, and religion. In addition, the essay takes into account race in the context of whether public opinion among African Americans in North Carolina differs systematically from the views of African Americans elsewhere in the South and the country. The primary question to be considered in each case is to what extent the Old North State is similar to or different from the rest of the South and the nation in terms of attitudes concerning politics and government.

❖ Public Opinion below the Mason-Dixon Line

Political observers widely perceive southern voters as conservative in their approach to politics and government, with an outlook rooted in a traditionalist southern Protestant culture of individual responsibility. In addition, adherents to this view see economic inequality as a natural result of differences in individuals' abilities and skills and how they use those abilities and skills (Black and Black 1987). That outlook translates into political values in which government should adopt a hands-off approach to economic matters and individuals should look to themselves to overcome life's obstacles and advance in society.

Mixed in with this outlook, however, is the acknowledgment that economic crises at times are so massive in scope and the resultant problems so intractable that the government must step in to help its citizens. Southerners were forced to accept federal government assistance during the Great Depression. But the catastrophic nature of the nation's economic collapse allowed southerners to view the depression as an extraordinary set of circumstances yet maintain their views about an unobtrusive government and the importance of the self-reliance of individualism as a fundamental political value (Black and Black 1987). John Shelton Reed (1986, 101) observes that the general attitude among an overwhelming number of southerners comes down to, "In the last analysis, you (or, at best, you and your neighbors) are on your own." Writing more recently, James M. Glaser (2005) observes that the increasing suburbanization of the South, with its sprawling subdivisions and car-oriented lifestyle, further contributes to an individualistic approach to life.

While southerners may prefer self-reliance and a less activist government, these values tend to vary by race and to a lesser extent by ideology in the South. Earl Black and Merle Black (1987) observe that the political culture of African Americans and a narrow segment of white populists holds that the government should be responsible for short-term assistance to low-income groups through the redistribution of wealth and power. Thus, while the South's overall political ideology is one of conservatism, economic liberalism prevails among African Americans and a small percentage of white residents. In addition, while regional differences may exist concerning whether government should help those who are less fortunate or whether they should rely on themselves, those regional differences are less likely to exist among African Americans. Katherine Tate (1994) found no regional variation between African Americans in the South and in other parts of the country regarding support for the idea that the national government should guarantee jobs for all citizens and provide jobs for the unemployed. Blacks in the South, however, were less likely to support the federal food stamp program.

Widespread conservative views also translate into mistrustful attitudes concerning government, with white southerners less likely to trust government than their counterparts outside of the region. Trust in government gradually declined in the South from the 1950s through the 1970s as the national government adopted civil rights and voting rights legislation. Analyzing American National Election Studies data, Black and Black (1987) note that the decline in trust was pronounced among white southerners, beginning with working-class whites in the 1960s and spreading to middle-class whites in the 1970s as a result of desegregation and the negative effects of inflation on southerners' standards of living.

The same is not necessarily true, however, for African Americans across the board. While Marc J. Hetherington (1998) finds that African Americans tend to distrust government nationally, Robert C. Smith and Richard Seltzer (1992) argue that African Americans' levels of trust in government vary by region. Blacks outside the South, while more politically knowledgeable and efficacious than their southern counterparts, tend to have lower levels of trust in government than do blacks in the South. The differences are consistent with what existed during the Black Power movement in northern cities during the late 1960s and early 1970s, in which alienation combined with political knowledge and efficacy to fuel activism.

In addition to greater levels of conservatism and political individualism and lower levels of trust in government among white residents, the South also is known for its high degree of religiosity. Reed (1986) notes that although some cultural differences between the South and the non-South diminished from the 1960s to the 1980s, the gap in the percentage of southern and nonsouthern survey respondents who said they attend worship services regularly remained the same or increased slightly during the same period, with southerners reporting higher levels of church attendance.

The greater degree of religiosity in the South translates into more conservative views regarding social issues as well as matters involving separation of church and state. Indeed, one of the more highly celebrated church-state disputes in the nation in recent years occurred in Alabama in 2003, when Chief Justice Roy Moore of the state Supreme Court was removed from the bench in a dispute over a monument to the Ten Commandments that Moore had erected in the state's judicial building (Gettleman 2003). While church-state disputes seem to occur on a regular basis around the country, higher levels of religiosity in the South tend to increase the intensity of these disputes.

❖ Distinctive Nature of North Carolina

Examining public opinion in the South requires taking into account potential variation within the region. Scholars argue that North Carolina is distinct from other parts of the South because of a number of political, economic, and social factors. As a result, public opinion on certain issues in North Carolina may differ from views in other parts of the South or from attitudes in areas outside of the South.

Writing in the 1940s, Key found that North Carolina differed from other southern states and was more like the rest of the nation in some respects:

> The prevailing mood in North Carolina is not hard to sense. It is
> energetic and ambitious. The citizens are determined and confident; they
> are on the move. The mood is at odds with much of the rest of the South—
> a tenor of attitude and of action that has set the state apart from its
> neighbors. Many see in North Carolina a closer approximation to national
> norms, or national expectations of performance, than they find elsewhere
> in the South. . . . It enjoys a reputation for progressive outlook and action
> in many phases of life, especially industrial development, education, and
> race relations. (1949, 205)

Economic factors played a large role in North Carolina's distinctiveness. The state had fewer sprawling plantations and thus was not nearly as reliant on slave labor before the Civil War as were other southern states. Indeed, North Carolina refused to follow other southern states in seceding from the union until Virginia and South Carolina had done so (Key 1949, 207). Key also found that heavy investment in public education, particularly at the university level, played an important part in moving the state forward during the twentieth century. Tobacco farming and textile manufacturing contributed to the state's strong economy. He also pointed to the citizenry's "willingness to accept new ideas, sense of community responsibility toward the Negro, feeling of common purpose, and relative prosperity" (210).

North Carolina's progressivism appears to have survived even as the state underwent significant political changes in the second half of the twentieth century. Jack D. Fleer (1968) and Charles Prysby (this volume) note that the Republican Party began to spread its influence from its historic stronghold in the state's mountain counties in the west in the 1940s, expanding into the industrialized and urbanized Piedmont and even into the heavily Democratic eastern end of the state. The Democrats maintained their statewide dominance into the 1960s, but the trend clearly favored a more competitive two-party state. North Carolina supported Richard Nixon for president in 1968 and 1972. After backing Democrat (and southerner) Jimmy Carter for president in 1976, North Carolina proceeded to support Republican presidential candidates in every election from 1980 through 2004.

Republican success at the state level was less clear-cut. Republicans were elected governor of North Carolina in three of five elections in the 1970s and 1980s, but Democrats then captured the office four consecutive times from 1992 through 2004. Democrats controlled both chambers of the state General Assembly until 1994, when Republicans gained control of the state House of Representatives. The Republican Party maintained control of the House in 1996. Although Democrats won control of the House in 1998, 2000, 2002, and 2004, the party's advantage typically consisted of only a few seats.

A combination of regional and national forces contributed to the rise of the Republican Party and creation of a two-party state. Southern Democrats became disenchanted with the national party's emphasis on racial equality beginning in the 1960s (Luebke 1998, 189). By the 1980s, the national Republican Party's emphasis on tax cuts and reducing the size of government also became an attractive message to North Carolina voters (Luebke 1998, 208).

The political forces at work in North Carolina similarly influenced the balance of power in other southern states (Glaser 2005). Luebke (1998) argues, however, that even with these widespread changes, North Carolina has remained distinct from the rest of the region in terms of its politics. The sizable migration of non-southerners into the state beginning in the 1980s has at least partially offset the growing conservatism of native North Carolinians. Less conservative newcomers have relocated to the metropolitan areas in the Piedmont section of the state, along with counties popular with retirees. Luebke cites as evidence of this moderating influence the results of exit polls for the 1990 and 1996 U.S. Senate races, in which former Charlotte mayor Harvey Gantt, a Democrat, lost to Senator Jesse Helms, a Republican. In both elections, Gantt, who is African American, won a majority of votes from white voters who had lived in North Carolina for less than ten years. "While native-born North Carolinians gave only about one-third of their votes to Gantt, their relative size in the statewide electorate was declining," Luebke writes (1998, 236).

The distinctiveness of North Carolina's political culture relative to the rest of the South appears to spring from two sources: the state's historical legacy of progressivism and the recent influx of more moderate voters from outside the South. One might expect, then, that public opinion in North Carolina might fall somewhere between that of the rest of the South and that of the rest of the nation on the ideological spectrum. Further, in light of recent demographic changes in the state, public opinion might be expected to vary based on whether one was born in North Carolina, elsewhere in the South, or outside the South.

❖ Data Analysis

I compare public opinion in North Carolina to public opinion in the South and outside the South using data from several sources: the Elon University Poll (a statewide telephone survey of adult North Carolinians conducted several times per year by the Center for Public Opinion Polling at Elon University in North Carolina) and several national polls obtained through the Roper Center for Public Opinion Research at the University of Connecticut.

Turning first to political ideology, evidence supports the assertion that North Carolina, in the aggregate, tends to be more conservative than the rest of the nation (see table 2.1). Twenty-seven percent of respondents in an April 2005 national survey conducted for the Kaiser Family Foundation identified themselves as politically conservative, and 25 percent said they were moderate. Each of these percentages is slightly lower than comparable data from an Elon University Poll conducted in February 2005, in which 32 percent of respondents identified themselves as conservative, and 33 percent said they were moderate.

Breaking down the national data by where respondents live and the state data by where they were born also reveals differences that are in line with expectations (see table 2.2). In the national sample, respondents living in the South were more likely than respondents living outside the South to say they were conservative (31 percent to 25 percent). Southerners also were less likely to identify themselves as liberals than were nonsoutherners (11 percent compared to 20 percent). Using a chi-square test to calculate the probability that the observed differences between southerners and nonsoutherners exist in the population shows that the probability that the differences result from chance is less than .1 percent.

In North Carolina, those who said they were born in the state or other parts of the South were more likely to identify themselves as conservative than those who said they were born outside of the South. The difference in percentages for moderates born outside the South was sizable—10 to 13 points—in comparison to those born in North Carolina or other parts of the South. This provides some evidence

TABLE 2.1. Comparing Ideology in North Carolina and the United States

Kaiser Family Foundation National Poll		Elon University Statewide Poll	
Would you say your views in most political matters are liberal, moderate, conservative, something else, or haven't you given this much thought?		When it comes to politics, do you usually think of yourself as very liberal, liberal, moderate or middle of the road, conservative, very conservative, or haven't you thought much about this?	
Liberal	17%	Very liberal/liberal	16%
Moderate	25	Moderate	33
Conservative	27	Very conservative/conservative	32
Something else	4		
Haven't given this much thought	25	Haven't thought much about this	18
Don't know/refused	2	No response	1
N	1,201		571
Dates 4/1/05–5/1/05		2/14/05–2/17/05	

Note: Percentages may not add to 100 due to rounding.

in support of the expectation that those who have moved to North Carolina from other parts of the country tend to have a moderating influence on the state's politics. But these differences must be viewed with some caution. The overall differences among the three groups—those born in North Carolina, those born in other parts of the South, and those born outside of the South—were not statistically significant.

Data for trust in government also revealed differences between the nation and North Carolina (see table 2.3). Thirty-four percent of those polled by National Public Radio, the Kaiser Family Foundation, and Harvard University in February and March 2003 said that they trusted the federal government nearly always or most of the time, compared with 29 percent in a North Carolina survey conducted by Elon University in October 2003. Sixty-four percent of the national sample said that they trusted the federal government only some or none of the time, compared with 70 percent in North Carolina. These findings appear to offer some support for the claim that trust in government is lower in the South, even in North Carolina.

Breaking down the national sample into those living in the South and outside the South, however, reveals no statistically significant differences (see table 2.4). Some variation does surface, however, in North Carolina. Eighty percent of survey

TABLE 2.2. Ideology and Southern Heritage

Kaiser Family Foundation National Poll			Elon University Statewide Poll			
Would you say your views in most political matters are liberal, moderate, conservative, something else, or haven't you given this much thought?			When it comes to politics, do you usually think of yourself as very liberal, liberal, moderate or middle of the road, conservative, very conservative, or haven't you thought much about this?			
	Lives outside South	Lives in South		Born outside South	Born in South outside N.C.	Born in N.C.
Liberal	20%	11%	Very liberal/liberal	17%	13%	16%
Moderate	26	24	Moderate	41	28	31
Conservative	25	31	Very conservative/ conservative	28	33	34
Something else	4	4				
Haven't given this much thought	24	29	Haven't thought much about this	13	24	19
Don't know/refused	2	1	No response	1	1	0
N	819	382		179	84	308
Chi-square = 39.6 5 df p < 0.001			Chi-square = 11.2 8 df p = 0.19			
Dates 4/1/05–5/1/05			2/14/05–2/17/05			

respondents who said that they were born in the South but outside North Carolina said that they trusted the government in Washington some or none of the time, compared with 71 percent of those born outside the South and 66 percent of native North Carolinians. The data provide additional evidence that nonsoutherners who have moved to North Carolina serve as a moderating influence, but native North Carolinians also are more likely to trust in government than those born elsewhere in the South.

To test for variation in political values regarding active government and individualism, I analyzed two questions from an Elon University Poll conducted in February 2005 and compared those questions with similar versions from a national poll conducted by the Kaiser Family Foundation, National Public Radio, and Harvard University in January and February 2001 (see table 2.5). Respondents in the North Carolina sample were more likely to say that the government is spending too little to fight poverty (58 percent) than those in the national sample (38 percent). North Carolinians were far less likely to say that the government was

TABLE 2.3. Comparing Trust in Government in North Carolina and the United States

Kaiser/NPR/Harvard National Poll		Elon University Statewide Poll	
How much of the time do you trust the federal government in Washington to do what is right—just about always, most of the time, only some of the time, or none of the time?		How much of the time do you think you can trust the government in Washington to do what is right?	
Just about always	7%	Just about always	3%
Most of the time	27	Most of the time	26
Only some of the time	52	Some of the time	59
None of the time	12	None of the time	11
Don't know/refused	2	Don't know/no response	1
N	1,339		492
Dates 2/5/03–3/17/03		10/27/03–10/30/03	

spending the right amount (19 percent) than were respondents in the national sample (36 percent). Although variation in question wording could account for some of the difference, it is unlikely that it completely explains the seventeen- to twenty-point gap between the samples on these views. In contrast to expectations, North Carolinians appear to prefer a more active government than residents of the country as a whole.

Further evidence of regional differences emerges when breaking down the national data by southerner/nonsoutherner and the North Carolina data by place of birth (see table 2.6). In the national sample, southerners were slightly more likely than nonsoutherners to say that the country is spending too much on assistance to the poor (22 percent to 16 percent). Among North Carolinians, those who were born in the South outside of North Carolina were more likely to say that the government is spending too much fighting poverty (21 percent, compared with 14 percent for native North Carolinians and 11 percent for those born outside of the South).

While the data point to regional and some intrastate variation in attitudes toward active government, the same was not entirely true of the political value of individualism. Drawing from the Elon and Kaiser/National Public Radio/Harvard surveys, I analyzed responses to similar questions about who is to blame for poverty—individuals or factors beyond individuals' control (see table 2.7). If respondents embraced the value of individualism, they would be more likely to say that people who are poor are not doing enough to help themselves. Respondents

TABLE 2.4. Trust in Government and Southern Heritage

Kaiser/NPR/Harvard National Poll		Elon University Statewide Poll			
How much of the time do you trust the federal government in Washington to do what is right—just about always, most of the time, only some of the time, or none of the time?		How much of the time do you think you can trust the government in Washington to do what is right?			
	Lives outside South	Lives in South		Born outside South	Born in South outside N.C.	Born in N.C.
Just about always	7%	8%	Just about always	4%	2%	3%
Most of the time	28	26	Most of the time	23	18	30
Only some of the time	52	52	Some of the time	63	59	56
None of the time	12	12	None of the time	8	21	10
Don't know/ refused	2	2	Don't know/ no response	1	0	1
N	871	468		161	63	268
Chi-square = 2.2 5 df p = 0.82		Chi-square = 14.5 8 df p = 0.07			
Dates 2/5/03–3/17/03		10/27/03–10/30/03			

in the national sample were more likely than those in the North Carolina data to have this view (48 percent and 37 percent, respectively). Breaking down the data by region in the national sample and place of birth in the North Carolina sample, however, provides a picture that is somewhat closer to expectations (see table 2.8). In the national sample, southerners were significantly more likely to assign responsibility to the poor for their plight than were nonsoutherners (55 percent to 45 percent). The differences in the North Carolina sample, broken down by place of birth, were not statistically significant. Overall, the national data provided stronger evidence than the North Carolina data that southerners are more likely to embrace the values of active government and individualism. This finding arguably provides further evidence that North Carolina is more moderate than the rest of the South in terms of political values, but the lack of statistical significance in the North Carolina data by place of birth weakens the argument.

The data concerning religiosity are less ambiguous (see table 2.9). A national survey conducted by Gallup for CNN and USA Today in September 2003 found that 40 percent of respondents said they attend church or synagogue almost every week or at least once a week. An Elon University Poll conducted in March 2005,

TABLE 2.5. Comparing Aid to Poor in North Carolina and the United States

Kaiser/NPR/Harvard National Poll		Elon University Statewide Poll	
In terms of the amount of money we as a country are spending on assistance to poor people, do you think we are spending too much, too little, or about the right amount?		When it comes to fighting poverty, do you think the government is spending too much, too little, or the right amount?	
Too much	18%	Too much	14%
Too little	38	Too little	58
About the right amount	36	The right amount	19
Don't know/refused	8	Don't know/no response	9
N	1,952		526
Dates 1/4/01–2/27/01		2/14/05–2/17/05	

TABLE 2.6. Aid to Poor and Southern Heritage

Kaiser/NPR/Harvard National Poll			Elon University Statewide Poll			
In terms of the amount of money we as a country are spending on assistance to poor people, do you think we are spending too much, too little, or about the right amount?			When it comes to fighting poverty, do you think the government is spending too much, too little, or the right amount?			
	Lives outside South	Lives in South		Born outside South	Born in South outside N.C.	Born in N.C.
Too much	16%	22%	Too much	11%	21%	14%
Too little	38	36	Too little	63	52	56
About the right amount	37	34	The right amount	19	22	19
Don't know/ refused	8	8	Don't know/no response	7	5	12
N	1,328	624		167	74	285
Chi-square = 9.5 4 df p = 0.05			Chi-square = 10.6 8 df p = 0.22			
Dates 1/4/01–2/27/01			2/14/05–2/17/05			

TABLE 2.7. Comparing Reasons for Poverty in North Carolina and the United States

Kaiser/NPR/Harvard National Poll		Elon University Statewide Poll	
In your opinion, which is the bigger cause of poverty today—that people are not doing enough to help themselves out of poverty or that circumstances beyond their control cause them to be poor?		In your opinion, what is more often to blame if a person is poor—lack of effort on their own part or circumstances beyond their control?	
People aren't doing enough to help themselves out of poverty	48%	Lack of effort	37%
Circumstances beyond their control cause them to be poor	45	Circumstances beyond their control	47
Don't know/refused	7	Don't know/no response	15
N	1,952		526
Dates 1/4/01–2/27/01		2/14/05–2/17/05	

however, found that 50 percent of North Carolinians said that they attend religious services every week or almost every week. The differences persist when the samples are broken down based on where the respondents lived at the time of the survey or where they were born (see table 2.10). Forty-seven percent of southerners surveyed in the Gallup/CNN/USA *Today* poll said that they attend church or synagogue at least once a week or almost every week, compared with 37 percent of nonsoutherners. In North Carolina, 55 percent of native-born North Carolinians said they attend religious services every week or almost every week, as did 52 percent of those born in other parts of the South and 42 percent of those born outside of the South. The results of both polls were statistically significant and support the assertion that attendance at worship services is higher among southerners than nonsoutherners. Whether those southerners were born in North Carolina or another state in the region appears to make little difference.

While levels of religiosity are higher in the South, do those differences extend to views about the separation of church and state (see tables 2.11–2.14)? To answer this question, I examined data generated by similar questions about displaying the Ten Commandments in public schools or government buildings. Seventy percent of the national sample approved of a monument to the Ten Commandments in a public school or government building, while the percentage supporting displays of the Ten Commandments in government buildings ranged from 72 to 77 percent in North Carolina. In each case, the difference between southerners and nonsoutherners was pronounced. In the national sample, 81 percent of southern-

TABLE 2.8. Reasons for Poverty and Southern Heritage

Kaiser/NPR/Harvard National Poll			Elon University Statewide Poll			
In your opinion, which is the bigger cause of poverty today—that people are not doing enough to help themselves out of poverty or that circumstances beyond their control cause them to be poor?			In your opinion, what is more often to blame if a person is poor—lack of effort on their own part or circumstances beyond their control?			
	Lives outside South	Lives in South		Born outside South	Born in South outside N.C.	Born in N.C.
People aren't doing enough to help themselves out of poverty	45%	55%	Lack of effort	40%	40%	35%
Circumstances beyond their control cause them to be poor	47	39	Circumstances beyond their control	45	41	50
Don't know/ refused	8	6	Don't know/ no response	15	18	14
N	1,328	624		167	74	285
Chi-square = 14.5 3 df p < 0.01			Chi-square = 2.8 6 df p = 0.84			
Dates 1/4/01–2/27/01			2/14/05–2/17/05			

ers supported monuments, compared to 65 percent of nonsoutherners (a statistically significant difference). In North Carolina, both native North Carolinians and those born in other parts of the South were more likely to support public displays of the Ten Commandments than were nonsoutherners who had moved to North Carolina. The results provide further evidence that outsiders who have moved to North Carolina from beyond the South have a moderating effect on public opinion in the state.

The data analysis to this point has compared North Carolina with national data and examined response patterns among North Carolinians who were born in the state or who moved there from somewhere else. While some regional differences in opinion have emerged, it is also useful to consider some of the measures in the context of race. Previous research on public opinion among African Americans

TABLE 2.9. Comparing Church Attendance in North Carolina and the United States

Gallup/CNN/USA *Today* National Poll		Elon University Statewide Poll	
How often do you attend church or synagogue—at least once a week, almost every week, about once a month, seldom, or never?		Do you go to religious services every week, almost every week, once or twice a month, a few times a year, or never?	
At least once a week	29%	Every week	34%
Almost every week	11	Almost every week	16
About once a month	16	Once or twice a month	16
Seldom	28	A few times a year	12
Never	15	Never	20
Don't know/refused	0	Don't know/no response	1
N	1,003		571
Dates 9/19/03–9/21/03		3/7/05–3/10/05	

TABLE 2.10. Church Attendance and Southern Heritage

Gallup/CNN/*USA Today* National Poll			Elon University Statewide Poll			
How often do you attend church or synagogue—at least once a week, almost every week, about once a month, seldom, or never?			Do you go to religious services every week, almost every week, once or twice a month, a few times a year, or never?			
	Lives outside South	Lives in South		Born outside South	Born in South outside N.C.	Born in N.C.
At least once a week	27%	34%	Every week	23%	34%	40%
Almost every week	10	13	Almost every week	19	18	15
About once a month	16	17	Once or twice a month	12	19	17
Seldom	30	25	A few times a year	12	11	13
Never	17	10	Never	33	17	14
Don't know/refused	1	0	Don't know/no response	1	1	1
N	722	281		179	84	308
Chi-square = 13.5 5 df p < 0.05			Chi-square = 33.5 10 df p < 0.001			
Dates 9/19/03–9/21/03			3/7/05–3/10/05			

TABLE 2.11. Support for Ten Commandments Nationally

Gallup/CNN/USA *Today* National Poll

Please say whether you approve or disapprove of each of the following: How about . . . display of a monument to the Ten Commandments in a public school or government building?

	National Sample	Lives outside South	Lives in South
Approve	70%	65%	81%
Disapprove	29	34	19
Don't know/refused	1	1	1
N	1,003	722	281

Chi-square = 23.3 3 df p < 0.001
Dates 9/19/03–9/21/03

TABLE 2.12. Support for Ten Commandments in North Carolina City Council Chambers

Elon University Statewide Poll

Do you support or oppose allowing the government to display the Ten Commandments on government property? Would you support or oppose displays in the following locations? Inside a city council chamber?

	Statewide Sample	Born outside South	Born in South outside N.C.	Born in N.C.
Support	77%	61%	76%	87%
Oppose	15	27	16	9
Don't know/no response	7	12	7	5
N	571	179	84	308

Chi-square = 43.4 4 df p < 0.001
Dates 3/7/05–3/10/05

indicates that differences may exist between blacks and whites in North Carolina and between blacks in North Carolina and elsewhere in the nation.

Turning first to the political values of active government and individualism, one would expect that African Americans would be more supportive of active government and less supportive of individualism than their white counterparts in North Carolina (see table 2.15). By a large margin—81 percent to 23 percent—

TABLE 2.13. Support for Ten Commandments in North Carolina Courtrooms

Elon University Statewide Poll

Do you support or oppose allowing the government to display the Ten Commandments on government property? Would you support or oppose displays in the following
locations? Inside a courtroom?

	Statewide Sample	Born outside South	Born in South outside N.C.	Born in N.C.
Support	76%	62%	74%	86%
Oppose	18	31	18	10
Don't know/no response	5	7	7	4
N	571	179	84	308

Chi-square = 38.7 4 df p < 0.001
Dates 3/7/05–3/10/05

TABLE 2.14. Support for Ten Commandments in North Carolina Public School Classrooms

Elon University Statewide Poll

Do you support or oppose allowing the government to display the Ten Commandments on government property? Would you support or oppose displays in the following
locations? Inside a public school classroom?

	Statewide Sample	Born outside South	Born in South outside N.C.	Born in N.C.
Support	72%	56%	74%	81%
Oppose	21	35	20	14
Don't know/no response	6	10	6	5
N	571	179	84	308

Chi-square = 36.3 4 df p < 0.001
Dates 3/7/05–3/10/05

African Americans in North Carolina are significantly more likely than whites to
believe that the government needs to spend more on fighting poverty. Contrary to
previous research showing no difference in support for active government based
on region, blacks in North Carolina also outpace their counterparts nationally in
supporting active government.

African Americans in North Carolina also are less likely than whites to embrace

TABLE 2.15. Comparing Aid to Poor by Race in North Carolina and the United States

Kaiser/NPR/Harvard National Poll			Elon University Statewide Poll		
In terms of the amount of money we as a country are spending on assistance to poor people, do you think we are spending too much, too little, or about the right amount?			When it comes to fighting poverty, do you think the government is spending too much, too little, or the right amount?		
	White	Black		White	Black
Too much	20%	10%	Too much	15%	5%
Too little	35	59	Too little	23	81
About the right amount	36	27	The right amount	52	7
Don't know/refused	9	4	Don't know/ no response	11	7
N	1,335	344		418	70
Chi-square = 50.4 4 df p < 0.001			Chi-square = 30.2 4 df p < 0.001		
Dates 1/4/01–2/27/01			2/14/05–2/17/05		

the values of individualism (see table 2.16). Only 22 percent of African American respondents agreed that poverty occurs because of a lack of effort, compared with 39 percent of white North Carolinians. In addition, blacks in North Carolina were less likely to endorse individualism than were blacks in the national sample.

Somewhat related to the values of active government and individualism is trust in government (see table 2.17). Previous research has found that trust in government is low in the South, primarily because of white disillusionment with the national government's support for civil rights and desegregation. Researchers have shown that southern blacks, conversely, are more trusting of government than are the region's whites and are more trusting than African Americans in other parts of the country. The data analyses show that African Americans in North Carolina are indeed slightly more trusting of government than are African Americans elsewhere, with 24 percent of the state's blacks saying that they trust the government just about always or most of the time, compared to 20 percent of blacks nationwide. Contrary to expectations, blacks in North Carolina were somewhat less trusting of government than were the state's whites. The differences by race, however, did not achieve statistical significance.

TABLE 2.16. Comparing Reasons for Poverty by Race in North Carolina and the United States

Kaiser/NPR/Harvard National Poll			Elon University Statewide Poll		
In your opinion, which is the bigger cause of poverty today—that people are not doing enough to help themselves out of poverty or that circumstances beyond their control cause them to be poor?			In your opinion, what is more often to blame if a person is poor—lack of effort on their own part or circumstances beyond their control?		
	White	Black		White	Black
People aren't doing enough to help themselves out of poverty	49%	38%	Lack of effort	39%	22%
Circumstances beyond their control cause them to be poor	44	55	Circumstances beyond their control	44	68
Don't know/refused	8	7	Don't know/no response	17	10
N	1,335	344		418	70
Chi-square = 10.1 3 df p < 0.05 Dates 1/4/01–2/27/01			Chi-square = 22.2 3 df p < 0.001 2/14/05–2/17/05		

❖ Discussion and Conclusion

The central premise of this essay consists of two assertions—that North Carolinians are more progressive than the rest of the South in their attitudes about government and that some of that difference results from the influx of nonsoutherners into the state since the 1980s. The analyses presented here provide some evidence to support these claims.

For example, trust in government was lower in North Carolina than in the rest of the nation, but newcomers to North Carolina from outside the South moderated that trend with higher levels of trust in government. In the realm of political values, North Carolinians were more likely than southerners as a whole to endorse active government and less likely to express attitudes in line with individualism.

North Carolina polled slightly ahead of the South as a whole in terms of church attendance and slightly behind in support for displays of the Ten Commandments on government property. While variation in opinion may occur in a number of areas, religion still appears to serve as a unifying force in the South in general

TABLE 2.17. Comparing Trust in Government by Race in North Carolina and the United States

Kaiser/NPR/Harvard National Poll			Elon University Statewide Poll		
How much of the time do you trust the federal government in Washington to do what is right—just about always, most of the time, only some of the time, or none of the time?			How much of the time do you think you can trust the government in Washington to do what is right?		
	White	Black		White	Black
Just about always	7%	4%	Just about always	4%	1%
Most of the time	30	16	Most of the time	29	23
Only some of the time	50	65	Some of the time	57	67
None of the time	12	16	None of the time	9	8
Don't know/ refused	1	0	Don't know/ no response	1	0
N	1,031	130		378	84
Chi-square = 19.4 5 df p < 0.01			Chi-square = 5.1 4 df p = 0.27		
Dates 2/5/03–3/17/03			10/27/03–10/30/03		

and in North Carolina in particular. Further reinforcing the point were the differences among nonsoutherners, native-born North Carolinians, and those who had moved to North Carolina from other parts of the South, with the latter two groups far more supportive of public displays of the Ten Commandments than were nonsoutherners.

The analyses also revealed interesting patterns according to race. African Americans in North Carolina were more likely to embrace the political value of active government and less likely to embrace the value of individualism than were white North Carolinians in the area of battling poverty. This finding accords with Key's assertion that North Carolina's general conservatism is offset in part by African Americans' liberal views on economic issues. Also in keeping with expectations, African Americans were somewhat more trusting of national government than their counterparts in the national sample.

While evidence suggests that North Carolina is distinct from the rest of the South in certain areas, some caveats must be borne in mind. The data analyses presented here rely in part on comparisons of state and national surveys in which questions were not always worded identically, and the contents of the rest of the questionnaires may have varied considerably. Those factors complicate comparisons. Also, the extent to which some of the subsamples of North Carolinians in the analyses were smaller than one hundred respondents may have made it more difficult to find statistically significant differences between native-born North Carolinians, other southerners, and newcomers. That differences emerged among those groups in some instances and approached significance in others indicates that larger samples might have yielded more conclusive results.

Even with these cautions, however, these analyses provide evidence that North Carolina differs from other parts of the South in certain respects in terms of public opinion. The Old North State is part of the region but is also distinct in some ways as a result of its history and of the influx of newcomers from outside the South. Obtaining a clear sense of how public opinion in North Carolina differs from and resembles that in the rest of the region and the nation requires considering these factors.

❖ Note

Thanks to Elon University for the use of data from the Elon University Poll.

❖ References

Black, Earl, and Merle Black. 1987. *Politics and Society in the South*. Cambridge: Harvard University Press.

CNN, *USA Today*, and Gallup Organization. 2003. Survey, September 19–21. <http://www.ropercenter.uconn.edu/ipoll.html>. Accessed July 13, 2006.

Fleer, Jack D. 1968. *North Carolina Politics: An Introduction*. Chapel Hill: University of North Carolina Press.

Gettleman, Jeffrey. 2003. "Alabama Panel Ousts Judge over Ten Commandments." *New York Times*, November 14, A-16.

Glaser, James M. 2005. *The Hand of the Past in Contemporary Southern Politics*. New Haven: Yale University Press.

Hetherington, Marc J. 1998. "The Political Relevance of Political Trust." *American Political Science Review* 92:791–808.

Kaiser Family Foundation. 2005. Survey, April 1–May 1. <http://www.ropercenter.uconn.edu/ipoll.html>. Accessed July 14, 2006.

Key, V. O., Jr. 1949. *Southern Politics in State and Nation*. New York: Knopf.

Luebke, Paul. 1998. *Tar Heel Politics 2000*. Chapel Hill: University of North Carolina Press.

National Public Radio, Kaiser Family Foundation, and Kennedy School of Government at Harvard University. 2001. Survey, January 4–February 27. <http://www.ropercenter.uconn.edu/ipoll.html>. Accessed July 13, 2006.

———. 2003. Survey, February 5–March 17. <http://www.ropercenter.uconn.edu/ipoll.html>. Accessed July 7, 2006.

Reed, John Shelton. 1986. *The Enduring South: Subcultural Persistence in Mass Society.* Chapel Hill: University of North Carolina Press.

Smith, Robert C., and Richard Seltzer. 1992. *Race, Class and Culture: A Study in Afro-American Mass Opinion.* Albany: State University of New York Press.

Tate, Katherine. 1994. *From Protest to Politics: The New Black Voters in American Elections.* Cambridge: Harvard University Press.

❖ Part II. Linkage Institutions

❖ 3. The Reshaping of the Political Party System in North Carolina

CHARLES PRYSBY

North Carolina's political party system was transformed during the second half of the twentieth century, as a formerly one-party, Democratic-dominated state became a competitive two-party state. The state's political changes were mirrored to varying degrees throughout the South, so any study of the change in North Carolina politics should be placed within the context of regional political change. This essay focuses on the development of the political party system in North Carolina, an emphasis that indicates a concern with more than just the growth of Republican voting in the state. The term "political party system" refers to a variety of aspects of the political parties, their relationships to each other, and their relationships with the electorate. This examination of these factors will reveal that deep and fundamental changes occurred in North Carolina's political party system over the past few decades.

❖ Components of the Political Party System

Change or development in a political party system can be analyzed along three dimensions: competition between the parties, party system cleavages, and party organizational strength. Each of these dimensions helps to define the nature of the political party system. The first of these dimensions, competition, is the most obvious feature of a political party system. Competition between parties is important in a democracy. Without sufficient competition between the parties, voters lack credible electoral alternatives and thus are less able to influence government. Competition in a two-party system is easily measured by examining two features of election outcomes: the division of the popular vote and the division of offices won. The closer the popular vote comes to an even division between the two parties, the more competitive the election. A pattern of highly competitive elections indicates that the party system is highly competitive (David 1972). Success in winning office also should be used to judge competitiveness (Ranney 1976). A highly competitive party system is one in which both parties regularly win office.

A second important dimension of a political party system is the nature of party cleavages. If political parties are supposed to provide voters with alternatives, then party differences in platforms and policies are crucial (Coleman 2003; David 1992;

Green and Herrnson 2002; Pomper 1971; Price 1984, 109–11; White 2001; White and Mileur 2002). A party system in which the two parties do not represent alternative viewpoints does not structure voters' electoral choices in a meaningful way. Past scholars have voiced such concerns about the American party system (American Political Science Association, Committee on Political Parties 1950; Broder 1971, 189–212; Sabato and Larson 2002, 164–66; Schattschneider 1942, 206–10). The extent of the policy differences between the parties is one important aspect of the nature of party cleavages. Another important aspect is the substantive basis of these policy cleavages. The literature on American political parties often views party cleavages as resulting from realignments of the party system. These realignments are relatively durable alterations of partisan loyalties in the electorate, usually involving changes in the social and issue bases of electoral behavior (Burnham 1970, 6–7; Key 1955, 1959; Petrocik 1981, 15–16; Sundquist 1983, 298–321). Furthermore, party system cleavages should be examined among political elites as well as within the electorate. The differences between politicians and activists within the two parties play a critical role in defining party cleavages. Observers commonly expect that partisan elites will be more ideologically polarized than will voters, but this tendency varies considerably (Jackson, Brown, and Bositis 1982; Jackson and Clayton 1996; McClosky, Hoffman, and O'Hara 1960).

A third aspect of a political party system is the parties' organizational strength. Parties have an organizational presence both in and out of government. American parties have been accused of being weak organizations, especially outside of government. Some analysts have seen American parties as little more than loose coalitions of office seekers (Crotty 1984). However, many scholars have found that American parties have greatly improved their organizational strength over the past two or three decades, especially at the national level (Bibby 1998; Coleman 1996; Herrnson 1988, 30–46; Longley 1980). Scholars now view American party organizations as playing an important service role by helping candidates in their election efforts (Aldrich 1995, 48–50; Crotty 1986; Herrnson 1988, 84–111; Hopkins 1986).

Party organizational strength can be assessed in terms of resources and activities. Resources include money and people (C. Cotter et al. 1984, 16–18; Gibson et al. 1983, 1985; Gibson, Frendreis, and Vertz 1989). Important election activities include recruiting candidates, providing resources and assistance to candidates, and attempting to get out the vote (Frendreis, Gibson, and Vertz 1990; Hogan 2003). Organizational activities between elections include ongoing public relations efforts, communication and party-building activities, and fund-raising efforts (Huckshorn et al. 1986). A strong party organization is active both during and between election campaigns.

The remainder of this essay analyzes North Carolina's political party system along these dimensions—party competition, party cleavages, and party organizational strength—with an emphasis on examining the changes in these aspects of the party system over the past few decades. The analysis also compares both the changes in and the current state of the North Carolina party system to the patterns found in other southern states and in the nation as a whole.

❖ Party Competition

The most obvious change in North Carolina's political party system is the growth of Republican voting and the development of two-party competition. The pattern of Republican growth in North Carolina resembles patterns elsewhere in the South, a topic addressed by a number of studies (Aistrup 1996; Bullock 1988; Lamis 1999a; Lublin 2004; Scher 1997). Republican strength emerged first in presidential elections. For example, the 1960 Republican presidential candidate, Richard Nixon, captured 48 percent of the two-party vote in North Carolina in his loss to John F. Kennedy, more than the Republican candidates for U.S. senator or governor won. Republican success further down the ballot was even more limited that year, as the GOP won only one of twelve U.S. House seats and just 10 percent of the state legislative seats. Eight years later, Nixon carried North Carolina on his way to the presidency, and he repeated that success in 1972. Democratic presidential candidate Jimmy Carter carried the state in 1976 but lost it in 1980 to Ronald Reagan, and Republicans have carried the state in every subsequent presidential election.

Table 3.1 shows the results of the past seven presidential elections, comparing the outcomes in the state to national and regional outcomes. Much of the change from one election to the next reflects either national or regional trends. For example, George H. W. Bush easily won the state in 1988 but only narrowly carried it in 1992, a difference that largely reflects the drop in Bush's national vote from 1988 to 1992 (Prysby 1991, 1994). We can also see that North Carolina has become more Republican than the nation as a whole in its presidential voting, just as the South has, a phenomenon discussed thoroughly by Earl Black and Merle Black (1992). In both 1996 and 2000, North Carolina was more than 7 percentage points more Republican than the country as a whole; this difference dropped to less than 5 points in 2004, possibly reflecting the presence of John Edwards on the Democratic ticket (Prysby 2005). Also interesting is the fact that North Carolina has moved from being slightly less Republican in its presidential voting than the rest of the South to being slightly more Republican than the region, with 2004 again the exception.

The growth of Republican voting in the South represented the leading edge in the breakup of the Solid South. Republican success in prominent statewide races, such as for governor or for U.S. senator, generally followed next; later came suc-

TABLE 3.1. Presidential Vote in North Carolina, the South, and the Nation, 1980–2004

	1980	1984	1988	1992	1996	2000	2004
North Carolina	51.1	62.0	58.2	50.5	52.5	56.5	56.2
South	53.6	62.6	58.8	49.9	50.0	55.5	57.6
Nation	55.3	59.2	53.9	46.5	45.4	49.7	51.4
North Carolina vs. South	-2.5	-0.6	-0.6	+0.6	+2.5	+1.0	-1.4
North Carolina vs. nation	-4.2	+2.8	+4.3	+4.0	+7.1	+7.7	+4.8

Source: Computed from data in *America Votes* (Washington, D.C.: Congressional Quarterly, various years), and from data obtained from the N.C. Board of Elections.

Note: Entries are the Republican percentage of the two-party vote for president. The South is defined as the eleven states of the Confederacy. The last two rows give the difference between the Republican vote in North Carolina and in the South and the nation, respectively. Positive numbers indicate than North Carolina is more Republican than the nation or the South.

cess further down the ballot (Aistrup 1996; Bullock 1988; Lamis 1990; Lublin 2004; Prysby 2000; Scher 1997; Shaffer, Pierce, and Kohnke 2000). This pattern characterizes electoral change in North Carolina. Table 3.2 presents election results from 1960 through 2006 for a variety of offices. We can see that the GOP was clearly the minority party in the state for both congressional and state elections during the 1960s. In 1972, Republicans James Holshouser and Jesse Helms won the gubernatorial and the U.S. Senate elections, respectively, marking the first time in the twentieth century that the GOP had won either office. However, Jim Hunt recaptured the governorship for the Democrats in 1976 and again in 1980, and the Democrats remained dominant in U.S. House and state legislative elections. Another milestone in Republican growth occurred in 1984, when the GOP won the governorship for the second time in the century, retained Helms's Senate seat in a hotly contested election, and made substantial gains in congressional and state legislative seats. A third crucial election occurred in 1994, when Republicans won a majority of the U.S. House seats and a majority of the state House seats for the first time in nearly one hundred years. By this time, two-party competition was firmly established in the state. Republicans were now highly competitive up and down the ballot, not just for the races at the top of the ticket.

A careful inspection of the data in table 3.2 shows that Republicans have been more successful in congressional elections than in state elections. Republicans have done particularly well in U.S. Senate elections. Senator Helms followed his initial election in 1972 with reelection victories in 1978, 1984, 1990, and 1996; Republican Elizabeth Dole was elected to Helms's seat following his retirement in

TABLE 3.2. Republican Strength in North Carolina, 1960–2006

			Republican Percentage of		
Year	U.S. Senate Vote	U.S. House Delegation	Gubernatorial Vote	State House Seats	State Senate Seats
1960	38.6	8.3	45.5	12.5	4.0
1962	39.6	18.2		17.5	4.0
1964		18.2	43.4	11.7	2.0
1966	44.4	27.3		21.7	14.0
1968	39.4	36.4	47.3	24.2	24.0
1970		36.4		20.0	14.0
1972	54.0	36.4	51.3	29.2	30.0
1974	37.3	18.2		7.5	2.0
1976		18.2	34.3	5.0	6.0
1978	54.5	18.2		11.7	12.0
1980	50.3	36.4	37.7	20.0	20.0
1982		18.2		15.0	12.0
1984	51.9	45.5	54.4	31.7	24.0
1986	48.2	27.3		30.0	20.0
1988		27.3	56.1	38.3	26.0
1990	52.6	36.4		30.8	28.0
1992	52.2	33.3	45.1	34.4	22.0
1994		66.7		55.8	48.0
1996	53.4	50.0	43.3	50.8	42.0
1998	47.9	58.3		45.0	30.0
2000		58.3	47.1	48.3	30.0
2002	54.4	53.8		50.0[a]	44.0
2004	52.3	53.8	43.5	47.5	42.0
2006		46.2	43.5	43.3	38.0

Sources: The 1960–90 figures were obtained from *America Votes* (Washington, D.C.: Congressional Quarterly, 1960–90) and *Statistical Abstract of the United States* (Washington, D.C.: U.S. Government Printing Office, 1960–92), various editions. The 1992–2006 figures were obtained from the N.C. Board of Elections.

Note: Entries in the U.S. Senate vote and the gubernatorial vote columns are the Republican percentage of the two-party vote. Entries in the other three columns are the percentage of seats won by Republicans. Seats not won by Republicans were won by Democrats.

[a]In 2002, Republicans won 61 of the 120 house seats, but shortly after the election, one Republican switched his party affiliation, leaving the house evenly divided between the two parties.

2002. The other Senate seat has alternated between the parties; it was won by Republican John East in 1980, by Democrat Terry Sanford in 1986, by Republican Lauch Faircloth in 1992, by Democrat John Edwards in 1998, and by Republican Richard Burr in 2004. While Republicans have won eight of the last ten U.S. Senate elections in the state, all were fairly close races. In each case, the winner had less than 55 percent of the two-party vote, indicating that Democrats have remained competitive. Republicans also won a majority of the U.S. House seats from 1994 through 2004, but Democrats remained a competitive minority during this time, and they recaptured a majority of the House seats in 2006.

State elections reveal a somewhat different picture than what we have just seen for congressional elections. Democrats have remained the majority party in state elections, holding the governorship since 1992 and maintaining control of the state legislature for most of this time period. Republicans have been very competitive, however. In the most recent gubernatorial elections that did not involve an incumbent running for reelection, 1992 and 2000, the Democratic candidates—Jim Hunt and Mike Easley, respectively—won with less than 55 percent of the two-party vote (Prysby 1994, 2002). In recent state legislative elections, Republicans have come close to being the majority party in the House and have been a strong minority party in the Senate. However, a slight trend toward the Democrats has existed in recent years, perhaps reflecting some of the divisions among Republicans in the state legislature.

Overall, North Carolina remains a competitive two-party state except in presidential elections. Republicans have held the advantage in congressional elections, but Democrats appear capable of winning a U.S. Senate seat and did win a majority of the U.S. House seats in 2006. Democrats have the advantage in state elections, but Republicans are capable of winning the governorship, especially in a year when no incumbent is running for reelection, which is a frequent situation since governors can serve only two consecutive terms. A GOP majority in at least one house of the state legislature also appears to be a realistic possibility in the near future. In this regard, North Carolina is more competitive than several other southern states, such as South Carolina or Texas, where the Republicans have established themselves as the more dominant party.[1]

❖ Party Cleavages and Coalitions

As political party competition developed in North Carolina, the nature of party cleavages and coalitions changed. The two parties appealed to different groups of voters, defined in both ideological and demographic terms. The two parties also became programmatically more distinct. Democrats, who had been fairly conservative in earlier decades, emerged as the more liberal party. Republicans became identified as clearly conservative. These developments took some time to become fully established, but by the 1990s, little doubt remained that a realignment had occurred. These developments are best viewed by first considering the changes in party cleavages in the electorate, then proceeding to an examination of differences among party officeholders and activists.

Demographically, Democratic voters differ from Republican voters along several lines: race, religion, social class, and gender. Table 3.3 contains results from exit polls for several recent elections. The three U.S. Senate elections shown involve different candidates and outcomes. In the 1996 contest, the very conservative Jesse Helms defeated a fairly liberal black Democrat, former Charlotte mayor Harvey Gantt, in a rematch of their 1990 battle. In 1998, Democrat John Edwards defeated incumbent Republican senator Lauch Faircloth. In 2004, Republican congressman Richard Burr defeated Erskine Bowles for the seat held by Edwards, who chose not to run for reelection. Bowles also ran and lost in 2002 to Elizabeth Dole, but no exit poll data are available for that election. Two of the three gubernatorial elections in table 3.3 involve Democrat Mike Easley, who defeated Richard Vinroot in 2000 and Patrick Ballantine in 2004. In the 1996 gubernatorial contest, Democratic governor Jim Hunt was reelected over Republican Robin Hayes. Although these six elections involve different candidates and different political circumstances, similar patterns are visible in table 3.3.

Race is clearly the most important demographic factor influencing voting in North Carolina. Close to 90 percent of blacks typically vote Democratic, whereas usually well below 50 percent of whites do so. Because blacks constitute about one-fifth of the electorate, a Democratic statewide candidate must form a biracial coalition to succeed. Doing so usually involves winning more than 40 percent of the white vote and around 90 percent of the black vote. As we can see from the data in table 3.3, victorious Democrats such as Edwards (running for Senate in 1998) and Easley (running for governor in 2000 and 2004) have done exactly that; unsuccessful Democrats such as Bowles (running for Senate in 2004) and Gantt (running for Senate in 1996) have not.

The importance of race in North Carolina politics reflects regional and national patterns. Throughout the South, blacks became an important element of the Democratic coalition following the civil rights revolution of the 1960s (Black and Black 1987, 126–51; Woodard 2006, 155–59). The 1965 Voting Rights Act, the Twenty-fourth Amendment to the U.S. Constitution, and other federal government actions greatly expanded the black electorate in the South by eliminating literacy tests, the poll tax, and other discriminatory practices that discouraged or prevented blacks from voting (Bass and DeVries 1976, 41–56; Scher 1997, 246–54). Moreover, because the civil rights legislation of the 1960s was pushed by Democratic president Lyndon Johnson and by northern liberal Democrats, the Democratic Party became identified as the party that supported federal government action against racial discrimination. In response, blacks became a very loyal part of the Democratic coalition, usually voting around 90 percent Democratic in national elections. In

TABLE 3.3. Exit Poll Results for North Carolina U.S. Senate and Gubernatorial
Elections, 1996–2004

| | Percentage Voting for Democratic Candidate | | | | | |
| | U.S. Senate Elections | | | Gubernatorial Elections | | |
	1996	1998	2004	1996	2000	2004
All voters	46	52	46	56	52	55
Race						
White	36	41	30	50	43	43
Black	89	91	87	87	89	87
Income						
Under $50,000	50	56	59	56	55	64
$50,000 and over	42	46	35	52	47	45
Gender						
Male	41	43	41	50	46	51
Female	50	59	50	61	57	57
Ideology						
Liberal	82	84	84	83	87	83
Moderate	56	65	55	67	60	65
Conservative	18	18	21	30	38	31
Party identification						
Democrat	78	86	89	86	87	90
Independent	45	55	47	58	49	59
Republican	13	11	6	22	15	19

Sources: Voter News Service 1996, 1998, and 2000 North Carolina Exit Polls; National Election
Pool 2004 North Carolina Exit Poll.
Note: Entries are the percentage of voters in the specified category who voted for the Democratic
candidate. Only the percentages for the Democratic candidates are shown; these were essentially two-candidate races, so the proportion of the vote not going to the Democrat went almost
entirely to the Republican.

southern states, where blacks comprise a significant minority, racial cleavages in
voting are especially important (Black and Black 1987, 126–51; Wattenberg 1991).
North Carolina falls in the middle of the region in the size of its African American
electorate; blacks constitute a smaller percentage of North Carolina's electorate
than is the case in the five Deep South states but are a higher percentage than in
the five other peripheral South states. Other minority groups, such as Hispanics,
currently represent a very small share of North Carolina's voters.

Religion is another important social or demographic factor in voting. Most
North Carolina voters are Protestants, so the key religious difference is not between Protestants and Catholics, which historically has been important in many

northern states. In North Carolina, the important difference is between whites who are more evangelical or fundamentalist Protestants, such as Southern Baptists, and those who are from more mainline Protestant denominations, such as Methodists or Presbyterians. Evangelical white Protestants are significantly more likely to vote Republican than are other white Protestants (Green 2002; Green et al. 2003). Also important is the voter's religiosity. Whites who are more religious—as measured by frequency of church attendance, for example—are more likely to vote Republican than those who are less religious, and those who are not at all religious are least likely to vote Republican (Green 2002; Green et al. 2003). Unfortunately, exit polls generally have not measured religiosity or denominational affiliation; as a result, this factor does not appear in table 3.3.

The religious patterns in North Carolina voting resemble those found throughout the South. Beginning in the 1980s, the Christian Right emerged as a potent political force, particularly in the South (Baker 1990; Smidt 1989). Concern over a number of religiously related moral issues and over issues involving questions of the separation of church and state divided more conservative white Protestants from more liberal ones. More religious and more fundamentalist or evangelical whites were more likely to take conservative positions on issues such as abortion, gay marriage, prayer in school, and displaying the Ten Commandments in government buildings. Those with more conservative positions on these issues were drawn to the Republican Party, and supporters of the Christian Right have emerged as one of the most Republican groups in the South (Green 2002; Green et al. 2003).

Social class or socioeconomic status has become a more important influence on voting than was the case in the past. Table 3.3 shows how income has been related to voting in recent North Carolina elections. For simplicity, income has been divided into just two groups, above and below fifty thousand dollars per year, which roughly divides the electorate in half during this period. Differences between these two groups are significant: Democrats consistently draw a higher percentage of their votes from voters with below-average incomes. The extent of the difference between the upper- and lower-income groups varies across the elections but averages about 10 percentage points. Income or class divisions appear to have become more important in North Carolina over the past two decades. This finding is consistent with other research, which has found that voting in the South increasingly is related to income (Black and Black 2002, 244–66; Nadeau and Stanley 1993; Petrocik 1987; Wattenberg 1991). This development has made the South more similar to the North in voting patterns, as class cleavages have characterized northern voting since the New Deal realignment of the 1930s.

Gender has also emerged as a significant partisan cleavage. The data in table

3.3 show that women have been consistently more likely to vote for Democratic candidates than have men. The difference usually is around 10 percentage points, comparable to the gap between the upper- and lower-income groups. The state's gender gap reflects a national tendency for women to be more Democratic that clearly emerged in the 1980s. Women tend to be more liberal on a variety of issues, especially social welfare issues, and thus have a greater inclination to vote Democratic (Seltzer, Newman, and Leighton 1997, 107–14).

In addition to these individual demographic characteristics, geographical factors play a role in elections. Regional patterns are clearly evident in voting; these regional differences are not included in the exit poll results but can be identified simply by analyzing the vote totals for different regions or localities. The traditional regional divisions have been between the east (the tidewater and coastal plain areas); the center, or Piedmont; and the west, or mountain area (Fleer 1994, 29–32; Fleer, Lowery, and Prysby 1988; Luebke 1998, 77–80). The east is the traditional base of Democratic strength, and it remains disproportionately Democratic, although less so than in the past. The west is the traditional source of Republican strength, and it remains disproportionately Republican. The Piedmont falls between these two regions in party strength. Another important geographical distinction involves urbanization. Most of the major urban areas are located in the center of the state, and an important difference exists between these urban areas and the rest of the Piedmont. The nonmetropolitan Piedmont has been very favorable to Republicans in recent elections, while Democrats have done better in the major cities (Prysby 2006). For example, in the 2000 gubernatorial election, the Democratic candidate, Easley, matched or exceeded his statewide percentage of the vote in four of the five major urban Piedmont counties, representing the cities of Raleigh, Durham, Greensboro, and Winston-Salem.[2] In the 2004 senatorial election, Bowles carried four of the five major urban Piedmont counties even though he lost the election.[3]

Geographical factors such as region of the state or urbanization are related to voting partly because they are related to race (Prysby 2006). Blacks are disproportionately located in the east, while the west has a relatively low percentage of blacks. The major urban Piedmont counties have substantial black populations, larger than those present in many of the other Piedmont counties. Region and urbanization are also related to religion and income. Urban areas also are more likely to be populated by people who moved to North Carolina from other states, including northern ones. Nevertheless, geography sometimes reflects historical and cultural factors, not just demographic differences. For example, Republican strength in the west can be traced to the Civil War era, when sympathy for the

Confederate cause was much lower in the mountain areas, where slaveholding was limited (Key 1949, 219–21).

All of these social and demographic cleavages have a common denominator. They influence voting insofar as they affect ideology and party identification. Groups that are more liberal are more likely to vote for Democrats; those that are more conservative are more likely to vote for Republicans. Ideology is related to social and demographic characteristics, which explains why such factors are related to partisan choice. The strong relationship between ideology and voting is clear in table 3.3. In each of the six elections examined, the Democratic candidate did far better among liberal voters, while the Republican candidate did much better among conservative voters. Conservatives outnumber liberals in the North Carolina electorate, so Democratic candidates usually have to attract a significant minority of conservative voters to win. Thus, the three successful Democratic gubernatorial candidates all won at least 30 percent of the conservative vote. The only election in the table where a Democrat won without doing well among conservatives was in 1998, when Edwards won the U.S. Senate seat.

Voting behavior also is strongly influenced by party identification, which is related to ideology. Voting has very much followed party lines in recent elections, particularly in 2004, when about 90 percent of Democrats voted for Bowles and Easley, the Democratic candidates in the senate and gubernatorial elections. Republicans also have been quite loyal in their voting, although they showed some tendency to defect in the 1996 and 2004 gubernatorial elections, both of which involved incumbents (Hunt and Easley) seeking reelection. In earlier decades, more voters defected from their party identification. Conservative Democrats provided an important source of votes for Republican candidates during the 1970s and 1980s. The support of such voters for Helms earned them the nickname "Jessecrats." By 2004, party identification and ideology were much more aligned. Conservative Democrats had diminished greatly in numbers, either because these individuals changed their party identification to match their ideology or because older conservative Democrats were replaced by younger conservative Republicans. This combination of individual change and generational replacement produced a gradual realignment of the electorate that had a substantial cumulative effect.

The realignment of the North Carolina electorate matched the more general realignment of the southern electorate. Throughout the region, conservative whites gradually shifted their partisan attachments from the Democrats to the Republicans, a movement that began after the civil rights era and continued until the end of the century (Carmines and Stanley 1990; Knuckey 2001). As a result, party identification and issue orientations became more tightly aligned. By the beginning of the twenty-first century, Democratic and Republican voters were far more polarized on issues than had been the case three decades earlier. Moreover, this polarization existed for a range of issues, including social welfare and moral issues as well as civil rights issues (Cowden 2001; Lublin 2004).

PARTY CLEAVAGES AMONG POLITICIANS AND ACTIVISTS

Realignment of the political parties in North Carolina is evident in the ideological differences between Democratic and Republican candidates. Several decades ago, the two parties were not nearly as ideologically distinct as they now are. The Democratic Party included many conservatives, as was true throughout the South. The Republicans, strongest at the time in the western part of North Carolina, included many moderates. The Republican Party's growth coincided with it becoming more clearly conservative. Democrats moved in the opposite ideological direction. Older conservative Democrats left office either through retirement or defeat or in some cases switched parties. New Democratic candidates and officeholders were generally more liberal. The realignment of voters described in the previous section contributed to this development. As the number of conservative Democratic voters decreased and the number of Republicans increased and as blacks became a significant part of the electorate, the Democratic primary electorate became more clearly liberal, making it more difficult for conservative Democratic candidates to win the nomination. Conversely, the Republican primary electorate became strongly conservative, ensuring that conservative Republicans would be nominated.

U.S. Senate elections clearly illustrate this trend. When Senator Helms was first elected in 1972, he became the most visible Republican in the state. He touted his conservatism and railed against liberals (Luebke 1990, 124–36). Each of his reelection campaigns attempted to paint his Democratic opponent as a liberal who was out of touch with North Carolina values. Helms's 1984 reelection effort against Jim Hunt, then completing his second term as governor, was very expensive, hard fought, and divisive. Helms attacked Hunt on a number of social issues, including ones with a racial aspect, such as the Martin Luther King Jr. holiday, enacted by Congress in 1983 (Luebke 1990, 137–55). Helms used a similar strategy in his next reelection effort, another costly and bitterly fought race. His opponent in 1990 was Harvey Gantt, an African American and a former mayor of Charlotte (Prysby 1996). In the final days of that campaign, Helms ran a controversial television advertisement that accused Gantt of favoring racial quotas (Luebke 1998, 181–84).

While Helms was the most visible conservative face in the North Carolina congressional delegation, the other Republican senators have been very conservative as well. Both East and Faircloth were ideologically close to Helms; both received substantial help from Helms's organization, the Congressional Club, in their election efforts; and both had very conservative Senate voting records. The two current Republican senators, Dole and Burr, do not use conservative rhetoric in the same way that Helms did, but they are fairly consistent conservatives in their voting in Congress. Burr had a lifetime American Conservative Union (ACU) rating of 91 percent for the ten years that he spent in the U.S. House before being elected senator in 2004. Senator Dole recorded an ACU score of 86 percent for her first two years in the Senate (ACU 2007).

The two most recent Democratic senators, Edwards and Sanford, were much more liberal in their congressional voting. Senator Edwards had an ACU rating of 10 percent for his single term, and Senator Sanford had an ACU score of 12 percent for his single term (ACU 2007). This is in sharp contrast to the voting patterns of earlier Democratic senators, who were much more conservative. For example, the two Democratic senators in 1972 had ACU scores of 67 percent and 100 percent (ACU 2007). Moreover, the losing Democratic candidates in recent years—Bowles in 2002 and 2004 and Gantt in 1990 and 1996—took positions that were clearly more liberal than those espoused by their Republican opponents (Prysby 1996, 1997b, 2004, 2005). Of course, Democratic candidates in North Carolina generally are less liberal than Democrats in other parts of the country and often emphasize their more moderate orientations. For example, during his 2004 campaign against Burr, Bowles stressed that he would be an independent thinker in the Senate. He also emphasized consensus issues, such as improving the economy, and avoided stressing specific policy proposals.

The sharpening ideological differentiation of the two parties, along with their increasing ideological cohesiveness, is clearly visible by examining the ACU scores for members of the U.S. House from North Carolina over the past few decades. Table 3.4 presents data on the ACU scores of North Carolina's congressional representatives for four selected years: 1972, 1982, 1992, and 2002. In 1972, Republicans were conservative, but so were Democrats, with an average ACU score only about 10 points lower than the average Republican score. We also can see that the most conservative Democrats were more conservative than the least conservative Republicans. By 1982, the difference in average ACU scores had increased to 30 points, and no overlap occurred in the ranges of scores for the two parties. Still, the Democrats overall were moderately conservative. By 1992, the Democrats were clearly liberal, with an average ACU score of 24, and in 2002, they were even more so. However, one Democrat (Mike McIntyre in the Seventh District) continued to post ACU scores of about 50 percent. Republicans in 2002 were uniformly conservative, with ACU scores over 90 percent.

Ideological differences between the parties in state elections are more difficult

TABLE 3.4. American Conservative Union Scores for U.S. Representatives from North Carolina, 1972–2002, Selected Years

	1972	1982	1992	2002
Democratic representatives				
Number of representatives	7	7	7	5
Mean ACU score	68	62	24	15
Highest score	100	75	58	48
Lowest score	40	47	4	0
Republican representatives				
Number of representatives	4	4	4	7
Mean ACU score	77	92	89	95
Highest score	90	100	92	96
Lowest score	70	82	84	92

Source: Computed from American Conservative Union (2007).
Note: ACU scores indicate the percentage of times that a member of Congress cast a conservative vote on the set of bills used to form the ACU index in the specified year.

to identify. Voting in the state legislature cannot be analyzed as easily as congressional voting, because ratings comparable to the ACU scores are not readily available. Moreover, candidates for the state legislature often do not clearly address policy issues. Nevertheless, the same tendencies that were identified for federal elections seem to apply to state elections. In recent gubernatorial elections, the Democratic candidate has taken more liberal positions than his Republican opponent. In 2000, for example, the Democratic candidate, Easley, and the Republican, Vinroot, differed on increasing state spending, school vouchers, state subsidization of prescription drug costs for senior citizens, a patient's bill of rights, environmental regulations, and abortion (Prysby 2002). In each case, Vinroot took a position that was more conservative than the one taken by Easley. In 1996, Hunt, the incumbent Democratic governor, presented himself as a moderate Democrat in his campaign against Hayes, a Republican state legislator who took very conservative positions on a number of issues (Prysby 1997b).

Ideological differences between the parties are extremely clear among local party leaders. A 2001 survey of county party chairs and other members of the county executive committees showed that Republican activists were strongly conservative. More than half called themselves very conservative, and most of the rest said that they were somewhat conservative. Democrats were somewhat more diverse in their ideological identification: about one-fifth claimed to be very liberal, about 40 percent somewhat liberal, and about 30 percent moderate in their ideological orientation (Prysby 2003). Analysis of the responses of activists to specific issue items reveals a similar pattern of polarization. A 1991 survey found the Republicans to be less conservative and the Democrats to be less liberal (Prysby 1995). Thus, during the 1990s, local Democratic and Republican Party leaders became more ideologically cohesive and more distinct. Moreover, party activists appear to be more polarized than do voters, with the elected officials falling somewhere between these two groups in their polarization.

These developments in North Carolina politics parallel those in other southern states. Throughout the region, similar changes in congressional delegations were taking place. Republican members of Congress were becoming more clearly conservative, while Democrats were becoming more consistently liberal (Berard 2001, 111–42). Accounts of politics in individual states report similar patterns of change (Bullock and Rozell 2006; Lamis 1990, 1999b). Studies of local party leaders and activists throughout the South indicate that the North Carolina patterns reflect regional changes (P. Cotter and Fisher 2004; McGlennon 1998; Steed 1998). Moreover, the trends in North Carolina and elsewhere in the South also characterize national developments. Over the past two decades, Democrats and Republicans at the national level have become more ideologically polarized, and this phenomenon is visible among both politicians and voters (Abramowitz and Saunders 1998).

Despite the growing ideological cohesiveness and distinctiveness of the two parties, both the Democrats and Republicans are far from homogeneous and united groups. Among Republicans, a division exists between those who are conservative on economic issues but more moderate on social issues and those who are very conservative on social issues, with the latter group often strongly represented by supporters of the Christian Right (Christensen and Fleer 1999; Luebke 1998, 213–15). The Democratic reliance on a biracial coalition sometimes creates tensions over a number of race-related issues (Prysby 2006). Democrats also have been divided between more moderate and more progressive supporters. Other divisions within the parties have been significant as well. Regional divisions of various sorts have played a role, as have personal conflicts and rivalries. Party factionalism often reflects several of these factors, which overlap in reinforcing patterns.

❖ Party Organizations

As Democrats and Republicans became more competitive in North Carolina, they became more concerned about developing stronger state party organizations. Party organizations can and do provide services to candidates. Stronger party organizations should enable a party to win more offices. When parties were less competitive, party organizations naturally were weaker. Democrats did not need a strong party organization to win elections when they were the dominant party in the state, while Republicans were too weak to create a strong organization. Growing two-party competition changed that situation. Beginning in the early 1980s, both parties began to establish strong state organizations. The development of the party organizations can be analyzed by examining the following indicators: headquarters, staffing, budgets, and activities.

In the 1970s, the Democratic and Republican state headquarters were limited operations, staffed by a few people and housed in rented office space. In the early 1980s, both parties purchased permanent office space, increased their staff, and expanded their budgets (Prysby 1997a). By 1984, the Democratic Party headquarters had increased to twelve individuals, with an additional fourteen staffers in two parallel campaign organizations. The state party budget was about $2 million. Republicans were equally well-off at this time. In 1988, the Republican state party headquarters had a staff of nine and a budget of $1.6 million. In addition, a separate organization, with a similar staff and budget, supported that year's campaign efforts. The party organizations provided a number of services to candidates, especially those running for lower-level offices, such as the state legislature. These services included assistance in fund-raising and campaign training seminars. Get-out-the-vote efforts were also important, especially for Democrats, who put considerable resources into that effort.

The state party organizations remained well financed and active during the 1990s (Prysby 1997a, 2003). For example, in 1994, when no statewide races appeared on the ballot, the Democratic state party headquarters had a budget of $1.3 million and a staff of fourteen. In 1998, the party had a budget exceeding $1.5 million and a staff of eleven. In 1999, when no state or federal elections took place, the party still had a staff of seven and a budget of $750,000. Republicans were equally if not better funded. Their state party budget amounted to about $2 million in 1996, plus an additional $3 million in the Victory '96 fund, the party's parallel campaign organization. The 1999 Republican budget totaled approximately $1 million.

In 2004, both parties had strong organizational efforts. Republicans had a $500,000 budget for their state headquarters and more than $6 million in their Victory '04 fund. The combined staff for these two organizations included seventeen individuals at the state headquarters plus additional field workers. The Democrats had close to $1 million in their state party budget for 2004, with more than $3 million in the parallel campaign organization. The Democrats' staff was even larger than the Republican staff. Both parties conducted particularly vigorous get-out-the-vote drives that year. Both parties also had separate legislative caucus funds, which were used for state legislative elections. These funds have grown considerably for both parties.[4]

Less information is available about the grassroots organizations for both parties, but what information we have indicates recent improvement at this level. Republicans first emphasized developing their state party organization but subsequently began to strengthen their county party organizations. Democratic county organizations historically were stronger because of the party's dominance, but these organizations seem to have languished during the 1980s and 1990s. Still, Democrats currently appear to match Republicans in level of county party organizational strength and have recently emphasized rebuilding the county organizations. For both parties, most counties have an active party chair and hold regular executive committee meetings and other events. Only a small number—those in the largest counties—have a permanent county party headquarters, but the majority establish county headquarters in election years. Surveys of local party leaders in 1991 and 2001 also suggest that considerable activity takes place at the county level. Moreover, the 2001 data indicate some increase in this activity (Prysby 2003).

The construction of stronger political party organizations in North Carolina parallels developments in the South as a whole. In most southern states, the weak state party organizations that existed throughout most of the twentieth century have been replaced by better staffed, better funded, and more active bodies. A number of studies of party organizations and party activists in the contemporary South suggest that in comparison to a few decades ago, state party headquarters are more important, party organizations do more to help their candidates, and more organizational activity occurs even between elections (Aldrich 2000; Bruce and Clark 2004; Clark, Lockerbie, and Wielhouwer 1998; Feigert and Todd 1998; Hogan 2004). However, considerable variation exists in the development of stronger party organizations across the South, both across states and between parties, and North Carolina appears ahead of most southern states in terms of having fairly strong organizations for both political parties.

❖ Conclusion

North Carolina's political party system has been transformed over the past several decades. Two-party competition is a reality. Republicans have gained a clear edge in federal elections, but Democrats remain competitive in congressional elections. Republicans have made sizable gains in state elections, but Democrats still retain a slight advantage there. Of course, if Republicans continue to increase their support in the state over the next decade, as they have for the past few decades, the state could become more solidly Republican across the board, but that development is far from a certainty. The growth of two-party competition has been accompanied by the realignment of the parties. Democratic officeholders and party activists are now more clearly liberal; their Republican counterparts are more clearly conservative. Voters have realigned in response to these changes, and divisions in the electorate along demographic and ideological lines are sharper than in the past. Finally, stronger party organizations have emerged, especially at the state level but more recently at the local level as well. For those who prefer a two-party system with stronger, more ideologically distinct parties, these developments are welcome.

❖ Notes

1. For discussions of politics in individual southern states, see Bullock and Rozell (2006) and Lamis (1999b).

2. Easley did worse than his statewide percentage in Mecklenburg County, which includes the largest city, Charlotte; however, his opponent, Vinroot, was a former mayor of Charlotte.

3. Bowles did not carry Forsyth County, home to Winston-Salem, but his opponent, Burr, had represented that county in Congress for ten years.

4. Information on party budgets, staff, and activities were obtained from interviews over the past twenty years with various state party officials, including Ken Eudy, Scott Falmlen, Christopher Geis, Christopher Hains, Wayne McDevitt, Jerry Meek, and Jim Van Hecke from the Democratic Party and Bill Cobey, Dan Gurley, Jack Hawke, Christopher Mears, Bill Peaslee, and Jane Rouse from the Republican Party.

❖ References

Abramowitz, Alan I., and Kyle Saunders. 1998. "Ideological Realignment in the U.S. Electorate." *Journal of Politics* 20:634–52.

Aistrup, Joseph A. 1996. *The Southern Strategy Revisited: Republican Top-Down Advancement in the South*. Lexington: University Press of Kentucky.

Aldrich, John H. 1995. *Why Parties?: The Origin and Transformation of Party Politics in America*. Chicago: University of Chicago Press.

———. 2000. "Southern Parties in State and Nation." *Journal of Politics* 62:643–70.

American Conservative Union. 2007. "Ratings of Congress." <http://www.acuratings.org/>. Accessed September 17, 2007.

American Political Science Association. Committee on Political Parties. 1950. *Toward a More Responsible Two-Party System: A Report of the Committee on Political Parties of the American Political Science Association*. New York: Rinehart.

Baker, Tod A. 1990. "The Emergence of the Religious Right and the Development of the Two-Party System in the South." In *Political Parties in the Southern States*, edited by Tod

A. Baker, Charles D. Hadley, Robert P. Steed, and Laurence W. Moreland, 135–47. New York: Praeger.

Bass, Jack, and Walter DeVries. 1976. *The Transformation of Southern Politics: Social Change and Political Consequences since 1945*. New York: Basic Books.

Berard, Stanley P. 2001. *Southern Democrats in the U.S. House of Representatives*. Norman: University of Oklahoma Press.

Bibby, John F. 1998. "Party Organizations, 1946–1996." In *Partisan Approaches to Postwar American Politics*, edited by Byron Shafer, 142–85. New York: Chatham House.

Black, Earl, and Merle Black. 1987. *Politics and Society in the South*. Cambridge: Harvard University Press.

————. 1992. *The Vital South: How Presidents Are Elected*. Cambridge: Harvard University Press.

————. 2002. *The Rise of Southern Republicans*. Cambridge: Harvard University Press.

Broder, David. 1971. *The Party's Over*. New York: Harper and Row.

Bruce, John M., and John A. Clark. 2004. "Organizational Activity and Communication: More Vibrant Southern Grassroots Organizations?" In *Southern Political Party Activists: Patterns of Conflict and Change, 1991–2001*, edited by John A. Clark and Charles Prysby, 185–96. Lexington: University Press of Kentucky.

Bullock, Charles S., III. 1988. "Regional Realignment from an Officeholding Perspective." *Journal of Politics* 50:553–74.

Bullock, Charles S., III, and Mark J. Rozell, eds. 2006. *The New Politics of the Old South: An Introduction to Southern Politics*. 3rd ed. Lanham, Md.: Rowman and Littlefield.

Burnham, Walter. 1970. *Critical Elections and the Mainsprings of American Politics*. New York: Norton.

Carmines, Edward G., and Harold W. Stanley. 1990. "Ideological Realignment in the Contemporary South: Where Have All the Conservatives Gone?" In *The Disappearing South: Studies in Regional Change and Continuity*, edited by Robert P. Steed, Laurence W. Moreland, and Tod A. Baker, 21–33, 179–81. Tuscaloosa: University of Alabama Press.

Christensen, Rob, and Jack D. Fleer. 1999. "North Carolina: Between Helms and Hunt No Majority Emerges." In *Southern Politics in the 1990s*, edited by Alexander P. Lamis, 81–106. Baton Rouge: Louisiana State University Press.

Clark, John A., Brad Lockerbie, and Peter W. Wielhouwer. 1998. "Campaign Activities." In *Party Organization and Activism in the American South*, edited by Robert P. Steed, John A. Clark, Lewis Bowman, and Charles D. Hadley, 119–33. Tuscaloosa: University of Alabama Press.

Coleman, John J. 1996. "Resurgent or Just Busy?: Party Organization in Contemporary America." In *The State of the Parties: The Changing Role of Contemporary American Parties*, 2nd ed., edited by John C. Green and Daniel M. Shea, 367–84. Lanham, Md.: Rowman and Littlefield.

———. 2003. "Responsible, Functional, or Both?: American Political Parties and the ASPA Report after Fifty Years." In *The State of the Parties: The Changing Role of American Contemporary Parties*, 4th ed., edited by John C. Green and Rick Farmer, 300–319. Lanham, Md.: Rowman and Littlefield.

Cotter, Cornelius P., James L. Gibson, John F. Bibby, and Robert J. Huckshorn. 1984. *Party Organizations in American Politics*. New York: Praeger.

Cotter, Patrick R., and Samuel H. Fisher III. 2004. "A Growing Divide: Issue Opinions of Southern Party Activists." In *Southern Political Party Activists: Patterns of Conflict and Change, 1991–2001*, edited by John A. Clark and Charles Prysby, 59–72. Lexington: University Press of Kentucky.

Cowden, Jonathan A. 2001. "Southernization of the Nation and Nationalization of the South: Racial Conservatism, Social Welfare, and White Partisans in the United States, 1956–92." *British Journal of Political Science* 31:277–302.

Crotty, William. 1984. *American Political Parties in Decline*. 2nd ed. Boston: Little, Brown.

———. 1986. "Local Parties in Chicago: The Machine in Transition." In *Political Parties in Local Areas*, edited by William Crotty, 157–95. Knoxville: University of Tennessee Press.

David, Paul T. 1972. *Party Strength in the United States, 1872–1970*. Charlottesville: University Press of Virginia.

———. 1992. "The ASPA Committee on Political Parties." *Perspectives on Political Science* 21:70–79.

Feigert, Frank B., and John R. Todd. 1998. "Party Maintenance Activities." In *Party Organization and Activism in the American South*, edited by Robert P. Steed, John A. Clark, Lewis Bowman, and Charles D. Hadley, 105–13. Tuscaloosa: University of Alabama Press.

Fleer, Jack D. 1994. *North Carolina Government and Politics*. Lincoln: University of Nebraska Press.

Fleer, Jack D., Roger C. Lowery, and Charles L. Prysby. 1988. "Political Change in North Carolina." In *The South's New Politics*, edited by Robert Swansbrough and David Brodsky, 94–111. Columbia: University of South Carolina Press.

Frendreis, John P., James L. Gibson, and Laura L. Vertz. 1990. "The Electoral Relevance of Local Party Organizations." *American Political Science Review* 84:225–35.

Gibson, James L., Cornelius P. Cotter, John F. Bibby, and Robert J. Huckshorn. 1983. "Assessing Party Organizational Strength." *American Journal of Political Science* 27:193–222.

———. 1985. "Whither the Local Parties?: A Cross-Sectional and Longitudinal Analysis of the Strength of Party Organizations." *American Journal of Political Science* 29:139–60.

Gibson, James L., John P. Frendreis, and Laura L. Vertz. 1989. "Party Dynamics in the 1980s: Change in County Party Organizational Strength, 1980–1984." *American Journal of Political Science* 33:67–90.

Green, John C. 2002. "Believers for Bush, Godly for Gore: Religion and the 2000 Election in the South." In *The 2000 Presidential Election in the South*, edited by Robert P. Steed and Laurence W. Moreland, 11–22. Westport, Conn.: Praeger.

Green, John C., and Paul S. Herrnson. 2002. "Party Development in the Twentieth Century: Laying the Foundations for Responsible Party Government." In *Responsible Partisanship?: The Evolution of American Political Parties since 1950*, edited by John C. Green and Paul S. Herrnson, 37–59. Lawrence: University Press of Kansas.

Green, John C., Lyman A. Kellstaedt, Corwin E. Smidt, and James L. Guth. 2003. "The Soul of the South: Religion and Southern Politics at the Millennium." In *The New Politics of the Old South: An Introduction to Southern Politics*, 2nd ed., edited by Charles S. Bullock III and Mark J. Rozell, 283–98. Lanham, Md.: Rowman and Littlefield.

Herrnson, Paul S. 1988. *Party Campaigning in the 1980s*. Cambridge: Harvard University Press.

Hogan, Robert E. 2003. "Candidate Perceptions of Political Party Campaign Activity in State Legislative Elections." *State Politics and Policy Quarterly* 2:66–85.

———. 2004. "Involvement in Campaign Activity among Southern Party Activists." In *Southern Political Party Activists: Patterns of Conflict and Change, 1991–2001*, edited by John A. Clark and Charles L. Prysby, 171–84. Lexington: University Press of Kentucky.

Hopkins, Anne H. 1986. "Campaign Activities and Local Party Organization in Nashville." In *Political Parties in Local Areas*, edited by William J. Crotty, 65–88. Knoxville: University of Tennessee Press.

Huckshorn, Robert J., James L. Gibson, Cornelius P. Cotter, and John F. Bibby. 1986. "Party Integration and Party Organizational Strength." *Journal of Politics* 48:976–91.

Jackson, John S., III, Barbara L. Brown, and David Bositis. 1982. "Herbert McClosky and Friends Revisited: 1980 Democratic and Republican Party Elites Compared to the Mass Public." *American Politics Quarterly* 10:158–80.

Jackson, John S., III, and Nancy L. Clayton. 1996. "Leaders and Followers: Major Party Elites, Identifiers, and Issues, 1980–92." In *The State of the Parties: The Changing Role of Contemporary American Parties*, 2nd ed., edited by John C. Green and Daniel M. Shea, 328–51. Lanham, Md.: Rowman and Littlefield.

Key, V. O., Jr. 1949. *Southern Politics in State and Nation*. New York: Knopf.

———. 1955. "A Theory of Critical Elections." *Journal of Politics* 17:3–18.

———. 1959. "Secular Realignment and the Party System." *Journal of Politics* 21:198–210.

Knuckey, Jonathan. 2001. "Ideological Realignment and Partisan Change in the American South, 1972–1996." *Politics and Policy* 29:337–60.

Lamis, Alexander P. 1990. *The Two-Party South*. 2nd expanded ed. New York: Oxford University Press.

———. 1999a. "The Two-Party South: From the 1960s to the 1980s." In *Southern Politics in the 1990s*, edited by Alexander P. Lamis, 1–49. Baton Rouge: Louisiana State University Press.

—, ed. 1999b. *Southern Politics in the 1990s*. Baton Rouge: Louisiana State University Press.

Longley, Charles H. 1980. "National Party Renewal." In *Party Renewal in America: Theory and Practice*, edited by Gerald M. Pomper, 69–85. New York: Praeger.

Lublin, David. 2004. *The Republican South: Democratization and Partisan Change*. Princeton: Princeton University Press.

Luebke, Paul. 1990. *Tar Heel Politics: Myths and Realities*. Chapel Hill: University of North Carolina Press.

—. 1998. *Tar Heel Politics 2000*. Chapel Hill: University of North Carolina Press.

McClosky, Herbert, Paul J. Hoffman, and Rosemary O'Hara. 1960. "Issue Conflict and Consensus among Party Leaders and Followers." *American Political Science Review* 54:406–29.

McGlennon, John J. 1998. "Ideology and the Southern Party Activist: Poles Apart or Reflecting the Polls?" In *Party Activists in Southern Politics: Mirrors and Makers of Change*, edited by Charles D. Hadley and Lewis Bowman, 79–94. Knoxville: University of Tennessee Press.

Nadeau, Richard, and Harold W. Stanley. 1993. "Class Polarization in Partisanship among Native Southern Whites, 1952–90." *American Journal of Political Science* 37:900–919.

Petrocik, John R. 1981. *Party Coalitions: Realignment and the Decline of the New Deal Party System*. Chicago: University of Chicago Press.

—. 1987. "Realignment: New Party Coalitions and the Nationalization of the South." *Journal of Politics* 49:347–75.

Pomper, Gerald M. 1971. "Toward a More Responsible Two-Party System? What? Again?" *Journal of Politics* 33:916–40.

Price, David E. 1984. *Bringing Back the Parties*. Washington, D.C.: CQ Press.

Prysby, Charles. 1991. "North Carolina: The Confluence of National, Regional, and State Forces." In *The 1988 Presidential Election in the South*, edited by Laurence Moreland, Robert Steed, and Tod A. Baker, 185–200. New York: Praeger.

—. 1994. "North Carolina: Conflicting Forces in a Confusing Year." In *The 1992 Presidential Election in the South*, edited by Robert Steed, Laurence Moreland, and Tod A. Baker, 139–55. New York: Praeger.

—. 1995. "North Carolina: Emerging Two-Party Politics." In *Southern State Party Organizations and Activists*, edited by Charles D. Hadley and Lewis Bowman, 37–54. Westport, Conn.: Praeger.

—. 1996. "The 1990 U.S. Senate Election in North Carolina." In *Race, Politics, and Governance in the United States*, edited by Huey L. Perry, 29–46. Gainesville: University Press of Florida.

—. 1997a. "North Carolina." In *State Party Profiles*, edited by Andrew A. Appleton and Daniel S. Ward, 234–43. Washington, D.C.: CQ Press.

—. 1997b. "North Carolina: Republican Consolidation or Democratic Resurgence?" In

The 1996 Presidential Election in the South, edited by Laurence W. Moreland and Robert P. Steed, 165–81. Westport, Conn.: Praeger.

———. 2000. "Southern Congressional Elections in the 1990s: The Dynamics of Change." *American Review of Politics* 21:155–78.

———. 2002. "North Carolina: Continued Two-Party Competition." In *The 2000 Presidential Election in the South*, edited by Robert P. Steed and Laurence W. Moreland, 169–79. Westport, Conn.: Praeger.

———. 2003. "North Carolina: The Development of Party Organizations in a Competitive Environment." *American Review of Politics* 24:145–64.

———. 2004. "A Civil Campaign in a Competitive State: The 2002 North Carolina U.S. Senate Election." In *Running on Empty?: Political Discourse in Congressional Elections*, edited by L. Sandy Maisel and Darrell M. West, 215–28. Lanham, Md.: Rowman and Littlefield.

———. 2005. "North Carolina: Color the Tar Heels Federal Red and State Blue." *American Review of Politics* 26:185–202.

———. 2006. "North Carolina: Two-Party Competition Continues into the Twenty-First Century." In *The New Politics of the Old South: An Introduction to Southern Politics*, 3rd ed., edited by Charles S. Bullock III and Mark J. Rozell, 161–86. Lanham, Md.: Rowman and Littlefield.

Ranney, Austin. 1976. "Parties in State Politics." In *Politics in the American States*, 3rd ed., edited by Herbert Jacob and Kenneth Vines, 51–92. Boston: Little, Brown.

Sabato, Larry J., and Bruce Larson. 2002. *The Party's Just Begun: Shaping Political Parties for America's Future*. 2nd ed. New York: Longman.

Schattschneider, E. E. 1942. *Party Government*. New York: Rinehart.

Scher, Richard K. 1997. *Politics in the New South: Republicanism, Race, and Leadership in the Twentieth Century*. 2nd ed. Armonk, N.Y.: Sharpe.

Seltzer, Richard A., Jody Newman, and Melissa Voorhees Leighton. 1997. *Sex as a Political Variable: Women as Candidates and Voters in U.S. Elections*. Boulder, Colo.: Rienner.

Shaffer, Stephen D., Stacie Berry Pierce, and Steven A. Kohnke. 2000. "Party Realignment in the South: A Multi-Level Analysis." *American Review of Politics* 21:129–54.

Smidt, Corwin. 1989. "Change and Stability in the Partisanship of Southern Evangelicals: An Analysis of the 1980 and 1984 Presidential Elections." In *Religion in American Politics*, edited by Charles Dunn, 147–60. Washington, D.C.: CQ Press.

Steed, Robert P. 1998. "Parties, Ideology, and Issues: The Structuring of Political Conflict." In *Party Organization and Activism in the American South*, edited by Robert P. Steed, John A. Clark, Lewis Bowman, and Charles D. Hadley, 85–104. Tuscaloosa: University of Alabama Press.

Sundquist, James L. 1983. *Dynamics of the Party System*. Rev. ed. Washington, D.C.: Brookings Institution Press.

Wattenberg, Martin P. 1991. "The Building of a Republican Regional Base in the South: The Elephant Crosses the Mason-Dixon Line." *Political Opinion Quarterly* 55:424–32.

White, John Kenneth. 2001. "Reviving the Political Parties: What Must Be Done?" In *The Politics of Ideas*, edited by John Kenneth White and John C. Green, 29–68. Albany: State University of New York Press.

White, John Kenneth, and Jerome E. Mileur. 2002. "In the Spirit of Their Times: 'Toward a More Responsible Two-Party System' and Party Politics." In *Responsible Partisan?: The Evolution of American Political Parties since 1950*, edited by John C. Green and Paul S. Herrnson. Lawrence: University Press of Kansas.

Woodard, J. David. 2006. *The New Southern Politics*. Boulder, Colo.: Rienner.

❖ 4. Interest Groups and Lobbying in North Carolina
Density, Diversity, and Regulation
ADAM J. NEWMARK

The N.C. Technological Development Authority (NCTDA), a private, nonprofit corporation devoted to increasing the number of technology companies in North Carolina, spends considerable resources on lobbying. Over a two-year period, the NCTDA paid $549,726 in lobbying and consulting fees to McClees Consulting. Some of this money was allegedly spent on trips, lavish hotel rooms, and expensive dinners. As a result, North Carolina's state auditor, Ralph Campbell Jr., submitted a special review of the NCTDA to Governor Michael Easley, the General Assembly, the secretary of the N.C. Department of Commerce, and the chair of the NCTDA's board of directors (Campbell 2001). According to the review, the NCTDA receives between 45 and 70 percent of its funding each year from General Assembly appropriations and federal grants. Although much of the lobbying effort was designed to raise large sums of money for the agency, these expenditures raise questions regarding the lobbying behavior of an organization that receives millions of dollars from the state and federal governments.

Given examples like the NCTDA, people often have negative connotations of lobbying, viewing the activity as "dirty politics" or assuming that lobbyists "buy politicians." At least some of this perception stems from the good-old-boy style of lobbying that often involves the provision of gifts in exchange for political favors (Rosenthal 2001). But a difference exists between questionable behavior and illegal activity. The example of the NCTDA may seem critical of interest organization and lobbyist behavior, but no laws were broken. Lobbyists and legislators interact with a multitude of actors in a political environment regulated by state statutes. This interest community, consisting of lobbyists, lawmakers, and state laws, determines what is legal and what is not. Despite public perceptions, most lobbying activity is not controversial. In fact, many people defend the profession for the vital role it plays in giving a voice to a multitude of interests and in informing both the public and lawmakers about a range of issues from pollution to estate taxes.

This essay examines the nature of interest organization activity in the states, paying particular attention to the role of interests and lobbying in North Carolina. The essay begins with a discussion of the changes in lobbying and interest organization activity. These changes have important implications for the composition of interests represented in the fifty states, including North Carolina. Next, the essay examines the numbers of interests and lobbyists in North Carolina before turning to the diversity of these interests. This allows us to assess whether certain interests are better represented than others in the state. Finally, the essay discusses states' efforts to regulate lobbyist behavior, which have important consequences, determining whether problems arise with lobbying influence and whether lawmakers are willing to take action to curb such behaviors.

❖ The Changing Environment of Organized Interests and Lobbying

For a number of reasons, many organizations now choose to lobby in the state capitals instead of or in addition to Washington. Political scientists Clive S. Thomas and Ronald J. Hrebrenar (1991, 1999) have written extensively on the proliferation of interests at the state level, pointing to the centralization of lobbying activity around state capitols. As discussed in the introduction to this book, the states have become much more active in a variety of policy areas, making them a key target for political interests. "Devolution" is a term that describes returning power and responsibility to the states, and interest groups have realized that their issues might be better dealt with at the state rather than national level. We have also witnessed a rise in new interests, such as those associated with technologies focusing on medical research, computers, and the Internet. Embryonic stem cell research, for example, was not an issue twenty years ago, yet today it is important to a number of interests.

Other interests spawn from larger organizations. The American Association of Retired Persons (AARP) lobbies in Washington, but AARP North Carolina also lobbies in Raleigh as well as many other state capitals. Similarly, the Sierra Club has a North Carolina chapter in addition to its national organization. Interest proliferation may also occur because of increasing specialization within a profession. Physicians are members of the American Medical Association, which is registered to lobby in Washington, but many doctors are also members of various state and national interest organizations, depending on their specialty. The 2006 lobbying registration list in North Carolina includes the N.C. Podiatric Medical Society, the N.C. Society of Eye Physicians and Surgeons, the N.C. Obstetrical and Gynecological Society, the N.C. Psychiatric Association, and Southeastern Orthopaedic Specialists. Although the American Medical Association meets many physicians' general needs, more specific issues such as stem cell research and reproductive rights, for example, would likely be of greater concern to the N.C. Obstetrical and Gynecological Society.

Along with increased specialization, we have also seen more single-issue organizations registered to lobby. Many organizations will register to lobby to facilitate the passage or defeat of a given bill. Some of these organizations have been registered for many years and continue to lobby even after the bill or issue is no longer on the legislative agenda. The N.C. Association of Convenience Stores and Freedom Works had a vested interest in the passage of the N.C. State Lottery Act, but these organizations have other issues that necessitate lobbying for many years to come. While the National Association for the Repeal of Abortion Laws (NARAL), Pro-Choice North Carolina, and Right to Life Inc. routinely register in the state, other organizations may register only when the legislature considers a bill to either extend or limit abortion rights. This is true in other issue areas as well. The Committee on State Taxation registered in North Carolina between 2001 and 2002 because of a tax bill dealing with related company expenses but did not register for the following time period because the bill was no longer on the legislative agenda.

Lobbying in the states has also become more sophisticated in recent years. Although the lobbying profession was traditionally dominated by men, it is now more common for women to work as lobbyists, at least in North Carolina. According to 2006 estimates, between 30 and 35 percent of the lobbyists in North Carolina are female. Many organizations hire contract firms, or "hired guns," because of their superior resources and contacts in the legislature (Thomas and Hrebenar 1999). North Carolina, for example, has a number of large lobbying firms, many of which have a variety of clients. For example, in 2006, contract lobbyist Jon Carr represented fifteen clients. including the N.C. Association of ABC Boards and the N.C. Pediatric Society. He holds a degree in business from the University of North Carolina at Chapel Hill and a law degree from Campbell University. Since 1993, he has worked for the law firm of Jordan, Price, Wall, Gray, Jones, and Carlton, collaborating with two other lobbyists.

Larger organizations and institutions in particular may even hire full-time lobbyists to represent their firms before the state legislature. The trend represents a movement away from the good-old-boy style of lobbying found in many statehouses in years past. Political scientist Alan Rosenthal (2001) has written about lobbyists who provided gifts, entertainment, and other benefits in exchange for a lawmaker's friendly ear. While the good old boys relied on friendships and personal appeal strategies to influence lawmakers, today's lobbyists are much more professional. However, the good-old-boy style of lobbying may not have disappeared completely. At the very least, lobbyists continue to maximize their personal relationships to facilitate interactions with lawmakers. While some condemn these relationships, others defend them on First Amendment grounds or because they are necessary for interests to be properly represented and for legislators to do their job.

National and state governments have also witnessed a rise in the numbers of political action committees (PACs). These organizations, often with loose connections to political parties or other political interests, play a financial role in supporting candidates. PACs sometimes distribute money to candidates and at other times spend money to support or defeat candidates (Rozell and Wilcox 1999). Unions often form PACs to support Democratic candidates, while business interests often favor Republican candidates (or sometimes both parties). The N.C. Pork Council is a PAC that distributes money to candidates in the state, including $2,000 in 2006 to Republican Virginia Foxx and $1,000 to Democrat Bob Etheridge, both members of the U.S. House of Representatives ("N.C. Pork Council" n.d.). This PAC's largest contributions to state legislators in 2006 included $1,000 to Democratic speaker of the North Carolina House James Black and $750 to Republican state senator Fred Smith (National Institute on Money in State Politics n.d.).

Another notable change in interest community composition stems from an increase in the number and type of institutions operating nationally and at the state level. Institutions generally have no members, at least in the traditional sense of a membership group. Institutions are typically businesses or corporations that register to lobby, though institutions also include universities, government agencies, and special districts. These organizations have vested interests in lobbying the legislature, whether for tax breaks in the corporate case or for budget allocations for universities or government agencies. Companies such as Du Pont or International Paper Company, which registered in North Carolina for 2006, may lobby for reduced taxation, decreased environmental regulation, or lower utility costs. The Town of Boone and City of Greensboro are two examples of other institutions registered in the state.

Taken together, these changes have led to what some scholars have referred to as the nationalization hypothesis—that is, state lobbying looks more and more like Washington lobbying. Accordingly, many state interest communities are looking more like each other, and many organizations are lobbying in a number of different state capitols (Thomas and Hrebenar 1991). David Lowery and Virginia Gray (1994) note that interest communities are similarly responsive to economic pressures, so many states may have similar interests. Thomas and Hrebrenar (1999) further suggest that many organizations are registered in many states. The National Rifle Association (NRA), U.S. Airways, United Parcel Service (UPS), and Verizon are registered in North Carolina and in other states where they conduct business or attempt to curry influence. A recent study noted that many organizations that were registered in a large number of states—for example, Anheuser-Busch Companies Inc. (forty-nine states), AT&T (forty-nine states), the Bankers Association (forty-eight states), and the Association of Realtors (forty-seven states)—were also registered in North Carolina (Wolak et al. 2002). Even the AFL-CIO registered in North Carolina (as well as forty-six other states), which may seem surprising given North Carolina's lack of support for unions.

Although many organizations register in more than one state, most do not. Of the 34,490 organizations registered to lobby the states in 1997, 53 percent were registered only in a single state. On average, organizations were registered in 1.6 states. Many of these organizations registered in the states are institutions, in this case small businesses, indicating that registrants reflect localized concerns rather than only large corporate interests (Wolak et al. 2002).

❖ The Number and Type of Interests and Lobbyists in the States

The number of interest organizations varies substantially from state to state. In 2006, 795 organizations, categorized as principals, were registered with the N.C. Secretary of State's Office, up from 713 registered in 2005. Each principal has one or more lobbyist—typically the chief executive officer, an in-house lobbyist, a contract lobbyist, a member of an organization who lobbies for a cause, or someone who registers because of a pet project (Thomas and Hrebenar 1999). BellSouth has fourteen lobbyists, and the N.C. Association of Electric Cooperatives Inc. and ElectriCities of North Carolina Inc. each has ten lobbyists. In 2006, 683 lobbyists registered in the state (up from 598 in 2005); some of them had multiple clients (of the 795 principals). Sometimes the clients were in similar issue areas, such as the lobbyist whose clients included the North Carolina Association of Rescue and Emergency Medical Services and the N.C. Firemen's Association. Other lobbyists may represent unrelated interests, like the lobbyist whose clients included the N.C. Association of ABC Boards and Daimler-Chrysler. Conversely, most lobbyists represented only a single client. Of the state's 683 registered lobbyists, 545 (about 80 percent) lobbied for a single client. For example, Louisa Warren represented the Common Cause Education Fund in North Carolina, a nonprofit, nonpartisan affiliate of the public interest organization Common Cause. She was also quite different from some of the contract lobbyists mentioned earlier. For example, she was new to lobbying, with a background involving work with other nonprofits and with the N.C. Coalition for Lobbying and Government Reform.

In 2006, North Carolina also had sixty-seven liaisons and departments that register to lobby the legislature, nearly three times as many as the twenty-three recorded the previous year. This group includes the office of the governor, the Department of Health and Human Services, the Department of Justice, the Ports Authority, and the University of North Carolina at Chapel Hill. Each of these entities has a vested interest in lobbying the legislature, some arguing for greater budgetary allocations and some working to pass legislation favorable to their issues of importance.

So why have we seen an increase in the number of interests in North Carolina, and why do some states have a larger number than other states? Scholars have encountered difficulty in explaining the density of interest systems (or number of interests). Pluralist scholars have argued that the number of interests is determined by the nature of the interests in the population. Therefore, if a large number of interests exists, a large number of groups should form. Mancur Olson Jr. (1982) argued that the number of interests was related to the amount of time since the political system's formation or its disturbance by crises such as war. Other observers have posited that government economic size would determine the number of interests (Mitchell and Munger 1991). Gray and Lowery (1996) employ population ecology models to explain interest system density, noting that the number and resources of constituents as well as interest certainty are more important determinants of density than are economic factors. Moreover, states have a carrying capacity that limits the number of interests the system can sustain.

Table 4.1 shows the number of lobbying registrants in the fifty states in 1999. The data show that the most populous states typically have a greater number of lobbying registrants than states with smaller populations. California, Florida, and Texas had 2,272, 2,149, and 2,135 registrants, respectively, reflecting the large number of issues in these states. California's issues consist not only of typical matters such as education and law enforcement but also of immigration issues and interests focusing on wine growers, citrus growers, the entertainment industry, tourism, technology, and resorts from the beach to the mountains. The state also includes a ballot initiative process that allows voters to decide on issues, and many interests may register to help influence these voters. Population is often important but does not always explain the number of registered organizations in a given state. North Carolina is the eleventh-most-populous state, yet it ranked twenty-fifth in the number of registrants. With 597 organizations in 1999, the state fell below the mean of 739 and the median of 593.5 organizations nationwide. At the bottom of the table are states such as Vermont, Hawaii, North Dakota, and Wyoming, each of which had fewer than 300 registered interests. Wyoming's 72 registrants represented a substantial decrease from the 273 registered two years earlier.

❖ The Diversity of State Interests

Another way to compare interest communities is in the diversity in the types of organizations registered. Early interest group scholars pondered the representative nature of the pressure system. Pluralists such as David B. Truman (1951) and

TABLE 4.1. Total Lobby Registrants in the Fifty States, 1999

State	Registrants	State	Registrants
California	2,272	Tennessee	590
Florida	2,149	Wisconsin	580
Texas	2,135	Iowa	560
Illinois	1,475	Colorado	540
New York	1,334	Alabama	512
Louisiana	1,279	Utah	512
Minnesota	1,223	Kentucky	464
Ohio	1,211	South Carolina	455
Arizona	1,092	Nebraska	441
Michigan	1,090	Montana	439
New Jersey	1,089	Arkansas	391
Massachusetts	1,075	Virginia	360
Missouri	1,010	Mississippi	349
Georgia	961	Idaho	338
Washington	952	New Hampshire	336
Nevada	935	Maine	333
Maryland	861	Rhode Island	324
Pennsylvania	834	Alaska	319
New Mexico	735	West Virginia	316
Indiana	669	South Dakota	311
Oregon	629	Delaware	310
Connecticut	627	Vermont	289
Oklahoma	611	Hawaii	202
Kansas	603	North Dakota	170
North Carolina	597	Wyoming	72

Mean = 739.22
Median = 593.5

Source: Data provided by David Lowery and Virginia Gray.

Arthur F. Bentley (1950) believed that people naturally joined groups; a multitude of interests, therefore, were represented. Robert Dahl (1956, 138) argued that "all active and legitimate" groups could be represented, and the result was a rather diverse set of interests rather than dominance by one or two powerful organizations. Others, including E. E. Schattschneider (1960), noted an elite dominance in the pressure system, where those with substantial resources indeed occupied a privileged position. Accordingly, businesses with substantial resources have a key monetary advantage when they register to lobby, allowing them to hire in-house lobbyists or expensive contract lobbying firms to help influence policy. McClees Consulting, the firm mentioned at the beginning of this essay, is an example of a contract firm. In 2006, Joseph McClees was listed as the lobbyist of record for fifteen different interests in the state of North Carolina. Bruce R. Thompson, another contract lobbyist, had twenty-five clients, including the Town of Cary, Dell Inc., and the Carolina Wireless Association.

The relevant question here concerns the diversity of the interests registered in the states—specifically, the diversity of North Carolina's interest community. Pluralists would argue that the diversity within an interest community simply reflects the diversity of interests in society. Thus, if there is an issue, cause, or concern, individuals will band together. Membership groups are voluntary organizations that are usually based on dues-paying members who have some common interest. Examples of membership groups include the American Association of Retired Persons North Carolina, the National Rifle Association of America, and the North Carolina chapter of the Sierra Club. As noted earlier, however, many interests that register do not have individuals as members. These institutions, often businesses or government agencies, comprise a substantial portion of the interests registered in the state. Associations are usually groups of institutions with a common reason to band together. For example, the N.C. Bankers Association is a registered association in the state, with more than 140 members, among them BB&T Corporation, Bank of America Corporation, First Citizens Bank and Trust, Asheville Savings Bank SSB, and North State Bank. These banks have common issues, and by joining an association, they try to maximize their clout through their numbers. The first three examples of these banks are also registered independently (as they are institutions), while the latter two are not. By registering individually *and* joining an association, organizations try to maximize their representation in front of the legislature. They often lobby for more particularized benefits individually while joining an association that represents their common interests.

One way to look at whether certain interests are better represented is simply to look at the organizations registered in the state. Table 4.2 shows the 776 registered interest organizations in North Carolina in 2006 by interest area. The five columns in table 4.2 from left to right include the interest area, those that are associations, institutions, membership groups, and the total. Seven hundred seventy six of North Carolina's interest organizations were coded into these categories. Many interests could easily fit into multiple categories on the table. Pfizer Inc. is a pharmaceutical corporation that could be classified under health or research and development, but it is a manufacturing company and is categorized as such. The most common interest areas in North Carolina as well as other states are sales/service/business consulting, health/human services, and manufacturing. These three categories make up about 39 percent of North Carolina's interests, indicating a moderate concentration. Business organizations are technically the most common

TABLE 4.2. Registered Interest Organizations in North Carolina by Interest Area, 2006

Interest Area	Associations	Institutions	Membership Groups	Total
Advocacy	11	16	30	57
Agriculture	6	4	6	16
Arts	1	3	3	7
Banking	1	7	2	10
Business (other)	12	13	3	28
Communications	6	17	1	24
Community organizations	0	4	4	8
Construction	6	6	1	13
Economic development	5	7	2	14
Education	8	7	10	25
Environment	3	6	13	22
Financial/economic	5	11	2	18
Government	4	25	1	30
Health/human services	22	59	14	95
Insurance	10	21	2	33
Labor	4	6	6	16
Legal	2	6	5	13
Manufacturing	13	62	0	75
Military/veterans	1	1	3	5
Police/fire	1	0	8	9
Political interest	0	4	14	18
Professional	6	0	30	36
Religion	1	2	1	4
Research/development	1	4	0	5
Senior adults	2	1	1	4
Service/sales/business consulting	46	80	9	135
Sports and recreation	4	5	6	15
Transportation	7	7	2	16
Unknown	0	2	0	2
Utilities	4	14	0	18
Welfare	1	5	3	9
Total[a]	191	399	186	776

Source: <http:www.secretary.state.nc.us/lobbyists/download.aspx>.
[a]Of the 795 total interest organizations in the state, 776 were coded based on the above categories.

interest, because businesses are found in many of the other categories, including communications, insurance, professional, or financial/economic. The table also suggests numerical institutional dominance, as approximately 51 percent of the organizations are institutions. The number is even higher if we include departments and legislative liaisons, which are not shown in the table. Associations and membership groups, conversely, make up 25 and 24 percent respectively of registered interests. The most common associations are similar to institutions in that they are often in the service/sales/business consulting, health/human services, or manufacturing fields, while membership groups are most likely advocacy or professional groups.

Another way to examine diversity is to investigate how North Carolina compares to other states in terms of the number of business, corporate, or industry-related interests. Figure 4.1 shows the number of firms in each state in the following areas or guilds relative to the total number of firms in that state: agriculture, banking, communications, construction, health, hotel, insurance, manufacturing, small business, sports, transportation, and utilities. This is of course only one way to examine the diversity issue. In fact, the figure offers little information regarding these organizations' activity. It does, however, give us a view of the numbers of organizations by type across states. In terms of business dominance, Hawaii has the highest percentage (70.7 percent) of its interests in these twelve categories, followed by Maryland (68.3 percent) and Vermont (67.8 percent). North Carolina ranks tenth, with about 63 percent of its interests in these categories, exceeding the national average of 59 percent. So, compared to the average state, North Carolina has more business interests as a percentage of its total registrants. At the other extreme, only 47 percent of Wyoming's and about 50 percent of Colorado's and Montana's interests fall into these categories.

Despite the institutional dominance that the data suggest, business interests are not necessarily uniform. So even if table 4.2 and figure 4.1 indicate that businesses dominate the lobbying rolls, all of these entities do not necessarily seek the same thing. Though business interests may generally favor low taxes, most of their lobbying efforts are aimed at very specialized benefits. The differences between the manufacturing and the service sectors are substantial, and their demands are hardly uniform. A company such as Du Pont may lobby for reduced environmental regulations, but the members of the National Bankers Association likely care little about this issue because it does not have a substantial effect on the banking business. Even in the well-represented health sector, it is likely that Johnson and Johnson, Johnston Memorial Hospital, the National Multiple Sclerosis Society, and Kerr Drug Inc. lobby the North Carolina statehouse for slightly different concerns.

With limitations on resources, these organizations focus on what is most important to them.

We also know relatively little from the data about the influence of these organizations even within the same sector. We know that twenty-two environmental organizations registered in North Carolina, but we do not know whether these organizations lobbied on the same side of issues or which interests are most influential. Some environmental interests may promote energy conservation by promoting wind-generated energy, yet bird conservationists may object to equipment that may harm these animals during flight. The N.C. Forestry Association and the Conservation Trust for North Carolina are clearly at odds over the state's forestlands. Still, the aggregate data are useful in assessing the diversity issue if not power and influence. We know from existing scholarship that certain types of organizations, including general businesses, teachers unions, and utilities, are often viewed as having substantial influence (Thomas and Hrebenar 1999), but variation in influence exists within these categories as well. In North Carolina, as in any state, Ford Motor Company and General Motors Corporation likely have greater political influence than Cascade Auto Glass, though we know that there are many more smaller interests registered than large multistate corporations (Wolak et al. 2002).

Finally, interest sectors seldom dominate public policy if the public pays attention. Some industries may find it profitable to pollute the environment, but if members of the public realize that their air or water quality is poor, they will pressure politicians to regulate the industry. This does not mean that tobacco interests or the health care industry have no influence over lawmakers, but it does suggest that these industries are limited in what they can do in the face of public opposition. Public opinion and issue saliency are important constraints on any interest sector that attempts to become too powerful. Politicians depend on reelection, so they pay attention when the public is watching. Recent research suggests that although business contributions positively influence business-related policies in the states, this influence is contingent on such factors as public opinion and countermobilization of other groups (Witko and Newmark 2005).

❖ Regulating Lobbying and Interest Organization Activity

The ethical questions raised at the beginning of this essay are germane at both the national and state levels. In 2006, Jack Abramoff, a prominent lobbyist, was convicted and sentenced to nearly six years in prison for charges including fraud, conspiracy, and corrupting public officials (Shenon 2006). Abramoff had ties to

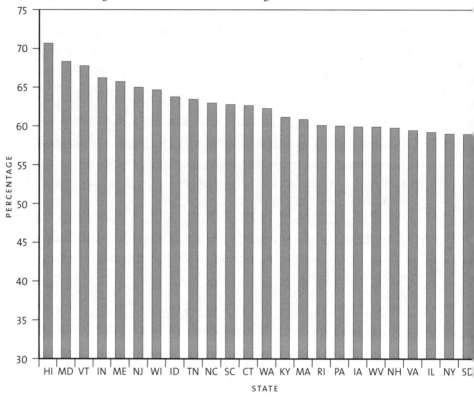

FIGURE 4.1. Percentage of Business-Related Interests Registered in the States

Source: Data provided by David Lowery and Virginia Gray (1997).

several prominent Republican U.S. lawmakers, including Bob Ney of Ohio and Tom DeLay of Texas, whose congressional careers have ended. Ney pled guilty to charges of corruption, while DeLay has been indicted and is waiting to stand trial for money laundering as of this writing. The states, too, have witnessed their share of lobbying scandals. In the 1990s, for example, South Carolina legislators were caught on camera selling their votes in exchange for money (Grimm 2003). South Carolina subsequently toughened its lobbying regulations, making them among the nation's most restrictive (Newmark 2005). In the early 1990s, the speaker of the Kentucky House, Don Blandford, and other legislators and lobbyists were sent to prison after being convicted on charges of corruption (Ensign 1997). These examples raise three important questions. First, how does lobbying regulation affect the number of interests or density of the interest community in the states? Second, what does lobbying regulation look like over time? Third, do stricter regulations result in behavioral changes among lobbyists and lawmakers?

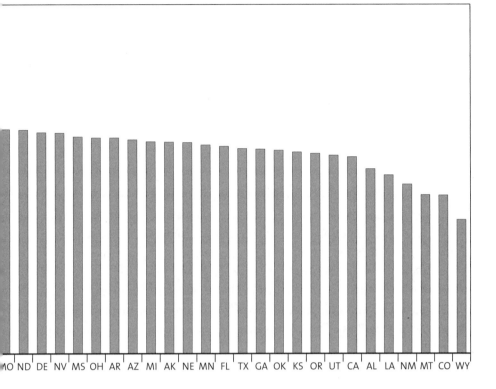

MO ND DE NV MS OH AR AZ MI AK NE MN FL TX GA OK KS OR UT CA AL LA NM MT CO WY

Scholars have examined how lobbying regulation influences the number of organizations that register to lobby in the states. When lobbyists and interest groups register with the secretary of state's office, they must complete paperwork and submit a relatively modest filing fee. Beginning in 2007, each lobbyist in North Carolina paid one hundred dollars to register plus an additional one hundred dollars for each principal the lobbyist represents. In addition, lobbyists are often required to disclose any gifts or other benefits they provide in total or over a set amount. The logic is that more difficult lobbying regulations will limit the number of organizations and lobbyists registering in the state. Margaret Brinig, Randall G. Holcombe, and Linda Schwartzstein (1993) find that regulations make it more costly to register, thereby influencing lobbying registration. Of course, increased costs predominantly affect organizations that are mostly inactive, because a larger or wealthy organization such as IBM will register whether the filing fee is fifty or two hundred dollars. Other scholars have found that lobbying regulations such as fees do not serve as barriers to registration and thus do not affect the density of the lobbying community (Hunter, Wilson, and Brunk 1991; Lowery and Gray 1997).

The states have implemented a number of good government reforms such as term limits and ethics legislation to ensure that public officials behave in an acceptable manner. Of course, what is deemed acceptable in one state may not necessarily be viewed the same way in another state. Lobbying regulations have been implemented to limit vote buying, bribery, or the provision of extravagant gifts in exchange for legislative favors. In the era of the good old boys, these behaviors were either accepted or overlooked, but they are now limited because of public pressure, media scrutiny, and a shift to more professional legislatures that somewhat resemble the U.S. Congress.

So how have the states regulated their interest groups and lobbying behavior? The states can regulate lobbying behavior in four ways. The first focuses on the scope of the definition of a lobbyist. More inclusive definitions of lobbying, such as those in states that consider lobbying by executive agencies or whether there is a compensation standard, generally reflect stricter lobby regulation. As of 2005, North Carolina's definition of "lobbyist" included only legislative lobbying and public employees, while South Carolina and Washington, for example, included these criteria as well as administrative agency lobbying and elected officials as lobbyists.

Second, the states can prohibit certain activities or types of gifts that may be given or received. Most would agree that handing a lawmaker a stack of hundred-dollar bills and asking him or her to support a given piece of legislation would be unlawful, but most activities are less blatant. Should a lobbyist be able to purchase a cup of coffee for a lawmaker? In Wisconsin and South Carolina, the answer is no. What about dinner? Is a vacation out of the question? In Georgia, lobbyists took lawmakers on a golf vacation involving exotic dancers (Newmark 2005; Salzer 1997). Following this incident, the state made few meaningful changes to its lobbying laws.

Third, as mentioned earlier, the state may require lobbyists and lawmakers to disclose gifts given or received in an attempt to induce lawmakers to exercise caution in accepting contributions or gifts. This strategy occasionally causes lawmakers to return gifts from sources that might hurt reelection chances.

Finally, the states regulate lobbying behavior by enforcing existing provisions with various penalties for violations. This is perhaps the most difficult type of regulation to examine because the penalties can be specific in one state and vague in another. The penalties can also vary widely—for example, State A may impose a minimum fine of $250 for violating a statute but specify no maximum, while State B may have a maximum fine of $1,000 for violating a similar statute but specify no minimum. However, states may not have similar statutes. Of course, to regulate lobbying, a state attorney general's office must be able and willing to pursue violations of statutory provisions.

Table 4.3 presents data on the extent to which the states have regulated their lobbyists between 1990 and 2003 (Newmark 2005). The data were obtained from the Council of State Governments' *Book of the States* and consist of the statutory definition of lobbying, prohibited activities, and disclosure requirements, which include the frequency of registration and reporting. States with stricter statutory definitions of what constitutes "lobbying" reflect stricter regulation than do states with narrower definitions. Much as with Cynthia Opheim's (1991) measure, this index is constructed based on whether the definition of lobbying includes seven criteria: (1) legislative lobbying, (2) administrative agency lobbying, (3) elected officials as lobbyists, (4) public employees as lobbyists, and whether the definition includes a (5) compensation standard, (6) expenditure standard, and (7) time standard. In addition, requirements for more frequent lobbying disclosure and reporting likely indicate more onerous laws overall.

To regulate lobbying, the states often prohibit certain activities or require disclosure of activities, gifts received, or contributions. Prohibited activities include four criteria: (1) making campaign contributions at any time, (2) making campaign contributions during the legislative session, (3) making expenditures in excess of a certain dollar amount per year, and (4) solicitation by officials or employees for contributions or gifts. Disclosure requirements include six types: (1) legislative/administrative action seeking to influence; (2) expenditures benefiting public officials or employees; (3) compensation received, broken down by employer; (4) total compensation received, (5) categories of expenditures, and (6) total expenditures. All categories were coded 1 if the state had a given requirement, and 0 if it did not. These values were summed to create an index ranging from 0 to 18, where higher values indicate greater levels of regulation. Thus, we now have a relative score across states and over time.

As of 2003, South Carolina regulates most heavily (with a score of 17), followed by Alaska (15), Maine (15), Texas (15), Washington (15), California (14), and Kentucky (14). The least regulated state is North Dakota (1), though Wyoming (5), Virginia (6), Oklahoma (6), North Carolina (6), Illinois (6), and Arizona (6) had relatively little regulation. As of 2003, North Carolina ranked near the bottom of the list. The second column from the right reports the 2003 score, which was added to the severity-of-penalties score (in parentheses). As the table indicates, most states increased the stringency of their lobbying laws; the average increase between 1990–91 and 2003 was 129 percent. South Carolina increased its lobbying regulation score by 750 percent, and Kentucky increased its score by 367 percent.[1] Both

TABLE 4.3. Changes in State Ranking of Lobbying Law Stringency, 1990–2003

State	1990–91	1994–95	1996–97	2000–2001	2002	2003	2003 Score (Penalties)	% Change from 1990 to 2003
South Carolina	2	14	16	17	17	17	21(4)	750
Alaska	10	11	11	13	15	15	17(2)	50
Maine	8	11	14	15	15	15	16(1)	87.5
Texas	10	16	15	15	15	15	18(3)	50
Washington	14	15	15	15	15	15	18(3)	7.14
California	7	12	14	14	14	14	16(2)	100
Kentucky	3	10	10	14	14	14	18(4)	366.67
Colorado	9	13	13	13	13	13	—	44.44
Connecticut	13	13	13	13	13	13	15(2)	0
Maryland	13	13	13	13	13	13	15(2)	0
Minnesota	9	11	12	13	13	13	15(2)	44.44
New York	8	12	12	12	13	13	17(4)	62.5
Utah	5	13	13	13	13	13	14(1)	160
Wisconsin	14	13	13	13	13	13	16(3)	-7.141
Hawaii	11	11	11	12	12	12	13(1)	9.09
Mississippi	4	7	12	12	12	12	15(3)	200
Missouri	5	12	12	12	12	12	14(2)	140
New Jersey	10	11	11	12	12	12	14(2)	20
Florida	5	8	8	11	11	11	13(2)	120
Massachusetts	9	10	11	11	11	11	13(2)	22.22
Michigan	10	11	11	11	11	11	15(4)	10
Montana	8	9	9	10	11	11	13(2)	37.5
Ohio	3	9	9	11	11	11	21(1)	266.67
Oregon	11	11	11	11	11	11	14(3)	0
Vermont	3	14	14	14	11	11	13(2)	266.67
Alabama	7	7	11	10	10	10	12(2)	42.86
Idaho	7	10	10	10	10	10	11(1)	42.86
Kansas	7	8	9	11	10	10	13(3)	42.86
Nevada	7	9	10	10	10	10	13(3)	42.86
Pennsylvania	6	7	7	12	10	10	14(4)	66.67
Rhode Island	7	7	9	9	10	10	13(3)	42.86
Arkansas	2	9	9	9	9	9	11(2)	350
Iowa	9	9	9	9	9	9	10(1)	0
Louisiana	2	8	8	9	9	9	12(3)	350
Tennessee	5	8	10	9	9	9	—	80
West Virginia	3	8	9	9	9	9	—	200
Delaware	4	5	5	8	8	8	11(3)	100
Georgia	1	8	8	8	8	8	9(1)	700
Indiana	11	8	8	8	8	8	11(3)	-27.27
Nebraska	8	9	8	8	8	8	11(3)	0
New Hampshire	5	8	8	8	8	8	10(2)	60

TABLE 4.3. (*continued*)

State	1990– 91	1994– 95	1996– 97	2000– 2001	2002	2003	2003 Score (Penalties)	% Change from 1990 to 2003
New Mexico	4	8	8	8	8	8	11(3)	100
South Dakota	1	7	7	7	7	7	8(1)	600
Arizona	3	3	5	6	6	6	9(3)	100
Illinois	1	6	6	6	6	6	8(2)	500
North Carolina	2	5	5	6	6	6	8(2)	200
Oklahoma	5	5	5	5	6	6	10(4)	20
Virginia	10		6	6	6	6	7(1)	-40
Wyoming	2	2	2	5	5	5	6(1)	150
North Dakota	4	4	1	1	1	1	2(1)	-75
Mean	6.54	9.35	9.72	10.34	10.34	10.34		129.13
Standard deviation	3.632	3.106	3.283	3.173	3.147	3.147		181.53

Source: Newmark (2005).

Note: The scores for each year are measured on a scale with a possible range from 0 to 18 points. Higher values indicate stricter lobbying laws. The second column from the right contains the 2003 score, which is added to the penalty score (in parentheses). The last column contains the percentage change from 1990 to 2003. Data for Colorado, Tennessee, and West Virginia are missing from the second-to-last column from the right because the relevant penalty statutes in these states were not comparable to the statutes in other states.

of these states have responded to lobbying and legislative scandals by substantially increasing their lobbying regulations. North Dakota and Wyoming, the two states with the least restrictive lobbying laws, also have lenient penalties for violating those relatively weak laws. Although North Carolina increased its regulation score by 200 percent over this period, it remained near the bottom of the fifty states as of 2003. The Abramoff scandal and the state scandal involving former North Carolina speaker James Black have resulted in much greater public attention to lobbying behavior. As Christopher A. Cooper details (this volume), Black was embroiled in a scandal involving lobbying and the passage of the N.C. lottery in 2005.

North Carolina addressed the regulation issue even before the scandal, on August 24, 2005, when the General Assembly ratified Senate Bill 612, which aimed to make the state's lobbying laws more stringent. Among the changes, the law now requires monthly disclosure of expenditures during the legislative session, reporting of gifts or payments of more than ten dollars, a six-month waiting period for former lawmakers who want to lobby, and reporting of lobbying by the executive branch. Another important series of changes in North Carolina's lobbying laws has been in enforcement. The secretary of state's office now has the authority to investigate violations and the ability to impose civil fines up to five thousand dollars. The current law enables the secretary of state to work with the attorney general to enforce the law. Some time will have to pass before we can assess the effectiveness and enforcement of North Carolina's new law, and even with stricter lobbying laws, enforcement requires action by the attorney general and conviction by a jury if a criminal trial takes place.

Lobbying reforms may also have altered lobbyists' and legislators' behavior. Many observers have noted the decline in the good-old-boy style of lobbying, but most of these assertions have been anecdotal. Still, many states have adopted laws that criminalize behaviors in which lobbyists previously engaged. Lobbyists likely adapt to more rigorous regulation of the profession by altering their strategies when dealing with lawmakers. For example, rather than attempting to appeal to lawmakers with gifts or other inducements, lobbyists now rely on the provision of information about the nature of potential legislation, how that legislation might affect a lawmaker's constituents, and what other lawmakers are planning to support it (Newmark 2003, forthcoming). Of course, the ideal situation involves the use of both personalized appeals and the provision of information. Thus, personal relationships between lawmakers and lobbyists facilitate the former's willingness to accept information from the latter.

To some extent, a disincentive exists for state legislators to regulate their behavior and that of lobbyists. As is the case with ethics reforms, many lawmakers' changes to state laws have fallen somewhat short (Rosenson 2005). Many lawmakers do not receive substantial compensation—in North Carolina, lawmakers receive only about fourteen thousand dollars plus expenses per year. Legislators may enjoy the occasional perks provided by lobbyists and in the absence of scandal may be unlikely to limit benefits, such as the occasional dinner, that they had hitherto received. Lobbyists also certainly do not want their access limited, as it is a primary means by which they achieve their objectives.

❖ Conclusion

Interest organizations and lobbyists are important components of North Carolina's political system. Individuals may have little political voice by themselves, but organized interests allow the public to become involved in the political process. Many scholars have argued that such involvement is key to democratic values. Proponents of gun rights might join the NRA because it provides an avenue to further their cause and allows them to interact with others who agree with them on the issue. Because the NRA is active in the states and nationally, the organization can influence policy at multiple levels of government. The presence of such groups facilitates residents' involvement. However, if the NRA's position becomes too inconsistent with the views of North Carolinians, other organizations likely will mobilize to oppose it. Similarly, for those concerned with protecting the environment, the North Carolina chapter of the Sierra Club would likely be of interest. Or the owner of a business that pumps out septic tanks might benefit from joining the N.C. Septic Tank Association.

In terms of diversity, North Carolina has a majority of institutions, many of which are business-related. This may appear disconcerting to those who believe that wealthy business interests dominate grassroots organizations. However, as we can see, it is unlikely that the banking industry has much in common with the manufacturers (aside from one sector offering loans and the other applying for them), so this numerical dominance may not necessarily limit other interests.

We also know that the states can be responsive to lobbying excesses. The states appear to restrict lobbying behavior when officials engage in questionable activities. Media scrutiny and public outrage at lobbying scandals may force lawmakers to restrict the benefits they can receive from lobbyists. North Carolina has been proactive in altering its lobbying laws; however, many people have argued that these changes are long overdue. We will have to see how these revisions alter the connections between lobbyists and legislators, though information likely will become a more important commodity for lobbyists if they are restricted in their gift provision (Newmark forthcoming). Because state legislatures are more active today than in the past, lawmakers rely on this information; the public, conversely, relies on interests to provide information on the amount of pollutants in the atmosphere or the status of a given piece of legislation. Interests also allow the public to participate in politics and to realize that others people may share certain issues or concerns. Pluralist scholars, of course, saw this phenomenon as a primary benefit of interest groups.

❖ Notes

I thank my former and current graduate assistants, Lara Crook and Joshua Hallingse, for their assistance in data collection.

1. The measure of lobbying stringency was updated for 2005 (not reported in the table); however, according to data provided by the *Book of the States*, a number of notable changes occurred across states between 2003 and 2005 that seemed inconsistent with either other data sources or current patterns of regulation across states and over time. Inquiries made regarding the data collection for the *Book of the States* reveal that data provided by the Council on

Governmental Ethics Laws may be inconsistent with previous years. Accordingly, the 2005 data are not reported. Still, some of the states appear to have changed their lobbying laws. As of 2005, Arizona may have had among the most restrictive laws.

❖ References

Bentley, Arthur F. 1950. *The Process of Government: A Study of Social Pressures*. Chicago: University of Chicago Press.

Book of the States. 1990–91, 1994–95, 1996–97, 2000–2001, 2002, 2003. Lexington, Ky.: Council of State Governments.

Brinig, Margaret, Randall G. Holcombe, and Linda Schwartzstein. 1993. "The Regulation of Lobbyists." *Public Choice* 77:377–84.

Campbell, Ralph, Jr.. 2001. "Special Review: N.C. Technological Development Authority, Inc."

Dahl, Robert A. 1961. *A Preface to Democratic Theory*. Chicago: University of Chicago Press.

Ensign, David. 1997. "Reforming Public Integrity Laws in an Era of Declining Trust." In *Book of the States*, 477–84. Lexington, Ky.: Council of State Governments.

Gray, Virginia, and David Lowery. 1996. *The Population Ecology of Interest Representation: Lobbying Communities in the American States*. Ann Arbor: University of Michigan Press.

———. 1998. "State Lobbying Regulations and Their Enforcement: Implications for the Diversity of Interest Communities." *State and Local Government Review* 30:78–91.

Grimm, Fred. 2003. "Election Reflection." *Miami Herald*, February 2. <http://www.miami.com/mld/miamiherald/news/columnists/fred_grimm/>. Accessed March 27, 2003.

Hunter, Kennith G., Laura Ann Wilson, and Gregory G. Brunk. 1991. "Social Complexity and Interest-Group Lobbying in the American States." *Journal of Politics* 53:488–503.

Lowery, David, and Virginia Gray. 1994. "The Nationalization of State Interest Group System Density and Diversity." *Social Science Quarterly* 75:368–77.

———. 1997. "How Some Rules Just Don't Matter: The Regulation of Lobbyists." *Public Choice* 91:139–47.

Mitchell, William C., and Michael C. Munger. 1991. "Economic Models of Interest Groups." *American Journal of Political Science* 35:512–46.

National Institute on Money in State Politics. N.d. "State at a Glance: North Carolina: Contributors." <http://www.followthemoney.org/database/StateGlance/contributor.phtml?si=200627&d=10619908>. Accessed November 17, 2006.

Newmark, Adam J. 2003. "Personal Relationships and Information Provision in State Lobbying: The Nature of Relationships and the Factors Affecting Them." Ph.D. diss., University of North Carolina at Chapel Hill.

———. 2005. "Measuring State Legislative Lobbying Regulations, 1990–2003." *State Politics and Policy Quarterly* 5:182–91.

———. Forthcoming. "Strategic Lobbying: The Nature of Legislator/Lobbyist Relations. *Journal of Political Science*.

"N.C. Pork Council, PAC Contributions to Federal Candidates, 2006 Cycle." N.d. <http://www.opensecrets.org/pacs/pacgot.asp?strID=C00235184&Cycle=2006>. Accessed November 17, 2006.

Olson, Mancur, Jr. 1982. *The Rise and Decline of Nations*. New Haven: Yale University Press.

Opheim, Cynthia. 1991. "Explaining the Differences in State Lobby Regulation." *Western Political Quarterly* 44:405–12.

Rosenson, Beth A. 2005. *The Shadowlands of Conduct: Ethics and State Politics*. Washington, D.C.: Georgetown University Press.

Rosenthal, Alan. 2001. *The Third House: Lobbyists and Lobbying in the States*. Washington, D.C.: CQ Press.

Rozell, Mark J., and Clyde Wilcox. 1999. *Interest Groups in American Campaigns: The New Face of Electioneering*. Washington, D.C.: CQ Press.

Salzer, James. 1997. "General Assembly Begins Session by Changing the Rules." *Augusta Chronicle*, January 14. <http://chronicle.augusta.com/stories/011497/met_openingday2.html>. Accessed October 16, 2007.

Schattschneider, E. E. 1960. *The Semisovereign People: A Realist's View of Democracy in America*. New York: Holt, Rinehart, and Winston.

Shenon, Philip. 2006. "Abramoff Set to Start Prison Term." *New York Times*, November 15. <http://www.nytimes.com/2006/11/15/washington/15abramoff.html>. Accessed September 19, 2007.

Thomas, Clive S., and Ronald J. Hrebenar. 1991. "Nationalization of Interest Groups and Lobbying in the States." In *Interest Group Politics*, 3rd ed., edited by Allan J. Cigler and Burdett A. Loomis, 63–80. Washington, D.C.: CQ Press.

———. 1999. "Interest Groups in the States." In *Politics in the American States: A Comparative Analysis*, edited by Virginia Gray, Russell L. Hanson, and Herbert Jacob, 113–43. Washington, D.C.: CQ Press.

Truman, David B. 1951. *The Governmental Process: Political Interests and Public Opinion*. New York: Knopf.

Witko, Christopher, and Adam J. Newmark. 2005. "Business Mobilization and Public Policy in the U.S. States." *Social Science Quarterly* 86:356–67.

Wolak, Jennifer, Adam J. Newmark, Todd McNoldy, David Lowery, and Virginia Gray. 2002. "Much of Politics Is Still Local: Multi-State Lobbying in State Interest Communities." *Legislative Studies Quarterly* 27:527–56.

❖ 5. Mass Media in North Carolina Politics

Watchdog Mutes Its Bark

FERREL GUILLORY

When I was growing up at the front edge of the baby boom in Baton Rouge, Louisi-ana, mornings at our house featured two immutable routines: the brewing of dark-roast coffee and the dividing of newspaper pages across the dining room table. While he sipped steaming black coffee, my father would make his way through the front news section and give special attention to the obituary page for the names of friends, associates, and clients. My brothers and I went first to the sports pages, in summer checking the baseball box scores and during football season studying the old Dunkle power ratings to see how the Louisiana State Tigers were faring. And when the legislature was in session, I would also study the roll-call votes printed daily in agate type. It seemed important to know how State Senator J. D. DeBlieux, Dad's friend who stood against the segregationists of the time, and other local law-makers had voted on the issues of the day.

When I moved from New Orleans to Raleigh in the early 1970s to join the *Raleigh News and Observer* as its chief Capitol correspondent and columnist, North Carolina was widely regarded as a strong newspaper state. Indeed, the progressive image that North Carolina projected across the South and to the nation rested in large part on the vigor of its journalism and the quality of its universities, especially the flagship in Chapel Hill. My daily routine included reading not only the *News and Observer* but also the morning newspapers from Charlotte, Greensboro, and Winston-Salem, all of which competed fiercely in covering government and poli-tics. My experience affirmed what Neal R. Peirce wrote in *The Border South States: People, Politics, and Power in the Five States of the Border South*: "North Carolina has a collection of daily newspapers which, to my mind, compared favorably with any other Southern or Border State's" (1975, 133).

From time to time, our newspaper reading in Baton Rouge would be accom-panied by dad's special breakfast: bacon fried in a skillet and eggs fried in the ba-con grease. In today's cholesterol-conscious world, hardly anyone I know regularly eats that sort of breakfast. And the world of high-anxiety mass media, competi-tion from new information technologies and Wall Street's insistence on high profit margins have led publishers and editors, in North Carolina as elsewhere, to reduce costs by providing a diminished diet of legislative reports, political campaign de-velopments, and similar hard news (Meyer 2004).

In the early 1960s, when I first entered the intersection of the press and politics, state capitals across the South featured hot leagues of journalistic competition. Overall, the writing and presentation were seldom graceful but rather were often formulaic, stodgy, and gray. Yet there prevailed a pervasive, innate dedication to watching governors and lawmakers govern, to following the debates—and the antics—among candidates for public office.

So, what is taking place at the beginning of the twenty-first century, at the intersection of the media and politics in North Carolina? What roles do the media play in the state's march of democracy? Has the watchdog's bark been muted? These are big questions, but insight can be gained from two stories, separated by a century.

❖ From Aggression to Retreat

In 1898, an election year, North Carolina's Democrats conducted an often brutal white-supremacy campaign to seize control of the state government from a coalition of Republicans and Populists known as Fusionists. In Wilmington, which then had a black-majority electorate, whites instigated a riot that led to the toppling of a Fusionist local government. White-owned newspapers, most notably the *Raleigh News and Observer*, did more than deliver detached accounts of events as they happened. Newspapers served as instruments of the Democratic political assault (N.C. Office of Archives and History 2006).

The press's role in the Democratic "redeemer" campaign is spelled out in the 1898 Wilmington Race Riot Commission's report to the 2006 session of the General Assembly. "One of the most visible components of the 1898 Democratic campaign was the use of newspapers," wrote the riot commission. The commission reported that Furnifold Simmons, chair of the Democratic Party campaign, used "men who could write, speak and ride." The riders wore red shirts and brandished weapons to intimidate blacks. The orators included Charles B. Aycock, who later became celebrated as a pioneering education governor. The writers provided articles for newspapers and campaign circulars. According to the state commission, "The *Raleigh News and Observer, Charlotte Observer*, and *Wilmington Messenger* and *Morning Star* led the barrage" (N.C. Office of Archives and History 2006).

As a leading ally, Simmons enlisted Josephus Daniels, who had purchased the *News and Observer* four years earlier with the intent of deploying it as a voice of the Democratic Party. "Using the *News and Observer* first as a barometer of public opinion and then as a weapon, Daniels and Simmons worked together to develop a strong argument against fusion and in favor of white supremacy in order to win the 1898 election. The paper slowly introduced the white supremacy issue to its readers, fed stories to other papers and worked the reading public into a frightened and tense frenzy. Especially powerful were the *News and Observer*'s editorial cartoons." As he and his newspaper changed over the years, Daniels acknowledged that his *News and Observer* had committed journalistic excesses during the 1898 campaign. Still, as the riot commission pointed out, the newspaper became a "powerful force" in shaping the politics of 1898 (N.C. Office of Archives and History 2006).

Now, fast-forward from the end of the nineteenth century to the beginning of the twenty-first century, and consider another moment in the ever-evolving media of North Carolina.

In the fall of 2005, the Knight Ridder Company, owner of the second-largest chain of newspapers the United States, offered itself to potential buyers. The chain included the *Charlotte Observer*, which had grown stronger after its purchase by the Knight family in 1954. His staff filled with anxiety and his newspaper facing rising costs, editor Rick Thames published a letter to readers on Sunday, January 8, 2006, under the headline, "Tight Times Allow Us to Rethink How Best to Bring You the News." Thames spoke of "an increasingly competitive business environment and new investor concerns for profit growth at all publicly traded companies." He said that the *Observer* would cut costs by reducing pages—about twenty pages per week, mostly in the Sunday and Monday issues. He promised continued "aggressive reporting . . . looking out for the public's best interest, while also helping people in our region live their lives well." He also wrote that editors had listened to interested readers and would respond: "You've told us, for example, that you'd like more news you can use, especially news about health, advice on managing money and career and tips on things to do for fun."

Josephus Daniels and Rick Thames provide symbolic bookends for an exploration of the mass media in the life of North Carolina. In one case, an owner-editor deploys his newspaper as a full-throated participant in politics, blatantly attempting to influence voters in a statewide struggle for power. In another case, a chain-hired editor devotes scarcer space to "news you can use" as he attempts to cope with economic pressures on his newspaper by drawing readers in with attention to their private pursuits.

❖ The New News Environment

Economic, demographic, and social shifts over the last third of the twentieth century dramatically transformed North Carolina. The traditional economic pillars of tobacco, textiles, and furniture collapsed, and the state became a jobs-producing machine in professional and managerial occupations, in services and in retail. Charlotte emerged as one of the nation's leading banking centers, and the Research Triangle matured, stimulating the development of a sprawling, suburban-style metropolitan region. Job growth attracted in-migrants, both blacks and whites, from elsewhere in the United States. Latino immigrants in search of jobs altered the ethnic mix. As in the American South generally, the elimination of old Jim Crow laws that segregated whites and blacks lifted a historical albatross and made North Carolina more attractive to new investments (State of the South 2000, 2002, 2004).

As commercial and journalistic enterprises, media companies inevitably have sought to adapt to the transformed economic and societal environment. Consider, for example, the *Raleigh News and Observer*. From its purchase by Daniels until the middle of the 1970s, the newspaper circulated across eastern North Carolina, so much so that about two-thirds of its midcentury readership lived outside of its home in Wake County. But as Raleigh, Cary, Wake Forest, Chapel Hill, and neighboring towns grew robustly—and as fuel prices rose—the *News and Observer* withdrew its daily delivery armada from the east and focused on building readership in the Research Triangle region.

In rural counties that have not grown robustly or have even declined in population, community newspapers and small-town radio stations have continued to serve a targeted local audience, much as they have for generations. At the same time, the mass media, based in metropolitan areas, have shifted not only their circulation patterns but also their journalistic focus. They have attempted to appeal to a more suburban and affluent audience composed of both native North Carolinians and recent arrivals. Furthermore, North Carolina's media have felt the same influences—that is, they have felt under siege, much like other U.S. media, as a consequence of declining newspaper readership, especially among young adults, a proliferation of television channels, and the rise of alternative communication vehicles on the Internet.

In the twenty-first century, media are plural. Anyone attempting to analyze the relationship of media and politics must take into account important variances among newspapers, magazines, television, and radio.

- Cable news/talk shows, journalism reviews, and national magazines regularly critique press and broadcast coverage of campaigning and governing. But they almost invariably focus on the big media of TV networks and major daily newspapers. Yet significant differences exist in how national and state campaigns are conducted and covered.

- A paradox pervades the media environment of the early twenty-first century. In North Carolina as well as across the United States, consolidation takes place simultaneously with diversification. Technology has given rise to a proliferation of delivery platforms for news, analysis, and opinion. But big media companies based outside of North Carolina, now own most of the state's major journalistic enterprises.

- Since the 1990s, North Carolina has served as a site for initiatives in the media's treatment of public affairs. For several years, the state emerged as a focal point in the development of "civic journalism." And two Raleigh-based broadcast companies sought to carve new paths in giving candidates and officeholders time to talk about their policy ideas.

- Today's newspaper editors and managers operate from a broadened definition of news. Declining circulation has sent editors and publishers scurrying to attract new readers with consumer-oriented features, narrative stories, and brilliant photos and infographics. Today's media tell readers more than in the past about business and finance, religion, child-rearing, food, and entertainment. The definition of news now includes the private as well as the public realm.

❖ Newspapers: From Play-by-Play Announcer to Referee

Gene Roberts stands in a long, distinguished line of North Carolinians who have made a mark on national journalism. After working for the *Goldsboro News Argus* and the *Raleigh News and Observer*, he went on to become editor of the *Philadelphia Inquirer* and managing editor of the *New York Times*. He later served as editor in chief of the State of the American Newspaper Project, which was funded by the Pew Charitable Trusts and turned out lengthy articles on trends and developments in newspapers that appeared in the *American Journalism Review* and in two books. During this period of his career, Roberts gave a lecture at the University of North Carolina (UNC) at Chapel Hill. He opened with a reminiscence:

> More than thirty-five years ago, I covered state government and the legislature, when it was in session, for the *Raleigh News and Observer* here in North Carolina. I would later cover the Kennedy assassination and its aftermath, big labor and the auto industry in Detroit, the civil rights movement across the South, and the war in Vietnam. Interesting assignments, all of them, but when it came to sheer competitiveness, there was no contest, really. The state capitol beat in Raleigh was the hottest league I ever played in. This had a lot to do, I think, with how seriously newspapers took state government coverage. Many of them considered it obligatory to have their own staff members on the scene, and they almost always assigned the cream of their crop of reporters. (1998)

Roberts mentioned several of his contemporaries, including Jay Jenkins and Joe Doster of the *Charlotte Observer*. Jenkins later became a legislative aide to UNC President William Friday, and Doster became publisher of the *Winston-Salem Journal*. Roberts also talked about Marjorie Hunter of the *Winston-Salem Journal*, who went on to the Washington bureau of the *New York Times*; Julian Scheer of the *Charlotte News*, who later joined the National Aeronautics and Space Administration as director of information during the heyday of spaceflight; and Roy Parker of the *News and Observer*, who subsequently served as editor of the *Fayetteville Times*.

Roberts's list of former legislative and campaign correspondents did not exhaust the record of North Carolina journalists who rose to a measure of fame and influence in American journalism. In addition to Charles Kuralt and David Brinkley, who became megastars of network news, Wallace Carroll, former publisher of the *Winston-Salem Journal*, served as James Reston's deputy Washington bureau chief for the *New York Times*; Tom Wicker was a longtime *New York Times* columnist and writer of books; Edwin M. Yoder Jr. edited the editorial pages of both the *Greensboro Daily News* and the *Washington Star*; and David Zucchino went from the *News and Observer* to foreign correspondents' posts with the *Philadelphia Inquirer* and *Los Angeles Times*. Even this list does not exhaust the record; rather, it illustrates the quality of journalism and journalists produced in North Carolina in the second half of the twentieth century.

In *The Border South States*, Peirce quoted Doster in making much the same point in his review of newspapers in the state's four largest cities. "Traditionally, all of these papers were well ahead of public opinion on civil rights, and focused their readers' attention on problems they might prefer to ignore," wrote Pierce. "Competition helps, too. Most southern and border states have one good paper; but with four solid dailies in the field, as Joe Doster, an old statehouse hand, put it, 'you could never sit on a story'" (1975, 134).

Over the course of the twentieth century, the relationship of newspaper editors to politics shifted. In the first half of the century, editors and publishers commonly took a direct role in political affairs. But after World War II, North Carolina newspapers generally adhered to the standard American practice of journalism. Akin to the separation of church and state, they put news on news pages and editorials on editorial pages. Editors and publishers sought to influence policy through their editorials, which they considered distinct from direct involvement in politics and government. Claude Sitton, formerly a *New York Times* correspondent in the South, succeeded Jonathan Daniels, Josephus's son, who served in President Franklin Roosevelt's White House, as editor of the *News and Observer* in the late 1960s. Sitton wrote lightning-bolt columns that won a Pulitzer Prize and insisted on aggressive reporting and strong editorials, but he saw himself as a newspaper editor, not a political activist.

Of course, newspapers still had a sense of responsibility for leadership in their communities. Under editor C. A. "Pete" McKnight and editorial editor David Gillespie, the *Charlotte Observer* played a crucial role in its city's temperate, let's-make-it-work reaction to a federal court's landmark ruling that instituted busing for school desegregation. Later, publisher Rolfe Neill was often listed among the business-civic titans who guided Charlotte into its New South, banking-center era.

In the half century after World War II, North Carolina newspapers, including two smaller community publications, won several Pulitzer Prizes, the most prestigious national awards for quality journalism. In 1951, the *Tabor City Tribune* won for taking on the Ku Klux Klan, and in 1990, the *Washington Daily News* took home the prize for documenting water contamination. Several Pulitzer winners dramatically influenced public policy in the state: the *Winston-Salem Journal and Sentinel* on the environment of the mountains; the *Charlotte Observer* on ameliorating brown lung suffered by textile workers; and the *Raleigh News and Observer* on restraining the growth of the hog industry. Table 5.1 displays a full list of North Carolina winners of Pulitzer Prizes.

Even as newspapers won Pulitzers and covered state politics and policy with the commitment that Roberts described, economic and demographic forces exerted their weight on the North Carolina press, much as they did to the press across the United States. As recently as the mid-1970s, most North Carolina cities had at least two daily newspapers. But the afternoon papers folded one by one: the *Charlotte News, Raleigh Times, Winston-Salem Sentinel, Greensboro Record, Fayetteville Times*, and other afternoon dailies no longer exist. Most afternoon papers had more of a local than a statewide influence, but by the end of the twentieth century, almost all North Carolina locales had only one editorial voice in the daily ink-on-paper media.

Another trend simultaneously took hold: North Carolina's newspapers shifted from local ownership to out-of-town chain ownership. By around 2005, all of the state's most powerful newspapers were owned elsewhere: the McClatchy Company, based in Sacramento, California, bought the *Charlotte Observer* from Knight Ridder newspapers (based in San Jose, California) and the *Raleigh News and Observer* from the Daniels family. The *Winston-Salem Journal* is owned by Media General, based in Richmond, Virginia, and the *Greensboro News and Record* is owned by Landmark Communications, headquartered in Norfolk, Virginia. In addition, the Gannett chain owns the *Asheville Citizen-Times*, the New York Times Company owns the *Wilmington Star-News*, and Paxton Media of Paducah, Kentucky, holds the *Durham Herald-Sun*. Out-of-state chain ownership has had varying effects on the coverage of state and local public affairs. Weak newspapers sometimes grow stronger when a chain brings in a higher level of professionalism; strong newspapers sometimes lose a measure of distinctiveness when a chain imposes standardization. At the outset of the twenty-first century and for the foreseeable future, North Carolina's major-city newspaper editors, whatever their devotion to local and state coverage, ultimately report to corporate authorities elsewhere.

Yet another big-picture development helped shape the course of North Carolina newspapers. What had been for decades a spread-out state of small towns and small cities, of farmers and mill workers, of a relatively small elite of affluent business and professional people along with a broad citizenry of people of modest means, of poor and near-poor, became something else through the 1980s and 1990s as economic change accelerated. A middle-class and upper-middle-class lifestyle took hold in the burgeoning suburbs of Charlotte, Raleigh, and other cities. Population growth and the rise in education and affluence, however, did not produce a corresponding growth in newspaper circulation. Circulation of North Carolina newspapers on Sunday, usually the day of highest sales, peaked in 1990 as a percentage of the state's population and has declined since (see table 5.2). In response, North Carolina's newspapers, like those throughout the rest of the United States, have reengineered their mix of news and features to appeal to nonreaders and to off-again, on-again readers.

In his Chapel Hill lecture, Roberts offered a stinging critique of what had resulted from this reengineering:

> It is nutty, and quite possibly suicidal, for a paper to cater to marginal
> and occasional readers at the expense of the regular and serious reader. In-
> creasingly, news coverage is being shaped by corporate executives at head-
> quarters far from the local scene. It is seldom done by corporate directive
> or fiat. It rarely involves killing or slanting stories. Usually it is by the ap-
> pointment of a pliable editor here, a corporate graphics conference there,
> that results in a more uniform look and cookie-cutter approach among a
> chain's newspapers, or it's by the corporate research director's interpretation
> of reader surveys that seek simply common-denominator solutions to com-
> plex coverage problems. Often the corporate view is hostile to government
> coverage. It has been fashionable for some years, during meetings of editors
> and publishers, to deplore "incremental" news coverage. Supposedly, it is
> boring, a turn-off to readers and—what's worse—it requires news hole. The
> problem with all of this is that governmental news develops incrementally.
> (1998)

TABLE 5.1. North Carolina Pulitzer Prize Winners, 1951–2005

Year	Paper	Individual (If Applicable)
1951	*Whitesville News and Reporter* and *Tabor City Tribune*	
1968	*Charlotte Observer*	Eugene Gray Payne
1971	*Winston-Salem Journal and Sentinel*	
1981	*Charlotte Observer*	
1983	*Raleigh News and Observer*	Claude Sitton
1988	*Charlotte Observer*	
1988	*Charlotte Observer*	Doug Marlette
1989	*Raleigh News and Observer*	Michael Skube
1990	*Washington Daily News*	
1996	*Raleigh News and Observer*	Melanie Sill, Pat Stith, and Joby Warrick

Source: <http://www.pulitzer.org>.

Under Roberts's direction, veteran journalists Mary Walton and Charles Layton conducted canvasses for the State of the American Newspaper Project in 1998, 2000, and 2002, recording answers from full-time reporters in all fifty state capitals. Their findings informed Roberts's assessment: "The original survey . . . demonstrated that during the decade of the 1990s, a period when state governments were acquiring enormous power and influence over the lives of average citizens, the commitment of resources by the newspaper industry declined precipitously" (Walton and Layton 2002). They found a climb in 2000, then a fallback in 2002. In North Carolina, the contingent of statehouse reporters remained relatively flat during this period.

In newsrooms in North Carolina and across the South, coverage of politics and government has not disappeared. Indeed, North Carolina has retained a corps of journalists devoted to serious coverage and analysis of state government and politics. Jack Betts, a Raleigh-based editorial writer for the *Charlotte Observer*, and his Charlotte-based editor, Ed Williams, have analyzed Tar Heel politics with care and concern for three decades. At the *Raleigh News and Observer*, Rob Christensen brings a perspective rooted in his study of history, and Pat Stith serves as the most dogged of investigative reporters, poking into the mistakes and misdeeds of the powerful. Still, the state government and politics beat no longer stands out so clearly as the preeminent beat. Coverage of population growth and sprawl, of religion and personal finance, of celebrities and of the day-to-day tragedies that

Category	Abstract
Public service	Campaign against Ku Klux Klan
Editorial cartooning	General
Public service	Strip mining
Public service	Brown lung
Commentary	
Public service	Misuse of funds by PTL-TV ministry
Editorial cartooning	
Criticism	Books and other literary topics
Public service	Contaminated water supply
Public service	Waste disposal in hog industry

befall regular folks shares space with news from the legislative building and the campaign trail. Of course, newspapers have long offered sports reports, advice columns, and comics. And yet, in a move symbolic of larger trends, the "Under the Dome" column of state government anecdotes, which ran daily on the front page in the *News and Observer* until the mid-1990s, was shifted to a designated page inside the second section. In the spring of 2006, the newspaper company added an "Under the Dome" blog to its newsobserver.com Web site.

❖ The Rise of "Civic Journalism"

Newspaper coverage of campaigns still bears the imprint of what is known as civic journalism. That is, the state's major newspapers work from the guiding concept that their coverage should be more voter-centered than candidate-centered, that they should be less tied to the candidates' agendas and to the "horse race" and more devoted to helping citizens make up their minds on how to vote (Project for Excellence in Journalism 2006).

In 1996, seven newspapers, as well as six commercial TV stations and WUNC public radio, formed the Your Voice, Your Vote consortium, which conducted joint polls on voters' opinions and joint interviews with candidates. The *New York Times* called the nation's attention to this civic-journalism approach to campaign coverage, and the *Times* story touched off a stormy debate in journalism circles. In 2000,

TABLE 5.2. Sunday News Circulation as Percentage of Population, 1970–2005

Year	North Carolina	South	United States
1970	18.12	21.84	24.21
1980	19.25	21.89	24.14
1990	21.92	23.70	25.18
2000	18.51	18.88	20.86
2002	17.07	17.56	20.09
2005	16.35	16.96	19.30

Source: "Ready Reckoner of Advertising Rates and Circulation," in *Editor and Publisher International Yearbook*, part 1, *The Dailies* (New York: Nielson Business Media).

a consortium was re-formed with fewer participants. By 2004, the civic journalism project had dissolved. It had been a costly enterprise, requiring participating news organizations to engage in significant coordination and thus consuming extensive amounts of staff time at a time when these organizations were still coping with the harsh financial effects of a recent recession.

Newspapers, of course, provided coverage beyond the Your Voice, Your Vote packages. Major newspapers worked diligently on "ad watches" that examined candidates' TV commercials—though not typically radio commercials—for tone and factual accuracy. In general, newspaper coverage had become driven far less by day-to-day campaign dynamics and more by the newspapers' decisions and agendas. Newspapers commented robustly about the decisions of both 2000 gubernatorial candidates—Democrat Mike Easley and Republican Richard Vinroot—to minimize daily campaigning and to devote much more time to raising money to pay for TV commercials.

A kind of circular dynamic seemed to have taken hold. Journalists acknowledge that they are much less likely than in the past to show up for candidates' press conferences and to report on stump speeches. Candidates and their strategists, in turn, ask themselves why they should spend time giving civic club luncheon speeches that reach only a few, mostly committed, voters when the media will not cover such speeches and when TV ads reach many more voters.

At least two results grow out of this media-political landscape. The first is that statewide races now have few markers—that is, moments that draw intense voter attention and thus help define candidacies. In the 1996 and 2000 campaigns, the markers included the Your Voice, Your Vote candidate interviews and televised debates. With the dissolution of the consortium, the lengthy candidate interviews have disappeared. Unlike presidential elections, in which debates have become inherent, debates in statewide campaigns remain not mandatory but rather a matter of negotiation among candidates. Thus, the second result is that in the relative dearth of day-to-day campaigning and coverage, TV commercials have become even more dominant in North Carolina's gubernatorial and senatorial elections.

Following the 2004 election, in which Easley won a second gubernatorial term, the Program on Public Life at the University of North Carolina at Chapel Hill convened a debriefing discussion among managers of statewide campaigns. Jay Reiff, manager of the Easley campaign, commented on how political coverage by newspapers plays out in the conduct of campaigns. Even as newspapers have tried to become more useful to voters, Reiff said that most newspaper coverage does "not move a whole lot of numbers"—a political professional's way of saying that news stories have little effect on public opinion. The principal role now filled by the press, Reiff said, is that of "referee"—newspapers blow the whistle on candidates when they issue statements, use data or propose policies, or otherwise report information that one campaign can use against the opposition. According to Reiff, "What really defined our race is what was on TV."

❖ Television: Commercials ahead of Journalism

Survey research regularly finds that U.S. citizens say they get most of their news about public affairs from television and local TV rather than from network or cable news programs (see table 5.3). If that is so, North Carolina residents learn much more about candidates for governor, U.S. senator, and other major offices from the candidates' commercials than from TV news reporting.

The Norman Lear Center of the Annenberg School at the University of Southern California, along with the NewsLab at the University of Wisconsin, has tracked local TV coverage of campaign news across the nation. In the 2000 campaign, WRAL, the Raleigh-based flagship station of Capitol Broadcasting, was one of only five stations among seventy-four surveyed nationwide that averaged more than three minutes of political coverage per thirty-minute newscast. Two North Carolina stations, WFMY in Greensboro and WSOC in Charlotte, devoted less than an average of ten seconds per newscast.

Laura Roselle, an associate professor of political science at Elon University, and several colleagues compiled a more detailed comparison of WRAL and WFMY in the November 2000 general election. The Roselle study found that WRAL broadcast a total of one hour, fifty-seven minutes, and fourteen seconds of election stories on the weekdays of October. During the same period, WFMY broadcast one hour, nineteen minutes, and fifteen seconds (Roselle 2003).

The numbers do not, however, tell the whole story. In fact, WRAL devoted much more time to North Carolina politics than did WFMY. The Greensboro station's time devoted to politics was inflated by the fact that Wake Forest University, which is in Winston-Salem and within WFMY's market area, hosted one of the three debates between Republican George Bush and Democrat Al Gore, and WFMY broadcast reports of the goings-on in the preparation and conduct of that debate.

In Raleigh, locally owned Capitol Broadcasting took the lead nationally in adopting the so-called five/thirty standard for campaign coverage—that is, devoting five minutes a night to candidate-centered discourse for thirty days prior to the election. Jim Goodmon, chief executive of Capitol, agreed to provide the time on his company's stations after meeting with representatives of the Alliance for Better Campaigns, a Washington-based organization funded by the Pew Charitable Trusts, and the University of North Carolina at Chapel Hill Program on Public Life, which served as the alliance's state partner in North Carolina.

In 2000, Capitol Broadcasting produced one minute, forty-five second "messages" from each of the three Republican and two Democratic candidates for governor. These messages appeared not only on WRAL but also on the company's smaller stations in Raleigh, Wilmington, and Charlotte. On WRAL, the messages appeared at the end of the noon, 6 P.M., and 11 P.M. news programs. Under the ground rules established by the broadcasting company, attacks on opponents were prohibited. Candidates were asked to address issues identified by the broadcaster as well as issues of their choice. In the general election, Capitol Broadcasting revised and extended the project, adding messages from candidates for lieutenant governor and attorney general. The broadcaster gave similar free time at the end of newscasts to candidates in 2002, 2004, and 2006.

In the 2000 campaign, WBTV, the Charlotte station owned by Jefferson-Pilot, produced a daily news report on campaign developments for the 6:30 P.M. newscast. The reporter (experienced political reporter Mike Cozza) and producer assigned to the project focused not only on the governor's race but also on congressional primaries in Charlotte-area districts. WBTV also had an investigative team look at campaign contributions.

From time to time, TV stations will spotlight a particular issue—for example, the approval of a state lottery or the investigation of a state House speaker—but state government and political news generally does not fit into the style and tone of local TV stations' daily news programs. WBTV's and WRAL's performances in delivering candidates' messages stand out as exceptions to the rule that coverage of the legislature and campaigns ranges from little to none.

For many years, the most extensive broadcast coverage of the N.C. General Assembly has come from the UNC Center for Public Television, which has a statewide network. During legislative sessions, UNC-TV has produced a weekly hour-long report on Friday evenings as well as shorter reports and interviews for its nightly, magazine-style half hour, *North Carolina Now*. While its coverage remains far more extensive than that provided by any other TV outlet, UNC-TV has actually pulled back from the daily half-hour legislative report that it previously provided.

State Government Radio, a relatively recent initiative of the Raleigh-based Curtis Media Group, introduced an additional element into the coverage of North Carolina public affairs. Designed to appeal to residents with an especially keen interest in or need to know about legislative, political, educational, and economic developments, State Government Radio has delivered daily reports both on a Curtis-owned radio station in the Triangle and on a Web site.

In campaigns, radio serves another function, targeting messages at selected audiences. Radio time is far less expensive than TV time, and radio audiences are fragmented because most stations cater to a certain demographic group rather than to a general audience. Campaigns, therefore, buy commercial radio time as a way of directing messages—whether a get-out-the-vote motivation or an attack on an opponent—to a particular subset of voters.

❖ Technology Spurs a Transition Time

Just as television transformed the practice of democratic politics across America, widespread broadband access to the Internet began to have dramatic effects on both politics and journalism in the earliest years of the twenty-first century. At its core, politics involves communication between those who would govern and their constituents. The Internet enables candidates to raise money without having to send out letters on paper and permits voters to watch TV spots without having to sit in front of the television set.

The Internet has also given rise to what many call a citizens media, in which "bloggers"—writers of Web logs—not employed or attached to a news-gathering company report and comment on public events. By the 2004 presidential election, blogging had emerged as a force in national politics, though its influence initially appeared more limited and uncertain in state politics and government. Still, alternatives to newspaper and TV punditry burgeoned in the mid-2000s. For example, Gary Pearce, a longtime adviser to North Carolina's former Democratic governor, James B. Hunt Jr., and Carter Wrenn, a veteran political organizer for Republican senator Jesse Helms, combined to produce an early blog, talkingaboutpolitics.com, that touched on state and national politics as well as Raleigh city issues.

Newspapers and television stations established their own news-oriented Web sites. Such sites initially provided news organizations with an additional distribu-

TABLE 5.3. Use of Media as Political Source by Age

Age	National Network News	Local TV News	Cable News Networks	Comedy Shows
Under 30	64	64	78	50
30–49	72	84	77	27
50–64	73	77	75	14
65+	74	77	68	11

Source: Pew Center for the People and the Press, <http://people-press.org/reports/
display.php37.ReportID=200>.

tion platform for news gathered for their traditional on-paper and on-air reports. Slowly but surely, however, newspaper and TV companies expanded their online offerings. Newspapers offered staff members opportunities to write online blogs as a supplement to their more traditional work. "Under the Dome" emerged as an online blog, and Jack Betts developed a blog on charlotte.com in addition to his regular commentary from Raleigh for the *Charlotte Observer*.

Both economic shifts and technological advances brought the mainstream media to a time of wrenching transition that will almost assuredly ripple through North Carolina politics and government. After all, how well a free press functions bears on the health of American democracy, in a state as well as nationally. When the McClatchy Company secured ownership of both the *Charlotte Observer* and the *Raleigh News and Observer*, the once-rival newspapers began sharing some articles written by their State Capitol staffs. In early 2007, the *News and Observer*'s editor, Melanie Sill, and managing editor, John Drescher, announced a major reorganization to create a "new newsroom," designed to produce more content with a smaller staff, to put breaking news on the newsobserver.com Web site, and to encourage more reader participation. While the Sill-Drescher memo held out the prospect of more "enterprise" reporting on North Carolina, the editors also described a redeployment of personnel to focus more of the *News and Observer*'s attention on local news in fast-growing Wake County.

❖ Helms and His Heirs

No assessment of the history of the mass media in North Carolina politics would be complete without taking former U.S. Senator Jesse Helms into account. He initially gained political power in North Carolina through his use of mass media—principally radio and television. As a Raleigh radio reporter, Helms played a key role in rousing supporters of Willis Smith to call for a runoff in the legendary 1950

Local Daily Newspaper	News Magazines	Internet	News Organization Web Sites	Late-Night Shows
56	35	44	31	44
60	30	40	34	27
65	30	27	27	15
65	30	11	15	23

Senate race against Frank Porter Graham. After Smith won, Helms joined the new senator's staff.

For eleven years beginning in the fall of 1960, Helms delivered "Viewpoint" editorials five days a week on WRAL-TV. A. J. Fletcher, a lawyer who owned WRAL, enlisted Helms to serve as a conservative voice in the state capital. His assaults on the civil rights movement, on antiwar protesters, on academics, and on what he considered "socialistic" government programs brought him both plaudits and derision during a decade of social, racial, and cultural change. His often fiery editorials, which had tremendous influence on the North Carolina's political dialogue, also brought him the wider recognition and the base of support that led to his successful 1972 candidacy for the U.S. Senate. He won reelection to four more terms.

When Helms retired from the Senate in 2003, his political apparatus had withered. Helms supported Elizabeth Dole and Richard Burr, both Republicans, in the two subsequent U.S. Senate elections, but they were not senators in the Helms mold. Indeed, Helms left no clear heir as a political candidate or as a TV editorialist. Since 2005, Capitol Broadcasting has aired a liberal editorialist, Chris Fitzsimon of N.C. Policy Watch, but his editorials have been broadcast on WRAL radio, not WRAL-TV.

The void Helms left at the press-politics intersection has been filled by a conservative force of another variety: an interlocking set of organizations largely funded by Art Pope, a Raleigh-based retail executive and former Republican state legislator. Pope finances not only organizations that advocate a rightward swing to public policy but also candidates in political campaigns, even engaging in Republican intraparty rivalry.

The hub of the Pope-funded organizations is the John Locke Foundation, begun in 1989. John Hood, the foundation's president and chair, appears regularly on television and radio and writes commentaries published in newspapers around the state. The foundation produces TV and radio programs and publishes the *Carolina*

Journal in both online and print forms. This publication tries to break news stories, as do newspaper journalists, and offers commentaries with a political and ideological purpose.

Pope and Helms long regarded the Daniels-owned *Raleigh News and Observer* as an adversary in a competition for the hearts and minds of North Carolina voters. Neither Pope nor Hood has emerged as the sort of mass-media figure that Helms became before running for the Senate. Still, like Helms, Pope, Hood, and their organizations have used mass media tools to advance a public agenda. Josephus Daniels would understand.

❖ References

Media Policy Program of the Campaign Legal Center. 2005. *Political Standard*, vol. 8.

Meyer, Philip. 2004. *The Vanishing Newspaper: Saving Journalism in the Information Age*. Columbia: University of Missouri Press.

N.C. Office of Archives and History. 2006. "1898 Wilmington Race Riot Commission." <http://www.ah.dcr.state.nc.us/1898-wrrc/>. Accessed October 20, 2007.

Peirce, Neil R. 1975. *The Border South States: People, Politics, and Power in the Five States of the Border South*. New York: Norton.

Project for Excellence in Journalism. 2006. "The State of the News Media 2006: An Annual Report on American Journalism." <http://www.stateofthemedia.org/2006/index.asp>. Accessed October 20, 2007.

Roberts, Gene. 1998. Reed Sarratt Lecture, University of North Carolina at Chapel Hill School of Journalism and Mass Communication, April 14. In possession of the author.

Roselle, Laura. 2003. "Local Coverage of the 2000 Election in North Carolina: Does Civic Journalism Make a Difference?" *American Behavioral Scientist* 46:600–616.

State of the South. 2000, 2002, 2004. Chapel Hill, N.C.: MDC.

Thames, Rick. 2006. "Tight Times Allow Us to Rethink How Best to Bring You the News." *Charlotte Observer*, January 8, 2A.

Walton, Mary, and Charles Layton. 2002. "Missing the Story at the Statehouse." In *Breach of Faith: A Crisis of Coverage in the Age of Corporate Newspapering*, edited by Gene Roberts and Thomas Kunkel. Fayetteville: University of Arkansas Press.

❖ **Part III. Governmental Institutions**

❖ 6. North Carolina Governors

From Campaigning to Governing

JACK D. FLEER

Fearing single-person rule, most American states gave very little power to their chief executives in the early years of the republic. Governors in North Carolina and most other states have evolved from this rather inauspicious past as administrative managers into state policy leaders. At the same time, governors have become powerful figures on the national political stage and have made attractive presidential candidates (Abramson, Aldrich, and Rohde 2006; Burden 2002).

The transition in the chief executive's position in North Carolina is a product of a more intense two-party system, the rise of public leadership, and new formal and political powers, including constitutionally enhanced budget powers, the opportunity for electoral succession, and the veto power. However, governors operate in a more complex and interdependent political environment derived from greater competition for state political leadership and extensive limitations on the exercise of major powers. In these respects, North Carolina's governor reflects similar positions in other states.

This essay considers the evolution and current state of the North Carolina governorship, focusing first on the formal and informal qualifications for becoming governor. This section describes how governors get into office, highlighting the increasingly competitive and expensive general elections. Next, the essay addresses the powers and activities of governors in office. The essay then examines the increasing importance of informal gubernatorial powers before concluding with a summary of North Carolina's gubernatorial power in comparative perspective.

❖ Becoming Governor: Formal and Informal Qualifications

Becoming a state governor involves meeting some rather modest official requirements and surviving a daunting series of political trials. As a result, many people are potential governors in a state, but very few survive the legal and electoral obstacles.

FORMAL AND INFORMAL REQUIREMENTS

The North Carolina Constitution requires that a governor be at least thirty years of age, a U.S. citizen for five years, and a state resident for two years. The governor is popularly elected, serves a four-year term, and can seek one successive additional term (North Carolina Constitution, Article 3, Section 3; *Book of the States* 2005). As table 6.1 indicates, these requirements resemble those of other states for their chief executives.

A review of the people who served as North Carolina's governor during the twentieth century reveals that in addition to the formal, legal requirements for being governor, a number of informal qualifications must also be met. The typical governor was born and reared in the state in a rural or small-town environment and is male, married, Caucasian, about fifty years of age at inauguration, Protestant, college educated (and in recent decades a recipient of a graduate degree), and an attorney; he also has had prior political experience (Crabtree 1958; *North Carolina Manual* 1911–2001).

Most of these characteristics describe governors across the nation. In other states, a slightly more diverse population of governors has emerged. In North Carolina, only white males have served as governor. In other states, the number of women, African Americans, and non-Protestants who have held governorships remains small. Only twenty-six women and two African Americans have been elected to the governorships of the various states since 1974 (Center for American Women and Politics 2006; Joint Center for Political and Economic Studies 2007). In the states of the old Confederacy, Virginians elected Douglas Wilder, an African American, in 1989, and Louisiana voters selected Kathleen Blanco in 2003. Female and nonwhite governors may become more common as more such persons are elected to lower-level political offices where they can gain the experience and exposure needed to win the governorship.

Despite Americans' claims that they do not like politicians, previous political experience remains a key variable influencing who becomes governor. Thad Beyle (2004) shows that from 1981 to 2002, 27 percent of the nation's governors served in a statewide elective position prior to being governor. Similarly, 18 percent served in the state legislature, and 16 percent served in the U.S. Senate or House. Only 14 percent of governors during this period came to the office with no political experience.

POLITICAL TRAILS AND TRIALS

In almost all states, including North Carolina, successful gubernatorial candidates must survive both primary nomination and general elections. These contests serve different functions, and each has its own challenges of campaign finance and candidate strategy. Since 1868, North Carolina governors have been elected every four years at the same time as U.S. presidential elections, a practice currently shared with ten states. Two states (New Hampshire and Vermont) elect their governors every two years. The office of governor tops the list of numerous state and national officials being chosen and influences other election outcomes. In North Carolina, nine other executive officials are also elected separately. Only six states elect that number of statewide executives or more (*Book of the States* 2005, 2006). This fragmented executive weakens North Carolina's governor relative to those in other states.

PARTY PRIMARIES

In North Carolina, the Primary Elections Act of 1915 established direct party primaries to nominate candidates for governor and other offices. North Carolina has closed primaries, meaning that participants must register for a particular party. However, Republicans relaxed this restriction in 1988 and Democrats did so in 1994, permitting independent or unaffiliated voters to participate. Most states use closed direct primaries to protect the integrity of nominations. Since 1989, candidates in North Carolina may be nominated in a primary with 40 percent of the votes cast, a unique procedure (Bibby 2003; North Carolina General Statutes n.d., chapter 163-111).

The significance of party primaries goes beyond nominations. The nominee for governor shapes a political party's policy agenda and becomes its principal spokesperson. Furthermore, a difficult primary election battle can undermine a candidate's general election prospects and a governor's strength in governing. When primaries are like public "family fights," they can damage a nominee. However, they are also useful in winnowing candidates and drawing attention to a nominee and a party.

In the twentieth century, most of North Carolina's nomination primaries were held in the Democratic Party until about 1960—receiving the Democratic nomination was tantamount to election. Beginning in 1972, nomination primaries became more frequent in the Republican Party. As two-party competition increased in the last third of the century, both Democrats and Republicans experienced changes in their primary contests and in general elections. Democratic primary contests normally derive from competing personal ambitions, while Republican contests more often occur between ideological competitors. Similar changes have affected primary nominations in other states where interparty competition grew.

Several major patterns of primary nominations in North Carolina and other states deserve consideration. Primary competition is greater in a state's majority party, in open-seat contests, when campaign financing is adequate, and when candidate quality is high. In North Carolina, these patterns mean that competition was greatest in the Democratic Party until recent decades and before succession was possible. In addition, candidates with larger treasuries are nominated regard-

TABLE 6.1. Qualifications for Governor, 2006

State	Minimum Age Requirement, Years	State Citizen Requirement, Years	U.S. Citizen Requirement, Years	State Resident Requirement, Years
Alabama	Yes, 30	Yes, 7	Yes, 10	No
Alaska	Yes, 30	Yes, 7	Yes, 7	Yes, 7
Arizona	Yes, 25	Yes, 5	Yes, 10	No
Arkansas	Yes, 30	Yes, 0	Yes, 0	Yes, 7
California	Yes, 18	No	Yes, 5	Yes, 5
Colorado	Yes, 30	Yes, 0	Yes, 0	Yes, 2
Connecticut	Yes, 30	No	Yes, 0	Yes, 0
Delaware	Yes, 30	No	Yes, 12	Yes, 6
Florida	Yes, 30	No	Yes, 0	Yes, 7
Georgia	Yes, 30	No	Yes, 15	Yes, 6
Hawaii	Yes, 30	No	No	Yes, 5
Idaho	Yes, 30	No	Yes, 0	Yes, 2
Illinois	Yes, 25	Yes, 3	Yes, 0	Yes, 3
Indiana	Yes, 30	No	Yes, 5	Yes, 5
Iowa	Yes, 30	No	Yes, 2	Yes, 2
Kansas	No	No	No	No
Kentucky	Yes, 30	Yes, 6	No	Yes, 6
Louisiana	Yes, 25	Yes, 5	Yes, 5	Yes, 5
Maine	Yes, 30	No	Yes, 15	Yes, 5
Maryland	Yes, 30	No	Yes, 0	Yes, 5
Massachusetts	No	No	No	Yes, 7
Michigan	Yes, 30	No	Yes, 0	Yes, 0
Minnesota	Yes, 15	No	Yes, 0	Yes, 1
Mississippi	Yes, 30	No	Yes, 20	Yes, 5
Missouri	Yes, 30	No	Yes, 15	Yes, 10
Montana	Yes, 25	Yes, 0	Yes, 0	Yes, 0
Nebraska	Yes, 30	Yes, 5	Yes, 5	Yes, 5
Nevada	Yes, 25	Yes, 2	Yes, 2	Yes, 2
New Hampshire	Yes, 30	No	No	Yes, 7
New Jersey	Yes, 30	No	Yes, 20	Yes, 7
New Mexico	Yes, 30	No	Yes, 0	Yes, 5
New York	Yes, 25	Yes, 0	Yes, 0	Yes, 1
North Carolina	Yes, 30	No	Yes, 5	Yes, 2
North Dakota	Yes, 30	No	Yes, 0	Yes, 5
Ohio	Yes, 18	No	Yes, 0	Yes, 0
Oklahoma	Yes, 31	No	No	No
Oregon	Yes, 30	No	Yes, 0	Yes, 3
Pennsylvania	Yes, 30	No	Yes, 0	Yes, 7
Rhode Island	Yes, 18	Yes, 30 days	Yes, 0	Yes, 30 days
South Carolina	Yes, 30	Yes, 5	Yes, 5	Yes, 5
South Dakota	Yes, 21	No	Yes, 0	Yes, 2

TABLE 6.1. (*continued*)

State	Minimum Age Requirement, Years	State Citizen Requirement, Years	U.S. Citizen Requirement, Years	State Resident Requirement, Years
Tennessee	Yes, 30	Yes, 7	Yes, 0	No
Texas	Yes, 30	No	Yes, 0	Yes, 5
Utah	Yes, 30	Yes, 5	Yes, 0	Yes, 5
Vermont	Yes, 18	Yes, 1	No	Yes, 4
Virginia	Yes, 30	No	Yes, 0	Yes, 5
Washington	Yes, 18	No	Yes, 0	Yes, 0
West Virginia	Yes, 30	Yes, 5	Yes, 0	Yes, 1
Wisconsin	Yes, 18	No	Yes, 0	Yes, 0
Wyoming	Yes, 30	Yes, 0	Yes, 0	Yes, 5

Source: *Book of the States* (2006, 153).

less of party, and higher-quality candidates prevail in most elections (Beyle 2004; Bibby 2003; Fleer 2007).

GENERAL ELECTIONS

After surviving the political minefield of primary nomination, gubernatorial candidates must of course win the general election as well. Since the 1950s, competition in North Carolina gubernatorial general elections has increased and become quite fierce. From 1950 to 1968, the Democrats were the state's majority party, and their candidates were advantaged even though the Republican Party was a substantial and strengthening minority. In 1972, James Holshouser became the first Republican governor elected in the century, and two-party competition received a boost. By the turn of the twenty-first century, neither Democrats nor Republicans had a clear majority in governor's races, and candidates from both parties had realistic prospects for victory depending on circumstances. Election results were erratic and depended on various factors.

Because neither political party has recently had a major advantage, factors such as candidate quality and status, national campaign influences, key issues debated, and turnout of various constituencies have determined election outcomes. Democrats remained advantaged but endured hard-fought battles unless an incumbent was running. The most convincing victories occurred either before two-party contestation had taken hold (1952–64) or when incumbents sought reelection (1980, 1988, 1996, and 2004). Narrower outcomes involved open-seat contests and closely fought national presidential elections where Republicans had an edge in the state.

In this newly competitive environment, general election outcomes are influenced by several factors, including party strength, incumbency, campaign finances, candidate quality, primary divisiveness, and national political trends. Party strength is measured by voter registration and voter party identification. In both cases, the large Democratic advantage from early in the period was eroded by increased Republican and unaffiliated voter registrations and by increased voter identifications as Republicans and independents. In the 1950s, three of four registrants were Democrats, but by 2004, those numbers had fallen below half of the electorate. Voter identification shows similar changes. Democrats comprised three-fifths of those who identified themselves as members of a party in 1968, but that share subsequently dropped to 38 percent in 2005. At the same time, Republicans increased from one-fifth to 30 percent of the electorate, and independents grew from one-fifth to 28 percent of identifiers by fall 2005. The political complexion of the state's electorate became more diverse. At the dawn of the new century, the electorate is closely divided among the two parties and unaffiliated voters. Political party remains important in deciding elections but has lost its dominance in tipping the scales (Comparative State Elections Project 1968; Carolina Poll 1986–2005; N.C. State Board of Elections 1965–2006). That pattern reflects developments in other states.

Each party had a major racial constituency: blacks supported Democrats, who received an average of 90 percent of the African American votes in 1988–2000, and an average of 57 percent of whites supported Republicans. Sex differences also exist: women are more supportive of Democrats (with an average rating of 55 percent during 1988–2000) and men supporting Republicans (an average of 54 percent during the period). Similar patterns prevail across the states (Bibby 2003; NBC and CBS 1988; Voter News Service 1996, 2000; Voter Research and Surveys 1992).

The incumbency advantage is well documented in American electoral politics. It is nowhere more pronounced than in the races for North Carolina governor—no incumbent governor has lost a reelection bid. Four Democratic governors (Luther Hodges, 1956; Jim Hunt, 1980, 1996; Mike Easley, 2004) and one Republican (Jim Martin, 1984) have won with margins ranging from 12 (Martin) to 34 (Hodges) points. North Carolina's incumbent reelection rate (100 percent) far exceeds the national rate (70 percent) (Beyle 2004; Bibby 2003).

A third factor affecting gubernatorial elections is campaign financing. As figure 6.1 reveals, some fluctuation has occurred, but campaign spending has generally increased since 1980. In fact, the 2000 campaign was more than twice as expensive in constant dollars as the 1980 contest.

Several patterns of campaign finance prevail. Incumbent governors generally raise and spend more money than challengers, who are not as well known. This pattern extends across the fifty states. In North Carolina, only Governor Jim Martin won reelection without greater resources than his opponent. In elections for open seats, the significance of money is not clear. Between 1968 and 2000, six gubernatorial elections had no incumbent candidate. In half, the top spender won; in half, he lost, including two cases (1972 and 1984) where a Republican won against well-financed Democrats in large part because of strong national party victories in the state. However, in each case, both major party candidates had adequate financing. Financial advantage does not guarantee electoral success in elections in North Carolina or nationwide (Beyle 2004; Jewell and Morehouse 2001).

While all candidates must raise enough money to compete, money alone cannot turn a lackluster candidate into a winning one. Candidate quality influences electoral success. Since the mid–twentieth century, the quality of North Carolina's candidates (measured by previous political experience) has risen impressively, especially in the Republican Party, where politically experienced candidates more often compete. By 2000, both major parties fielded high-quality gubernatorial nominees, although the Democrats more often had the edge. In every election where the two candidates had different quality rankings, the higher-ranked candidate won. This pattern also holds true for other states (Krasno 1994; Squire 1992).

The effects of a primary can reverberate through the general election campaign. Between 1952 and 2004, North Carolina's Democratic Party had more divisive primaries (six) than the Republican Party (four), reflecting in part the Democrats' electoral advantage in much of the period. Intraparty competition is more common in the putative majority party because of its favorable general election position. Also, political fragmentation has been more common among Democrats than Republicans. Republicans had fewer major candidates competing and more incentive to rally around nominees to maximize their general election majority. In two instances (1972 and 1984), primary divisiveness in the Democratic Party contributed to fall victories for Republicans when combined with other relevant factors (Jewell and Morehouse 2001; Kenny and Rice 1987).

National politics also strongly influences North Carolina elections because presidential and gubernatorial elections coincide. Beginning in 1972, the Republican Party has gained a substantial advantage in North Carolina presidential elections. No Democratic presidential nominee has won in the state since 1976. The most common pattern is for a Democratic governor to be elected alongside a Republican presidential nominee. However, in three instances, Republicans won both offices. Since the beginning of the twentieth century, Democratic gubernatorial candidates have outpolled their presidential ballot mates in every election except 1936, with an average margin of 9 points. Conversely, Republican presidential candidates regularly do better than Republican gubernatorial candidates. In twenty-

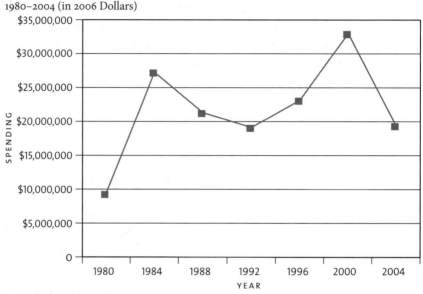

FIGURE 6.1. North Carolina Gubernatorial Campaign Spending, 1980–2004 (in 2006 Dollars)

Source: Beyle and Jensen (2006).

four of twenty-eight elections between 1900 and 2004, gubernatorial candidates have had larger margins, with an average advantage of 7 points. Nationally, the winning presidential candidate's party lost governorships in almost half of state elections between 1952 and 2000 (Bibby 2003). In North Carolina, Republican Party candidates for these two top positions have frequently campaigned together, working in a coordinated fashion to win office. Democrats have more often kept distance between their state and national slates, although these relationships have varied over time.

❖ Being Governor: Major Gubernatorial Powers

Once elected, governors are constrained in their activity by the formal institutional powers of the office. At the same time, governors have a considerable amount of informal power that derives from the individual in office rather than from the rules and constraints of the institution itself.

INSTITUTIONAL POWERS

The governor's formal institutional powers include: (1) tenure potential; (2) state budget control; (3) executive appointment power; (4) veto authority; (5) the number of separately elected executives; and (6) political party control of executive and legislative bodies. For each power, state governors are scored from 1 to 5 to denote their relative strength, with a higher score indicating greater strength. The cumulative score gives an overview of gubernatorial powers across the states and places each governor in context. An examination of scores of several powers in 1965 and 2007 reveals changes and continuities in North Carolina and across the states (Beyle 2007; Schlesinger 1965).

Tenure potential combines length of term and possibility of successive terms. Governors who have four-year terms and may seek reelection are stronger than those with shorter terms and no option for succession. The current norm is four-year terms with two successive terms, as in North Carolina. Between 1965 and 2007, North Carolina governors' scores increased from 3 to 4; the national score in 2007 was 4. The change in North Carolina derives from the passage of a 1977 constitutional amendment permitting two successive terms for governors and lieutenant governors, duplicating actions in many states.

Control of the state budget includes responsibility for its preparation, subject to legislative approval, and for its implementation with or without legislative approval. The Schlesinger/Beyle index includes a governor's authority to recommend a budget and the legislature's authority to alter those recommendations. The North Carolina governor's budget powers were scored in 1965 as 4 and in 2007 as 3. The lower score results from the General Assembly's efforts to assert itself in budget making and oversight and to involve legislative committees in budgetary shifts after budget approval. However, a 1971 constitutional provision making the governor the chief proposer and administrator of the state budget belies this scoring. In the Schlesinger/Beyle scoring, the median state score dropped from 5 in 1965 to 3 in 2007, reflecting the growing capacity and will of legislatures across the nation to influence state budget making and administration.

The strength of executive appointment powers and the number of separately elected executive officials range widely across the nation. A governor who can appoint all major executive officials without legislative confirmation is more powerful than one who shares executive leadership with many separately elected officials and whose appointments are subject to confirmation. Most governors believe that their success in office depends in large part on their ability to select executive colleagues. North Carolina's governor is restrained significantly by the fact that nine state executive officials are elected separately but is enhanced by a robust appointment power. On the two dimensions, North Carolina's governors received a 1965 score of 1 on separately elected officials and 2 on executive appointments. Forty-two years later, the first score remained unchanged, while the second increased to 3.5. Nationally, both dimensions had scores of 3 in 2007.

For eighty years, North Carolina was the only state to deny its governor veto power. The addition of veto power in 1996 was modest relative to other state governors but represented a major step in North Carolina. The range of veto powers among governors includes the presence or absence of item veto, the size of a legislative majority required to override a veto, and the types of legislation on which a veto may be invoked. In 2007, the fifty-state average score on veto power was 4.5, denoting item veto and requiring a three-fifths or two-thirds legislative majority to override. North Carolina governors had a score of 2, with no item veto and a three-fifths majority in each chamber required to override. The types of legislation subject to veto are limited to general statewide measures except constitutional amendments and redistricting laws.

The sixth dimension is a political power related to party control of the two policymaking branches of state governments. In recent years, divided state governments have become more common across the nation. Partisan differences can weaken a governor's influence over legislative decisions. As legislative and gubernatorial politics in North Carolina has become more competitive, an opposition party is more likely to control one or both legislative houses. In the power index, the highest score (5) is given when a governor has majorities of at least 75 percent of membership in both houses. Lower scores are given for smaller majorities and for opposition party control. In 1965, North Carolina scored 5; in 2007, that number had dropped to 4. The average nationwide score in 2007 was 3.

As table 6.2 indicates, North Carolina's gubernatorial powers are categorized as weak relative to those of other state governors. On the Schlesinger/Beyle power index, the North Carolina governor's score changed only modestly between 1960 and 2007. Similar modest changes are recorded for the nation's governors collectively, although some states—for example, Florida, North Dakota, and West Virginia—have experienced considerably more change (Beyle 2007; Schlesinger 1965). The North Carolina governor's powers have increased modestly in tenure potential, appointments, and veto authority, although budget power has decreased. The number of separately elected executives has not varied, and party control has been variable, with increased electoral competition in executive and legislative politics.

As table 6.2 and the previous discussion make clear, the institutional powers of North Carolina's governor have increased modestly over the past half century. In addition, the public leadership provided by governors across the nation has been enhanced by advances in technology and communications, which have enabled governors to travel and communicate widely and easily, thereby personalizing the office.

At the same time, several circumstances restrict gubernatorial power—a more assertive legislature, more frequently divided government, and continued executive branch fragmentation. Powers remain balanced among the changing partners in state policymaking.

❖ The Increasing Importance of Informal Powers

An analysis of three major gubernatorial powers provides insights into the sources and limitations of authority exercised by a state chief executive. Continuities and changes in the roles of public leader, legislative leader, and executive leader elucidate a governor's powers in North Carolina and other states and draw particular attention to the rise in informal powers—the governor's ability to secure policy and political goals through nontraditional, informal means.

GOVERNORS AS PUBLIC AND POLITICAL LEADERS

Public leadership involves activities public officials use to "promote themselves and their policies before the American people." The idea is to advocate policies, mobilize support, and secure laws or executive actions with the prospect of achieving governing success (Kernell 1997, ix). In the vernacular, governors go over the heads of legislators and other officials to shape public opinion and generate policy support. Winning support for legislation and administrative actions redounds to a governor's benefit by making him/her appear to be an effective leader. A reputation for success helps to secure support for other policies, higher performance approval ratings, and where possible reelection. Effective public governorship can contribute to such a reputation.

Governors in North Carolina and other states have many means of communicating with the public and shaping public opinion. State of the State speeches and other messages before the legislature and in the media help governors set a policy agenda and publicize policy priorities and solutions. Periodic news conferences, small group meetings with civic and professional associations, public outreach programs, and visits to public schools, industrial sites, and health facilities, for example, can bring public attention to what the governor believes are important issues and policy responses.

Looking at these various means of communicating with the public in North Carolina, the number of major speeches has remained the same, the frequency of formal news conferences appears to have declined, and the number of small group meetings and events has increased over the past half century. The number of legislative sessions, which has not changed since 1974, determines the major speech schedule. Precise data on news conferences are not readily available. Increases in the number of meetings and events are derived from data published in each governor's public papers. These data show an average of 105 such events per year in

TABLE 6.2. Gubernatorial Institutional Power Scores, 1960 and 2007

State	1960	2007	% Change
Alabama	3.8	2.8	-26
Alaska	NA	4.1	N/A
Arizona 2.5	3.4	36	
Arkansas	2.8	3.6	29
California	4.3	3.2	-26
Colorado	3.5	3.9	11
Connecticut	3.8	3.6	-5
Delaware	2.5	3.5	40
Florida	2.0	3.6	80
Georgia	3.0	3.2	7
Hawaii	NA	3.4	N/A
Idaho	3.5	3.3	-6
Illinois	4.5	3.8	-16
Indiana	3.0	2.9	3
Iowa	3.0	3.8	27
Kansas	2.8	3.3	18
Kentucky	3.5	3.3	-6
Louisiana	3.3	3.4	-3
Maine	2.8	3.6	29
Maryland	4.0	4.1	2.5
Massachusetts	3.0	4.3	43
Michigan	3.5	3.6	3
Minnesota	3.5	3.6	3
Mississippi	1.8	2.9	61
Missouri	4.0	3.6	-10
Montana	4.0	3.5	-12.5
Nebraska	3.0	3.8	27
Nevada	3.5	3.0	-14
New Hampshire	2.5	3.2	28
New Jersey	4.5	4.1	-9
New Mexico	2.8	3.7	32
New York	4.8	4.1	-15
North Carolina	2.3	2.9	26
North Dakota	1.8	3.9	117
Ohio	3.8	3.6	-5
Oklahoma	3.3	2.8	-15
Oregon	4.0	3.5	-12.5
Pennsylvania	4.3	3.8	-11
Rhode Island	2.5	2.6	4
South Carolina	1.8	3.0	67
South Dakota	2.8	3.0	7
Tennessee	3.5	3.8	9
Texas	1.8	3.2	78

TABLE 6.2. *(continued)*

State	1960	2007	% Change
Utah	4.0	4.0	0
Vermont	2.5	2.5	0
Virginia	4.3	3.2	-26
Washington	4.3	3.6	-16
West Virginia	2.0	4.1	105
Wisconsin	3.0	3.5	17
Wyoming	4.0	3.1	-22.5
Average	3.2	3.5	9

Source: Beyle (2007).
Note: Change computed as (2007 power - 1960 power)/1960 power.

1965–76 but an average of more than 330 per year between 1981 and 2001 (Brown 2001; Mitchell 1971, 1974, 1982a, 1982b; Poff 1987, 1992, 1996, 2000).

Regardless of the means used by individual governors, effective use of media in whatever venue is desirable under the circumstances. Governors vary in their ability and willingness to communicate with the public. But governors require frequent communication to achieve policy goals and to maintain public support. In this regard, governors depend on the media for some forms of public communication. The relationship between governors and mass media is necessarily and desirably adversarial. Each has a job to perform, and each must respect the other's functions. As the mass media have become more skeptical of public officials in recent decades, governors have become more willing to seek alternative means of reaching the public. But they cannot escape their reliance on mass media, only reduce it.

Hunt, who served as North Carolina's governor for sixteen years, stated, "The most important power of the governor . . . is public leadership, public education, the 'bully pulpit.'" He explained, "It's important that people know and have some connection with their leaders, their governor. . . . It's important that, at the state level, . . . people know you as more than a face on television. . . . It's important if you're going to get people to really tie in [to do more]." Hunt illustrated, "When I went out as I did so many times and had town meetings about education in schools, I would talk about our statewide Smart Start initiative. I'd talk about our effort to raise standards for teachers and raise pay to the national average. I would talk about our accountability system. . . . I would take it right down to that school, to that county, that city. Get people talking about what they were doing, getting them thinking about how they can advance these ideas and move this agenda ahead" (Hunt 2001). This process is the practice of public leadership.

Public job performance ratings are one means—a principal immediate device—by which governors can determine their effectiveness in public communication and leadership. Many influences come to bear on how residents respond to the question "Do you approve or disapprove of the way [Governor X] is handling his job?" Performance ratings on governors became readily available beginning in the 1970s. Figure 6.2 presents data regarding the public perceptions of four North Carolina governors from 1977 to 2005.

Public evaluations of governors contain a positivity bias. Governors across the nation generally receive greater approval than disapproval in such polls. This finding holds true for all of North Carolina's recent governors. Positive responses were greater than negative responses in seventy-six of eighty-four polls examined in the period (Beyle, Niemi, and Sigelman 2005; Edwards 1990; Fleer 2007).

Studies of presidential performance ratings have also found that approval declines over their term in office and that recent presidents have on average lower ratings than their predecessors. How do North Carolina governors compare? No clear pattern emerges over this period. Hunt lost support during his first stint in office (1973–85) but gained support during his second (1993–2001); Martin's approval ratings dropped over his governorship (1985–93); and Easley's support increased during his first term (2001–4). Similarly, approval levels have not declined steadily since the beginning of the period but rather have been erratic. Factors other than the passage of time are involved.

North Carolina's governors compare favorably with those of other states. In 1987, Martin ranked third among ten governors, with a higher-than-average positive rating. A study of forty-seven governors in 1995, while Hunt was in office, showed him with a score of 74, well above the group average of 54. In 2003, Easley's performance rating was average among the thirty-five governors for whom data were available (Beyle 2004; Rosenthal 1990).

Why has public leadership by governors become more prominent? In the past half century, state electorates have become more volatile, with fewer people grounded in strong party identification and declining loyalty among those who report such grounding. Equally important has been the growth of unaffiliated and independent voters. Both developments contribute to more frequent ticket splitting and divided government. Media changes also contribute. Newspapers and electronic media provide less coverage of public affairs than was previously the case. Correspondents covering state politics are seen as less engaged and experienced with officeholders and as more adversarial. Public events are more likely to receive media attention if they are dramatic and have local dimensions. Governors

FIGURE 6.2. North Carolina Gubernatorial Approval, 1977–2005

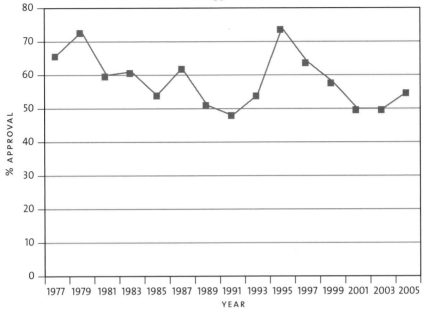

Source: Beyle and Jensen (2006).

hope to sidestep the media through direct voter appeals. Third, new technology and means of communications affect governors' relationships with their publics. Air travel, e-mail, Internet, fax machines, mobile phones, and other electronic devices have facilitated voter contact with governors and have enabled governors to do their jobs outside the office, nearer to the people. Finally, expectations for public leadership have risen. Residents expect governors to visit communities, address organizations, and show voters what the government is doing to improve their lives. Governors will differ in their effectiveness as public leaders, but few if any will be able to escape this role.

LIMITATIONS ON PUBLIC LEADERSHIP

Limitations exist on a "going public" strategy and its effectiveness. Governors vary in personal and communications skills. Many actors vie to set the state policy agenda; governors do not have a monopoly on this activity. Governors also cannot determine the circumstances within which they govern: intervening and unexpected events can grab public attention and require significant course changes. Despite a governor's desire to get close to the people, an era of public discontent and cynicism has eroded people's trust in their leaders.

❖ Governors as Legislative Leaders

Legislators, media, and citizens have high expectations for gubernatorial leadership of the legislature. Governors often are evaluated on their success in translating policies into laws. This part of a governor's job receives more attention than just about anything else he/she does after being elected. To succeed, governors need to marshal numerous resources at their command—constitutional, legal, political, and personal. A survey of several major powers and influences illuminates legislative leadership.

Agenda setting lies at the core of this function for all governors and is most clearly visible in biennial State of the State and budget messages grounded in state constitutions. Governors use these messages to set forth legislative and budgetary priorities and programs. Gubernatorial messages receive wide media attention as road maps showing where governors intend to lead legislatures and states. The power to initiate is also based on the governor's constitutional responsibility as director of the budget. Most major legislation requires allocation of public funds through the budget. The 2005–6 North Carolina budget included expenditures from a $17.2 billion general fund and $33.4 billion overall (North Carolina Constitution, Article 3, Section 5.2; N.C. General Assembly 2005).

A second group of legislative powers and influences derives from governors' political and personal resources. Included are the public and political resources discussed earlier, a governor's legislative orientation and reputation, and personal and institutional lobbying by the governor's office. As the principal statewide elected governmental official, the governor is a state's major policy spokesperson. As the head of one of the major state political parties, a governor leads a coalition of supporters from within and without the legislature on behalf of an agenda. The weight of this influence relates in part to the size and loyalty of a governor's legislative party delegation. As a state's chief executive, a governor commands the personnel and resources of major departments, agencies, boards, and commissions on behalf of his/her program.

Use of these resources depends heavily on a governor's attitude toward the legislature and will and skill to use the powers at the governor's disposal—that is, legislative orientation and legislative reputation. A governor's legislative orientation is a product of accumulated experiences, including previous service or work with legislators, respect for the legislative role, and attitude toward the legislature in the larger policymaking process (Beyle 2004; Rosenthal 1990). Recent North Carolina governors have varied widely on this dimension, from Holshouser and Hunt, who had legislative experience and were appreciative of the legislature, to Martin, who had no state legislative experience and respected the legislative role but had difficulties with the legislative process and leadership while governor. These attitudes, of course, involve not only the views of a governor but also the views of legislators and their leaders.

Governors lobby legislators with a variety of tools, including breakfasts in the mansion, phone calls, district visits with members, appointments, and preferments. One major gubernatorial decision involves the selection of a legislative liaison, a staff representative to the legislative houses and their members. Governors Holshouser (1998) and Hunt (2001) have stated that choosing a liaison constituted one of the most important decisions they made. Legislative liaisons frequently are chosen for their legislative experience in or with the General Assembly, their commitment to the governor's program, and their personal rapport with legislators. However, Hunt cautioned, "The legislative counsel can only be as effective as the governor is standing behind him."

Legislators recommend constituents, acquaintances, and friends for the numerous gubernatorial appointments to executive commissions, boards, and agencies and judicial posts. A recent study reveals that between 1994 and 1997, North Carolina legislators suggested more than sixty-six hundred appointments of people seeking jobs, promotions, and transfers in state government (Krueger 1997). Governors may use these requests and other preferments to negotiate support for legislation.

A key element in executive-legislative relations is legislative party control and divided government. Governors have little clout in determining or influencing the outcomes of legislative elections because of the power of incumbency, gerrymandered districts, and candidate-centered campaigns. However, election outcomes can greatly influence the prospects for a governor's program in the assembly. In recent decades, many states have experienced divided government. Since 1972, divided government has been as common as unified government in North Carolina. Republican governors have faced Democratic legislative majorities in both chambers, while Democratic governors have dealt with Republican House majorities and an evenly split House. Either case brings major challenges in building legislative coalitions and securing passage of laws.

Veto is the most recent constitutional major power acquired by North Carolina's governors. All other state governors had this power at least eighty years earlier, and more than four-fifths of states allow their governors item veto. As a legislative tool, the veto is better as a threat than when it is used in a confrontation. The ability to veto forces governors to become directly involved in almost every major legislative decision. Governor Hunt did not veto any measures during his fourth term. Governor Easley vetoed eight measures between 2001 and 2007. None of these vetoes were overridden by the General Assembly. During the mid-1990s, governors across the nation vetoed fewer than 4 percent of all bills (Beyle 2004; *Book of the States* 2005; N.C. Office of the Governor 2007).

While governors are major actors in the legislative arena, their powers and influence over bills are limited. Other political actors have competing agendas and can press priorities with the public and media. Small legislative majorities and divided governments can impede the building of support. Declining public approval and undisciplined party support can weaken a governor's sway over legislators. Vetoes may be overridden by three-fifth votes in assembly houses. During the 1990s, overrides occurred in fewer than 3 percent of cases, but the numbers vary widely among the states. Furthermore, North Carolina's governors do not have the power to veto line items. Earmarked funds and special provisions in bills can restrict a governor's budget powers and inhibit the ability to manage state revenue and expenditures, especially when balanced budgets are threatened. In addition, the legislature has unlimited power to change a governor's budget recommendations.

Hunt (2001) has reflected on what works in legislative leadership: (1) a governor's respect for the legislative process; (2) a precisely articulated agenda that legislators are persuaded to own; (3) making clear the consequences if legislators do not accede to the people's demands for legislative action; and (4) positive leadership. These conditions represent a tall order for legislative success and demonstrate the challenges a governor faces.

❖ Governors as Chief Executives

The 1971 North Carolina Constitution included two changes that enhanced the power of the state's chief executives. According to Article 3, "The executive power of the State shall be vested in the Governor." In the previous constitution, the provision read, "The executive department shall consist of a Governor, in whom shall be vested the supreme executive power of the State." The new wording makes the governor the chief executive, increasing his/her authority within the branch and the government. This power includes responsibility and authority to "take care that the laws be faithfully executed." Second, the constitution provides for the governor to be director of the budget, a provision made initially in the Executive Budget Act of 1925. As director, the governor has two responsibilities: (1) to prepare and recommend a budget to the General Assembly and (2) to monitor revenue and expenditures "to ensure that the State does not incur a deficit for any fiscal period" (North Carolina General Statutes n.d., chapter 143, sections 1–34.7; North Carolina Constitution, Article 3, Section 5). These provisions increase a governor's authority to manage state finances, often without legislative concurrence. The two powers combine to provide the core of a governor's executive power and ability to manage the government. Over this period, governors across the nation saw their budget powers decrease.

One major administrative authority for any governor is the power to appoint numerous executive officials in departments, in agencies, on boards, and on commissions. In an average year, a North Carolina governor makes one thousand appointments. Most appointees do not require confirmation by the legislature and serve at the pleasure of the governor. Several major boards (for example, the State Board of Education, the Utilities Commission) must have members confirmed by one or both legislative houses, and some of these posts have fixed terms. The North Carolina governor's appointment power is strong relative to that of other governors (Beyle 2007; Dinnes and Richardson 1996).

In making appointments, a governor may provide a diverse group of residents with opportunities for service and governmental authority. The appointments of members of the governor's cabinet and boards and commissions include more women and minorities than the elected members of the Council of State. In 1973, for example, Governor Holshouser named the first woman to head a North Carolina state department; four years later, Governor Hunt named the first African American to serve as a department secretary in the state. No African American was elected to the council until 1992, and no woman until 1996. Between 1973 and 2005, five women and one African American served on the council, and seventeen women and seven African Americans served as appointed secretaries (*North Carolina Manual* 1973–2006). Data on the political party affiliations of appointees are not available.

On boards and commissions, similar advances have been made in enhanced representativeness of members during administrations headed by both major political parties. Martin and Hunt's appointees between 1977 and 1993 included nearly 28 percent women, 12 percent African Americans, and 2 percent other ethnic minorities. In Governor Hunt's second two terms, the proportions increased to 36 percent women and 17 percent ethnic minorities. During his first term, 35 percent of Governor Easley's appointees were women. For all four administrations, the percentages are higher than for elected positions and have increased (Coble, Bryan, and Maddox 1984; N.C. Department of the Secretary of State 2001–4; N.C. Office of the Governor 1990, 1998, 2003).

The criteria used by recent governors in selecting appointees include program and personal loyalty; knowledge and commitment to the subject area; personal integrity and motivations for service; political compatibility; and diversity in geographic origins, gender, and race/ethnicity. Potential problem areas for appointments include adequate and competitive compensation; political background (that is, history as a campaign worker and/or contributor); disclosure of economic interests; and public scrutiny. The significance of these problem areas varies with circumstances and appointees (Fleer 2007; Martin 1998; Scott 1998).

Other major executive powers include service as commander in chief of the National Guard; the right to grant pardons, reprieves, and commutations to convicted criminals; the authority to reorganize administrative agencies; and the ability to act as the state's representative in intergovernmental forums.

The North Carolina Constitution charges the governor with the faithful implementation of state laws. That is one of the governor's numerous responsibilities, especially in his/her capacity as chief executive. Gubernatorial oversight of the executive branch through personnel and budgetary powers is challenging, to say the least. Formal and informal powers enhance a governor's ability to achieve supervisory control of the vast and varied state bureaucracy.

However, size, variety, and fragmentation restrict that control. The bureaucracy includes twenty departments, more than three hundred boards and commissions, several independent agencies, and more than seventy thousand employees, only a small fraction of whom are political appointees. Civil service employees are recruited through the Office of State Personnel, housed in the Department of Administration. These employees are protected from partisan interference and characterized by stability of service. A governor's office seeks to oversee these far-flung operations through its personal staff and appointed departmental secretaries. The roles of public leader, legislative leader, and state budget director extend a governor's influence over the state administration.

Finally, the personal attributes of a particular governor contribute to his/her ability to secure meaningful oversight. Governors vary in the priority they assign to this task, in their experience with large-scale public administration, and in their personal skills at team building and maintaining loyalty and fidelity among public employees. Bureaucratic oversight demands much time and devotion when other duties are also calling. Effective oversight is possible but is not easily achieved.

LIMITATIONS ON EXECUTIVE POWERS

All of a governor's executive powers are limited. A governor's ability to gain and maintain control of an administration confronts the size and fragmentation of the executive branch. While the 1971 Executive Organization Act limited the number of departments to twenty-five and sought to rationalize the distribution of boards and commissions among those departments, the executive office is not a monolith and involves large budgets and numerous personnel. A key factor in North Carolina and some other states is the large number of independently elected executives on the Council of State; none of those executives except the lieutenant governor has term limits.

Where governors have the power to appoint numerous officials, a governor's personal attention to appointees and their performance is restricted. Some board members are appointed by other officials, such as the lieutenant governor, the speaker of the House, the Senate president pro tempore, and association officials. Some appointees require legislative confirmation. Finally, a governor's removal power is constrained by recent court decisions protecting First Amendment freedoms.

Budgeting as a managerial tool is also limited. The legislature has budget-making power and can change a governor's recommendations. The General Assembly's Division of Fiscal Research, the House and Senate Appropriations Committees, and other legislative oversight committees dissect, deliberate, and decide on the state's budget. Funds can be earmarked and special provisions placed in the budget. These tactics limit a governor's flexibility in managing funds, even in the face of the constitutional requirement for a balanced budget. Finally, North Carolina's governors, unlike those in forty-three other states, cannot veto individual items in bills involving money.

What does being an effective chief executive require? Governors Hunt (2001) and Martin (1998) listed loyalty from a committed executive team, a clear focus on the governor's agenda, frequent communication with team members, and hard work. Once again, governors face immense demands for leadership.

❖ Summary and Conclusion

Compared to other governors, North Carolina's governor is weak in institutional powers. Major weaknesses derive from the large number of separately elected executive officials and the absence of a line-item veto. These limitations, if they are overcome, require strategic use of formal powers such as appointments and budget control as well as significant reliance on the personal attributes and skills of an incumbent. Thus, the relative success of North Carolina's governors depends more on the skills of the people elected and their performance in office than on the institutional powers of the office.

Race and sex remain major factors in the office of governor in North Carolina and other states. Among people who are qualified to hold the office, white males have major advantages. To date, no woman or ethnic minority has been a major candidate for governor in North Carolina, and few have been in other states. Since the first woman elected in her own right became a governor in 1974, twenty-five women have served as governors in nineteen states, and two African Americans have served as governors. Indeed, few candidates from these groups compete for the offices, although the number of women candidates in particular has recently grown.

Excluded groups can improve their prospects for office by serving in lower-level offices. More women and ethnic minorities recently have been elected to statewide offices, but progress remains slow. As Christopher A. Cooper's essay in this volume recounts in more detail, at the beginning of the current century, 22 percent of legislators and 27 percent of statewide elected executive officials across the states were women. For African Americans, the comparable figures are 6 percent and less than 1 percent (Center for American Women and Politics 2006; Joint Center for Political and Economic Studies 2007). Governors can use appointments to provide opportunities to improve the officeholding qualifications for women and ethnic minority candidates, and North Carolina's governors have done so.

Race and gender differences are significant in voting for governors in North Carolina. Racial polarization is a factor, as blacks support Democrats and whites support Republicans, a phenomenon that is repeated in other states. Since 1980, a gender gap too has existed in national and state politics, with women tending to favor Democrats and men supporting Republicans. This pattern moderated in 2004 but remains a factor in North Carolina's gubernatorial elections and other state and national contests (Abramson, Aldrich, and Rohde 2006; Keefe and Hetherington 2003).

The evolution of the office of governor in North Carolina and other states has been influenced by developments that make securing and holding the office more democratic—that is, an increasingly diverse group of people is involved in the selection of governors and in determining whether they maintain public support for their policies. Increased political competition in the states, the frequency of divided governments, and emergence of the public leadership role have contributed to this gubernatorial evolution.

At the dawn of the twenty-first century, governors in many states, including North Carolina, operate in political environments that are more competitive than was previously the case. In North Carolina and across the South and the nation, two-party competition has increased. In the 1950s and 1960s, twenty-five states were classified as two-party competitive, while eight states (all in the South) were one-party Democratic. By 1999–2003, thirty-one states were two-party competitive, and none fell into the one-party Democratic or Republican categories (Bibby and Holbrook 2004; Ranney 1965). A venue in which either major political party has a realistic chance of winning the governor's mansion increases candidates' and officeholders' attention to public opinion as well as voter participation.

Similarly, the incidence of divided government has increased in the states. In the 1950s, an average of fifteen states had governments in which different parties controlled the executive and at least one legislative house. By 1999–2004, that number had almost doubled to an average of twenty-nine (National Conference of State Legislatures 2004). Divided governments require state chief executives to implement governing strategies that differ from those used when governments are unified. Since the 1970s, divided governments have been frequent in North Carolina and across the fifty states.

Finally, the emergence and prominence of governors' public leadership role means that they operate closer to the people to maintain support and to manage divisions in public opinion in the electorate and legislatures. Governors have become more responsive to and influenced by public opinion as they seek to shape public attitudes and develop governing coalitions. Governors across the states are increasingly engaged in a "race for representation" with legislatures often controlled by political opponents (Roeder 1994; Rosenthal 1998).

Governors in North Carolina, as elsewhere, sit at the center of the process by which public policy is made and share that responsibility with many actors. To succeed, governors must provide leadership in many areas, select able teams, provide manageable agendas, and communicate effectively with those who put them in office. The office of governor provides significant power but also demands great responsibility and skills.

❖ Note

I am grateful to Jeevan Chelladurai, a Wake Forest University graduate, who contributed to research on this essay.

❖ References

Abramson, Paul R., John H. Aldrich, and David W. Rohde. 2006. *Change and Continuity and the 2004 Elections.* Washington, D.C.: CQ Press.

Beyle, Thad. 2004. "The Governors." In *Politics in the American States*, 8th ed., edited by Virginia Gray and Russell Hanson, 194–231. Washington, D.C.: CQ Press.

———. 2007. "Gubernatorial Power: The Institutional Power Ratings for the 50 Governors of the United States." <http://www.unc.edu/<tilde>beyle/gubnewpwr.html>. Accessed October 6, 2007.

Beyle, Thad, and Jennifer Jensen. 2006. "The Gubernatorial Campaign Finance Database." <http://www.unc.edu/<tilde>beyle/guber.html>. Accessed October 6, 2007.

Beyle, Thad, Richard Niemi, and Lee Sigelman. 2005. "Job Approval Ratings, 1958–2005." <http://www.unc.edu<tilde>beyle/jars.html>. Accessed October 6, 2007.

Bibby, John. 2003. *Politics, Parties, and Elections in America*. 5th ed. Chicago: Nelson-Hall.

Bibby, John, and Thomas M. Holbrook. 2004. "Parties and Elections." In *Politics in the American States*, 8th ed., edited by Virginia Gray and Russell Hanson, 62–99. Washington, D.C.: CQ Press.

The Book of the States. 2005, 2006. Lexington, Ky.: Council of State Governments.

Brown, William, ed. 2001. "Hunt Papers." Vol. 4, "Chronological Control." In possession of the author.

Burden, Barry C. 2002. "United States Senators as Presidential Candidates." *Political Science Quarterly* 117:81–102.

Carolina Polls. 1986–2005. Chapel Hill, N.C.: Odum Institute for Research in Social Science. <http://www.irss.unc.edu/odum/jsp/content_node.jsp?nodeid=241>. Accessed September 14, 2007.

Center for American Women and Politics. 2006. "CAWP Fact Sheet: History of Women Governors." <www.rci.rutgers.edu/<tilde>cawp/Facts/Officeholders/govhistory.pdf>. Accessed September 14, 2007.

Coble, Ran, Jim Bryan, and Lacy Maddox. 1984. *Boards, Commissions, and Councils in the Executive Branch of North Carolina State Government*. Raleigh: N.C. Center for Public Policy Research.

Comparative State Elections Project. 1968. Chapel Hill, N.C.: Institute for Research in Social Science.

Crabtree, Beth G. 1958. *North Carolina Governors, 1585–1958*. Raleigh: N.C. Department of Archives and History.

Dinnes, Robin, and Robin Richardson, eds. 1996. *Directory of North Carolina Boards and Commissions*. Raleigh: N.C. Department of the Secretary of State.

Edwards, George C., III. 1990. *Presidential Approval: A Sourcebook*. Baltimore: Johns Hopkins University Press.

Fleer, Jack. 1994. *North Carolina Government and Politics*. Lincoln: University of Nebraska Press.

———. 2007. *Governors Speak*. Lanham, Md.: University Press of America.

Holshouser, James. 1998. Interview by Jack D. Fleer, March 13 (C328). Southern Oral History Program Collection #4007, Southern Historical Collection, Wilson Library, University of North Carolina at Chapel Hill.

Hunt, James B. 2001. Interview by Jack D. Fleer, July 6 (C330), August 15 (C331), October 3 (C332). Southern Oral History Program Collection #4007, Southern Historical Collection, Wilson Library, University of North Carolina at Chapel Hill.

Jewell, Malcolm E., and Sarah M. Morehouse. 2001. *Political Parties and Elections in American States*. 4th ed. Washington, D.C.: CQ Press.

Joint Center for Political and Economic Studies. 2007. "African-American Federal and State-wide Elected Administrative Officeholders, 1963–2007." <www.jointcenter.org>. Accessed October 8, 2007.

Keefe, William J., and Marc J. Hetherington. 2003. *Parties, Politics, and Public Policy in America.* 9th ed. Washington, D.C.: CQ Press.

Kenny, Patrick J., and Tom W. Rice. 1987. "The Relationship between Divisive Primaries and General Election Outcomes." *American Journal of Political Science* 31:31–44.

Kernell, Samuel. 1997. *Going Public: New Strategies of Presidential Leadership.* 3rd ed. Washington, D.C.: CQ Press.

Krasno, Jonathan S. 1994. *Challengers, Competition, and Reelection: Comparing Senate and House Elections.* New Haven: Yale University Press.

Krueger, Bill. 1997. "Many Legislators Approach State Agencies about Hirings." *Raleigh News and Observer*, June 7, A1.

Martin, James G. 1998. Interview by Jack D. Fleer, February 27 (C334). Southern Oral History Program Collection #4007, Southern Historical Collection, Wilson Library, University of North Carolina at Chapel Hill.

Mitchell, Memory R., ed. 1971. *Messages, Addresses, and Public Papers of Daniel Killian Moore, Governor of North Carolina, 1965–1969.* Raleigh: N.C. Department of Archives and History.

―――. 1974. *Addresses and Public Papers of Robert Walter Scott, Governor of North Carolina, 1969–1973.* Raleigh: N.C. Division of Archives and History, Department of Cultural Resources.

―――. 1982a. *Addresses and Public Papers of James Baxter Hunt, Jr., Governor of North Carolina.* Vol. 1, *1977–1981.* Raleigh: N.C. Division of Archives and History, Department of Cultural Resources.

―――. 1982b. *Addresses and Public Papers of James Eubert Holshouser, Jr., Governor of North Carolina, 1973–1977.* Raleigh: N.C. Division of Archives and History, Department of Cultural Resources.

National Conference of State Legislatures. 2004. "Divided Government in the States." <www.ncsl.org/programs/legman/elect/divgov.htm>. Accessed September 12, 2007.

NBC and CBS. 1988. North Carolina Exit Poll. In possession of the author.

N.C. Board of Elections. 1968–2006. Voter Registration Statistics. <www.sboe.state.nc.us>. Accessed October 11, 2007.

North Carolina Constitution. 1971. <http://www.ncga.state.nc.us/Legislation/constitution/ncconstitution.html>. Accessed September 24, 2007.

N.C. Department of the Secretary of State. 2001–4. "Appointments Reporting, July 1, 2001–June 30, 2004." <http://www.secretary.state.nc.us/apprpt/>. Accessed October 11, 2007.

N.C. General Assembly. 2005. "2005 Appropriations Act." <www.ncga.state.nc.us/Sessions/2005/Bills/Senate/S622>. Accessed October 11, 2007.

North Carolina General Statutes. N.d. <http://www.ncga.state.nc.us/gascripts/Statutes/StatutesTOC.pl>. Accessed September 24, 2007.

North Carolina Manual. 1911–2006. Raleigh: N.C. Department of the Secretary of State.

N.C. Office of the Governor. 1990. Memo to author, December 27. In possession of the author.

———. 1998. Memo to author, March 31. In possession of the author.

———. 2003. Memo to author, May 1. In possession of the author.

———. 2007. "Gov. Easley Vetoes Bill That Gives Businesses Unfair Breaks." Press Release. August 30. <www.governor.state.nc.us/NEWS>. Accessed October 11, 2007.

Poff, Jan-Michael, ed. 1987. *Addresses and Public Papers of James Baxter Hunt, Jr., Governor of North Carolina.* Vol. 2, *1981–1985.* Raleigh: N.C. Division of Archives and History, Department of Cultural Resources.

———. 1992. *Addresses and Public Papers of James Grubb Martin, Governor of North Carolina.* Vol. 1, *1985–1989.* Raleigh: N.C. Division of Archives and History, Department of Cultural Resources.

———. 1996. *Addresses and Public Papers of James Grubb Martin, Governor of North Carolina.* Vol. 2, *1989–1993.* Raleigh: N.C. Division of Archives and History, Department of Cultural Resources.

———. 2000. *Addresses and Public Papers of James Baxter Hunt, Jr., Governor of North Carolina.* Vol. 3, *1993–1997.* Raleigh: N.C. Division of Archives and History, Department of Cultural Resources.

Ranney, Austin. 1965. "Parties in State Politics." In *Politics in the America States: A Comparative Analysis*, edited by Herbert Jacob and Kenneth N. Vines, 61–99. Boston: Little, Brown.

Roeder, Phillip W. 1994. *Public Opinion and Policy Leadership in the American States.* Tuscaloosa: University of Alabama Press.

Rosenthal, Alan. 1990. *Governors and Legislatures: Contending Powers.* Washington, D.C.: CQ Press.

———. 1998. *The Decline of Representative Democracy: Process, Participation, and Power in State Legislatures.* Washington, D.C.: CQ Press.

Schlesinger, Joseph. 1965. "The Politics of the Executive." In *Politics in the American States: A Comparative Analysis*, edited by Herbert Jacob and Kenneth N. Vines, 207–37. Boston: Little, Brown.

Scott, Robert W. 1998. Interview by Jack D. Fleer, February 4 and 11 (C336). Southern Oral History Program Collection #4007, Southern Historical Collection, Wilson Library, University of North Carolina at Chapel Hill.

Squire, Peverill. 1992. "Challenger Profile and Gubernatorial Election." *Western Political Quarterly* 45:125–42.

Voter News Service. 1996. "Voter News Service General Election Exit Poll" [computer file]. ICPSR version. New York: Voter News Service. <www.icpsr.umich.edu.cocoon.ICPSR/STUDY/06989.xml>. Accessed October 11, 2007.

———. 2000. "Voter News Service General Election Exit Poll" [computer file]. ICPSR

03527-v2. New York: Voter News Service. <www.icpsr.umich.edu.cocoon.ICPSR/ STUDY/03527.xml>. Accessed October 11, 2007.

Voter Research and Surveys. 1992. "North Carolina Exit Poll, General Election, 1992." ICPSR 9852. New York: Voter Research and Surveys. <www.ciser.cornell.edu/ASPs/search-athena.asp>. Accessed October 11, 2007.

❖ 7. The People's Branch

Reassessing the N.C. General Assembly

CHRISTOPHER A. COOPER

Jim Black's political career began rather inauspiciously. The Democrat from Matthews, North Carolina, won a spot in the General Assembly in 1981 but lost his first reelection bid. Despite this early stumble, Black ran and won his seat back during the following election cycle. Before long, the middle-aged optometrist and political novice had become a remarkably effective and powerful legislator, serving eleven terms and occupying the position of speaker of the House for a record-tying four terms. In a state shifting toward the Republican Party, Black helped the Democrats retain control of the state legislature longer than many political observers believed possible.

As the 2002 election returns poured in, Black's time in power appeared to be coming to a close. After years of Democratic control, the Republicans gained a two-seat majority, and the partisan tide in the General Assembly seemed to be shifting. Before the new legislature could be sworn in, however, Michael Decker, a conservative Republican, switched from the Republican Party to the Democrats, erasing the razor-thin Republican majority and creating a partisan tie in the General Assembly. Observers viewed this switch as surprising for a number of reasons, not the least of which was that Decker's district leaned strongly Republican, giving Democratic candidates in the same election only 31 percent of the presidential vote, 42 percent of the gubernatorial vote, and 37 percent of the vote for chief justice (Beyle 2002, 10). As we would later learn, Black was intimately involved in these negotiations to persuade Decker to switch, which benefited not only Black's party but also his political career. After weeks of behind-the-scenes negotiations, Black helped broker a deal to create a co-speakership arrangement under which he would share power with Republican Richard Morgan.

Just when things seemed to be going well for Black, the bottom fell out. He became embroiled in three separate but equally damaging scandals. In the first, he was accused of using political influence to pass lottery legislation and provide lottery contracts to a private company, Scientific Games. The scandal began when his former aide, Meredith Norris, failed to register as a lobbyist despite clearly attempting to influence lawmakers to pass the lottery. Black also appointed Kevin Geddings, a political operative and public relations veteran, to the state's lottery commission. While appointing a political consultant to a public commission might appear unseemly, the real problems began when it was revealed that Geddings had undisclosed business dealings with Scientific Games, the same lottery vendor that had gotten Black's aide into trouble less than a year earlier. Geddings was eventually sentenced to four years in prison (Kane and Curliss 2007b).

The second scandal did not begin in the halls of the Capitol or even in the city of Raleigh but in the unlikeliest of places, an International House of Pancakes bathroom. As the story broke, the state alleged that Decker's decision to switch parties was influenced not by Black's superior political skills but rather by an old-fashioned bribe. According to sources in the state bureau of investigation, Decker agreed to switch parties in exchange for fifty thousand dollars and the promise of a government job for his son (Robertson 2007). The state contends that Black kept his end of the bargain and soon laundered checks and cash to Decker and hired Decker's son as a legislative assistant. In April 2007, Decker agreed with this version of events and was sentenced to four years in prison (Kane and Curliss 2007a). Although Black never admitted guilt, calling Decker "untrustworthy," he eventually entered an Alford plea in superior court, not admitting to the act but agreeing that a court would likely find him guilty (Robertson 2007).

Black's third and final scandal began when he accepted twenty-nine thousand dollars from two chiropractors in Charlotte-area bathrooms, reminding one of the chiropractors, "This is just between me and you—don't you ever tell anybody about this." In exchange for these cash transfers, Black promised to push for a bill to lower copayments for chiropractic services. Black pleaded guilty to bribery on February 15, 2007 (Robertson 2007).

Stories about Black's trials and tribulations dominated North Carolina's headlines for almost two years and reinforced many citizens' negative beliefs about their legislature. Even prior to the Black scandal, North Carolinians viewed their legislators with a skeptical eye. A 1994 poll of state residents revealed that only 28 percent rated the General Assembly's performance as "excellent or good," the lowest such proportion of all public state institutions (Hardin 1994, 7). Twenty years earlier, the *Raleigh News and Observer* expressed similar discontent with the people's branch:

> The State Legislative Building stands as one of the most outwardly handsome temples built to democracy in America. Its glistening marble, lush carpets, resplendent brass and tinkling fountains could grace a Taj Mahal. But the marble is but a veneer glued to cinder block. And the proceedings echoing through the temple's chambers these past three months have been as democratic as the Cadillacs clustered in its basement. (Bass and DeVries 1995 [1976], 225–26)

Although it is easy to focus on these negative headlines, a closer inspection of the North Carolina legislature reveals a representative body that performs much good for the state. The legislature may occasionally endure a high-profile scandal, but most legislators are not the scurrilous, unethical, and downright seedy individuals that many observers believe them to be. Legislative behavior is also much more systematic and predictable than a quick reading of the headlines may suggest. Legislators are goal-seeking political actors who are embedded in political and social institutions that affect their behavior and provide incentives and disincentives for political action. Many of these institutions remain constant across states. For example, with the exception of Nebraska, state legislatures are bicameral institutions with two chambers, an upper house that generally has fewer members and longer terms and a lower house with less prestige and power. Despite these similarities, considerable variation exists in state legislatures' election procedures, lawmaking powers, and rules. These differences provide intriguing cases for those interested in legislative politics and allow us to better understand how institutions affect the practice of democracy.

This essay compares the operation of North Carolina's state legislature to other state legislatures, thereby providing a more systematic look at the people's branch. To this end, the essay is organized around legislators' three primary goals—getting elected and reelected, achieving political power, and passing good public policy (Fenno 1973). Throughout each of these sections, we pay particular attention to the ways North Carolina's arrangement of legislative institutions affects political outcomes.

❖ Election and Reelection

In North Carolina, 50 senators serve about 161,000 constituents each, and 120 legislators in the lower house represent about 67,000 constituents apiece. Most legislative candidates' primary goal is to win election to one of these 170 seats and once elected, to stay in office. After all, candidates who never win election cannot pass policy or achieve power. Given the importance of election and reelection, three questions immediately surface: (1) Who is elected to the legislature? (2) How often are legislators reelected? (3) What factors influence election and reelection to the legislature?

WHO SERVES IN THE LEGISLATURE?

Like most U.S. political institutions, state legislatures are not very diverse. Across the country, state legislatures include fewer women, ethnic and racial minorities, and other traditionally underrepresented groups than appear in the general population. The picture is not all negative, however. Because of the lower cost of running for office as well as the compact nature of state legislative districts, women and minorities appear in greater numbers in state legislatures than in the U.S. Congress.

North Carolina has a reputation as an early pioneer on issues of women's representation (Bass and DeVries 1995 [1976]). Today, North Carolina's legislature appears fairly average on both measures. Figure 7.1 provides graphic evidence of this trend as it relates to female representation. The solid line represents the average percentage of women in America's state legislatures from 1983 to 2007. The dashed line presents the percentage of women in the North Carolina legislature during the same period. The number of women in the North Carolina legislature as well as other legislatures across the country has increased over the past twenty-five years, and today about 25 percent of North Carolina's legislators are women, compared with 24 percent in the country as a whole. North Carolina fares even better when compared to its immediate neighbors South Carolina (9 percent women), Virginia (17 percent women), and Georgia (20 percent women).

A number of reasons account for North Carolina's good standing on gender equity (particularly in relation to its neighbors). Women may fare well in North Carolina elections because higher campaign costs impede the election of women to office and North Carolina's elections rank as some of the least expensive in the country (Carroll 1994). The lingering effects of district structure have also aided female representation. Through the mid-1980s, some North Carolina legislators were still elected in multimember districts, a structure that is generally associated with higher proportions of women in office (Arceneaux 2001). Finally, beginning in the 1990s, North Carolina experienced higher-than-average rates of legislative turnover, creating open seats for potential female candidates (Moncrief, Niemi, and Powell 2004).

Despite these institutional advantages, the people themselves may be the primary impediment to female representation. Kevin Arceneaux (2001) finds that states with more feminist populations elect female candidates in greater numbers than states with less progressive attitudes about women. North Carolina has the thirty-fifth-most feminist population of the thirty-nine states for which data are available, trailing such southern states as South Carolina, Georgia, Tennessee, and Louisiana (Brace et al. 2002). Taken together, the advantages afforded women institutionally and the cultural impediments to female representation lead to a state that falls almost exactly in the middle of national gender representation.

The proportion of women in the legislature tells only part of the story about representation. North Carolina also fares well in terms of women in committee chairs—27 percent of North Carolina's committee chairs are women, the tenth-

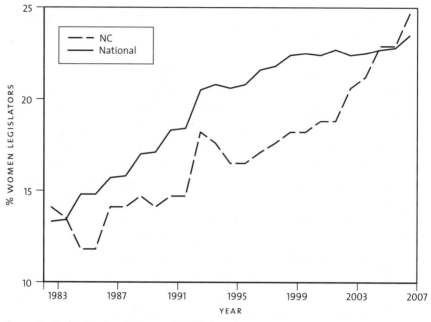

FIGURE 7.1. Female Representation in State Legislatures, 1983–2007

Source: Center for American Women and Politics (2007).

highest rate in the country. The picture looks even more positive when comparing North Carolina to its immediate neighbors—South Carolina has no female committee chairs, only 4 percent of Virginia's chairs are women, and Georgia has only 10 percent (Center for American Women and Politics 2005).

Electing women to office has important influences on the policy process. Women tend to serve on different committees (Thomas and Welch 1991) and support different policies than men do (Thomas 1994). In addition, women are more likely to perform casework (Richardson and Freeman 1995) and constituent service (Thomas 1994). The effects of women in office may even extend beyond the internal workings of the state house. Lonna Rae Atkeson (2003) finds that having more viable female candidates creates greater levels of political engagement among women.

While women are traditionally underrepresented, minorities face even more daunting odds against serving in the legislature. As late as 2001 (the last year for which national data are available), only 5.7 percent of lower house legislators and 4.6 of upper house legislators nationally were African American (Bositis 2001). The numbers regarding Asians, Hispanics, and other ethnic groups are even smaller. In 2001, 15 percent of North Carolina's state legislators in both houses were African American. By 2005, the numbers had not increased in the state Senate and had increased only slightly (from eighteen black legislators to nineteen) in the lower house (Guillory 2006). In 2007, none of the African Americans in either chamber represented the Republican Party.

The proportion of women is relatively consistent across states, but the proportion of a state's population that is African American varies considerably, radically altering the potential candidate pool and the voting patterns of the electorate. Not surprisingly, the number of African Americans in the state is the most important factor influencing the election of African Americans to the state legislature. Figure 7.2 clearly demonstrates this point, with the percentage of the voting age population in a state that is black arrayed along the X axis and the percentage of a state legislature that is black is on the Y axis. The southern states are labeled by name, while all other states are represented as dots. The solid line displays the line of best fit. States that fall above this line have more African Americans in the legislature than would be expected given the number of African Americans in the population relative to other states. In states below the line, African Americans are underrepresented. North Carolina falls just below the line, suggesting that blacks, at 15 percent of the legislature and 21 percent of the general population, are slightly underrepresented in the state legislature, but the state looks fairly average when compared to other states. Some southern states, such as Virginia, look particularly poor on black representation, while Alabama's legislative numbers are in rough parity with those of the population as a whole. About 87 percent of the variation in black legislative representation is explained solely by the percentage of blacks in the voting-age population.

Similar to the findings about female representation, minority state legislators also have different political priorities and behave differently in office than their white counterparts. Studies show that black state legislators propose and vote for different policies, even while controlling for the push and pull of district opinion (Haynie 2001). Chris T. Owens's (2005) study echoes this conclusion, finding that when more African Americans are elected to office, the state's budget priorities change. Black legislators are also more likely to serve on committees of particular importance to the African American community (Haynie 2001). Minority representation clearly matters both symbolically and substantively.

A host of other demographic factors beyond race and gender affect the makeup of state legislatures. Service in the state legislature has long been known as well suited for people in certain occupations—people with flexible schedules can serve in the legislature without sacrificing their "real work." The distribution of occupations in the legislature is important because if certain occupations dominate the legislature, the legislature may be more likely to pass measures that benefit those groups. In earlier times, farmers dominated state legislatures. Over the past cen-

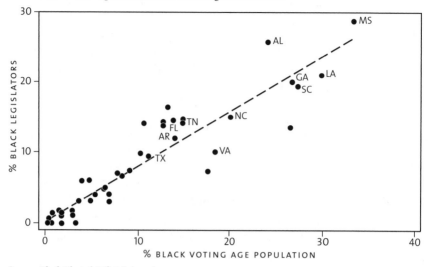

FIGURE 7.2. Black Representation in State Legislatures, 2001

Source: *Black Elected Officials* (2001).

tury, the proportion of farmers has fallen dramatically from 25 percent of state legislators nationally in 1909 to 7 percent by 1999. Business has recently taken over as the most-represented occupation in state legislatures across the country, with 27 percent of legislators declaring business as their occupation in 1999. Government employees come in second at 16 percent of all legislators, with attorneys a close third at 15 percent (Squire and Hamm 2005, 133–34).

An analysis of the occupational makeup of North Carolina state legislators in 2006 reveals that the state follows national trends fairly closely (see table 7.1). When asked to list their primary occupations, 34 percent of legislators in the lower house reported working in business, 31 percent were retired, and 13 percent were lawyers. Only 1 percent considered farming to be their primary occupation.[1]

Although they still lack parity with the population, state legislatures are among the country's most representative political bodies. North Carolina falls somewhere in the middle of all fifty states in terms of the electing women and minorities. The state is certainly not a leader in these areas, but little evidence suggests that it is a laggard, either. Its occupational makeup also resembles that of other states. We now turn our attention to the question of how often legislators are reelected and what institutions affect their reelection.

HOW OFTEN ARE LEGISLATORS REELECTED?

With very few exceptions, when state legislators run for reelection, they win. Despite near-certain victory, not all legislators seek reelection. They may not run

TABLE 7.1. Self-Reported Occupations of Members of the N.C. House
of Representatives, 2006

Occupation	%
Business	34
Retired	31
Lawyer	13
Full-time legislator	4
Educator/teacher/professor	4
Minister	3
Medical professions	3
Homemaker	2
Contractor/construction	2
Self-employed	2
Farmer	1
Media/journalist	1
N	120

Source: <http://www.ncga.state.nc.us/House/House.html>.

again because they may seek higher office. They may simply retire. They also may be forced out by term limits, death, scandal, or arrest. Because of these factors, turnover, defined as the number of new legislators divided by the number of total legislators in a given year, is considerably higher than reelection rates would suggest. Nationally, turnover is trending downward, a finding that suggests increasing stability in legislative bodies. Table 7.2 compares the rates of legislative turnover in North Carolina to turnover averages in all fifty states. In North Carolina, turnover in both houses is higher than the average in all time periods but one. These differences are particularly pronounced during the 1990s in the lower house and the 1970s in the upper house.

State legislatures experience turnover and reelection at dramatically different rates. For example, the Alabama Senate had 40 percent turnover during the 1990s, but only 11 percent of the Pennsylvania House turned over during the same period. While few systematic factors influence retirement, the factors that affect reelection—professionalism, term limits, and district structure—are easier to explain.

WHAT FACTORS INFLUENCE ELECTION AND REELECTION?

Legislative professionalism is one of the most commonly cited institutional factors affecting reelection rates. Professionalism describes the institutional resources available to a state legislator, commonly understood as salary, staff support, and time in session (Mooney 1995). Professional legislators make more money, have

TABLE 7.2. Legislative Turnover in North Carolina Compared to Other States, 1971–2000

	1971–80	1981–90	1991–2000
N.C. House	34%	25%	34%
50-state House average	32	24	25
N.C. Senate	38	27	23
49-state Senate average	29	22	23

Source: Moncrief, Niemi, and Powell (2004).

more staff, and remain in session longer than their less professional counterparts. In short, professional states come closer to resembling the U.S. Congress, the paragon of legislative professionalism.

After members of a professional legislatures are elected, they receive a series of advantages that increase their odds of reelection. For example, members of professional legislatures have more travel resources (Holbrook and Tidmarch 1991) and more contact with their constituents (Maestas 2003). Like members of Congress who use subsidized travel, staff resources, and the franking privilege to increase their public perceptions, senators and representatives in professional legislatures mobilize these resources to increase their reelection chances.

Figure 7.3 presents the professionalism score of each state along the Y axis and the percentage of the legislature with outside careers along the X axis. All states are represented by dots; only North Carolina is labeled.

Professionalism scores can be interpreted as a percentage of Congress's professionalism. For example, a legislature receiving a professionalism score of .5 has about half the resources of the U.S. Congress; a legislature receiving a score of 1 would have the same resources as Congress. California is considered the most professional state legislature, with 57 percent of the staffing, salary, and session length of Congress. New Hampshire, where state legislators make only $100 a year (less than .1 percent of the salary of a member of Congress), and serve each January through June, falls at the bottom of this list. As figure 7.3 suggests, North Carolina lies near the middle, with a score of .149 (15 percent as professional as Congress). North Carolina's legislators make $13,951[2] and have the thirtieth-most staffers per legislator. The legislature convenes in early January, but there is no formal limit on session length. Odd-numbered years are considered to be regular sessions, and even-numbered years are short sessions, but strangely enough, no rule prevents the short session from being longer than the long session. North Carolina's legislators have voted on adding a formal limit on session length, but such a measure has never passed.

FIGURE 7.3. Comparing Professionalism and Outside Careers in State Legislatures, 1998

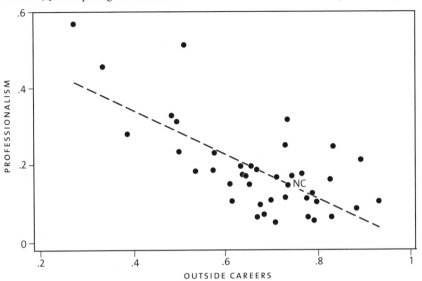

Sources: Squire (2000); Maddox (2004).

The variations in professionalism produce a number of other incentives for candidates and legislators. Because of the low salary, few individuals in New Hampshire can afford to quit their day jobs when they enter the state legislature. A legislator in California, however, serves year-round and is paid almost $100,000 per year, making it neither advantageous nor feasible to hold a second job. The Y axis of figure 7.3 presents the proportion of the legislature that holds outside employment (Maddox 2004).

The line's downward trend shows the that the relationship between professionalism and outside careers is negative, suggesting that legislators in more professional bodies are less likely to hold outside employment. While 27 percent of California legislators have outside careers, 93 percent of legislators in a relatively unprofessional state such as Indiana pursue careers outside the legislature. Given North Carolina's legislative salary, it is not surprising that almost three-quarters of North Carolina state legislators hold outside employment, the fourteenth-highest percentage among the forty-one states for which data are available.

Term limits are perhaps the most obvious institutional influence on turnover rates. Fifteen states have now placed limits, generally via public referendum, on the number of terms that a legislator can serve (National Conference of State Legislatures 2006). While North Carolina has not adopted term limits, it is instructive to examine how the use of term limits could change the composition and operation of the North Carolina legislature.

As one might expect, term limits lead to more legislative turnover. Gary Moncrief, Richard Niemi, and Lynda Powell (2004, 377) find that "the presence of an implemented term limit law increases turnover by an average of 18 to 19 percentage points." In a legislature like North Carolina's, which has traditionally experienced a turnover rate of around 30 percent, term limits could put that number in excess of 50 percent.

Many observers expected that term limits would have other effects on the composition of the legislature. Conventional wisdom might suggest that the person who is willing to spend time, money, and other resources to run for a temporary office differs substantially from someone who is willing to run for an office that could span multiple decades. Thus far, the data do not support this hypothesis (Carey et al. 2006). The most extensive study of term limits to date concluded that people elected in term-limited and non-term-limited states do not differ demographically or politically. According to John Carey, Richard Niemi, and Lynda Powell (2000, 39), "Few if any changes in demographic representation occurred in the immediate aftermath of the adoption of term limits." The authors continue with a prediction for the future: "The most likely scenario is that over the next decade, there will be increasing numbers of new faces in the state capitols of term-limited states, but the new faces will look remarkably like those they have replaced."

District structure is the final institutional component that affects turnover as well as the characteristics of the people who serve. While most state legislators elect their members in traditional single-member districts, some states still elect legislators in multimember districts, where more than one candidate is chosen in each district. In these elections, voters are instructed to choose two or more candidates from a slate of potential nominees.

North Carolina elected a large number of legislators through multimember district systems through the mid-1980s. When multimember districts are present, constituents are less likely to be able to identify their legislators. Because name recognition is lower, it stands to reason that multimember districts would increase legislative turnover. Moncrief, Niemi and Powell (2004) find that multimember districts produce about 3.9 percent greater turnover than their single-member-district counterparts. While North Carolina no longer uses multimember districts, their effects still reverberate throughout the state's legislature.

❖ Power inside the Institution

After legislators are elected to office, they seek power inside the institution. With power comes many advantages, including the ability to affect legislation, increased media attention, and a higher presence on the national political stage. Some legislators gain power behind the scenes, but most take the most direct path to power—a leadership position in the institution.

Legislative leaders can block or pass legislation through coalition building on either side of the partisan divide. They serve as the de facto spokespersons for the legislature, their party, and oftentimes the entire lawmaking side of state government. They may also serve as mentors for rising political stars while increasing their own political stock (Jewell and Whicker 1994).

Both the North Carolina House and the Senate have eight major elected leadership positions, about average across the country. Senate leaders include the president (who is always the lieutenant governor), president pro tem, majority leader, majority whip, majority caucus chair, minority leader, minority whip, and minority caucus chair. The House leadership looks remarkably similar, but the president and president pro tem are replaced by the speaker and speaker pro tem. Other states may have many more leadership positions (for example, Connecticut, which has forty-nine in the House alone), or far fewer (Louisiana, which has two) (Squire and Hamm 2005).

The speaker of the House is one of the few offices that exists in all state legislatures, making it a particularly important office to consider. Judging by power of appointment, control over committees, the available resources, the legislative procedures in place, and tenure in office, North Carolina has the fourteenth-most-powerful speaker in the nation (Clucas 2001). Joe Hackney (D–Chapel Hill) held the position during the 2007–8 session.

As in most states, leadership positions in North Carolina are typically filled by the party caucus. In the House, only the speaker and speaker pro tem are elected by the entire body. In the Senate, the lieutenant governor serves as the president of the chamber, while the entire Senate elects the president pro tem.

Within each party, some signs indicate that the most effective legislators are the ones who move into leadership positions and onto powerful committees. Gerard Padro I. Miquel and James M. Snyder (2006) find that a relatively ineffective legislator in North Carolina has a .22 probability of being appointed to a powerful committee, while an effective legislator has a .31 probability, an increase of 50 percent.

Each chamber also includes a number of minor leadership positions, the most obvious of which is committee chair. Each of the twenty-two standing committees in the Senate and thirty-two in the House has a chair. In North Carolina, the president pro tem both appoints the committee chairs and determines the composition of each committee in the Senate, while the House process is governed by the speaker. Most states employ similar systems.

Given the political party's important role in committee assignments and leadership positions, party control is a vital component of legislative power. All else being equal, legislators who find themselves in the majority can expect to wield more power in the institution than their counterparts in the minority. As Charles Prysby's essay in this volume recounts, North Carolina tends to be controlled by Democrats at the state level, and the state legislature is no exception. As of 2006, Democrats held a twenty-nine–twenty-one lead in the Senate and a sixty-three–fifty-seven lead in the House.

Of course, leadership positions are not the only path to power. Some legislators become powerful and effective lawmakers without gaining leadership positions. North Carolina has one of the best available data sources for assessing power and effectiveness. During each legislative session since 1977, the nonprofit N.C. Center for Public Policy Research has published a ranking of the most effective legislators. The data are collected from surveys sent to state legislators, lobbyists, and Capitol news correspondents and give us a fairly nonpartisan and objective look at what makes a North Carolina legislator effective and powerful.

Previous work on legislative effectiveness (analyzing data through 1992) reveals that the number of bills introduced and the amount of time served in the legislature are strong predictors of legislative effectiveness (Miquel and Snyder 2006). This research also finds that effectiveness has important implications for the future of a legislator's career. More effective legislators are likely to get elected to higher office sooner and more easily.

Tables 7.3–7.5 present a series of cross-tabs testing the effects of tenure, sex, and party affiliation on effectiveness in the lower house of the N.C. General Assembly. To make the data easily interpretable, the effectiveness scores are divided into two categories. Legislators in the top half of effectiveness are coded 1, while legislators in the bottom half are coded 0. Legislators who have served fewer than the mean number of terms (4.2 terms) are coded as less experienced, and those above the mean are coded as experienced. Sex is coded as male/female and party affiliation is coded as Republican/Democrat.

Effectiveness appears along the rows of each of the tables and the relevant predictor (time in office, sex, or party) appears in the columns. The percentages are computed by column. Table 7.3 shows that 57 percent of the legislators who have served more than the average number of terms are in the top half of effectiveness, verses 45 percent of the legislators who have served fewer terms. Table 7.4 suggests that gender may also be an important predictor of effectiveness. Two-thirds of female legislators are in the top half of effectiveness, while less than half of male legislators are considered effective. Finally, table 7.5 demonstrates that party may also exert some influence on effectiveness, as two-thirds of Democrats but only one-third of Republicans are in the top half of effectiveness. This effect likely re-

TABLE 7.3. Effect of Time in Office on Effectiveness in N.C. General Assembly

	Less than Average Terms	More than Average Terms	Total
Less effective	50 (55%)	20 (43%)	60 (50%)
Effective	33 (45%)	27 (57%)	60 (50%)
Total	73 (100%)	47 (100%)	120 (100%)

Source: N.C. Center for Public Policy Research (2005).

TABLE 7.4. Effect of Gender on Effectiveness in N.C. General Assembly

	Female	Male	Total
Less effective	13 (41%)	47 (53%)	60 (50%)
Effective	19 (66.67%)	41 (47%)	60 (50%)
Total	32 (100%)	88 (100%)	120 (100%)

Source: N.C. Center for Public Policy Research (2005).

TABLE 7.5. Effect of Party on Effectiveness in N.C. General Assembly

	Republican	Democrat	Total
Less effective	39 (68%)	21 (33%)	60 (50%)
Effective	18 (32%)	42 (67%)	60 (50%)
Total	57 (100%)	63 (100%)	120 (100%)

Source: N.C. Center for Public Policy Research (2005).

sults from a history of Democratic control of the legislature rather than from an independent effect of party.

While instructive, these cross-tabs may hide some important relationships. To test these relationships more rigorously, I conducted a multiple regression (not shown) where the dependent variable represents the effectiveness ranking (between 1 and 120) and the independent variables represent sex, party, and time in office. This regression allows us to test whether these relationships remain statistically significant after other variables are controlled for.

The regression results suggest that party and time in office are both statistically significant and robust relationships, whereas sex is not significant after other factors are controlled for and the full range of effectiveness is considered. In fact, the average Democratic state legislator is about thirty-two places higher on the effectiveness scale than the average Republican, holding gender and time in office constant. Likewise, for each term in office, a legislator can expect to move up about two and a half places on the effectiveness ranking, holding sex and party constant.

❖ Passing Policy

In addition to achieving reelection and gaining power inside the institution, legislators want to create good public policy. They do so primarily by moving legislation through the chamber and via bureaucratic oversight.

LEGISLATIVE VOTE CHOICE

In the 1997–98 legislative session, North Carolina legislators introduced 3,370 bills and enacted 758, a per-member average of 19.8 introductions and 4.5 enactments and an average of 1.7 enacted bills per day. To put these numbers in perspective, the U.S. House averages .8 enactments per member. Among the states, the North Carolina legislature falls near the middle. The average state enacts 5.7 bills per member, with a high of 17 in California to a low of 1 in Vermont (*Book of the States* 2006).

Hidden in the consideration of overall bill passage rates are thousands of individual voting decisions. Vote choice by individual legislators in North Carolina may appear chaotic, but it is actually fairly systematic and can be predicted quite well by considering the influence of partisanship, constituency pressure, and personal opinion as well as the influence of other legislators, interest groups, the media, and the governor.

Partisanship. Party identification is the most obvious and robust factor affecting voting behavior. Any analysis of voting patterns in the North Carolina state legislature reveals that Democrats tend to vote with Democrats and Republicans tend to vote with Republicans. Although exceptions to this trend occur, parties in the North Carolina legislature provide ready-made coalitions on most issues.

A common question about "party effects" asks whether party voting patterns result from party affiliation or from ideology. After all, North Carolina Democrats might vote together because they share ideology, not because party exerts a separate and unique effect. Two recent articles inform our discussion of party, and while they do not focus specifically on North Carolina, the findings apply to the Tar Heel State.

Gerald C. Wright and Brian F. Schaffner's (2002) comparison of voting patterns in the nonpartisan Nebraska legislature and the partisan legislature in Kansas demonstrates that without official party labels, voting patterns vary considerably by bill. Even beyond serving as a label for people of similar ideologies, party provides an important structure to voting patterns. Jeffery A. Jenkins's (1999) work comparing the nonpartisan Confederate House of Representatives to the partisan U.S. House demonstrates similar results—party, even when separated from ideology, affects vote choice in significant ways.

Constituency Pressure. Almost every study of legislative voting behavior suggests that next to party affiliation, constituent opinion is perhaps the most important influence on how a legislator votes. For example, although State Senator David Hoyle is a Democrat, he represents a fairly Republican district in North Carolina (a district where only 33 percent of the voters voted for Al Gore in the 2000 election) and is therefore extremely unlikely to vote with the Democratic Party as often as his Democratic colleague David Weinstein, who represents the most Democratic district in the state (Guillory 2003).

In North Carolina, much of the constituency effect can be seen by examining long-standing regional differences in public opinion. Legislators from the eastern part of the state are likely to introduce and vote for bills aimed to help the agricultural industry. Likewise, legislators from the mountains may seek policies to help bolster the tourism dollars that flow to that part of the state. In his analysis of voting patterns from 1987 to 1997, Paul Luebke (1998, 53) finds that even when holding party constant, region exerts a separate and independent influence. He explains,

> Democrats from the western Piedmont and Coastal Plain were most likely
> to adopt traditionalist positions. Democrats from the metro Piedmont and
> from other North Carolina cities tended to support modernizer policies as
> well as the occasional populist political initiative. Modernizer Democrats
> hailed from every region of the state, but they were the most common in
> the metro Piedmont counties along Interstate 85.

Of course, all legislators are not equally subject to constituency pressure. Some state-level institutions lead legislators to follow constituent opinion more than others. For example, in term-limited states, when legislators do not face the prospect of reelection, they have less incentive to respond to constituents and may make decisions more independently (Carey et al. 2006). The lack of reelection incentives leads to a form of democracy somewhat closer to the trustee model of representation, where legislators believe that they are put into office to make decisions on behalf of the common good or statewide interests. This approach offers a direct contrast to the delegate model of representation, where legislators believe that they are put in office to follow the direct wishes of their constituents (Rosenthal 1998). Similarly, in multimember districts, legislators do not have to respond to the average voter, making them more likely to move to the extremes (Richardson, Russell, and Cooper 2004).

Personal Opinion. Legislators do not arrive in the legislature as blank slates. In addition to party and constituency pressures, they are also affected by their personal predispositions and individual circumstances. Although there is relatively little work on how legislators are affected by personal factors, a recent study by Barry C. Burden (2007) suggests that legislators cannot be separated from their pasts. For example, Burden finds convincing evidence that smokers vote differently on tobacco issues than do nonsmokers, even after controlling for a host of other factors. In North Carolina, like most other states, there is little doubt that personal habits and opinions affect what a legislator considers good public policy.

Other Legislators. One common thread among legislative bodies is the need for coalition building. A legislator acting in isolation cannot pass policy or further an agenda. Political party is probably the most important ready-made coalition, but it is not the only one. Legislators are social beings and depend on other legislators to gather information and enact policy. Luebke's book on North Carolina politics highlights this important trend. When he wrote the first edition of his book (published in 1990), Luebke was a sociologist with an interest in politics. By the time he wrote the second edition (published in 1998), he had also served in the North Carolina House. When asked the biggest insight he gained from his insider's perspective, he replied, "As an academic outsider I had misunderstood the importance of personal relationships" (1998, x). Systematic studies of legislative voting behavior show similar trends. Laura W. Arnold, Rebecca D. Deen, and Samuel C. Patterson (2000) find that personal friendships exert an important influence on legislative voting behavior, even after controlling for a laundry list of other factors. Some evidence even indicates that legislators are more likely to vote in accord with legislators who sit close to them on the chamber floor (Masket 2006).

Interest Groups. As Adam Newmark's essay in this volume explains, interest groups and lobbyists use various means to attempt to influence a legislator's view of what constitutes good public policy. The most obvious tactic is directly contacting legislators. When lobbyists contact legislators, their common currency is information. Legislators are overwhelmed and rarely keep up with every issue on the legislative agenda. Particularly in a state such as North Carolina, which has limited legislative staff, legislators often rely on others in the policy community to provide information and help make decisions. Interest groups and lobbyists are happy to assist. While they certainly supply "interested information" that presents their point of view in a positive light, the information they supply is almost always correct. If it were not, lobbyists would lose influence and credibility with legislators.

Lobbyists also try to affect media coverage to influence public opinion and in turn legislative vote choice (Cooper, Nownes, and Johnson 2007). Legislators may find indirect lobbying, as this practice is known, more complicated than direct lobbying, but it is often quite effective. By using both indirect and direct means of lobbying, lobbyists and interest groups in North Carolina help shape the agenda and influence legislative vote choice.

One particularly well-known North Carolina lobbyist is John Hood of the John Locke Foundation. Hood (also discussed in Ferrel Guillory's essay in this volume) and his organization engage in both inside and outside lobbying. Like all good lobbyists, Hood and the John Locke Foundation attempt to influence legislators by direct contact. They approach legislators in the halls of the Capitol and on the streets of Raleigh to push information and work to convince legislators of his organization's views. Hood also uses indirect lobbying by writing policy reports and other publications he hopes will be read by the media and by interested publics. If Hood can raise the awareness of any of his issues, he will be better able to influence legislators' opinions about what constitutes good public policy.

The Media. As Ferrel Guillory's essay in this volume discusses in more detail, newspaper reporters, television journalists, and increasingly bloggers and nontraditional journalists are also important influences on the legislative agenda. State legislators understand public opinion primarily through what they read in the media (Herbst 1996). If journalists and editorial page writers print stories about a particular issue, legislators will likely respond. The *Raleigh News and Observer's* Rob Christensen is known as a particularly important journalist. What he writes certainly affects the legislative agenda as well as individual legislators' vote choices. While this influence may be obvious, journalists also affect the legislative agenda through their informal relationships with legislators (Cooper and Johnson 2006). North Carolina's delegation of Capitol reporters includes a number of well-respected and experienced figures who have influence with legislators even beyond what is written in the paper or reported on television.

The Governor. Not very long ago, occupants of the office of governor were sarcastically referred to as good-time Charlies and were thought to be political figures that were neither particularly qualified nor skilled at lawmaking. Fortunately, this view of governors is disappearing. Governors today are skilled politicians and influential actors in state and national politics. In fact, mere mentions of policy items by the governor may shift legislative agendas and legislative decision making (Ferguson 1996). As Jack D. Fleer's essay in this volume suggests, North Carolina's governors are no different. Since the mid-1990s, they have also enjoyed the power to veto bills that are not to their liking. Legislators in North Carolina who work at cross-purposes with the governor may encounter difficulty in passing policy.

BUREAUCRATIC OVERSIGHT

Most scholarly literature and popular attention focuses on how legislators achieve their desired public policy outcomes through the legislative process, but a second, extremely important, means of accomplishing the same ends is through bureaucratic oversight. The seventeen state departments pass many important rules that have the force of law. For example, the Department of Agriculture and Consumer Services creates rules that determine who can and cannot operate an animal shelter. The Department and Environment and Natural Resources levies fines on individuals and businesses that harm water quality, and the Department of Transportation determines how long a driver's license is valid.

The state legislature still has a number of weapons in its arsenal to watch over and influence the bureaucracy, including the power to approve many agency heads, the power to affect the creation and termination of agencies, and perhaps most importantly, significant power over the budget (Elling 2004). In North Carolina, legislators may introduce bills to fight a rule created by the bureaucracy and approved by the rules review commission (*Book of the States* 2006, 130).

Of course, state legislatures vary in their capacity to perform bureaucratic oversight. Professional states have a greater capacity to adequately oversee the bureaucracy, removing much of the power to govern from the agency itself and placing it squarely in the legislature (Potoski and Woods 2001).

❖ Conclusion

A quick read of the headlines may suggest that legislative behavior is unpredictable, but this essay has argued that much legislative behavior is often quite predictable. From the election cycle to legislators' ability to gain power to voting patterns, much of legislative behavior can be understood, if not predicted, by considering both institutional context and individual legislator characteristics.

In addition to demonstrating that legislative behavior is more systematic than the headlines may suggest, this essay has highlighted the legislature's ability to change. The North Carolina state legislature has altered institutions, eliminating multimember districts, increasing professionalism, and becoming more careerist. As the institutions have changed, so have the people occupying the legislature. The representation of women and minorities is increasing. In addition, the occupational makeup has shifted. Gone are the days of the farmer-legislator. Today's legislators in Raleigh are more comfortable in courtrooms and classrooms than in the fields.

The institution retains a number of important challenges in the years to come, foremost among them the question of how to deal with an increasing workload while staffing, salary, and session length pose challenges to efficient operations. While the legislature has become more inclusive, much room remains for forward movement in electing women and minorities to office.

The North Carolina legislature was designed to be a representative body; for it to work properly, not only must the legislature itself and its occupants change and evolve but so must the way the citizens of North Carolina view and interact with their legislature. With frequent headlines reminding citizens of scandal, it is easy to feel less efficacious toward the state legislature. While some skepticism may be healthy, citizens of the Tar Heel State must work harder to educate themselves about their legislature and remember that most legislators are not unethical but rather are good public servants whose behaviors are influenced by their context and surroundings.

❖ Notes

1. For those interested in a historical perspective, data on state legislator occupation from 1971 to 2005 can be found in Guillory (2006).

2. This does not include additional benefits such as retirement. North Carolina legislatures receive a competitive retirement plan, including a 7 percent employee contribution rate (*Book of the States* 2006).

❖ References

Arceneaux, Kevin. 2001. "The 'Gender Gap' in State Legislative Representation: New Data to Tackle an Old Question." *Political Research Quarterly* 54:143–60.

Arnold, Laura W., Rebecca D. Deen, and Samuel C. Patterson. 2000. "Friendship and Votes: The Impact of Interpersonal Ties on Legislative Decision Making." *State and Local Government Review* 32:142–47.

Atkeson, Lonna Rae. 2003. "Not All Cues Are Created Equal: The Conditional Impact of Female Candidates on Political Engagement." *Journal of Politics* 65:1040–61.

Bass, Jack, and Walter DeVries. 1995 [1976]. *The Transformation of Southern Politics: Social Change and Political Consequence since 1945.* Athens: University of Georgia Press.

Beyle, Thad. 2002. "2002 North Carolina Election Primer." *North Carolina DataNet* 32:1–12.

Black Elected Officials: A National Roster. 2001. Washington, D.C.: Joint Center for Political and Economic Development.

The Book of the States. 2006. Lexington, Ky.: Council of State Governments.

Bositis, David A. 2001. *Black Elected Officials: A Statistical Summary.* Washington, D.C.: Joint Center for Political and Economic Studies.

Brace, Paul, Kellie Sims-Butler, Kevin Arceneaux, and Martin Johnson. 2002. "Public Opinion in the American States: New Perspectives Using National Data." *American Journal of Political Science* 46:173–89.

Burden, Barry C. 2007. *The Personal Roots of Representation.* Princeton: Princeton University Press.

Carey, John, Richard Niemi, and Lynda Powell. 2000. *Term Limits in the State Legislatures.* Ann Arbor: University of Michigan Press.

Carey, John, Richard Niemi, Lynda Powell, and Gary Moncrief. 2006. "Term Limits in the State Legislatures: Results from a New Survey of 50 States." *Legislative Studies Quarterly* 31:105–36.

Carroll, Susan J. 1994. *Women as Candidates in American Politics.* 2nd ed. Bloomington: Indiana University Press.

Center for American Women and Politics. 2005. *Women State Legislators: Leadership Positions and Committee Chairs 2005.* New Brunswick, N.J.: Eagleton Institute of Politics, Rutgers University.

————. 2007. *CAWP Fact Sheet: Women in State Legislatures.* New Brunswick, N.J.: Eagleton Institute of Politics, Rutgers University.

Clucas, Richard A. 2001. "Principal-Agent Theory and the Power of State House Speakers." *Legislative Studies Quarterly* 26:319–38.

Cooper, Christopher A., and Martin Johnson. 2006. "Politics and the Press Corps: Reporters, State Legislative Institutions, and Context." Paper presented at the annual meeting of the American Political Science Association, Washington, D.C.

Cooper, Christopher A., Anthony J. Nownes, and Martin Johnson. 2007. "Interest Groups and Journalists in the States." *State Politics and Policy Quarterly* 7:39–53.

Elling, Richard C. 2004. "Administering State Programs: Performance and Politics." In *Politics in the American States: A Comparative Analysis*, 8th ed., edited by Virginia Gray and Russell Hanson, 261–89. Washington, D.C.: CQ Press.

Fenno, Richard. 1973. *Congressmen in Committees.* New York: Scott Foresman.

Ferguson, Margaret. 1996. "Gubernatorial Policy Leadership in the Fifty States." Ph.D. diss., University of North Carolina.

Fleer, Jack. 1994. *North Carolina Government and Politics*. Lincoln: University of Nebraska Press.

Guillory, Ferrel. 2003. "North Carolina General Assembly Elections, 2002." *North Carolina DataNet* 34:9–11.

———. 2006. "Look at the Legislature: Who Serves." *North Carolina DataNet* 40:6–7, 12.

Hardin, John. 1994. "Rating North Carolina Public Institutions and Elected Officials." *North Carolina DataNet* 4:6–7.

Haynie, Kerry. 2001. *African American Legislators in the American States*. New York: Columbia University Press.

Herbst, Susan. 1996. *Reading Public Opinion: How Political Actors View the Democratic Process*. Chicago: University of Chicago Press.

Holbrook, Thomas, and Charles Tidmarch. 1991. "Sophomore Surge in State Legislative Elections, 1968–1986." *Legislative Studies Quarterly* 16:49–63.

Hunter, Kathleen. 2004. "Evenly Split Legislatures No Longer Rare." <www.stateline.org>. Accessed September 13, 2007.

Jenkins, Jeffery A. 1999. "Examining the Bonding Effects of Party: A Comparative Analysis of Roll-Call Voting in the U.S. and Confederate Houses." *American Journal of Political Science* 43:1144–65.

Jewell, Malcolm E., and Marcia Lynn Whicker. 1994. *Legislative Leadership in the American States*. Ann Arbor: University of Michigan Press.

Kane, Dan, and J. Andrew Curliss. 2007a. "Decker Gets 4 Years, Fine for Payoffs." *Raleigh News and Observer*, April 28. <http://www.newsobserver.com/1179/story/568656.html>. Accessed June 15, 2007.

———. 2007b. "Defiant Geddings Gets 4 Years." *Raleigh News and Observer*, May 8. <http://www.newsobserver.com/114/story/571936.html>. Accessed May 30, 2007.

Luebke, Paul. 1990. *Tar Heel Politics: Myths and Realities*. Chapel Hill: University of North Carolina Press.

———. 1998. *Tar Heel Politics 2000*. Chapel Hill: University of North Carolina Press.

Maddox, Jerome. 2004. "Working outside the House (and Senate): Outside Careers as an Indicator of Professionalism in American State Legislatures." *State Politics and Policy Quarterly* 4:211–26.

Maestas, Cherie. 2003 "The Incentive to Listen: Progressive Ambition, Resources, and Opinion Monitoring among State Legislators." *Journal of Politics* 65:439–56.

Masket, Seth. 2006. "Where You Sit Is Where You Stand: Measuring the Impact of Seating Proximity on Legislative Voting." Paper presented at the annual conference on State Politics and Policy, Lubbock, Texas.

Miquel, Gerard Padro I., and James M. Snyder. 2006. "Legislative Effectiveness and Legislative Life." *Legislative Studies Quarterly* 31:347–81.

Moncrief, Gary, Richard Niemi, and Lynda Powell. 2004. "Time, Term Limits, and Turnover: Trends in Membership Stability in U.S. State Legislatures." *Legislative Studies Quarterly* 24:357–81.

Mooney, Christopher Z. 1995. "Measuring U.S. State Legislative Professionalism: An Evaluation of Five Indices." *State and Local Government Review* 26:70–78.

————. 2001. "State Politics and Policy Quarterly and the Study of State Politics: The Editor's Introduction." *State Politics and Policy Quarterly* 1:1–4.

National Conference of State Legislatures. 2006. "The Term Limited States." <http://www.ncsl.org/programs/legismgt/about/states.htm>. Accessed September 13, 2007.

Owens, Chris T. 2005. "Black Substantive Representation in State Legislatures: 1971–1994." *Social Science Quarterly* 86:779–91.

Potoski, Matthew, and Neal D. Woods. 2001. "Designing State Clean Air Agencies: Administrative Procedures and Bureaucratic Autonomy." *Journal of Public Administration Research and Theory* 11:203–22.

Richardson, Lilliard E., and Patricia K. Freeman. 1995. "Gender Differences in Representation among State Legislators." *Political Research Quarterly* 48:169–79.

Richardson, Lilliard E., Brian E. Russell, and Christopher A. Cooper. 2004. "Legislative Representation in a Single-Member versus Multi-Member District System: The Arizona State Legislature." *Political Research Quarterly* 57:337–44.

Robertson, Gary D. 2007. "Black Enters Plea in State Court." *Greensboro News and Record*, February 20. <http://www.newsobserver.com/1179/story/568656.html>. Accessed June 15, 2007.

Rosenthal, Alan. 1998. *The Decline of Representative Democracy*. Washington, D.C.: CQ Press.

Squire, Peverill. 2000. "Uncontested Seats in State Legislative Elections." *Legislative Studies Quarterly* 25:131–46.

Squire, Peverill, and Keith Hamm. 2005. *101 Chambers: Congress, State Legislatures, and the Future of Legislative Studies*. Columbus: Ohio State University Press.

Thomas, Sue. 1991. "The Impact of Women on State Legislative Policies." *Journal of Politics* 53:958–76.

————. 1994. *How Women Legislate*. New York: Oxford University Press.

Thomas, Sue, and Susan Welch. 1991. "The Impact of Gender on Activities and Priorities of State Legislators." *Western Political Quarterly* 44:445–56.

Wright, Gerald C., and Brian F. Schaffner. 2002. "The Influence of Party: Evidence from the State Legislatures." *American Political Science Review* 96:367–90.

❖ 8. North Carolina's Judicial System

The Forgotten Branch of Government

RUTH ANN STRICKLAND

In U.S. politics, the judiciary has often taken a backseat to the executive and leg-islative branches of government. Legislators serve as the peoples' representatives, developing and amending rules and regulations. Similarly, executives have a hand in both lawmaking and the day-to-day administration of government, holding an elevated position in the public consciousness. Lost in this political cacophony is the judicial branch. This situation is unfortunate, given the judiciary's central role in politics and the courts' importance in shaping politics and policy across the American states. The state courts, especially state supreme courts, play a major role in policymaking and rule on issues ranging from education policy and equal opportunity to criminal procedure and voting rights. For an example of the policy influence of the N.C. Supreme Court, see figure 8.1.

This essay compares North Carolina's judicial branch to those in other states, beginning with an outline of the historical development of the judicial structure in the Tar Heel State. The essay also outlines the contemporary organizational structure in North Carolina and compares this structure to the organizational fea-tures of other states. Following these comparisons, the essay turns to the issues of judicial selection and the contours of judicial campaigns. After discussing politics and campaigns, the essay turns to budgeting and court funding before concluding with an examination of the ever-important role of diversity in the North Carolina judiciary.

What emerges from this essay is a picture of a judiciary that has been adaptable, open to change, and in many cases quite innovative. At the same time, however, the North Carolina judiciary is haunted by a lack of diversity and a tendency toward political infighting.

❖ Historical Development of North Carolina's Judicial Structure

Before major court reform took place during the 1960s, hundreds of courts existed in North Carolina, including domestic relations courts, mayor's courts, county courts, recorder's courts, and justices of the peace. Created by the General Assem-bly, these courts were set up to meet the localized needs of the towns and coun-ties they served. Some courts ran full time, while others operated sporadically,

FIGURE 8.1. Access to an Adequate Education and State Financing Responsibilities

Leandro v. State of North Carolina, 346 NC 336 (1997)

Arguing that low-income school districts had not provided their schoolchildren with an adequate education due to inadequate funding, the low-income school districts sued the state of North Carolina in *Leandro*. Although the North Carolina Constitution holds that the state is obligated to provide a "general and uniform system of free public schools" with equal opportunities given to all students, the N.C. Supreme Court held that the state's constitution does not require equal funding of all school districts. However, the Court in *Leandro* found that every student has a right to a sound basic education and that the state is obligated to provide adequate funding in pursuit of this goal. The Court even specified what a "sound basic education" should be, including the following:

(1) sufficient ability to read, write, and speak the English language and sufficient knowledge of fundamental mathematics and physical science to enable the student to function in a complex and rapidly changing society;

(2) sufficient fundamental knowledge of geography, history, and basic economic and political systems to enable the student to make informed choices with regard to issues that affect the student personally or affect the student's community, state, and nation;

(3) sufficient academic and vocational skills to enable the student to successfully engage in postsecondary education or vocational training; and

(4) sufficient academic and vocational skills to enable the student to compete on an equal basis with others in further formal education or gainful employment in contemporary society.

Leandro began a conversation about the adequacy of state school funding, particularly in low-income school districts where funding comes primarily from property taxes. This case also established that North Carolina schoolchildren have educational rights that the judicial branch will monitor and protect. *Leandro* changed the landscape of educational policy and has resulted in other disputes as school districts continue to litigate for their students' needs.

conducting business only for short periods each week. Some judges were trained attorneys, whereas others were laypersons who devoted most of their time to other careers. Judges' salaries and the administrative costs of court operations varied from court to court, sometimes even within a single county. Some court officials were compensated by the fees they levied and provided their own offices and facilities (*North Carolina Manual* 2001–2).

Under this decentralized system, the Supreme Court (the appellate court) and the Superior Court (general jurisdiction trial court) were funded by the state, while lower courts were funded by towns, cities, and counties. The sheer number of courts and the practice whereby some justices of the peace received fees based on findings of guilt led to reforms (*Judicial System* 2005).

In 1955, a number of citizens called for a professionalization of North Carolina's judicial system, with reforms such as full-time salaried judges and more centralized state control. In a 1962 referendum, the state's citizens supported an amendment authorizing a radical overhaul of the judicial branch. In 1965, the General Assembly approved recommendations for a new court structure and established the conditions set forth in Article 4 of the North Carolina Constitution (*North Carolina Manual* 2001–2). (See figure 8.2 for a detailed description of North Carolina's General Court of Justice.)

One recommendation urged the creation of an intermediate appellate court to assist the overburdened Supreme Court. Furthermore, reformers sought to amend Article 4 to establish a unified statewide and state-operated judicial system consisting of the Appellate Division, the Superior Court Division, and the District Court Division. Both reforms were accepted, and the judicial branch now contains two trial divisions, the District Court and the Superior Court, and two appellate levels, the Court of Appeals and the Supreme Court. Counties had previously controlled funding of the courts, but under the new model, the state assumed responsibility for funding and administering almost all court operations. Counties retain some responsibilities, such as providing and maintaining courthouses. Some municipalities that have additional district court seats because of high caseloads continue to provide court facilities as well. Key characteristics of North Carolina's unified court system include centralized budgeting, standardized rulemaking, state funding for all court officials and prosecutors, a uniform fee structure, and centralized administration by the Administrative Office of the Courts. For example, all court personnel are now paid by the state and the Administrative Office of the Courts, and the chief justice of the Supreme Court develops one budget for the whole judicial system (Brannon 2001).

❖ Contemporary Organizational Structure of the North Carolina Courts

The Supreme Court is North Carolina's court of last resort and hears civil and criminal cases on appeal. While a combination of civil and criminal cases arise in all states, the North Carolina judiciary sees a greater percentage of criminal cases—almost 70 percent—than any other state in the country. Even more striking is the fact that more than 90 percent of these criminal cases are murder cases. Conversely, only about 31 percent of cases decided by the N.C. Supreme Court are

FIGURE 8.2. N.C. General Court of Justice

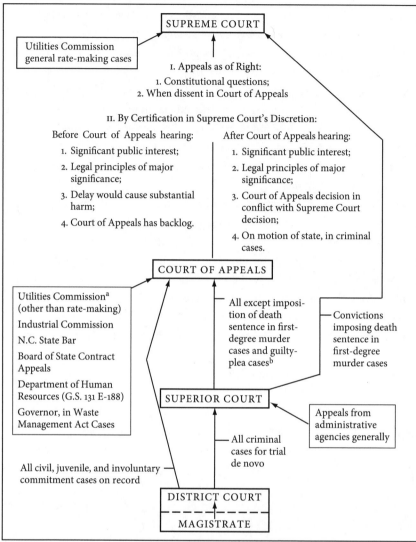

Source: Reprinted with permission of the School of Government, © 2004. This copyrighted material may not be reproduced in whole or in part without the express written permission of the School of Government, CB#3330 UNC Chapel Hill, Chapel Hill, NC 27599-3330; telephone, 919-966-4119; fax, 919-962-2707; Web site, <www.sog.unc.edu>.

[a]Appeals from the agencies must be heard by the Court of Appeals before the Supreme Court can hear them.

[b]Postconviction-hearing appeals and reviews of valuation of exempt property under G.S. Ch. 1c are final with the Court of Appeals.

classified as civil, the smallest proportion in the country (Brace and Hall 2005, 186–87).

The chief justice and the six associate justices of the Supreme Court are elected for eight-year terms in nonpartisan elections. The Supreme Court's only original case jurisdiction involves censure and removal of judges after a nonbinding recommendation from the Judicial Standards Commission. The court's jurisdiction encompasses all cases involving constitutional questions. It may review Court of Appeals cases involving issues of public interest or cases of major importance and criminal cases on appeal by right from the superior courts. All first-degree homicide convictions involving death row sentences automatically go to the Supreme Court for review. Automatic review may also occur in N.C. Utilities Commission general rate cases. The Court may grant discretionary review and hear appeals directly from trial courts in cases that involve a substantial public interest or significant legal principles or in instances where delay in hearing a case would result in substantial harm (*North Carolina Manual* 2001–2). The Supreme Court sits only en banc, meaning that all its members must be present on each case, and the chief justice presides over oral arguments before the court (*Fiscal Year 2003–2004 Annual Report*).

Established by constitutional amendment in 1965, the other appellate court, the Court of Appeals, consists of fifteen judges elected to eight-year terms in nonpartisan elections. Most of the Court of Appeals's caseload consists of cases appealed from civil and criminal trial courts (although those involving the death penalty go to the Supreme Court). The Court of Appeals also hears cases from the N.C. Industrial Commission and reviews decisions and final orders from various administrative agencies (*North Carolina Manual* 2001–2).

The Court of Appeals hears cases in panels of three judges, facilitating efficiency by allowing the court to hear arguments in separate cases at the same time. The chief justice of the Supreme Court selects a judge to serve as chief judge of the Court of Appeals. The chief judge assigns appellate judges to panels, making sure that all judges sit roughly an equal number of times (*North Carolina Manual* 2001–2).

North Carolina's Superior Court Division consists of forty-seven superior court districts, which serve as trial courts of general jurisdiction, hearing all felony cases and certain misdemeanor cases. Superior courts also have original jurisdiction over civil disputes exceeding ten thousand dollars and hear appeals from most administrative agencies. Superior court jurisdiction, however, does not extend to probate and estate matters, domestic relations, certain matters first heard by the clerk of the superior court, or juvenile cases regardless of the amount of money involved in the controversy.

Superior court judges are constitutionally required to rotate from one district to another in their division. Judges serve in one judicial district for six months and then move to another district. As a result of this rotation system, judges may have to commute up to one hundred miles from their homes or even establish second homes in districts where they temporarily serve. Rotation has given rise to some controversies regarding such issues as the costs of traveling and the problem of "judge-shopping" by attorneys who seek to delay a case or find a judge who they feel is more sympathetic to their case. It may also mean that more than one judge may hear the same case by sitting in on it a different stages. At the same time, some advantages accrue from this system, such as avoiding favoritism that could result from a judge always holding court where he or she lives. This system creates state-wide uniformity in procedure and prevents localized rulemaking (*Judicial System* 2005).

Each district's voters elect its superior court judge, who runs on a nonpartisan basis and serves an eight-year term. The governor appoints thirteen special superior court judges to hold court as needed around the state. These appointed judges may reside in any county but also can be assigned anywhere in the state. A special superior court judge could, theoretically, at least, sit in all one hundred counties at some point. Usually, however, the appointed judges are assigned to counties close to where they live (*Judicial System* 2005).

The jurisdiction of North Carolina's 235 district court judges is complex, as they handle almost all misdemeanor and infraction cases in addition to all juvenile proceedings, mental health commitments, and domestic relations cases. The clerk of superior court holds exclusive jurisdiction over probate of wills and administration of estates and trusts. In other civil matters, superior and district trial divisions share authority. District courts hear civil cases involving ten thousand dollars or less, while the superior courts hear civil cases exceeding ten thousand dollars (*Judicial System* 2005). Civil disputes may be tried before a jury, with appeals available to the Court of Appeals.

Appointed for two-year terms by the senior resident judge, magistrates—judges who hear minor claims—serve under the district court division. They have both civil and criminal jurisdiction. In criminal cases, they issue arrest and search warrants, preside over initial appearances, and set conditions for pretrial release. For relatively minor infractions and misdemeanors, such as traffic, littering, wildlife, boating, and alcoholic beverage violations, they may accept guilty pleas, set punishment, and even preside over trials. Fines charged for these violations are set by a uniform state schedule (*Judicial System* 2005). In civil matters, magistrates may accept guilty pleas in worthless-check cases involving two thousand dollars or less. As of October 1, 2004, they may try small-claims cases involving up to

TABLE 8.1. General Court of Justice Caseload: Case Filings, 1980–2004

Court	1980–81	1987–88	1989–90	2003–4
District courts	1,520,826	2,004,447	2,270,456	2,802,559
Superior courts	82,441	105,704	128,215	334,232
Court of appeals	1,222	1,351	1,408	1,758
Supreme court	231	309	295	182

Sources: For 1980–90, Fleer (1994); for 2003–4, *Fiscal Year 2003–2004 Annual Report.*

five thousand dollars (*Judicial System* 2005). At these simple proceedings, lawyers are usually not present, and the trial occurs before a bench rather than a jury. North Carolina has more than seven hundred magistrates, with at least one in each county (*Fiscal Year 2003–2004 Annual Report*).

The workload of most North Carolina courts has risen steadily. In 1989–90, 2.2 million cases were filed with the district court; in 2003–4, that number rose to 2.8 million. In superior court, 128,215 cases were filed in 1989–90 and 334,232 were filed in 2003–4. The Court of Appeals had 1,408 filings in 1989–90 and 1,758 in 2003–4. Only the Supreme Court experienced a decrease in filings, from 295 in 1989–90 to 182 in 2003–4. Table 8.1 gives the caseloads of the appellate, superior, and district court divisions.

Two specialized courts, family court and drug treatment court, address problems that are best handled outside of the traditional adversarial system. Judges in these two courts dispense therapeutic justice—that is, they try to solve problems through counseling and treatment rather than by levying harsh penalties. Therapeutic justice encourages judges to address the underlying issues that bring families to court or cause drug abuse. Family and drug treatment courts take a holistic approach by attempting to solve the underlying problems that keep recycling people through the system (Sullivan 1999).

Family courts are based in the district court division and first operated in North Carolina in April 1999. They handle divorce, child custody, adoption, and domestic abuse cases. In family court cases, each family is assigned one judge, who hears all issues related to that particular family. Previously, each family issue was treated as a separate case, with different judges randomly assigned to each case. Family courts encourage families to resolve disputes through mediation; having a single judge handle all of the matters involving a particular family enables that judge to see the big picture and to look after the family's overall needs. Former N.C. Supreme Court chief justice Henry E. Frye said that family court is a "kinder, more user-friendly way to deal with families" (Turnbull 1999, 1B). Family court judges rely on case managers, who direct families to community services such as mediation, anger-management counseling, divorce education, and drug counseling.

In North Carolina, drug treatment courts began providing treatment and case-tracking services in 1996. North Carolina operates seventeen adult treatment courts in thirteen judicial districts. The state also has drug courts for juveniles and family drug treatment courts for parents trying to regain custody of their children. Adult defendants who have committed violent felonies in the past five years are not eligible to participate in drug treatment court (Kim 2004).

To be eligible for participation, a defendant must be addicted, must wish to participate, must not be charged with drug trafficking, and must be able to participate in community punishment. The criminal justice workgroup—including the judge, prosecutor, defense attorney, probation officer, community policing officer, treatment provider, and case manager—collaborate in nonadversarial proceedings to ensure that the defendants receive access to appropriate treatment and are held accountable for their actions while in the program. Unlike defendants who plea-bargain or plead guilty on drug offenses and go to jail, drug treatment court participants must stay in treatment, undergo drug tests, attend school or have jobs, perform community service, pay court fees as well as other legal obligations such as child support, and attend frequent court hearings. According to the Administrative Office of the Courts, those who participate in drug treatment courts are less likely to cycle through the courts again (*Judicial System* 2005; Kim 2004).

In 1995, the N.C. Commission on Business Laws and the Economy recommended creation of a special court to handle business litigation ("Commission Recommends" 1995). The N.C. Supreme Court issued a rule that created a special superior court judge for complex business cases. Trying to ease some of the workload of trial courts, business courts are assigned intricate commercial cases that could take weeks before the state's already backlogged Superior Court Division. These complex cases usually include product-liability suits, cases involving numerous corporations, and shareholder litigation. The first state business court began operations in Greensboro and has since expanded to Charlotte and Raleigh (Collins 2005, B1; Weigl 2005, B5). After a case is assigned to business court, one judge will shepherd the case from pretrial to trial. In regular superior court proceedings, by contrast, judges rotate (*Judicial System* 2005).

North Carolina's business courts are among the nation's most technologically sophisticated. They have high-definition television monitors and rostrums equipped with CD-ROM/DVD players, videotape machines, and computer touch-screen technology. Judges typically have two laptop computers, allowing them to control all courtroom technology. Attorneys can use the touch screen to access exhibits and to contact witnesses for videoconferences. Witnesses can use touch-screen technology to highlight important documents. These courtrooms are also equipped for electronic filing of records and automatically update the parties via e-mail about new filings (Nowell 2001). These technological features help judges and attorneys speed up complicated cases and make for greater efficiency in court operations.

North Carolina's court structure has been simplified and consolidated into three tiers. The courts are also managed centrally by the chief justice of the Supreme Court and the Administrative Office of the Courts. Finally, the state puts forward a centralized budget for the courts and finances most court operations. The court system operates uniformly: jurisdiction, procedure, personnel, and costs are the same in all counties and judicial districts. The General Assembly sets uniform court fees and costs for all judicial districts. The courts are more professional because all justices and judges must be admitted to the bar and court personnel are full time and receive salaries and benefits. The increase in professionalization has also occurred because the Judicial Standards Commission set and monitors ethical and professional standards and behavior (Fleer 1994, 133–34).

With the creation of the Administrative Office of the Courts, judges have acquired greater independence and the General Assembly is less likely to micromanage their affairs. The executive branch plays a major role in filling vacancies that occur between elections but is still not involved in the day-to-day management of the courts. The Administrative Office of the Courts enables judges and justices to devote their time to judicial rather than administrative tasks, enhancing the courts' efficiency. Uniform procedures and guidelines enhance fairness and equal treatment under the law (Fleer 1994, 149–50).

Consolidated trial courts make for better judicial accountability and result in more comprehensible and user-friendly institutions. Streamlining the courts has also resulted in a reduction of costs, as all courts use the same stationery, order supplies in bulk, and have less equipment to purchase and maintain. North Carolina courts have experienced a more even distribution of workload, making them more responsive and accountable. With increased staff and cross-training, consolidated courts can respond more quickly to inquiries and cases are disposed of in standard amounts of time (Mikeska 2000, 47–48).

Elsewhere in the United States, some states use general-jurisdiction trial courts to hear and decide cases, whereas others use a multitiered system with general-, limited-, or special-jurisdiction courts. A number of states, like North Carolina, employ specialized courts to meet their unique needs—Colorado, for example, has a water court, and Hawaii has a land court. States have arranged their appellate court structures according to their caseloads. Some states, such as Rhode Island and Vermont, have no intermediate appellate courts, while others, such as North

Carolina and New Jersey, have intermediate appellate courts with primarily mandatory jurisdictions, and still others, including Louisiana and Virginia, have intermediate courts with primarily discretionary jurisdictions. Tennessee and Alabama have two intermediate courts, one for civil appeals and one for criminal appeals. States follow a total of seven different patterns for designing their appellate court structure (Flango and Flango 1997). Minnesota, with only three courts, is clearly among the nation's most consolidated court systems.

Consolidated trial court structures, such as those in New Jersey and North Carolina, generally provide better judicial accountability. Courts structured in this way are more easily understood by the public and are simpler to access and use. Consolidation has been acclaimed for reducing court costs, distributing workloads more evenly, and promoting greater efficiency in case processing (Mikeska 2000, 47–48). However, in states such as New York, court performance may be enhanced by decentralization, which allows the courts to respond to local needs. Table 8.2 illustrates the contrasts in court structure.

❖ Selection of North Carolina Judges and Justices

The selection of judges has changed during the course of North Carolina's history. In 1776, judges were appointed for life by the General Assembly. In 1868, constitutional change mandated that judges be elected in partisan elections for eight-year terms. Governor James B. Hunt created a merit selection panel in 1977 to help him fill vacancies in the Superior Court Division and used this panel until he left office in 1985.

North Carolina gradually moved away from use of partisan elections. Effective in 1998, the General Assembly established nonpartisan elections for superior court judges and provided that they would be elected by voters in each district, rather than statewide. The General Assembly established nonpartisan elections for district court judges in 2002 and two years later provided for the nonpartisan election of Supreme Court and Court of Appeals judges.

The General Assembly has frequently considered bills that would move away from election of appellate judges and toward merit selection. Under a merit-based process, a nonpartisan nominating committee draws up a list of qualified candidates, and the governor appoints someone from the list. The appointed judge then goes up for a noncompetitive retention election in regularly scheduled cycles. Despite support from a sizable minority of North Carolinians, efforts to institute some form of merit selection failed in 1974, 1977, 1989, 1991, 1995 and 1999 (American Judicature Society n.d.).

To qualify for a judgeship in North Carolina, candidates must be at least twenty-

TABLE 8.2. Examples of Differences in Court Organizational Structures

State	Courts
Minnesota	Supreme Court
	Court of Appeals
	District Court
New Jersey	Supreme Court
	Appellate Division of Superior Court
	Superior Court: Civil, Family, General Equity, and Criminal Divisions
	Municipal Court
	Tax Court
New York	Court of Appeals
	Appellate Divisions of Supreme Court
	Supreme Court
	County Court
	Court of Claims
	Surrogates' Court
	City Court
	Family Court
	District Court
	Civil Court of the City of New York
	Criminal Court of the City of New York
	Town and Village Justice Court
North Carolina	Supreme Court
	Court of Appeals
	Superior Court
	District Court
Virginia	Supreme Court
	Court of Appeals
	Circuit Court
	District Court

Source: National Center for State Courts, 2004 State Court Structure Charts, <http://www.ncsconline.org/D_Research/Ct_Struct/Index.html>.

one years old and must be licensed to practice law. The second qualification was added to the North Carolina Constitution in 1981 after a layperson with no judicial experience and no law degree was nominated as a candidate for Supreme Court chief justice. Prior to 1990, when judicial elections were partisan, the great majority of judges were Democrats (Fleer 1994, 140). Since that time, North Carolina's elections—including judicial races—have become increasingly competitive, and being a Democrat is no longer a prerequisite for success in nonpartisan contests. As noted throughout this volume, North Carolina is now a competitive two-party state, and neither political party can take citizen loyalty for granted. Between 1990 and 2000, fourteen separate Supreme Court races took place in six elections: Democratic candidates won eight of the seats, and Republicans won six (Beyle 2002, 10).

Although nonpartisan elections are the official mode of judicial selection in North Carolina, political parties still play a prominent role, just as in other states. For example, Republican and Democratic Party Web sites still supported candidates for appellate court judgeships in 2004 ("Partisanship Clings" 2004, A8).

Observers have generally praised the move from partisan to nonpartisan elections as a positive step in the belief that they give the appearance of impartiality and make judicial decision making seem less tainted by partisan factionalism (Newman and Isaacs 2004, 16). For example, 81 percent of citizens surveyed in 2002 believed that judges should be elected, and 89 percent agreed that judges should be chosen through nonpartisan elections. Respondents also indicated that they had had little information on which to base their votes in the most recent judicial elections. Despite the near-uniform support for nonpartisan elections, public support is more nuanced than it may appear at first. Ninety percent of likely voters expressed concern about low-information races, a concern that many scholars share about nonpartisan contests. Furthermore, large majorities of those surveyed believed that the costs of running a judicial campaign were too great, that campaign contributions influence judicial decision making, and that judicial campaign reforms were necessary (Gutermuth 2002).

As this survey demonstrates, North Carolina's populist tinge remains a strong cultural force that makes adoption of gubernatorial appointive or merit selection options less likely to gain acceptance. North Carolina voters are likely to believe the idea that such processes take the selection of judges out of the hands of the people and put them in the hands of the elites (Anderson 2004, 797).

When selecting judges for the state high courts, eight states use partisan election, thirteen use nonpartisan election, six use legislative or gubernatorial appointment, and twenty-four use merit selection. Thirty-nine states have intermediate appellate courts, with six using partisan election, eleven using nonpartisan election, eighteen using merit selection, and four using gubernatorial or legislative appointment. At the trial court level, nine states select all general-jurisdiction trial court judges through partisan elections, seventeen states have nonpartisan elections for these judges, sixteen use merit selection, four use a combination of these methods, and five use gubernatorial or legislative appointment (American Judicature Society 2004). Tables 8.3–8.5 summarize the initial methods used to select state trial and appellate court judges in the United States.

TABLE 8.3. Initial Method of Judicial Selection in the States: Trial Courts of General Jurisdiction

Selection Method	States
Merit selection	Alaska, Colorado, Connecticut, Delaware, District of Columbia, Hawaii, Iowa, Maryland, Massachusetts, Nebraska, Nevada, New Mexico, Rhode Island, Utah, Vermont, and Wyoming (16 states)
Partisan election	Alabama, Illinois, Louisiana, New York, Ohio, Pennsylvania, Tennessee, Texas, and West Virginia (9 states)
Nonpartisan election	Arkansas, California, Florida, Georgia, Idaho, Kentucky, Michigan, Minnesota, Mississippi, Montana, North Carolina, North Dakota, Oklahoma, Oregon, South Dakota, Washington, and Wisconsin (17 states)
Gubernatorial (G) and legislative (L) appointment	Maine (G), New Hampshire (G), New Jersey (G), South Carolina (L), and Virginia (L) (5 states)
Combined methods (merit selection and competitive elections)	Arizona, Indiana, Kansas, and Missouri (4 states)

Source: American Judicature Society (2004).

TABLE 8.4. Initial Method of Judicial Selection in the States: Intermediate Appellate Courts

Selection Method	States
Merit selection	Alaska, Arizona, Colorado, Connecticut, Florida, Hawaii, Indiana, Iowa, Kansas, Maryland, Massachusetts, Nebraska, New Mexico, New York, Oklahoma, Tennessee, and Utah (17 states)
Partisan election	Alabama, Illinois, Louisiana, Ohio, Pennsylvania, and Texas (6 states)
Nonpartisan election	Arkansas, Georgia, Idaho, Kentucky, Michigan, Minnesota, Mississippi, Montana, North Carolina, Oregon, Washington, and Wisconsin (12 states)
Gubernatorial appointment	California and New Jersey (2 states)
Legislative appointment	South Carolina and Virginia (2 states)

Source: American Judicature Society (2004).

TABLE 8.5. Initial Method of Judicial Selection in the States: Courts of Last Resort

Selection Method	States
Merit selection	Alaska, Arizona, Colorado, Connecticut, Delaware, District of Columbia, Florida, Hawaii, Indiana, Iowa, Kansas, Maryland, Massachusetts, Missouri, Nebraska, New Mexico, New York, Oklahoma, Rhode Island, South Dakota, Tennessee, Utah, Vermont, and Wyoming (24 states)
Partisan election	Alabama, Illinois, Louisiana, Michigan, Ohio, Pennsylvania, Texas, and West Virginia (8 states)
Nonpartisan election	Arkansas, Georgia, Idaho, Kentucky, Minnesota, Mississippi, Montana, Nevada, North Carolina, North Dakota, Oregon, Washington, and Wisconsin (13 states)
Gubernatorial appointment	California, Maine, New Hampshire, and New Jersey (4 states)
Legislative appointment	South Carolina and Virginia (2 states)

Source: American Judicature Society (2004).

Legal scholars often reject or seek modifications to elections, whether partisan or nonpartisan. They frequently view elections as a threat to judicial independence because of the fund-raising activities associated with getting elected. The involvement of special interest groups in judicial selection, these scholars believe, can create the appearance of impropriety. Finally, the appearance of judicial responsiveness to special interest groups could undermine public confidence in the judiciary (Baum 2003; Behrens and Silverman 2002; Geyh 2003; Larkin 2001; Tarr 2003). At the same time, nonpartisan elections stand out as the method that elects the highest percentages of female and minority judges to general jurisdiction and appellate state courts.

Judicial scholars favor appointment-based selection, claiming that this form of selection preserves judicial independence and could ultimately open judicial appointments to a more diverse pool of qualified candidates. If elections are used, many observers argue that these contests should be nonpartisan to prevent judges from resembling partisan advocates and for public funding of judicial campaigns to avoid the appearance of impropriety or corruption (Committee for Economic Development, Research and Policy Committee 2002).

❖ Judicial Politics and Campaigns

Judicial campaigns have become more politicized, with judicial candidates, interest groups, and political parties spending more on television advertisements. Since 2000, only two states with contested Supreme Court elections—Minnesota and North Dakota—have refrained from using television ads. In four of every five states, ads were run by candidates, political parties, and interest groups whenever candidates ran head-to-head. In 2002, $10.6 million was spent on air wars. In 2004, the amount of spending more than doubled to $24.4 million, with one out of every four dollars raised by judicial candidates going to airtime costs. The tone of one in five television advertisements was negative in 2004, compared to fewer than one in ten negative ads in 2002 (Goldberg et al. 2004, vii–1). West Virginians were beset by a particularly vitriolic judicial campaign between incumbent justice Warren McGraw and challenger Jim Rowe. Together, they aired 1,608 television ads at a cost of $677,922 (Goldberg et al. 2004, 5).

Not only have ads become more acrimonious and negative, but candidates devote more time to stating their opinions on controversial issues. Instead of focusing on their qualifications, judges now tout their political views. In Mississippi, Judge Samac Richardson expressed opposition to gay marriage; Judge Lloyd Karmeier in Illinois stated that he was tackling the medical malpractice crisis (Goldberg et al. 2004, 9–11). In Georgia and Kentucky, candidates in the 2003–4 election cycle were inundated with questionnaires asking for their positions on issues such as abortion. Although candidates may have objected to the assault on judicial ethics and impartiality, many potential judges did not resist this pressure. In North Carolina, some candidates used the state's new voter guides to make pledges and issue promises, but none of the candidates who played the hot-button issue card were elected (Goldberg et al. 2004, 23–31).

Judicial campaigns in North Carolina, as in many other states, had usually been low-key affairs. However, when Henry Frye spent $907,491 in 2000 in an unsuccessful bid for the chief justiceship, the stakes increased considerably (Robertson 2004). Questions arose over how campaign fund-raising might impinge on judicial impartiality. Even with nonpartisan elections, the 2004 judicial campaigns were heated. Seeking an appeals court seat, Doug Berger, a state industrial commissioner, attacked incumbent judge Linda McGee for her participation in three court rulings (Eisley 2003, B5). The evidence suggests that nonpartisan elections are not a panacea for the ills afflicting judicial politics. To deal with the role of money in judicial campaigns, North Carolina instituted full public financing for appellate judicial candidates in 2004.

In 2004, when two Supreme Court seats were open, judicial reformers watched

North Carolina very closely for the same type of acrimonious campaigning that had occurred elsewhere. It was the first year that the public financing measure had taken effect, and interest group activity was remarkably low—in fact, the Brennan Center for Justice, a nonpartisan public policy and law institute, found no independent interest group expenditure activity. Under the new law, independent expenditures of more than $201,000 in opposition to a publicly funded candidate trigger the "rescue fund" provision, under which the State Board of Elections gives the publicly financed candidate extra campaign money. The new law also covers party committee expenditures and may explain why interest group activity was so low (Frasco 2007, 771).

Since 1997, North Carolina has had an open rule, allowing judicial candidates to announce their positions on various issues. A High Point attorney running for district court had filed a federal lawsuit challenging the state's gag order, and the N.C. Supreme Court struck down the gag rule in the code of judicial conduct. The practice in North Carolina preceded the U.S. Supreme Court's decision in *Republican Party of Minnesota v. White* (2002). In 1998, Superior Court Judge George Wainwright, running for a seat on the Supreme Court, wrote in a fund-raising letter that he favored the death penalty and victims' rights. Thus, North Carolina became one of the first states to permit judicial candidates to discuss controversial issues (Christian 1998, B1).

Instead of imposing gag rules, North Carolina has asked candidates voluntarily to restrain themselves. Nevertheless, some candidates have made pledges and issued promises. In his personal campaign literature, Edward Brady, a 2002 candidate for the state's Supreme Court, advertised his "core conservative values," stating in letters to potential constituents that he "supported an abortion ban except in cases of rape, incest, or danger to the mother's life, and he would defend citizens' Second Amendment rights." The partisanship is not one-sided. Bob Hunter, running for different seat on the Supreme Court, wrote in a campaign letter that the "North Carolina Supreme Court has become dominated by Republicans—and it is time for a change!" This level of partisanship may have motivated the General Assembly to make statewide appellate judicial contests nonpartisan (Eisley 2002, B1).

In 2004, three men running for statewide court positions, John Tyson, Paul Newby, and Bill Parker, stated their personal stances on issues ranging from abortion and gay marriage to the death penalty and displaying the Ten Commandments in public buildings. These candidates justified publicly taking these positions as part of an effort to enable voters to make informed choices. Gregory Wallace, a Campbell University law professor, argues that because judicial opinions often reflect a judge's personal views and values, voters have a right to know what judges believe. Other observers worry that pushing opinions so blatantly may make residents wonder about a judge's impartiality and ability to rule on a case without placing personal values above the law (Eisley 2004, B1).

Nationally, judicial candidates in 2003–4 raised more than $46.8 million, with winners in forty-three races averaging $651,586 (a significant jump from the $450,689 average in 2002). Approximately 64 percent of appellate judge candidates' campaign funds came from public financing. In states with judicial elections, incumbents were more successful than challengers, and big spenders on television ads were the winning candidates in twenty-nine of thirty-four races. The average cost of winning increased by 45 percent from 2002 to 2004 (Goldberg et al. 2004, 1).

Although money has been a factor in North Carolina's judicial elections, it has caused fewer problems than fund-raising activities in states such as Illinois, Ohio, West Virginia, and Texas. Reformers have grown concerned about money and its influence because campaign contributions can create the appearance of a quid pro quo. In 1998, when Associate Justice I. Beverly Lake of the N.C. Supreme Court ruled that each retiree would receive $799 in tax refunds, his campaign sent letters to retirees requesting that they "look back and recall what Justice Lake's wisdom and demeanor have meant to each of us" (Scherer 2001).

In 2002, North Carolina's Supreme Court and Court of Appeals candidates raised $1.3 million. Two-thirds of the money was drawn from attorneys and special interest donors such as political action committees sponsored by physicians who oppose medical malpractice lawsuits, banks, insurance companies, and labor unions. Between 1998 and 2002, spending by Court of Appeals candidates increased by 60 percent, and spending by Supreme Court candidates increased by 11 percent. In 2002, six of seven Republican appellate candidates won election; somewhat surprisingly, outspending the opponent was not a predictor of success. But in 1998, all seven candidates who spent the most won, regardless of party affiliation. In 2004, expenditures in contests for two Supreme Court seats were very low (Weiss 2005, 20). Nevertheless, the rise in spending for judicial elections raised concerns and made public financing of judicial campaigns more attractive to elites and reformers (Democracy N.C. 2004).

North Carolina became the first state to offer full public financing to qualified appellate court candidates. In reaction to the first million-dollar Supreme Court race in 2000, reformers pushed for changes in judicial campaign financing. Under the program, candidates may qualify for funding if they limit their private fund-raising in the year before the race to less than $10,000; collect between $33,000 and $69,000 in small amounts ($10–$500) from at least 350 voters registered in the state (with no political party or political action committee funds allowed);

file their intent to participate in the program with the Board of Elections between January 1 and the date of the state primary; and finish first or second in the state's primary election. Court of Appeals judicial candidates typically receive $137,000, and Supreme Court judicial candidates receive $201,300. If outspent by privately financed candidates, publicly financed candidates may receive "rescue" funds to help them remain competitive. Of the sixteen qualifying candidates in 2004, fourteen participated in the program. In 2004, the rescue funds were not dispersed because none of the candidates who participated in the program were outspent by privately financed candidates (Goldberg et al. 2004, 38–39).

❖ Budgeting and Court Funding

About thirty years ago, as part of the court consolidation movement, court funding shifted from local to the state level. Today, the state funds almost 70 percent of the costs of operating state trial courts. Such state financing brings both advantages and disadvantages. During economic hard times, the courts often suffer the most. As the "forgotten branch," the state judiciaries often do not receive due consideration in the budgeting process. North Carolina's courts are no exception to this rule.

During budget shortfalls and economic downswings, the state legislature can slash court funding. In his 2001 State of the Judiciary address, Lake, now the chief justice of the N.C. Supreme Court, put forward an urgent plea for increased funding of the courts. He argued that even before the budget crisis, North Carolina's courts had been underfunded. Facing a $3.6 million cut out of an $18.5 million budget for high-priority items, Lake argued that the courts' ability to serve the residents of North Carolina would be impaired. He outlined critical shortages in funding for such items as phone lines for courtrooms under construction, renting space for the business court in Greensboro, and salaries of court personnel ("Judiciary Funding Urged" 2001, A3). After Lake's pleas failed to get results, he stated that the cuts might cause courts to shut down on Fridays, forcing court employees to take vacation time or unpaid leave (Mooneyham 2001; "State Courts Too Poor Already" 2002, 8A).

Again in 2003, Lake begged the N.C. General Assembly for funding, noting that the budget for the state court system has dropped from $317 million in 2001 to $304 million in 2003. Citing the rise in the courts' annual caseload—11 percent from 2000 to 2003—Lake again called for better technology, more court clerks, and more court reporters so that the courts could process cases faster ("Chief Justice Says" 2003). In 2005, Lake cited the loss of experienced judges, who, he noted, could earn twice as much practicing law in a medium-sized firm ("Lake Says"

2005). Lake later announced that the courts might suspend consideration of civil cases until prosecutors caught up with the criminal caseload. With declining budgets and increasing caseloads, Lake believed that public safety and defendants' rights to speedy trials were threatened ("N.C. Chief Justice" 2005).

North Carolina's are not the only state courts in financial trouble. State court judges in New Hampshire also bemoaned the status of their underfunded courts ("Court Funding" 2003, A10). Similarly, Chief Justice Mary Ann McMorrow asked Illinois lawmakers to increase court funding in times of budget shortfalls (Vock 2003, 1). In 2002, layoffs and trial delays were likely in Alabama's courts unless the state legislature provided adequate court funding ("Chief Justice Warns" 2002). Alabama Supreme Court Chief Justice Roy Moore later declared a four-month statewide moratorium on jury trials because of a $2.7 million funding shortfall, resulting in much political feuding between Moore and Alabama governor Don Siegelman (Ellis and Temple 2002).

Statewide financing of courts resulted from good intentions and has yielded some positive results: (1) state-funded systems tend to produce more overall funding than locally funded systems; (2) state-funded systems reduce inequities between poorer and wealthier jurisdictions; (3) state-funded systems are more economical and produce savings through bulk purchases and shared infrastructure; and (4) state-funded systems improve planning and management, with better internal controls and accounting procedures. However, statewide financing also has drawbacks: (1) state revenues are less stable and are more subject to recession than are local funding sources; (2) more groups compete for access to state revenues, putting courts at the bottom of the totem pole; (3) interbranch relations suffer as legislative-judicial and executive-judicial tensions arise over the proper allocation of scarce resources; and (4) statewide financing stifles innovation as those at top, such as the Administrative Office of the Courts, allocate resources and determine priorities for innovation, allowing little variance (Hudzik and Carlson 2004).

Most state courts need state legislative funding because of reliance on centralized financing. In North Carolina, the constitution requires that court operating expenses be paid from state funds and that the courts be open and administered without favor, denial, or delay. Since the state court unification trend in the 1970s, courts have faced increasing demands. Cases have become more complex and time-consuming, juvenile crime has risen, business litigation has become more complicated, and changes in family law have increased burdens on the courts. These changes have necessitated increases in the number of in judges' staffers, trial court administrators, and court reporters as well as district attorneys and clerks. Court security issues have taken center stage since September 11, 2001, and funding needs in this area have increased. Inadequate funding of the courts has prevented them from updating court technology and has resulted in unacceptable workload increases for judges and others in the courtroom workgroup. The lack of state funds has increased court reliance on court fees—the hidden tax on residents who use the courts—and nonstate revenues such as grants from federal, local, and private sources. For judicial independence and accountability, state funds are essential (Medlin and Billings 2003). Despite the importance of state funding, only nine state court systems—those in Alaska, Connecticut, Hawaii, Kentucky, Maine, Massachusetts, New Hampshire, Rhode Island, and Vermont—are almost completely financed by the state.

The power of the purse held by state legislatures clearly can constitute a trump card if inadequate funding weakens judicial independence and the maintenance of a separation-of-powers balance. Some state judges have taken drastic actions. In 2002, Chief Justice Kay McFarland of the Kansas Supreme Court ordered across-the-board increases in court fees to overcome a $3.5 million budget shortfall. McFarland explained that "while there are things that the people of Kansas may have to give up in these trying fiscal times, justice cannot and must not be one of them" (Webb and Whittington 2004, 14). Exercising the doctrine of inherent judicial power, McFarland took the actions she felt necessary to carry out the constitutional functions of the courts. Her actions were not sanctioned by the constitution or legislative statute and provoked some discussion as to whether the doctrine should be extended to budgetary matters.

Statewide financing is a growing trend. How state legislatures and executives respond to the problems associated with this development may determine whether other chief justices follow the McFarland example. John Medlin and Rohad B. Billings (2003, 14) argue that judicial appropriations should be nonreverting—that is, the governor should not be able to confiscate court monies to balance the budget. In addition, Medlin and Billings suggest that court funding should be allocated on a single-sum basis, allowing the courts to move funds among programs as needed, and budget cuts should be determined by the chief justice, not the governor.

❖ Diversity on the State Bench

With the overwhelming number of cases being filed and resolved in state courts and the increasingly diverse populace, a healthy debate has arisen regarding the diversity of state courts. Some observers argue that judges are not representatives in the same way that legislators are and that judicial independence might be threatened if a "representative" judiciary were sought (Graham 2004, 160). Other scholars argue that descriptive representation, which promotes the idea that society's institutions should mirror its demographic composition, enhances perceptions of institutional fairness and equity. Proponents of descriptive representation argue that a mostly white and male judiciary may create a legitimacy crisis in the eyes of those who perceive the courts as an instrument of bias (Wynn and Mazur 2004, 786–87).

Research indicates that the presence of women and minorities on the bench makes a difference. For example, at the federal court level, female judges often are the strongest proponents of women's rights. The presence of just one female on the bench is one of the best predictors of favorable sex-discrimination rulings for women plaintiffs. Some studies even assert that women on the bench may eventually develop jurisprudence with a different voice (Palmer 2001, 237). Some evidence suggests that women judges are often harsher than men in sentencing, are more likely to incarcerate, and are likely to impose longer sentences (Steffensmeier and Hebert 1999). Studies indicate that black judges are more evenhanded than are white judges in sentencing defendants of both races and are slightly more lenient toward black defendants in sentencing (Welch, Combs, and Gruhl 1988). As a whole, this literature on judicial decision making suggests that race, ethnicity, and sex significantly influence how judges decide cases, even after a host of other factors are controlled for.

How well are minorities and women represented in the state judiciary? In 2003, 10 percent of North Carolina's appellate and state trial court judges of general jurisdiction were female, well below the national mean of 21 percent. Other states that fell far short of the national mean included Alabama, Arkansas, Delaware, Georgia, Indiana, Maine, Mississippi, Missouri, South Carolina, Tennessee, Virginia, and West Virginia. Hawaii, Massachusetts, Maryland, Minnesota, Nevada, and Rhode Island had percentages of female judges well above the mean (Williams 2004). If the trial courts of limited jurisdiction are included, female representation increases to 23 percent in North Carolina (O'Brien 2003).

Margaret Williams (2004) finds that southern states fare worse than others in the representation of women and that nonpartisan elections increase the number of women on state courts. Incumbency often helps male judges get reelected but is a less significant factor for female judges. Furthermore, women require greater sums of money to compete for judicial seats than do men (Reid 2004). In North Carolina as in many other states, female judicial candidates face a less favorable electoral environment than do their male counterparts.

According to 2001 data collected by the American Bar Association, 14 percent of all judges in North Carolina are African American, while North Carolina's population is 21 percent African American, 1.2 percent American Indian, and 4.7 percent Latino (American Bar Association n.d.). Despite the advantages afforded by nonpartisan elections, North Carolina courts rank forty-seventh in the proportion of African Americans on the bench after accounting for the proportion of African Americans in the state's population (Graham 2004).

Judges of color are underrepresented on the state bench nationally. Barbara L. Graham (2004, 173) reports that judges of color (including African American, American Indian, Latina/Latino, and Asian/Pacific Islander) constitute 10.3 percent of state and intermediate appellate court judges, 9.8 percent of general-jurisdiction trial court judges, and 7.1 percent of limited-jurisdiction court judges. Of the 30,059 judges studied in 2001, only 8 percent were people of color.

In 2001, ten states had no African American judges in the major trial courts and appellate courts—Idaho, Maine, Montana, Nebraska, New Hampshire, New Mexico, North Dakota, South Dakota, Vermont, and Wyoming. Of the nineteen states with African American voting-age populations of at least 10 percent, a rank ordering illustrates the best and the worst diversity records. South Carolina, Mississippi, North Carolina, New York, and Texas had the worst records, while Michigan, Illinois, Virginia, New Jersey, and Maryland had the best records. Asian/Pacific Islanders are not represented in twenty-nine states. Of states with significant numbers of Asian/Pacific Islanders in the voting-age population, Hawaii and Washington had the highest representation, while California, New Jersey, and New York had extreme underrepresentation. Latina/o representation, although somewhat better than Asian/Pacific Islander representation, still lags far behind the African American presence on the bench. Twenty-two states had no Latina/o representation on the bench, while New Mexico was the only state that achieved close to parity between the Latina/o population and Latina/o presence on the bench (Graham 2004, 171–75).

Table 8.6 indicates the total number of judgeships per state with the number and percentage of women, African American, Hispanic, Native American, and Asian/Pacific Islander judges per state court system. This table illustrates that state courts are not very representative of the people they serve. This lack of diversity disturbs scholars who support descriptive representation, leading to calls for judicial diversity task forces as one way to start addressing the issue (Graham 2004).

❖ Conclusion

North Carolina's court system has been remarkably adaptable and open to change. The state's judiciary has been quite innovative in areas such as business courts, drug treatment, and public financing of appellate court judicial campaigns. The trend toward court consolidation and the move toward a more unified court system have helped the courts improve their efficiency and accountability. Perhaps because of advances in these areas, North Carolinians hold their courts in high

TABLE 8.6. Diversity of State Court Judges, 2001

State	Total Judges	Women Judges (%)	African American Judges (%)	Hispanic Judges (%)	Native American Judges (%)	Asian Judges (%)
Alabama	159	20 (12.6)	6 (3.8)	0 (0)	0 (0)	0 (0)
Alaska	42	9 (21.4)	1 (2.4)	0 (0)	0 (0)	1 (2.4)
Arizona	185	38 (20.5)	4 (2.2)	19 (10.3)	1 (0.5)	3 (1.6)
Arkansas	134	17 (12.7)	15 (11.2)	0 (0)	0 (0)	0 (0)
California	1,611	357 (22.2)	79 (4.9)	89 (5.5)	2 (.12)	52 (3.2)
Colorado	155	24 (15.5)	4 (2.6)	13 (8.4)	0 (0)	0 (0)
Connecticut	196	40 (20.4)	18 (9.2)	5 (2.5)	0 (0)	0 (0)
Delaware	29	5 (17.2)	2 (6.9)	0 (0)	0 (0)	0 (0)
Florida	596	129 (21.6)	29 (4.9)	25 (4.2)	1 (0.2)	0 (0)
Georgia	207	35 (16.9)	20 (9.7)	0 (0)	1 (0.5)	0 (0)
Hawaii	54	14 (25.9)	1 (1.8)	0 (0)	0 (0)	30 (55.6)
Idaho	47	7 (14.9)	0 (0)	1 (2.1)	0 (0)	0 (0)
Illinois	558	127 (22.8)	63 (11.3)	7 (1.3)	0 (0)	2 (0.4)
Indiana	315	48 (15.2)	11 (3.5)	3 (0.9)	0 (0)	1 (0.3)
Iowa	132	18 (13.6)	2 (1.5)	0 (0)	0 (0)	1 (0.8)
Kansas	177	13 (7.3)	5 (2.8)	1 (0.6)	0 (0)	0 (0)
Kentucky	132	30 (22.7)	3 (2.3)	0 (0)	0 (0)	0 (0)
Louisiana	275	64 (23.3)	50 (18.2)	0 (0)	0 (0)	0 (0)
Maine	23	4 (17.4)	0 (0)	0 (0)	0 (0)	0 (0)

TABLE 8.6. (*continued*)

State	Total Judges	Women Judges (%)	African American Judges (%)	Hispanic Judges (%)	Native American Judges (%)	Asian Judges (%)
Maryland	166	46 (27.7)	28 (16.9)	1 (0.6	0 (0)	0 (0)
Massachusetts	94	40 (42.6)	11 (11.7)	3 (3.2)	0 (0)	2 (2.1)
Michigan	245	57 (23.3)	35 (14.3)	3 (1.2)	0 (0)	0 (0)
Minnesota	295	77 (26.1)	8 (2.7)	2 (0.7)	1 (0.3)	1 (0.3)
Mississippi	113	22 (19.5)	20 (17.7)	0 (0)	0 (0)	0 (0)
Missouri	174	30 (17.2)	14 (8.0)	2 (1.1)	0 (0)	0 (0)
Montana	49	8 (16.3)	0 (0)	0 (0)	0 (0)	0 (0)
Nebraska	68	9 (13.2)	0 (0)	0 (0)	0 (0)	0 (0)
Nevada	63	20 (31.7)	2 (3.2)	1 (1.6)	0 (0)	0 (0)
New Hampshire	33	7 (21.2)	0 (0)	0 (0)	0 (0)	0 (0)
New Jersey	436	98 (22.5)	31 (7.1)	13 (3.0)	0 (0)	2 (0.4)
New Mexico	90	18 (20.0)	0 (0)	23 (25.5)	1 (1.1)	0 (0)
New York	536	91 (16.9)	50 (9.3)	14 (2.6)	0 (0)	3 (.5)
North Carolina	114	13 (11.4)	16 (14.0)	0 (0)	0 (0)	0 (0)
North Dakota	47	8 (17.0)	0 (0)	0 (0)	0 (0)	0 (0)
Ohio	451	99 (21.9)	12 (26.6)	3 (0.7)	0 (0)	0 (0)
Oklahoma	99	18 (18.2)	2 (2.0)	0 (0)	0 (0)	0 (0)
Oregon	184	45 (24.4)	2 (1.1)	3 (1.6)	1 (1.1)	1 (1.1)
Pennsylvania	425	91 (21.4)	31 (7.3)	3 (0.7)	0 (0)	1 (0.2)

TABLE 8.6. (*continued*)

State	Total Judges	Women Judges (%)	African American Judges (%)	Hispanic Judges (%)	Native American Judges (%)	Asian Judges (%)
Rhode Island	27	9 (33.3)	2 (7.4)	0 (0)	0 (0)	0 (0)
South Carolina	60	7 (11.7)	6 (10%)	0 (0)	0 (0)	0 (0)
South Dakota	43	9 (20.9)	0 (0)	0 (0)	0 (0)	0 (0)
Tennessee	180	29 (16.1)	11 (6.1)	0 (0)	0 (0)	0 (0)
Texas	512	130 (25.4)	18 (3.5)	59 (11.5)	0 (0)	3 (0.6)
Utah	82	12 (14.6)	1 (1.2)	1 (1.2)	1 (1.2)	2 (2.4)
Vermont	37	13 (35.1)	0 (0)	0 (0)	0 (0)	0 (0)
Virginia	168	20 (11.9)	16 (9.5)	0 (0)	0 (0)	0 (0)
Washington	206	63 (30.6)	11 (5.3)	0 (0)	1 (0.5)	6 (2.9)
West Virginia	70	3 (4.3)	3 (4.3)	0 (0)	0 (0)	0 (0)
Wisconsin	264	37 (14.0)	6 (2.3)	2 (0.7)	0 (0)	0 (0)
Wyoming	30	3 (10.0)	0 (0)	0 (0)	0 (0)	0 (0)

Sources: American Judicature Society; *The Directory of Minority Judges of the United States* (Chicago: American Bar Association, 2001).

Note: The American Bar Association data, as presented in the American Judicature Society Web site on diversity of the bench, may have overlapping categories. For example, an African American judge may also be female. Also, the diversity on the bench data includes only the trial courts of general jurisdiction and the major appellate courts.

esteem. Citizen complaints center not on the administration of justice but rather on ancillary issues such as adequate parking at courthouses (*Court Performance Survey* 2003).

Less inspirational is the lack of diversity of judges on the North Carolina bench and the political infighting that has occurred over court funding. Like other state court systems, North Carolina's has been slow to improve its diversity. Structural changes in law school recruitment and judicial selection may be required to remedy the problem. Underrepresented groups often perceive the courts as unfair and illegitimate, damaging the courts. Another troubling problem is that chief justices, including North Carolina's, must beg state legislatures for adequate court financing, hindering court operations and the administration of justice. Elected officials must find a more equitable funding formula if North Carolina's courts are to meet the needs of the new century.

❖ References

American Bar Association. N.d. "National Database on Judicial Diversity in State Courts." <http:www.abanet.org/judind/diversity/home.html>. Accessed February 19, 2006.

American Bar Association. Standing Committee on Judicial Independence. N.d. "Fact Sheet." <http:www.abanet.org/judind/jeopardy/fact.html>. Accessed February 19, 2006.

American Judicature Society. N.d. "Judicial Selection in the States." <http://www.ajs.org/js/NC_history.htm>. Accessed December 28, 2005.

———. 2004. *Judicial Selection in the States: Appellate and General Jurisdiction Courts.* Des Moines, Iowa: American Judicature Society.

Anderson, Seth. 2004. "Perspectives: Judicial Elections versus Merit Selection: Examining the Decline in Support for Merit Selection in the States." *Albany Law Review* 67:793–801.

Baum, Lawrence. 2003. "Symposium: Perspectives on Judicial Independence: Judicial Elections and Judicial Independence: The Voter's Perspective." *Ohio State Law Journal* 64:13–41.

Behrens, Mark A., and Cary Silverman. 2002. "The Case for Adopting Appointive Judicial Selection Systems for State Court Judges." *Cornell Journal of Law and Public Policy* 11:273–314.

Beyle, Thad. 2002. "The N.C. Supreme Court Power Shift, 1990–2000." *North Carolina DataNet* 31:10–11.

Brace, Paul R., and Melinda Gann Hall. 2005. "Is Judicial Federalism Essential to Democracy?: State Courts in the Federal System." In *The Judicial Branch*, edited by Kermit L. Hall and Kevin McGuire, 174–99. New York: Oxford University Press.

Brannon, Joan G. 2001. *Guide to the North Carolina Judicial System.* Raleigh: N.C. Administrative Office of the Courts.

"Chief Justice Says N.C. Courts Need More Money." 2003. *Associate Press State and Local Wire*, April 29.

"Chief Justice Warns of Layoffs, Trial Delays in State Court." 2002. *Associated Press*, March 29.

Christian, Paula. 1998. "Issues Now Fair Game in Judicial Races." *Greensboro News and Record*, January 11, B1.

Collins, Eric. 2005. "Elon Law School Will House Court; a Judicial Branch Focusing on Complex Business Cases Might Also Open a Location in Mecklenburg County." *Greensboro News and Record*, July 3, B1.

"Commission Recommends Separate Business Court." 1995. *Greensboro News and Record*, January 25, B4.

Committee for Economic Development, Research and Policy Committee. 2002. *Justice for Hire: Improving Judicial Selection*. New York: Committee for Economic Development.

"Court Funding; It's All a Matter of Priorities." 2003. *Manchester (New Hampshire) Union Leader*, March 4, A10.

Court Performance Survey. 2003. Raleigh: N.C. Administrative Office of the Courts.

Democracy N.C. 2004. "Choosing Judges: Money Given in Past Races Is Restricted, Replaced under New Program." February. <http://www.democracy-nc.org/nc/judicialcampaignreform/whosfunding.shtml>. Accessed November 4, 2007.

Eisley, Matthew. 2002. "Getting Mileage from Parties." *Raleigh News and Observer*, October 23, B1.

———. 2003. "Appeals Race Gets Personal." *Raleigh News and Observer*, December 11, B5.

———. 2004. "Bench Hopefuls Bank on Personal Beliefs." *Raleigh News and Observer*, October 31, B1.

Ellis, Kristi Lamong, and Chanda Temple. 2002. "Moore Defends Cutbacks in State Courts as Necessary; 'We Simply Do Not Have the Money' Says Chief Justice." *Birmingham (Alabama) News*, April 26.

Fiscal Year 2003–2004 Annual Report: North Carolina Courts. Raleigh: Research and Planning Division, N.C. Administrative Office of the Courts.

Flango, Victor E., and Carol R. Flango. 1997. *Examining the Work of the State Courts*. Williamsburg, Va.: National Center for the State Courts.

Fleer, Jack D. 1994. *North Carolina Government and Politics*. Lincoln: University of Nebraska Press.

Frasco, Jason B. 2007. "Full Public Funding: An Effective and Legally Viable Model for Campaign Finance Reform in the United States." *Cornell Law Review* 92:733–93.

Geyh, Charles Gardner. 2003. "Symposium: Perspectives on Judicial Independence: Why Judicial Elections Stink." *Ohio State Law Journal* 64:43–79.

Goldberg, Deborah, Saram Samis, Edwin Bender, and Rachel Weiss. 2004. *The New Politics of Judicial Elections 2004: How Special Interest Pressure on Our Courts Has Reached a 'Tipping Point'—and How to Keep Our Courts Fair and Impartial*. Edited by Jesse Rutledge. Washington, D.C.: Justice at Stake Campaign.

Graham, Barbara L. 2004. "Diversity, Impartiality, and Representation on the Bench Symposium: Toward an Understanding of Judicial Diversity in American Courts." *Michigan Journal of Race and Law* 10:153–81.

Gutermuth, Randall. 2002. "American Viewpoint: Key Survey Findings." <http://ncvotered.com/downloads/5_9_02_report.pdf>. Accessed September 13, 2007.

Hudzik, John K., and Alan Carlson. 2004. "State Funding of Trial Courts: What We Know Now." *American Bar Association Judge's Journal* 43:11–14, 26.

The Judicial System in North Carolina. 2005. Raleigh: N.C. Administrative Office of the Courts.

"Judiciary Funding Urged." 2001. *Raleigh News and Observer*, March 27, A3.

Kim, Ann S. 2004. "Courts Mix Therapy, Threat; New Approach to Justice—Tackling Causes of Crime." *Raleigh News and Observer*, May 14, B1.

"Lake Says N.C. Judge Salaries Too Low, Fears Exodus." 2005. *Associated Press State and Local Wire*, August 6.

Larkin, Elizabeth A. 2001. "Judicial Selection Methods: Judicial Independence and Popular Democracy." *Denver University Law Review* 79:65–89.

Medlin, John, and Rohad B. Billings. 2003. "Judicial Independence Requires More Resources and Greater Management Flexibility." *North Carolina State Bar Journal* 8:8–15.

Mikeska, Jennifer L. 2000. "Court Consolidation: Reinventing Missouri State Courts." <http://www.ncsconline.org/D_ICM/programs/cedp/papers/Research_Papers_2000/Court%20Consolidation.pdf>. Accessed September 13, 2007.

Mooneyham, Scott. 2001. "Chief Justice Considers Scaled-Back Court Operations." *Associated Press State and Local Wire*, October 22.

Newman, Sandra Shultz, and Daniel Mark Isaacs. 2004. "Historical Overview of the Judicial Selection Process in the United States: Is the Electoral System in Pennsylvania Unjustified?" *Villanova Law Review* 49:1–53.

"N.C. Chief Justice: Courts May Suspend Consideration of Civil Cases." 2005. *Associated Press State and Local Wire*, October 11.

North Carolina Manual: The Judicial Branch. 2001–2. Raleigh: N.C. Office of the Secretary of State.

Nowell, Paul. 2001. "Special Business Court Offers High-Tech Help for Merger Litigants." *Associated Press State and Local Wire*, June 13.

O'Brien, Kelley. 2003. "Measuring Citizen Engagement: The North Carolina Civic Index." *Popular Government* 69:5–12.

Palmer, Barbara. 2001. "'To Do Justly': The Integration of Women into the American Judiciary." *PS: Political Science and Politics* 34:235–39.

"Partisanship Clings to Judicial Candidates; Party Labels Officially Have Been Dropped in Races for N.C. Supreme Court and Court of Appeals; So Why Won't the Politicians Let Them Go?" 2004. *Greensboro News and Record*, September 7, A8.

Reid, Traciel V. 2004. "Perspectives: Judicial Elections versus Merit Selection: The Competitiveness of Female Candidates in Judicial Elections: An Analysis of the North Carolina Trial Court Races." *Albany Law Review* 67:829–42.

Republican Party of Minnesota v. White. 536 U.S. 765 (2002).

Robertson, Gary D. 2004. "Trial Begins for Appeals Court Campaign Plan—Publicly Funded General Election Is Linked to Limits in Primaries." *Charlotte Observer*, February 15, 4B.

Scherer, Michael. 2001. "State Lines: Is Justice Undermined by Campaign Contributions?" Capital Eye, Summer. <http://www.opensecrets.org/newsletter/ce76/statelines.asp>. Accessed October 16, 2007.

"State Courts Too Poor Already." 2002. *Wilmington Morning Star*, March 26, 8A.

Steffensmeier, Darrell, and Chris Hebert. 1999. "Women and Men Policymakers: Does the Judge's Gender Affect the Sentencing of Criminal Defendants?" *Social Forces* 77:1163–96.

Sullivan, John. 1999. "New Court Offers a Family Focus." *Raleigh News and Observer*, June 1, B1.

Tarr, G. Alan. 2003. "Symposium: Selection of State Appellate Judges: Reform Proposals: Rethinking the Selection of State Supreme Court Justices." *Willamette Law Review* 39:1445–70.

Turnbull, Amy E. 1999. "Will Start in February; 'Kinder' Family Court Coming to Pender, New Hanover." *Wilmington Morning Star*, December 10, 1B.

Vock, Daniel C. 2003. "Increase Court Funding, Chief Justice Pleads." *Chicago Daily Law Bulletin*, March 7, 1.

Webb, Gregg, and Keith E. Whittington. 2004. "Judicial Independence, the Power of the Purse, and Inherent Judicial Powers." *Judicature* 88:12–19, 45.

Weigl, Andrea. 2005. "Business Court Adds Two Judges." *Raleigh News and Observer*, August 31, B5.

Welch, Susan, Michael Combs, and John Gruhl. 1988. "Do Black Judges Make a Difference?" *American Journal of Political Science* 32:126–36.

Williams, Margaret Susan. 2004. "Women Judges: Accession at the State Court Level." Ph.D. diss., Ohio State University.

Wynn, Andrew James, Jr., and Eli Paul Mazur. 2004. "Perspectives: Judicial Elections versus Merit Selection: Judicial Diversity: Where Independence and Accountability Meet." *Albany Law Review* 67:775–91.

❖ 9. Conflict or Cooperation?

Local Governments, Intergovernmental Relations, and Federalism in North Carolina

SEAN HILDEBRAND AND JAMES H. SVARA

Most of the essays in this volume emphasize the importance of state-level political institutions and actors for understanding North Carolina politics. This essay offers a slightly different perspective by focusing on the characteristics of local government in North Carolina and investigating when and how the state cedes power to localities. The essay also investigates the state's intergovernmental relations, the interface between state and local governments, an increasingly salient topic in American politics.

Although important, local governments in North Carolina, as in all states, have both positive and negative attributes. On the positive side, North Carolina's local governments are generally well run, with civic-minded elected officials and professionally competent administrators. Almost all of North Carolina's counties and all but the smallest cities use the council-manager form of government. Cities can expand their boundaries into unincorporated areas of counties as growth occurs, and cities and counties cooperate in many areas. North Carolina has also reduced the number of school districts and avoided the proliferation of special districts that are common in other states but sometimes contribute to confusion among officials and residents about who is responsible for dealing with problems. The North Carolina state government is heavily involved in the "local" services of education and roads, and this financial contribution to some extent equalizes the quality of these services across the state.

Conversely, North Carolina local governments have less positive features. The state has many cities and counties, and their legal authority to control their own affairs is ambiguous. In addition, there are limitations on local autonomy, and many opportunities for state government intervention arise. Rather than undermining local governments, however, a complex mix of provisions and practices appears to enhance the position and integrity of local government. The state also ranks nineteenth in per-capita federal aid to state and local governments.

This essay takes a closer look at these positive and negative features of intergovernmental relations, beginning with a review of the distinctiveness of local governments in the Tar Heel State. Next, the essay examines governmental structure at the substate level, focusing specifically on cities and towns, counties, school districts, and special districts. The essay then highlights dimensions of federalism, such as state control and local autonomy, home rule, functional responsibilities of cities and counties, administrative discretion permitted to local governments, fiscal affairs, local revenues, local expenditures, grants-in-aid, unfunded mandates, and the amount of resources North Carolina receives from the federal government. The essay moves on to address three key challenges facing local governments—growth, education, and social policy issues—before concluding with some remarks on the status of local government, intergovernmental relations, and federalism.

❖ A Closer Look at North Carolina's Distinctiveness

Unlike its neighbor Georgia, North Carolina lacks a single dominant city. Charlotte, with a 2004 population approaching 600,000, is distancing itself from the other large cities, but six additional cities have populations exceeding 100,000, nineteen boast populations between 25,000 and 99,999, and forty-three have between 10,000 and 24,999 citizens. Overall, North Carolina has 547 municipalities and 100 counties. Because of the state's early reliance on agriculture and the limited means of transportation, the state allowed the incorporation of many municipalities. Counties also needed to be small enough to permit residents to travel on horseback to the county seat in a day's time. North Carolina resembles other older states such as Georgia, with 159 counties, and Missouri, with 115. Newer states, in contrast, tend to have fewer counties—Arizona, for example, has only fifteen. California, with a population of more than 35 million and a land area slightly larger than North Carolina, South Carolina, Virginia, and West Virginia combined, has only fifty-eight counties. Table 9.1 illustrates the differences among the fifty states in the number of counties, municipalities/townships, and special districts.

Historical circumstances explain much of North Carolina's distinctiveness. The state has a tradition by which the state government assumes responsibility for residents' basic needs rather than relying largely on local governments to do so. Since the early 1800s, the state has stressed centralized authority and responsibility. For improvements in government services, North Carolinians have stressed centralized authority, responsibility, and improvements in government services (Liner 1995).

After almost eighty years during which the scope and quality of services expanded, the Great Depression ended this growth and produced a fundamental reordering of responsibility for services. The state took over funding of rural highways, the minimum costs of education, and county prisons. It abolished independent school districts, putting the schools under county control, and tightened the

TABLE 9.1. Number of Municipalities, Counties, and Special Districts per State, 2002

State	Number of Municipalities and Townships	Number of Counties	Number of Special Districts
Alabama	451	67	525
Alaska	149	12[a]	14
Arizona	87	15	305
Arkansas	499	75	704
California	475	57	2,830
Colorado	270	62	1,414
Connecticut	179	8[b]	387
Delaware	57	3	260
Florida	404	66	626
Georgia	531	159	180
Hawaii	1	3	15
Idaho	200	44	798
Illinois	2,722	102	3,145
Indiana	1,577	91	1,125
Iowa	948	99	542
Kansas	1,926	104	1,533
Kentucky	424	119	720
Louisiana	302	60[a]	45
Maine	489	16	222
Maryland	157	23	85
Massachusetts	351	5[c]	413
Michigan	1,775	83	332
Minnesota	2,647	87	403
Mississippi	296	82	458
Missouri	1,258	114	1,514
Montana	129	54	592
Nebraska	977	93	1,146
Nevada	19	16	158
New Hampshire	234	10	148
New Jersey	566	21	276
New Mexico	101	33	628
New York	1,545	57	1,135
North Carolina	547	100	319
North Dakota	1,692	53	764
Ohio	2,250	88	631
Oklahoma	590	77	560
Oregon	240	36	927
Pennsylvania	2,564	66	1,885
Rhode Island	39	5[b]	75
South Carolina	269	46	301

TABLE 9.1. (*continued*)

State	Number of Municipalities and Townships	Number of Counties	Number of Special Districts
South Dakota	1,248	66	376
Tennessee	349	92	475
Texas	1,196	254	2,245
Utah	236	29	300
Vermont	284	14	152
Virginia	229	95	196
Washington	279	39	1,173
West Virginia	234	55	342
Wisconsin	1,850	72	684
Wyoming	98	23	546

Source: U.S. Census Bureau (2002).

[a] Louisiana uses the term "parish" and Alaska uses the term "borough" when describing county-level governments.

[b] Connecticut and Rhode Island have eliminated the use of counties for traditional government purposes, handing over all powers to the state. Boundaries remain for judicial purposes only.

[c] Massachusetts has abolished several county governments in recent years.

fiscal controls on local governments. In response to the availability of federal assistance, counties uniformly received responsibility for public welfare and had an incentive to establish health departments. In the 1960s, the state took over responsibility for all courts and covered the court system's operating expenses, although counties retained responsibility for constructing and maintaining court facilities. Other major changes since the 1930s have broadened the annexation authority of cities and expanded the state's shared revenues. In 1959 and 1967, changes in state law broadened the powers of cities and counties to plan, to zone, and to regulate land development and promoted greater cooperation between cities and counties. Constitutional amendments in the 1970s limited new municipal incorporations and provided greater flexibility in local government financing.

Providing context for a discussion of governmental structure in North Carolina requires a consideration of the dramatic rise in the state's metropolitan population. The 2005 Census estimates that 77 percent of the state's population is metropolitan, compared to 57 percent ten years earlier. Not only are these metropolitan areas growing, they are also spreading. In 1990, twenty-five of North Carolina's one hundred counties were classified as part of the Census Bureau's standard metropolitan statistical areas; in 2000, thirty-five counties had this designation.

❖ Governmental Structure at the Substate Level

The United States has many different kinds of local governments—towns, townships, cities, counties, school districts, and special districts—and they are used in many different combinations. For example, Hawaii and Alaska have created an atypical, highly centralized system of state control. The other states use combinations of various kinds of local governments. Some southern states rely largely on cities and counties, and New England states use cities and towns. At the extreme of complexity are mid-Atlantic states and Wisconsin, which have all types. Half of the states fall in between and employ a conventional combination of cities, counties, school districts, and special districts. North Carolina is part of a southern group, along with Maryland, Virginia, and Tennessee, that relies on cities and counties with school districts under the counties (Stephens and Wikstrom 2006).

Because of the confusing nature of the federal system, citizens in most states have a poor understanding of who provides a range of traditional bureaucratic services such as police, welfare, schools, mental health, and highways. In North Carolina, cities typically provide police protection, counties deliver welfare services, and in most cases a school district operating under the county delivers public education. In many parts of the state, mental health services are provided by a special district that covers several counties. Streets and highways are the combined responsibility of cities and the state government. Like all states, different types of governments have different purposes and serve differently defined segments of the population.

Although the state often grants power to cities, counties, and other types of local governments, the state retains complete authority over how local governments are arranged within state boundaries. The state retains all powers over local government except as it chooses to share them or delegate them to local governments. How much power the states should delegate to localities has been the subject of debate, and a general trend toward expanded "home rule" has occurred, as part of which local governments receive increased power and autonomy.

The states provide services to residents and exercise authority directly and through centralized and decentralized agencies with differing powers and relationships. The state obviously operates a wide range of programs from offices in the State Capitol, but it also has decentralized offices or installations to provide services throughout the state. The highway department has regional offices, and the highway patrol has stations throughout the state. Furthermore, freestanding operations such as state parks and universities are scattered geographically. These entities, though state run, may develop local ties. For example, a university may draw members of its board of trustees from the surrounding area and provide services in connection with local governments while serving students from other areas. Thus, the fact that the state runs a program does not mean that it is available only in the capital. Moreover, the fact that a program is run by the state does not assure that the state legislature and executive branch will exert unchallenged control over its operations.

CITY AND TOWN GOVERNMENT STRUCTURE

In the United States, local government structure is based on two major constitutional principles: separation of powers (between a strong mayor and council found in mayor-council cities) and the unitary model (which incorporates some of the elements of parliamentary government found in council-manager cities). The choice between these principles determines how elected officials will be organized, what powers they will have, and how they will be connected to the government's administrative staff to execute decisions and provide services to citizens. In addition, an implicit organizing principle commonly found in very small governments might be called government by elected committee. Although this form of government is called mayor-council, this small-town version features shared duties, no sharply defined separation of powers, and a limited number of staff. The general pattern in North Carolina includes all three approaches.

Government by committee is found in small towns with limited resources. Towns with more staff and resources add an administrator who serves the mayor and council. Towns adopt the council-manager form of government when seeking more clearly to assign responsibilities and organize activities. Counties used to follow a similar pattern: some were run by a commission alone, others had a commission and an administrator with limited responsibilities, and still others had a commission with a county manager. Now, all of North Carolina's counties operate with the county equivalent of the council-manager form. Table 9.2 lists the forms of government found in each state. Table 9.3 shows in-depth data for North Carolina, broken down by city size.

As table 9.3 suggests, all North Carolina cities with populations greater than ten thousand use the council-manager form, as do 85 percent of cities between with between five thousand and ten thousand residents and 74 percent of cities with populations between twenty-five hundred and five thousand. Ninety-one counties have managers, three have appointed the chair of the county commission as manager, and five have administrators who, though lacking all the formal powers of the manager, are by and large the equivalent of managers (*1995 Directory*).

In the small-town mayor-council form of government, elected officials serve as the governing body and help run the town's operations. The mayor chairs the coun-

TABLE 9.2. Form of Local Government by State, 2001

State	Mayor-Council	Council-Manager	Com-mission	Town Meeting	Repre-sentative Town Meeting	Number of Local Govern-ments
Alabama	83.3%	13.0%	3.7%			54
Alaska	8.3	83.3	8.3			12
Arizona	8.3	91.7				48
Arkansas	92.6	7.4				27
California	2.5	97.5				279
Colorado	10.2	89.8				59
Connecticut	23.2	28.0		46.3	2.4	82
Delaware		100.0				4
Florida	10.0	87.3	2.7			150
Georgia	39.4	60.6				66
Idaho	90.5	9.5				21
Illinois	55.9	39.9	4.2			213
Indiana	79.4	16.2	2.9	1.5		68
Iowa	54.4	45.6				79
Kansas	37.3	62.7				59
Kentucky	75.9	24.1				54
Louisiana	100.0					27
Maine	4.8	74.7		20.5		83
Maryland	48.0	52.0			25	
Massachusetts	12.0	18.3		56.0	13.7	175
Michigan	16.8	83.2				167
Minnesota	34.7	65.3				118
Mississippi	88.5	3.8	7.7			26
Missouri	50.0	48.3	1.7			118
Montana	57.9	42.1				19
Nebraska	69.7	27.3	3.0		33	
Nevada		100.0				10
New Hampshire	3.0	33.3	3.0	48.5	12.1	33
New Jersey	66.3	28.3	5.4			166
New Mexico	42.9	57.1				21
New York	79.8	19.2	1.0			104
North Carolina	6.4	93.6				109
North Dakota	33.3	16.7	50.0			6
Ohio	62.7	36.8	0.5			193
Oklahoma	15.4	84.6				65
Oregon	8.3	91.7				60
Pennsylvania	26.9	71.0	2.1			193
Rhode Island	34.6	46.2		11.5	7.7	26
South Carolina	53.7	46.3				41
South Dakota	43.8	12.5	43.8			16

TABLE 9.2. (*continued*)

State	Mayor-Council	Council-Manager	Com-mission	Town Meeting	Repre-sentative Town Meeting	Number of Local Govern-ments
Tennessee	44.9	51.0	4.1			49
Texas	16.4	83.2	0.4			232
Utah	61.9	38.1				42
Vermont		71.9		28.1		32
Virginia	3.7	96.3				54
Washington	56.5	39.1	4.3			69
West Virginia	44.0	56.0				25
Wisconsin	65.6	32.0	0.8	1.6		122
Wyoming	81.8	18.2				11
All states	36.3	56.4	1.5	4.9	0.9	3,745

Source: International City/County Management Association (2001).
Note: Only cities over 2,500 are included.

cil, and both have authority over the town's policy. The mayor also bears ultimate responsibility for the administration of town government, although council members may share this responsibility. Small towns use several different approaches for supervising staff and contract employees.[1] The mayor alone may provide such supervision, or council members, either singly or in committees, may oversee departments.

In the mayor-council towns with an administrator, the council appoints the administrator, decides what duties the administrator will be assigned, and determines whether he or she will have authority to act alone or will simply advise and assist the mayor and council. In many mayor-council-administrator town governments in North Carolina, however, the administrator operates much like a city manager.

The council-manager form is based on the unitary model of organizing government. The council possesses all governmental authority except for those functions it delegates to the manager, and the system thus lacks checks and balances. This form provides for specialization of roles but not separation of powers. The council and mayor occupy the overtly political roles in government, set policy, and select the city manager. The manager provides policy advice and recommendations to the council and directs the bureaucratic administrative apparatus. This broad division of functions includes considerable power sharing. The city manager also provides policy leadership in helping to frame the agenda and has latitude and therefore influence in the way that policy goals are converted into programs and

TABLE 9.3. Form of Government by Size of City in North Carolina, 2004

Government	Under 1,000	1,000–2,499	2,500–4,999	5,000–9,999
Mayor-council	179	30	10	2
Mayor-council administrator	28	33	12	5
Council-manager	23	54	64	40
Number of cities	230	117	86	47

Source: N.C. League of Municipalities (2006).

services. The council, conversely, has the potential to oversee the city's administrative performance by appraising the manager's performance (and whether the manager will continue in office) and through its ability to secure information about the performance of administrative staff in general. Elected officials are not supposed to get involved in specific administrative matters and usually do not.

The mayor typically serves as the presiding officer of the council and has identical powers to other council members, except for the veto power, which is granted in 28 percent of council-manager cities across the nation. Mayors, directly elected in 73 percent of these cities, can be an important source of policy guidance and coordination of participants, although they rarely exercise any administrative authority (*Municipal Yearbook* 1998). In North Carolina, most mayors do not vote in the city council except to break a tie. Although this differentiation of roles has been justified as a benefit to the mayor, who does not have to expend political capital on votes that are one-sided, the provision can weaken the mayor if it causes the other members of the council to view the mayor as removed from the council's decision-making process (Wheeland 1990).

The manager is the executive officer of the municipality, with extensive authority to direct staff, formulate and expend the budget (after approval by council), and control operations. The manager is appointed by the council with no voter involvement and serves at the pleasure of the council without term. The manager is typically the only staff member hired by the council (in some cities, the city attorney and/or clerk are selected by the council as well), and the manager has authority to hire all other employees. If the council is displeased with a staff member, the council can only attempt to persuade the manager to make the change and, if unsuccessful, either accept the situation or fire the manager. Elected officials usually respect the insulation of staff members from political interference, providing the manager some degree of autonomy over the bureaucracy.

The structure of council-manager government promotes cooperative relation-

10,000–24,999	25,000–49,999	50,000–99,999	100,000–249,999	250,000–599,999
0	0	0	0	0
0	0	0	0	0
43	9	9	5	2
43	9	9	5	2

ships among officials (Svara 1990). To be sure, tensions can emerge among elected officials or between elected officials and the staff, but without separation of powers, officials do not have to contend with structural impediments to cooperation, and positive relationships are more common. For example, in a survey of city managers in North Carolina, more than 90 percent reported that the city council and city manager have a good working relationship (Svara 1989)

COUNTY GOVERNMENT STRUCTURE

In general, the same features that are found in city government are also found in county government. Thus, the working relationship between the county commission and the county manager also tends to be positive. Similar to city councils, county commissions in North Carolina consist of three to eleven members, chosen at the same time as national and state officials in even-numbered years.

Despite these similarities, differences in the structure of counties affect how they function. The commissioners retain residual authority over certain management functions not found in cities. Consequently, county managers' organizational authority is somewhat ambiguous. The manager assures that the policies of the governing board are executed and directs and supervises the administration of all offices under the control of the governing board. The manager has the power to prepare and submit the annual budget and capital program to the governing board. Whereas the city manager also has complete authority over personnel appointments, the approval of the county commission is required unless delegated to the manager by resolution. The county commission appoints its clerk, county attorney, county assessor, and tax collector.

North Carolina's county organizational structure is more fragmented than the typical city structure under the council-manager form. Unlike city government, where the manager may hold sole line authority, additional elected officials at the county level, including the sheriff and the register of deeds, have line authority, including the power to hire and discharge staff. In addition, county governments have quasi-independent agencies that are responsible for major human service functions. The boards and commissions in these major departments have a formal role in policymaking, budgeting, and selection of the director. In both situations, these "subordinate" officials may play the county governmental process according to different standards than the county manager, ignore the manager's organizational authority, explicitly mobilize political supporters, and directly communicate and make deals with the county commission.

Despite these characteristics, most county governments do not appear in practice to be highly fragmented. The manager has major assets to support his or her influence over all the departments of county government, both those under the manager's direct authority and those that are not. These assets include proximity to the board of commissioners, commissioners' respect for the professional criteria the manager uses to make recommendations, and the manager's budget authority. The managers also rely on persuasion, active communication, and collaborative leadership to overcome the structural fragmentation. The end result is a negotiated structure that operates in an integrated way (Svara 1993)

SCHOOL DISTRICT STRUCTURE

As Hunter Bacot's essay on education policy in this volume details, North Carolina has 117 school districts—1 for each county, plus 17 community-based districts. As with cities and counties, the school system structure includes board members, who are elected by voters in all but three community-based school districts, where the city council appoints school board members. Little uniformity exists in the size and shape of school districts—that is, they vary considerably in land area, enrollment size, and school size. As Bacot discusses, the state constitution assures all children the right to a "sound, basic education," in accordance with the *Leandro* decision, which requires the state to provide additional assistance to districts that cannot afford to meet these requirements (*Leandro v. State of North Carolina* 1997, 2004). Many districts continue to explore the issue of school choice, considering the establishment of charter, magnet, and vocational schools.

THE OTHER GOVERNMENTS: SPECIAL DISTRICTS AND REGIONAL COUNCILS

North Carolina has made relatively little use of special districts. For purposes of comparison, North Carolina has 319 special districts, while Illinois has 3,145 and Louisiana has 45. In North Carolina, most special districts are of two types: soil and water conservation (ninety-eight) and housing and community development (ninety-one). There are no independent school districts, and many districts (109) share legal boundaries with a single county (U.S. Census Bureau 2002).

Governing regions, both in North Carolina and throughout the nation, are relatively weak. Throughout the country, there are virtually no examples of a regional government structure that covers an entire urban region. The common approach is to use a mechanism that can encourage voluntary cooperation. Composed of representatives of member governments, regional councils are long-established organizations created to foster regionalism. Regional councils are agents of the local governments that constitute each region, but they also serve important purposes for higher levels of government. Some tension over their purpose, however, arises from the fact that the funding for regional councils comes primarily from federal and state sources, and most of this funding is not available to support the core functions of promoting regional cooperation and services to local governments. Thus, potential confusion arises over the identity and function of regional councils. The state of North Carolina has never explicitly set regional goals or clearly defined the working relationships of organizations that deal with regional affairs. Regionalism in North Carolina has essentially consisted of what the regional councils have chosen to do (Svara 1998).

Regional councils typically fulfill eight major functions: (1) serving as a regional forum, (2) regional planning, (3) service to local governments, (4) providing data centers, (5) promoting cooperative ventures, (6) promoting environmental protection, (7) promoting economic development, and (8) administering federal and state programs. Of these, only planning and intergovernmental program administration are directly linked to the purposes of creating regional councils (along with economic development for five regions started for this purpose). The other functions have emerged as regional councils worked with member governments. There are no provisions for direct citizen participation in the selection of regional councils, although the members may have been elected to their respective city councils or county commissions.

Organization on an even larger scale has occurred in the area of economic development. Starting in 1995, North Carolina has undertaken a new strategy for economic development by supporting seven large regions organized as economic development partnerships or commissions. Each partnership has the ability to recruit and assist businesses in the region and provides a single point of contact for those seeking further information about the area's economic development agenda, skills of the local workforce, incentives from local governments, and other related data.

❖ Dimensions of Federalism

A variety of tools can promote control and coordination across levels of government. In varying combinations, state and federal governments can control how local governments operate, what tasks they perform, and how much freedom and local autonomy they have to initiate their own approaches. The state and federal government may also provide financial resources to help localities accomplish tasks, although higher-level governments can also take money away from localities.

STATE CONTROL AND LOCAL AUTONOMY

Several characteristics contribute to state control of local government affairs in North Carolina. First, North Carolina remains a Dillon's Rule state, meaning that localities have only powers expressly granted by the state (Richardson, Gough, and Puentes 2003). Second, the state is responsible for rural roads and covers a majority of basic educational expenses. Third, all local government bonds or notes must be approved and sold by the Local Government Commission, an agency of the state government. Finally, the state extensively uses special legislation (applying only to a single city or county), but this practice is often criticized as state interference in a locality's affairs. The prevailing opinion among public officials in the state, however, is that these characteristics benefit local governments. State involvement in roads and education has relieved the fiscal burden on local governments. The bonding restrictions have reduced the cost of borrowing, helped to protect governments from excessive debt, and encouraged national investor rating services to give the state higher bond ratings. In 2004, Fitch rated all $4.3 billion of the state's outstanding general obligation bonds as AAA as a consequence of "the state's very moderate debt burden and excellent debt structure, as well as the long-term prospects for an expanding and diversifying economy" ("Fitch Rates" 2004). Local legislation promotes flexibility and experimentation.

Furthermore, state policies generally enhance the position of general-purpose local governments. Municipalities may expand through unilateral annexation, and existing cities are protected from new incorporations close to their borders. Policy and common practice limit the role of special districts. Counties have fiscal responsibility for schools, provide for the construction of school facilities, and have broad authority to provide urban-type services. Cities and counties are permitted to share in the provision of services and to transfer functions.

Local governments in North Carolina operate under extensive state control, although the state has given considerable power to cities to control their own expansion and development and to counties to provide a wide range of services. The

General Assembly has virtually complete power to create or abolish municipal corporations, and it can alter their boundaries, change their structures, and grant and take away their legal powers. Still, the state has typically not used these powers arbitrarily or to the severe disadvantage of local governments except in control over revenue sources, as we shall see.

LEGAL/TRADITIONAL FEATURES OF HOME RULE IN NORTH CAROLINA

Local bills receive extensive, although not unlimited,[2] use in North Carolina. The state legislature uses special acts to bring municipalities into existence and to give powers that are not generally available to selected local governments. Municipal reformers in the late nineteenth and early twentieth centuries believed that this practice constituted an invitation for state interference and political manipulation of local affairs, but local legislation is now generally viewed as a tool for flexibility and responsiveness to local needs. As a rule, if a county's legislative delegation supports the proposed local bill, the entire General Assembly will approve the measure. Exceptions would apply to local changes that were controversial or were viewed as having important statewide consequences.

Local laws initially approved as experiments may be converted to general legislation (Lawrence and Wicker 1995). For example, Raleigh received permission to carry out satellite annexation in 1967. Other cities received similar authority in the next two legislative sessions, in 1969 and 1971, and in 1974, the General Assembly passed an act that permitted such annexations statewide. General laws apply to all cities statewide or to cities of a particular class, such as all cities above a certain size. North Carolina does not, however, have a general classification system under which cities of different sizes have different powers.

A city may be created only by an act of the legislature, and the General Assembly may incorporate an area with or without a local referendum. Two approaches to creating new municipalities exist. The more common way is for a legislator to introduce a bill for that purpose and to work to secure its passage (Lawrence and Wicker 1995). The alternative approach is to first refer the proposal to the Joint Legislative Commission on Municipal Incorporation.[3] Once approved, the incorporation may be either immediate or subject to the approval of residents of the area to be incorporated. Thus, the approval of residents is possible but not required. From 1981 through 1994, the legislature approved incorporation for forty-nine communities, although residents in ten of these areas voted against incorporation. Since 1995, legislation for thirty-eight additional incorporations passed the General Assembly, with twenty-one becoming cities (Lawrence and Wicker 1995).

The legislature creates municipalities on a fairly regular basis but rarely uses its power to abolish municipalities. In fact, the legislature has exercised this power only at the request of residents of the area, normally because a city government has become inactive (Lawrence and Wicker 1995).

Creating and abolishing municipalities may be the most obvious ways the legislature can exert power over the local government structure in North Carolina, but there are also other means. The legislature also creates the framework for consolidating two or more government structures into one (North Carolina General Statutes n.d., chapter 153A, sections 401–5). In these cases, the governments interested in consolidation create a charter or governmental study commission. The commission may call for a referendum on its proposed plan of governmental consolidation. If approved by a majority of voters, the consolidation becomes effective when enacted by the General Assembly. Since 1933, eight referenda have occurred on consolidating the primary city and county governments in four counties (Lawrence and Wicker 1995). None has succeeded. The highest proconsolidation vote of 42 percent occurred in the 1995 referendum in Wilmington–New Hanover (where referenda had also occurred in 1933, 1973, and 1987). Two counties that have also previously rejected the idea, Durham and Mecklenburg, continue to consider consolidation.

Limited home rule exists for charter revisions that pertain to the form of government and the structure of the governing board. Cities may adopt the council-manager or mayor-council form of government (or add an administrator to the mayor-council form), alter the size of the council, terms of office, or the nature of members' constituencies (at-large, district, or a combination), the use of partisan ballots, and the method of selecting the mayor). The city council may change the charter by ordinance, following a public hearing, with no referendum. It may propose a change and allow voters to determine whether it will be accepted. Residents can also force a referendum by petition of 10 percent of the city's voters or five thousand residents, whichever is less. Citizens may also initiate ballot measures, with the same requirements for signatures as with petitions. As a fourth method of change, the General Assembly may alter a city's charter. Other types of changes in the charter must be approved by the legislature.

Table 9.4 illustrates the options available to citizens of North Carolina as well as the other states when considering referendums, initiatives, and recalls at the state level. While these options are available for local ordinances, North Carolina, like fifteen other states, does not permit these measures for change within state government and policy. States that allow such input from its citizens are mostly concentrated in New England, the Midwest, and the western half of the nation.

Counties may adopt the county-manager form of government by resolution (North Carolina General Statutes n.d., chapter 158A, section 81). They may alter the board of commissioners with respect to number of members, terms of office, mode of election, and selection of the chair from among already-elected members or by direct election for a two- or four-year term (North Carolina General Statutes n.d., chapter 158A, sections 58–60). A resolution approved by the county commissioners is subject to referendum.

A 1972 constitutional amendment indicated the state's preference for annexation of newly developing areas outside cities over incorporation of new municipalities (North Carolina Constitution, Article 7, Section 1). New municipalities may not be incorporated within prescribed distances from an existing municipality with a population of more than five thousand. The limits are one mile for a city of this size, three miles for a city of ten thousand or more, four miles for a city of twenty-five thousand or more, and five miles for a city of fifty thousand or more. The General Assembly may override these restrictions only by a three-fifths vote of the members of each house, and such overrides have been rare.

Cities in North Carolina enjoy extensive authority to take in developing areas on their doorsteps—or even a step or two further away. The state's approach to local affairs favors expanding existing municipalities. A key aspect of this approach is that cities have unilateral authority to take in urbanized areas on their borders. Cities have had the power to initiate annexation of contiguous areas developed for urban purposes since 1959. As long as cities meet the required conditions in the area to be annexed, follow prescribed procedures, and make services available in the annexed areas, cities are free to annex without approval by the residents of the area to be taken into the city. Annexation can occur across county lines without approval of the county affected.

Annexation may occur in North Carolina via three other methods as well: annexation by legislative act, voluntary annexation of areas contiguous to the city, and voluntary annexation of areas not contiguous to the city. The legislative method is normally used only at a city's request to meet circumstances that are not accommodated by the standard method, such as annexation of land for public facilities surrounded by areas of limited development or annexation involving rivers and lakes. Voluntary annexation of contiguous areas can be approved by the city council after receiving a petition from all the owners of real property within the area to be annexed. Satellite areas can be annexed, also upon the petition of property owners, if five conditions are met: (1) the area is no more than three miles from the city limits, (2) none of the area is closer to another city than to the annexing city, (3) entire subdivisions are included in the annexation, (4) the total area does not

TABLE 9.4. Use of Initiatives, Referenda, and Recall Elections by State, 2006–2007

| State | Statutes | | | Constitution | | |
	Initiative Type	Citizen Petition Referendum	Legislative Referendum	Initiative	Legislative Referendum	Recall Election
Alabama	No	No	No	No	No	No
Alaska	Direct	Yes	No	No	Yes	Yes
Arizona	Direct	Yes	Yes	Direct	Yes	Yes
Arkansas	Direct	Yes	Yes	Direct	Yes	No
California	Direct	Yes	Yes	Direct	Yes	Yes
Colorado	Direct	Yes	No	Direct	Yes	Yes
Connecticut	No	No	No	No	No	No
Delaware	No	No	No	No	No	No
Florida	No	No	No	Direct	Yes	No
Georgia	No	No	No	No	No	Yes
Hawaii	No	No	No	No	No	No
Idaho	Direct	Yes	Yes	No	Yes	Yes
Illinois	No	No	Yes	Direct	Yes	No
Indiana	No	No	No	No	No	No
Iowa	No	No	No	No	No	No
Kansas	No	No	No	No	No	Yes
Kentucky	No	Yes	Yes	No	Yes	No
Louisiana	No	No	No	No	No	Yes
Maine	Indirect	Yes	Yes	No	Yes	No
Maryland	No	Yes	Yes	No	Yes	No
Massachusetts	Indirect	Yes	Yes	Indirect	Yes	No
Michigan	Indirect	Yes	Yes	Direct	Yes	Yes
Minnesota	No	No	No	No	No	Yes
Mississippi	No	No	No	Indirect	Yes	No
Missouri	Direct	Yes	Yes	Direct	Yes	No
Montana	Direct	Yes	Yes	Direct	Yes	Yes
Nebraska	Direct	Yes	Yes	Direct	Yes	No
Nevada	Indirect	Yes	Yes	Direct	Yes	Yes
New Hampshire	No	No	No	No	No	No
New Jersey	No	No	No	No	No	Yes
New Mexico	No	Yes	Yes	No	Yes	No
New York	No	No	No	No	No	No
North Carolina	No	No	No	No	No	No
North Dakota	Direct	Yes	Yes	Direct	Yes	Yes
Ohio	Indirect	Yes	Yes	Direct	Yes	No
Oklahoma	Direct	Yes	Yes	Direct	Yes	No
Oregon	Direct	Yes	Yes	Direct	Yes	Yes
Pennsylvania	No	No	No	No	No	No

TABLE 9.4. (*continued*)

State	Statutes			Constitution		
	Initiative Type	Citizen Petition Referen-dum	Legislative Referen-dum	Initiative	Legislative Referen-dum	Recall Election
Rhode Island	No	No	No	No	No	Yes
South Carolina	No	No	No	No	No	No
Tennessee	No	No	No	No	No	No
Texas	No	No	No	No	No	No
Utah	Direct and indirect	Yes	Yes	No	Yes	No
Vermont	No	No	No	No	No	No
Virginia	No	No	No	No	No	No
Washington	Direct and indirect	Yes	Yes	No	Yes	Yes
West Virginia	No	No	No	No	No	No
Wisconsin	No	No	No	No	No	Yes
Wyoming	Direct	Yes	No	No	Yes	No

Source: National Conference of State Legislatures (2004).

exceed 10 percent of the existing city area, and (5) the city can provide full services to the satellite area (North Carolina General Statutes n.d., chapter 160A, section 58.1).

North Carolina statute permits nearby cities to enter into an agreement under which they divide the territory that each will eventually annex (North Carolina General Statutes n.d., chapter 160A, sections 58.21–28). The agreements, which may last for up to twenty years, encourage orderly planning for the extension of boundaries and facilities and alert residents in areas adjacent to such cities of likely changes in boundaries (Liner 1995, 47). In the absence of an agreement, a dispute between cities that wish to take in the same area is resolved in favor of the one that first adopted a resolution of intent under the nonvoluntary approach or that first received petitions under the voluntary approach (Lawrence and Wicker 1995).

Most annexations result from one of the voluntary methods, but most people and property are annexed under the involuntary method (Lawrence 2007b). Between 1999 and 2004, North Carolina had 4,130 annexation actions covering more than 183,000 acres and roughly 178,000 people, about 2 percent of the state's population. During this period, four cities added more than 10,000 people through annexation: Charlotte (33,736), Raleigh (22,100), Wilmington (20,437), and Fayetteville (11,392). Annexation clearly remains an important tool cities use to bring newly developing areas within city boundaries.

According to the state's General Statutes, a municipality may exercise planning controls in areas up to one mile outside its boundaries (North Carolina General Statutes n.d., chapter 160A, section 360). This authority may not be exercised, however, if the county is already enforcing zoning, subdivision regulations, and the state building code in the prospective extraterritorial jurisdiction zone. When the city enforces zoning or subdivision regulations, it must make some provision for citizens in the outlying area to have a voice in decision making by the planning agency and the zoning board of adjustment. The city must ask the county commissioners to appoint outside members to these two bodies, with the number of people appointed and their voting power determined by the city.

FUNCTIONAL RESPONSIBILITIES ASSIGNED TO CITIES AND COUNTIES

Cities and counties generally have complementary functions. Cities are responsible for public safety, public works, community development, recreation, and human relations functions, whereas counties are responsible for social services, schools, and traditional county functions. Counties serve all residents, whether or not they live in incorporated areas.

Despite this common division of labor, considerable overlap exists between the two bodies. Counties are authorized to engage in most of the functions that cities can provide, and vice versa. The major exceptions to this overlap of powers (often called dual authority) are human services provided by counties and streets and sidewalks provided by cities (Liner 1995). The latter exception makes it advantageous for developing areas to be annexed by municipalities because they could not obtain a full range of city-type services from counties. Conversely, counties' (or in certain cases, municipalities') ability to provide other services in unincorporated areas helps reduce the need for the creation of special districts. Moreover, residents of outlying areas commonly object to having to pay both municipal and county taxes.

The state authorizes various forms of intergovernmental cooperation. Governments can contract with other governments for virtually all the functions they can provide. Counties contract with cities for extension of city infrastructure, and cities contract with counties for services. Certain functions are also commonly transferred to the county after development of the function within municipalities (Lawrence 2007a). Library systems, hospitals, and solid waste disposal are now largely county functions. Functional consolidation of city and county services has also occurred, particularly in the area of planning.

Highways are the shared responsibility of cities and the state (North Carolina

General Statutes n.d., chapter 136, section 66.1). Public roads and streets outside of cities and those that handle travel into and through cities are the responsibility of the state. Other streets and roads within cities are the responsibility of city governments. Planning for thoroughfares in cities is also a shared responsibility, and the city's thoroughfare plan must be approved by the state. In addition, the state board of transportation is required to consult with county commissioners annually about secondary road needs.[4]

ADMINISTRATIVE DISCRETION PERMITTED LOCAL GOVERNMENTS

The General Assembly has delegated to cities and counties broad authority for personnel administration. Cities are authorized to create, change, abolish, and consolidate city offices and departments and to determine how to organize the city government. The only restrictions pertain to altering offices defined by law.[5]

The same grant of authority applies to the board of county commissioners as is found in cities, but state law determines a wide range of appointments. The sheriff and register of deeds are elected and have authority to appoint and remove staff. Appointments in the health and social services departments, in area mental health authorities, and in local emergency management agencies must be made in accordance with the provisions of the State Personnel Act (Bell and Wicker 1999). Cooperative extension employees are jointly appointed by the board of commissioners and the state Cooperative Extension Service. The boards of elections and education also control their own staff.

FISCAL AFFAIRS

As a consequence of widespread fiscal distress in local governments during the Great Depression, North Carolina established tight financial controls over local governments. Lee Carter (1995, 80–81) asserts that "state oversight of local government finance is more centralized in North Carolina than in any other state, both through the financial laws under which local governments operate and through the activities of the" Local Government Commission. The commission's powers include the approval of financing and sales of debt and authorization of general obligation bonds as well as the establishment of other policies and providing arbitration in situations such as the amount of payments to be made by municipalities when portions of fire districts are annexed. The Local Government Commission prefers to act in an advisory role but backs up that role with substantial regulatory powers.

Commission staff members exert substantial influence over the complex sphere of local government financial and debt management. Commission personnel meet with local officials from governments considering debt financing and review the

TABLE 9.5. Revenues and Expenditures of Municipalities and Counties in North Carolina, 2005

Municipalities			Counties		
Revenues	Per capita	Percentage	Revenues	Per capita	Percentage
Property tax	376	22	Property tax	512	44
Sales tax	164	10	Sales tax	190	16
Inter-governmental	211	12	Inter-governmental	235	20
Sales and services	116	7	Sales and services	125	11
Utility	639	37	Other tax	51	4
Miscellaneous	204	12	Miscellaneous	62	5
Total	$1,710	100	Total	$1,175	100
Expenditures	Per capita	Percentage	Expenditures	Per capita	Percentage
Utility	653	36	Education	353	28
Debt service	181	10	Debt service	113	9
Public safety	339	19	Human services	352	28
General government	136	8	General government	107	8
Transportation	210	11	Public safety	177	14
Other	287	16	Other	166	13
Total	$1,806	100	Total	$1,268	100

Source: N.C. Department of the State Treasurer (2006).

financial condition and proposed methods for repaying the debt. The staff also investigates whether any problems exist that should be corrected before funds can be borrowed and consults with officials regarding the method of financing. In the case of non-general-obligation bonds, staff members take an active role in negotiating the arrangements and terms of the bonds. Formal approval of the Local Government Commission is necessary before any debt is issued.

LOCAL REVENUES

The property tax is the largest unrestricted local government revenue source and the one that can be altered with greatest flexibility.[6] Table 9.5 summarizes the major city and county revenue sources. Although it is the local governments' tax, the state can affect this revenue source by exempting or providing reduced valuations for certain types of property, or by applying reduced tax rates as long as such rates apply uniformly across the state (North Carolina General Statutes n.d., chapter 105, sections 275–278.9). The state excludes the first twenty thousand dollars in property value for low-income, elderly, or totally and permanently disabled homeowners. Half of the lost property tax is reimbursed to local government. In 1994 and 1995, the state exempted business inventories from the tax base and eliminated an intangibles tax that had been collected by the state and largely returned to local governments. The state reimburses local government for these lost revenues, but there is a perennial concern that state legislators will conclude that the state cannot afford these payments to cities.

North Carolina has a broad constitutional limitation that prevents local governments from levying property taxes "except for purposes authorized by general law . . . unless the tax is approved by a majority of the qualified voters" of the jurisdiction (North Carolina Constitution, Article 5, Section 2[5]). The state collects and distributes to counties 2 percent local-option sales taxes.[7] Half is returned to the county from which it was collected, and the other half—the result of two separate .5 percent local options—is pooled statewide and allocated among the counties on a per-capita basis. Thus, this portion operates as a state revenue-sharing program with some equalization of resources on the basis of population. When the General Assembly alters the overall state sales tax, it may also affect this local revenue source. In 2005, the legislature reduced the sales tax on food from 4 to 3 percent, but it left the local 2 percent share unchanged. If the movement to eliminate the food tax completely ultimately succeeds, it is easy to imagine that the local share might also be cut.

Local governments may also choose to use other revenue sources such as taxes on privilege licenses, cable television franchises, animals, motor vehicle licenses, and 911 services. Local acts permit local governments in about seventy counties to levy occupancy taxes on hotel and motel rooms (Lawrence and Millonzi 2007). Local governments can also impose a variety of user charges for services, such as water and sewer. A range of fees must or can be imposed, including development impact fees and charges for regulatory services. Cities and counties share in the net profits of state Alcoholic Beverage Control stores.

LOCAL EXPENDITURES

City and county expenditures, summarized in table 9.5, indicate the functional differentiation of the two local governments. Cities emphasize utilities, public safety, and transportation; counties emphasize education and human services. As noted, the Local Budget Fiscal and Fiscal Control Act creates the framework for controlling expenditures (North Carolina General Statutes n.d., chapter 159, sections 7–42). This law requires that the budget be balanced and that funds be budgeted before they can be spent. The act restricts expenditures from any source of revenue to spending for "public purposes." The courts have interpreted this provision to mean that governments should not enter functions traditionally provided by the private sector (Lawrence 2007a).

STATE GOVERNMENT GRANTS-IN-AID TO LOCALITIES

In the early twentieth century, the state relied on local governments to fund and administer most public services. Over time, state government has progressively increased its share of the total state and local revenues. In 1900, local governments accounted for more than three-quarters of the taxes levied by all levels of government to support state and local functions; by 1992, that number had dropped to 21 percent. The state share increased from 23 to 55 percent, while the federal share expanded from less than 1 percent to 24 percent (Liner 1995). When direct spending by state and local government are compared, the state share of the total is more than three-quarters for higher education, public welfare, and highways (*Significant Features* 1992). In addition, state sources provide two-thirds of the total (including federal) and 71 percent of the state-local expenditures for public education (*Significant Features* 1992). The next-largest state contribution is 32 percent of the expenditures for health and hospitals.

Finally, North Carolina state taxes are shared with local governments. Beer and wine taxes are shared with both cities and counties, the state franchise tax and gasoline tax are shared with cities only, and the real-estate transfer tax is shared solely with counties. The major state reimbursements are the equivalent of the amount formerly raised through the intangible and business inventories taxes.

UNFUNDED MANDATES IMPOSED BY STATE GOVERNMENT ON LOCALITIES

Given the nature of the relationship between state and local governments in North Carolina, the concept of unfunded mandates is not particularly meaningful as a discrete set of controls. The state sets the terms for a wide range of activities in local governments, most of which have financial implications for local governments. The state rarely provides full funding to offset the costs of compliance or service provision, although virtually none of its mandates is totally unfunded (McLaughlin and Lehman 1996). In the mid-1990s, the ten most expensive state mandates for cities and counties were adequate facilities for public schools, local share of Medicaid costs, local share of Aid to Families with Dependent Children costs, various water testing requirements, wastewater monitoring, solid waste recycling, landfill construction regulations and increased tipping fees, pension benefits for law enforcement officers, compliance with federal Occupational Safety and Health Act (state administered), fire inspections, and watershed protection (McLaughlin and Lehman 1996). The list likely would be similar today.

GIVING AND TAKING FROM THE FEDERAL GOVERNMENT
IN NORTH CAROLINA

In a federal system, some states will receive more benefits from the federal government than others. Federal assistance to North Carolina exceeded $70 billion in 2002, with $48 billion funding direct expenditures or obligations. When this amount is compared to what North Carolinians pay in taxes, the state comes out ahead. For the 2004 fiscal year, residents received $1.10 for every dollar paid in taxes to the federal government. Among other southern states, Georgia, Florida, and Texas were about even, whereas Tennessee ($1.29), South Carolina ($1.35), Kentucky and Louisiana ($1.41), Virginia ($1.60), and Mississippi ($1.70) received bigger returns than did North Carolina. In contrast, the northeastern and midwestern states combined received only 89 cents for each dollar contributed. It might seem that North Carolina would benefit from its many military installations, but this is not the case. North Carolina's level of per-capita military spending is only 91 percent of the national average.

Table 9.6 illustrates the amount of grants and aid received by all fifty states during the third quarter of 2006. While Louisiana, Florida, and Mississippi receive the greatest amount of federal aid as they continue to recover from the recent swarm of hurricanes and other natural disasters, North Carolina found itself near the middle of the pack in per-capita assistance received. The state receives more than Virginia, Tennessee, Georgia, and Kentucky but far less than South Carolina and West Virginia. However, these figures may be subject to changes in the natural as well as political environment should new projects and needs receive greater attention and funding.

❖ Challenges Faced by Local Government

In 1995, the General Assembly created the N.C. Progress Board, an independent agency that sets goals and tracks the state's progress in several key policy areas, including economic development, education, and social policy issues. The board's 2005 report showed mixed results in terms of progress, likely a result of budget concerns early in the twenty-first century.

TABLE 9.6. Total Federal Assistance Received by States during Third Quarter, 2006 (in Thousands of Dollars)

State	Total Grants	Total Assistance	Total Loans	Total Miscellaneous	Overall Total	Per-Capita Rank
Alabama	1,724,597	5,155,552	814,693	1,080,207	8,775,049	10
Alaska	643,744	357,089	133,877	137,121	1,271,831	11
Arizona	2,012,755	5,173,316	597,513	1,216,709	9,000,293	40
Arkansas	972,678	3,085,790	355,092	389,548	4,803,108	20
California	12,652,839	29,298,363	2,012,557	12,854,631	56,818,390	31
Colorado	1,245,150	3,251,703	876,789	587,656	5,961,298	48
Connecticut	1,169,804	3,589,135	400,817	994,243	6,153,999	18
Delaware	288,270	808,164	106,700	585,318	1,788,452	6
Florida	4,430,210	20,210,105	2,059,521	53,307,929	80,007,765	3
Georgia	2,957,957	7,106,847	1,319,567	2,468,043	13,852,414	37
Hawaii	430,263	1,061,370	53,657	714,501	2,259,791	17
Idaho	445,530	1,122,632	244,732	303,157	2,116,051	41
Illinois	4,310,381	11,767,885	1,083,644	1,306,682	18,468,592	42
Indiana	2,798,363	5,988,667	710,614	700,801	10,198,445	26
Iowa	886,039	2,953,305	318,778	222,409	4,380,531	38
Kansas	757,161	2,591,960	271,234	230,828	3,851,183	44
Kentucky	1,569,010	4,434,828	394,190	518,295	6,916,323	24
Louisiana	10,499,683	4,657,446	5,234,259	12,886,542	33,277,930	1
Maine	658,292	1,381,364	133,425	237,955	2,411,036	13
Maryland	1,931,473	4,723,986	564,294	1,378,652	8,598,405	35
Massachusetts	2,919,560	6,952,020	314,108	1,402,991	11,588,679	14
Michigan	2,662,490	10,387,903	957,489	781,442	14,789,324	39
Minnesota	1,456,879	4,191,753	681,236	318,802	6,648,670	47
Mississippi	7,024,194	3,100,984	1,855,914	2,373,317	14,354,409	2
Missouri	2,071,529	5,946,972	693,819	550,669	9,262,989	27

State					Rank
Montana	475,082	897,771	143,884	150,137	1,666,874	16
Nebraska	350,705	1,586,291	212,927	341,255	2,491,178	43
Nevada	534,261	1,745,040	243,261	734,193	3,256,755	46
New Hampshire	378,986	1,113,095	125,977	206,868	1,824,926	45
New Jersey	2,561,352	8,585,697	806,153	6,345,243	18,298,445	5
New Mexico	842,488	1,662,752	212,095	377,679	3,095,014	28
New York	10,497,844	20,394,348	974,672	3,931,516	35,798,380	12
North Carolina	3,076,352	7,855,618	819,089	3,728,175	15,479,234	19
North Dakota	300,591	644,998	132,497	195,395	1,273,481	9
Ohio	3,511,663	11,451,491	1,342,739	984,208	17,290,101	36
Oklahoma	1,171,588	3,628,912	434,825	338,185	5,573,510	32
Oregon	1,165,797	3,345,382	300,296	1,224,673	6,036,148	25
Pennsylvania	4,524,557	14,858,219	800,272	2,026,187	22,209,235	15
Rhode Island	598,885	1,139,369	87,483	363,210	2,188,947	8
South Carolina	1,492,983	4,075,300	348,558	4,745,919	10,662,760	4
South Dakota	283,310	743,068	122,380	88,968	1,237,726	29
Tennessee	2,054,964	6,082,545	634,275	588,865	9,360,649	33
Texas	5,682,997	17,543,705	3,085,046	13,413,528	39,725,276	22
Utah	750,564	1,435,303	521,806	180,558	2,888,231	50
Vermont	307,923	571,801	58,000	101,090	1,038,814	23
Virginia	2,195,946	6,090,672	2,128,675	2,511,533	12,926,826	21
Washington	2,718,861	5,252,752	687,120	1,198,524	9,857,257	34
West Virginia	838,090	2,384,019	119,722	437,484	3,779,315	7
Wisconsin	1,009,811	4,933,098	489,423	382,518	6,814,850	49
Wyoming	217,188	429,963	74,134	84,599	805,884	30

Source: U.S. Census Bureau (2006).

Growth and economic development can provide new opportunities and improve the well-being of residents of the state. Alternately, growth and economic development can have negative consequences for the environment and quality of life and can strain resources when the cost of infrastructure and services for new residents exceeds the additional revenue generated.

Cities and counties have broad authority to engage in activities related to community and economic development, industrial promotion, and urban renewal. Counties may also create special authorities that issue industrial revenue bonds, subject to the approval of the Department of Commerce and the Local Government Commission. To attract new development, local governments may provide public services and facilities, such as water and sewer and streets and roads (cities only). In addition, local governments may acquire property and build public facilities that will support private development, such as off-street parking. North Carolina has provided cities and counties with broad authority to build industrial parks, assemble other potential industrial sites, construct and lease or sell shell buildings, and prepare sites for industrial properties or facilities (North Carolina General Statutes n.d., chapter 158, section 7.1).

Sparked by recent debates over the *Kelo v. New London* decision, which upheld a city's right to take property for economic development, the question of eminent domain has become an important issue in intergovernmental relations. In North Carolina, cities and counties may acquire property through eminent domain for a variety of purposes (North Carolina General Statutes n.d., chapter 40A, section 3[b]). If the owner of the property questions the appropriateness of the action or objects to the amount offered, the court oversees the determination of just compensation that reflects the property's fair market value. According to the North Carolina General Statutes, chapter 158, section 7.1, localities may spend money "for the purposes of aiding and encouraging the location of manufacturing enterprises," including additional incentives not mentioned earlier, although the total investment in economic development programs cannot exceed 0.5 percent of a government's tax base. Under the redevelopment statute (North Carolina General Statutes n.d., chapter 160A, section 512), local governments may make property available to private developers, either directly or after improvements have been made, as long as redevelopment procedures have been followed.

General-obligation bonds may be used to support these activities if approved in a referendum, and revenue bonds may be used without voter approval to finance a public service enterprise improvement if sufficient revenue will be generated to retire the debt. The state constitution does not, however, permit local governments to offer property-tax exemptions or special classifications if they are not available statewide. No such special classifications have been enacted, so local economic development officials may not offer them to developers (Lawrence and Wicker 1994).

As the state continues to grow, various levels of government have been somewhat slow to meet demands for additional infrastructure. The state recently expanded the One North Carolina Fund to lure new businesses or to provide funds to expand enterprises already located in the state. However, the state continues to have several problems with the adequacy of transportation infrastructure and with air/water pollution. The N.C. Department of Transportation's long-range plan anticipates a $29 billion shortfall over the next twenty-five years as the state tries to keep up with growth by expanding and updating key routes and developing new roadways. Residents in urban areas across the state have pondered the creation of light rail mass transit systems or similar types of public transportation development. Charlotte has an aggressive plan to develop a coordinated system of light rail, trolley car, and bus service to serve the entire metropolitan area by 2025. The Triangle Transit Authority has plans to operate a regional rail service by 2009, although the prospects of federal funding for this service declined after the project's rating was lowered in 2005 (Triangle Transit Authority 2007).

EDUCATION: CLOSING THE PERFORMANCE GAP

As North Carolina continues to grow, creating and maintaining a quality public educational system remains a priority for state and local governments. Spending for education at all levels (K–12 and colleges) accounts for 55 percent of the state's general operating budget. During the 2002–3 school year, the state provided school districts with an average of 60 percent of their operating budgets. Local governments provide an additional 31 percent, with federal programs accounting for the remainder. Districts in Kentucky (59.5) and West Virginia (60) receive nearly the same percentage of revenue from their state governments, but the majority of southeastern states place a heavier burden on local government sources to finance public education. North Carolina, however, spends $6,635 per pupil on educational expenses, which is less than all of its closest neighbors with the exception of Tennessee ($6,200) (U.S. Census Bureau 2006a).

In recent years, North Carolina's students have improved their performance on standardized tests. Oddly, the state ranks high compared to the rest of the nation in elementary test scores but low in high school indicators such as SAT scores. In addition, North Carolina's four-year high school graduation rate remains one of the lowest in the nation. While the number of advanced degrees per capita is high, basic educational attainment rates, such as the percentage of the population with high school diplomas or college degrees, fall in the bottom half of the nation. Chapter 12 provides a more detailed discussion of education.

SOCIAL POLICY ISSUES

Like most states, North Carolina spends a large portion (34 percent) of its general operating budget on social welfare issues, including welfare, criminal justice, and health care. In North Carolina, poverty remains a major problem, particularly among children: 18 percent of children live below the poverty line (N.C. Progress Board 2006). The three-year average poverty rate is trending upward as well. In addition, the state ranks fortieth in median household income, earning 88 percent of the national median (N.C. Progress Board 2006).

While the state enjoys strong medical resources, many health problems related to lifestyle choices and lack of insurance coverage exist. Adults in the state have high rates of smoking (25 percent) and obesity (24 percent), both of which are leading contributors to major health problems and thus to health care costs. North Carolina ranks thirty-fourth in the nation in the number of citizens with some type of health insurance coverage (84 percent). To partially address the needs of those without coverage, the state recently expanded Medicaid coverage for children, pregnant women, and the elderly. North Carolina Health Choice for Children helps children from working families obtain free or reduced-cost comprehensive medical coverage and provides vaccines to all children through age eighteen.

The state has seen marked improvements in the rates of violent and property crime. However, these rates remain high in comparison to the nation and region. In particular, the property crime rate stands at 119 percent of the national average (N.C. Progress Board 2006.

❖ Conclusion

North Carolina has a unique system of local government structure and intergovernmental relations. Its high reliance on the council-manager form of government in cities and counties contributes to a distinct governing style in which elected officials stress a governing role and appointed managers and staff support the council and provide competent policy implementation and service delivery. The similarity of governmental structure in cities and counties reinforces a generally cooperative relationship between these local governments.

In the area of local autonomy, North Carolina is characterized by apparent contradictions. The legal framework for intergovernmental relations is heavily tilted toward the state, which plays a very large fiscal role and controls many aspects of local finance. The state provides for and pays for a wide range of governmental functions. Despite this high level of state activity, considerable local flexibility occurs. Appreciation of the ability to craft special arrangements through local bills appears to outweigh dissatisfaction about having to go to the General Assembly for permission to innovate. General-purpose governments are strongly supported, and counties do not face competition from special districts. Cities and counties have considerable freedom to develop cooperative approaches to providing and delivering services. For the most part, municipalities do not have to contend with increasing governmental fragmentation on their borders and can develop orderly approaches to absorbing newly developing areas. Local governments depend on state government for revenues and remain vulnerable to changes in state policy on reimbursements and shared taxes, but localities also have some measure of freedom from taxpayer revolts because local property tax rates are relatively low. North Carolina's reasonably coherent state-level policy for local government and intergovernmental relations simultaneously constrains and empowers city and county governments.

The trend in North Carolina is toward more local autonomy, although the basic state-dominated relationship remains intact. Local units are receiving more freedom to negotiate issues such as school performance and alternatives to welfare but are also expected to be more accountable for results. Selected local governments have received new revenue options, including a hotel/motel tax in sixty-six counties and thirty-three municipalities, a prepared food and beverage tax imposed by nine local governments, a local land transfer tax in seven counties, and an amusement tax in two units (McLaughlin 1996). Tension continues to exist between state and local officials, but it is not always evident and is not always bad. As the general counsel of the county government association put it, "Sometimes there is more tension than at others" (quoted in McLaughlin 1996, 50).

The major potential issue facing all governments is the state's continuing commitment to funding shared revenues. For cities, the biggest issue is preservation of unilateral annexation; for counties, the primary concern is how devolution of human services will affect state-local relations.

North Carolina's governmental tradition does not square well with consideration of local autonomy as a concept, nor are issues that have been common in national discussions framed in the same way in this state. Providing public services in North Carolina is a joint endeavor that includes state and local governments. Responsibilities are intermixed. The terms of the relationship are established by the state, but an integral part of the approach is to protect the status of general-purpose local governments as major actors in these joint undertakings. The notion that separate spheres of state and local action exist and that local governments have identifiable prerogatives that amount to a measurable level of autonomy is largely absent. What might be viewed elsewhere as intrusiveness, interference, or restriction is generally accepted as part of the way that state and local governments go about meeting citizens' needs.

❖ Notes

Portions of this essay appeared in James H. Svara, "North Carolina," in *Home Rule in America: A Fifty State Handbook*, edited by Dale Crane, Platon N. Rigos, and Melvin B. Hill Jr. (Washington, D.C.: CQ Press, 2001), 312–21. Used with permission of the editors.

1. In towns with populations under five thousand, the mayor and council members may serve as department heads. Small towns often contract for legal and other services rather than having their own staff.

2. The North Carolina Constitution, Article 2, Section 24, imposes some limitations on local bills. They cannot be used, for example, in matters pertaining to health, sanitation, and the abatement of nuisances; to change the names of cities; to authorize the laying out of highways; and to regulate labor, trades, mining, or manufacturing.

3. See North Carolina General Statutes n.d., chapter 120, sections 158–74. The review can also be initiated by petition of 15 percent of the population in the areas proposed for incorporation (North Carolina General Statutes n.d., chapter 120, section 163).

4. North Carolina General Statutes n.d., chapter 136, section 44.8. The recommendations should be followed "insofar as they are compatible with its [the board's] general plans, standards, criteria, and available funds."

5. Under North Carolina General Statutes n.d., chapter 160A, section 146, cities cannot abolish positions required by law (for example, the city attorney), combine offices when forbidden by law, or discontinue or reassign functions assigned by law to a particular office.

6. Utility revenue is a larger source for cities but is tied closely to the service provided—that is, it is not a general revenue.

7. North Carolina General Statutes n.d., chapter 105, articles 39 (one-cent local-option sales tax passed in 1971), 40 (half-cent option passed in 1983), and 42 (half-cent option passed in 1985).

❖ References

Bell, A. Fleming, and Warren J. Wicker, eds. 1999. *County Government in North Carolina*. 4th ed. Chapel Hill: Institute of Government, University of North Carolina at Chapel Hill.

"Boundary Changes, 1990–95." 1997. In *The Municipal Yearbook, 1997*, 35–37. Washington, D.C.: International City/County Management Association.

Carter, K. Lee. 1995. "State Oversight of Local Government Finance." In *State and Local*

Government Relations in North Carolina: Their Evolution and Current Status, 2nd ed., edited by Charles Liner, 71–82. Chapel Hill: Institute of Government, University of North Carolina at Chapel Hill.

Condliffe, Simon, Edward C. Ratledge, and Sean Hildebrand. 2003. "Financing Public Education in Delaware." <http://www.cadsr.udel.edu/DOWNLOADABLE/DOCUMENTS/EdFinDistrictsFinal.pdf>. Accessed May 24, 2007.

"Fitch Rates North Carolina's $744MM GOs 'AAA.'" 2004. *Business Wire*, March 3. <http://www.findarticles.com/p/articles/mi_m0EIN/is_2004_March_3/ai_113861387>. Accessed May 24, 2007.

Hoke County Board of Education et al. v. State of North Carolina. 2004. N.C. Case 530PA02. <http://www.aoc.state.nc.us/www/public/sc/opinions/2004/530-02-1.htm>. Accessed May 24, 2007.

International City/County Management Association. 2001. *Form of Government Survey Data.* Washington, D.C.: International City/County Management Association.

Lawrence, David M. 2007a. "City and County Governing Boards." In *County and Municipal Government in North Carolina*, edited by David M. Lawrence. Chapel Hill: Institute of Government, University of North Carolina. <www.sog.unc.edu/pubs/cmg/cmg03.pdf>.

———. 2007b. "Incorporation, Abolition, and Annexation." In *County and Municipal Government in North Carolina*, edited by David M. Lawrence. Chapel Hill: Institute of Government, University of North Carolina. <www.sog.unc.edu/pubs/cmg/cmg02.pdf>.

Lawrence, David M., and Kara A. Millonzi. 2007. "Revenues." In *County and Municipal Government in North Carolina*, edited by David M. Lawrence. Chapel Hill: Institute of Government, University of North Carolina. <www.sog.unc.edu/pubs/cmg/cmg13.pdf>.

Lawrence, David M., and Warren Jake Wicker. 1995. *Municipal Government in North Carolina.* 2nd ed. Chapel Hill: Institute of Government, University of North Carolina at Chapel Hill.

Kelo v. New London.

Leandro v. State of North Carolina. 1997. 346 NC 336 179 PA 96.

———. 2004. 122 N.C. App. 1, 11, 468 S.E.2d. 543, 550.

Liner, Charles D., ed. 1995. *State and Local Government Relations in North Carolina: Their Evolution and Current Status.* 2nd ed. Chapel Hill: Institute of Government, University of North Carolina at Chapel Hill.

McLaughlin, Mike. 1996. "A Tax Menu for Local Government: Yes or No?" *North Carolina Insight* 16:99–101.

McLaughlin, Mike, and Jennifer Lehman. 1996. "Mandates to Local Government: How Big a Problem?" *North Carolina Insight* 16:42–75.

Miller, Joel. 1993. "Annexations and Boundary Changes in the 1980s and 1990–1991." In *The Municipal Year Book*, 100–109. Washington, D.C.: International City/County Management Association.

Municipal Yearbook. 1998. Washington, D.C.: International City/County Management Association.

National Conference of State Legislatures. 2004. "Initiative, Referendum, and Recall Data." <http://www.ncsl.org/programs/legismgt/elect/initiat.htm>. Accessed May 26, 2007.

1995 Directory of North Carolina County Officials. Raleigh: N.C. Association of County Commissioners.

North Carolina Constitution. 1971. <http://www.ncga.state.nc.us/Legislation/constitution/ncconstitution.html>. Accessed September 24, 2007.

N.C. Department of the State Treasurer. 2006. "City and County Revenue Expenditure Data." <http://www.treasurer.state.nc.us/lgc/units/unitlistjs.htm>. Accessed May 24, 2007.

North Carolina General Statutes. N.d.<http://www.ncga.state.nc.us/gascripts/Statutes/StatutesTOC.pl> Accessed September 22, 2007.N.C. League of Municipalities. 2006. Personal communication, August 28.

N.C. Progress Board. 2006. *2005 North Carolina 20/20 Update Report.* <http://www.ncprogress.org/PDF/2020report_2005.pdf>. Accessed May 24, 2007.

Richardson, Jesse, Jr., Meghan Zimmerman Gough, and Robert Puentes. 2003. "Is Home Rule the Answer?: Clarifying the Influence of Dillon's Rule." <http://www.brookings.edu/es/urban/publications/dillonsrule.pdf>. Accessed May 24, 2007.

Significant Features of Fiscal Federalism. 1992. Vol. 2. Washington, D.C.: Advisory Commission on Intergovernmental Relations.

Stephens, Ross, and Nelson Wikstrom. 2006. *American Intergovernmental Relations: A Fragmented Federal Polity.* New York: Oxford University Press.

Svara, James H. 1989. "Understanding Council Roles and Responsibilities: Resent Research Findings." In *Partnerships in Local Governance: Effective Council/Manager Relations,* 10–19. Washington, D.C.: International City Management Association.

——. 1990. *Official Leadership in the City: Patterns of Conflict and Cooperation.* New York: Oxford University Press.

——. 1993. "The Possibility of Professionalism in County Government." *International Journal of Public Administration* 16:2051–80.

——. 1998. *Official Leadership in the City: Patterns of Conflict and Cooperation.* New York: Oxford University Press.

Triangle Transit Authority. 2007. "Current Project Status." <http://www.ridetta.org/Regional_Rail/Current_Status/currProjectStatus.html>. Accessed May 24, 2007.

U.S. Census Bureau. 2002. *2002 Census of Governments,* GC92-1 (1) Washington, D.C.: U.S. Government Printing Office.

——. 2006a. "Annual Survey of Local Government Finances." <http://www.census.gov/govs/www/estimate04.html>. Accessed October 22, 2007.

——. 2006b. "Federal Assistance Award Data System." <http://www.census.gov/govs/www/faads.html>. Accessed May 26, 2007.

Wheeland, Craig M. 1990. "The Mayor in Small Council-Manager Municipalities: Are Mayors to Be Seen and Not Heard?" *National Civic Review* 79:337–49.

❖ Part IV. Public Policy

❖ 10. Environmental Politics in the Tar Heel State

An Ambivalent Legacy

DENNIS O. GRADY AND JONATHAN KANIPE

With the passage of the federal Clean Air and Clean Water Acts of the early 1970s, states across the nation became embroiled in one of the most controversial, contentious, and important policy issues confronting modern politics—environmental protection. North Carolina was no different. For more than thirty years, policymakers in the Tar Heel State have tried to balance the responsibility for protecting the state's water, air, natural beauty, and residents from environmental dangers while promoting expansion of the state's economy to provide for an ever-growing population. In some ways, two generations of political leaders have been exceptionally successful at this balancing act, and in other cases this equilibrium has been much more difficult to achieve.

Environmental politics covers the policies, processes, and actors involved in advocating, developing, opposing, and enforcing standards for clean water, air pollution, toxic waste disposal, land use, and energy utilization. While the federal government has primary responsibility for setting standards for air quality, water quality, and toxic substances, state governments bear primary responsibility for enforcing those standards (Rabe 2006). States make choices about how to enforce federal environmental laws, enact their own measures, and determine the level of resources devoted to implementing environmental legislation. According to University of Michigan environmental policy professor Barry Rabe (2006, 36), states "collectively issue more than 90 percent of all environmental permits, complete more than 75 percent of all environmental enforcement actions, and rely on the federal government for less than 25 percent of their total funding on environmental and natural resource concerns." So, while green activists roam the halls of Congress pushing environmental legislation, they also prowl the halls of the General Assembly to ensure that state lawmakers address environmental issues.

By its very nature, environmental politics is inherently intergovernmental and contentious. From an intergovernmental perspective, the federal government, state governments, and local governments have both unique and overlapping responsibilities. For example, the federal Environmental Protection Agency (EPA), created in 1970 by President Richard M. Nixon through executive order, bears responsibility through the Clean Air Act for establishing standards for the level of various substances in the air called criteria pollutants. The N.C. Division of Air Quality, however, bears responsibility for monitoring the air at various stations across the state and for providing mitigation strategies if the air at any location falls below acceptable levels. The same arrangement holds true for clean water, with the N.C. Division of Water Quality working with local governments across the state because they bear primary responsibility for treating wastewater and delivering safe drinking water. The implementation of environmental regulation thus is essentially an intergovernmental partnership or a shotgun wedding, depending on one's perspective. Also, environmental problems rarely respect state boundaries, creating challenges as states attempt to negotiate agreements over low-level nuclear waste disposal, sulfur dioxide migration, and interbasin water diversion. Environmental politics is enormously complex because it runs on both the vertical (federal-state-local) and the horizontal (state-to-state) planes of the intergovernmental system.

Environmental politics is inherently contentious because environmental regulation requires private entities to refrain from engaging in certain activities, resulting in restricted freedom of choice and/or increased costs of production. Enforcing environmental policy involves telling powerful actors what they cannot or must do. Prior to the enactment of the framework environmental legislation of the early 1970s, companies freely and legally poured tons of toxic chemicals into the atmosphere, dumped billions of gallons of waste into the water, and buried millions of vats of multisyllabic compounds in the earth. Following the passage of these landmark statutes, the costs of cleaning the production processes of the industrial age were either passed along to consumers or sliced from companies' profit margins. Resistance and controversy inevitably result and play out on the political stage.

Environmental politics consequently offers an interesting lens through which to examine state politics. Powerful forces are pitted against one another at a big-stakes policy table. In this essay, we will describe how the game has been played in North Carolina for the past three decades. We will take a look at the actors involved, the structure of the policy arena, and how North Carolina compares to other states before turning to three recent case studies that illustrate how the actors have interacted over specific issues.

❖ Environmental Policy Actors

At the state level, environmental policy is hammered out among a distinct set of actors, each with a uniquely important role to play. On the executive side sits the Department of the Environment and Natural Resources (DENR), an umbrella agency containing the operating divisions that enforce most of the environmental laws promulgated by Congress, the General Assembly, and federal and state regulatory agencies. DENR is the lead executive agency for environmental policy. Playing less dominant but still important roles in the executive branch are the Department of Transportation, which deals with a host of transportation policies that impact the environment; the Department of Agriculture, which deals with pesticide regulation; the Division of Community Development (within the Department of Commerce), which provides planning assistance to local governments in areas such as smart growth and zoning; and the Department of Administration, which houses the N.C. State Energy Office and the state's motor fleet. On the legislative side are committees in both the House and Senate with original jurisdiction over policy areas concerning everything from agriculture to tax policy. Also sitting at the table is an important group of independent regulatory commissions with powers over parts of the environmental policy scene generally unknown to even the most attuned resident. From the sidelines, one can hear the exhortations of the various lobbying forces that have grown in both size and power over the past three decades. And from time to time, the state's major newspapers have played important roles in clarifying the issues for the public at large.

DEPARTMENT OF THE ENVIRONMENT AND NATURAL RESOURCES

Created in 1973, during Governor James Holshouser's administration (1973–77), DENR is an executive agency whose secretary is appointed by and serves at the pleasure of the governor. The evolution of the department's name is indicative of the way environmental policy has been viewed over the decades. Governor Holshouser initially named it the Department of Natural and Economic Resources, thus signaling the marriage of commerce and environmental enforcement. Holshouser was the first Republican governor in North Carolina since Reconstruction, and his moderate, Main Street Republicanism is manifest in this selection of the name for the first cabinet level environmental agency. When James Hunt (1977–85, 1993–2001) succeeded Holshouser as governor, he spun economic development into the Department of Commerce and attached community development to the newly named Department of Natural Resources and Community Development. Hunt appointed Howard Lee, former mayor of Chapel Hill and faculty member at the University of North Carolina School of Social Work, as its secretary. Given Lee's background, community development received more attention than natural resources during Hunt's first terms in the governor's mansion. With the 1984 election of the state's second post-Reconstruction Republican governor, James Martin (1985–93), a doctorate-level chemist, former faculty member at Davidson College, and former member of the U.S. Congress, came a slightly different view on the role of environmental protection. He transferred community development to the Department of Commerce and added health to the environmental equation with

FIGURE 10.1. N.C. Department of Environment and Natural Resources
Organizational Chart

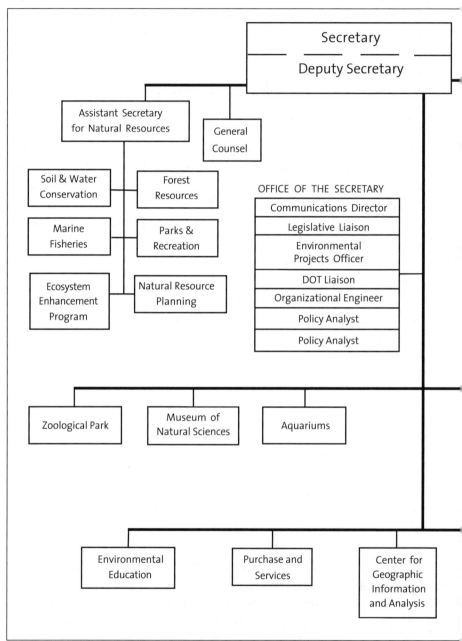

Source: N.C. Department of Environment and Natural Resources.

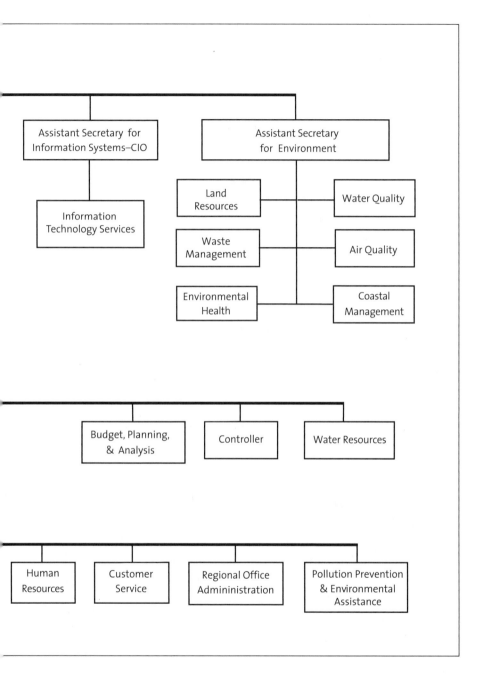

the newly minted Department of Environment, Health, and Natural Resources. After Hunt reclaimed the governorship, he returned the health portfolio to the Department of Health and Human Services in 1996 and gave the environmental agency the name it bears today. Governor Michael Easley (2001–) has done little to date in the way of restructuring state government. Today the agency is organized as figure 10.1 depicts.

As figure 10.1 shows, the DENR's scope of responsibilities is large, running literally from A (aquariums) to Z (zoological park). Areas of environmental concern are divided between natural resources (such as soil and water, marine fisheries, ecosystem enhancement programs, forest resources, parks and recreation, and natural resource planning) and environment (land resources, waste management, environmental health, water quality, air quality, and coastal management). The department also provides staff to the regulatory agencies under its administrative structure, which we will explain later. During the 2004–5 fiscal year, the department carried out these responsibilities with an appropriated budget of approximately $250 million (not including federal funds or fees) and four thousand employees (N.C. Office of Management and Budget 2005).

According to Bill Holman (2005), an informed observer of the state's environmental scene and former secretary of the agency, the organization has a conservative culture and focuses at the division level on specific details of policy implementation. DENR is more a collection of individual regulatory entities than a broad environmental policy leader. He observed, "DENR's not clear what its mission really is—assisting in economic development or protecting health and the environment." Table 10.1 gives a brief description of the primary environmental enforcement agencies within the DENR.

THE GENERAL ASSEMBLY

Since environmental politics became a relevant public policy issue in 1972, eighteen sessions of the General Assembly have occurred. During this time, the Democrats have been in control of all of the Senate sessions and fifteen House sessions. (Exceptions occurred in 1995–97, 1997–99, and 2003–5, an unusual session during which the House was tied 60–60, allowing James Black [D-Mecklenburg] to form a bipartisan co-speakership with Richard Morgan [R-Moore]).

Even though Democrats have dominated the legislative branch for most of this period, environmental interests have not enjoyed continual support. While the national Democratic Party is more environmentally focused, the North Carolina party, for the most part, could be characterized as moderate to conservative (Erickson, McIver, and Wright 1987).

Like all state legislative assemblies (with the exception of Nebraska), the N.C.

TABLE 10.1. N.C. Department of Environment and Natural Resources Divisions

Division	Environmental Focus and Impact
Air Quality	Monitors air quality
	Inspects and approves permits for emissions sources
	Enforces state and federal air quality regulations
Coastal Management	Protects and conserves North Carolina's coastline through planning and management
	Carries out regulations enacted by legislature
	Conducts investigations into land use, coastal erosion, and protection of public beach access
Marine Fisheries	Protects state's marine resources
Conservation and Community Affairs	Promotes and plans for North Carolina's long-term conservation efforts
	Protects land and water resources
	Leads statewide conservation plan with government agencies, private organizations, landowners, and public
Parks and Recreation	Developed plan to build and renovate new state parks and recreation areas and protect those in current use
	Conserves areas of natural beauty and ecological features for use by public
Soil and Water Conservation	Protects North Carolina's soil and water resources
	Presents programs and information on pollution management
	Provides financial and technical assistance to North Carolina's 96 soil and water conservation districts
Water Resources	Provides management for river basins, water conservation, and water resources
	Works with federal agencies on major water projects within state

Source: N.C. Department of Environmental and Natural Resources (2005).

General Assembly is bicameral, with 50 members in the Senate and 120 in the House. Also as in all legislatures, the real work of the body takes place in committees. Table 10.2 shows the primary House and Senate committees with responsibility for some aspect of environmental policymaking.

As the number of environmentally related committees indicates, environmental legislation can face a tortuous route through the legislative process. It would not be

TABLE 10.2. N.C. General Assembly Environmental Committees and Jurisdictions, 2003–2005

Committee	Issue Jurisdiction
Similar House and Senate Committee	
Rules	Controls flow of legislation from other committees to floor of respective chambers
	Acts as leaders' "ace in the hole" in processing environmental legislation
Transportation	Handles legislation dealing with stormwater runoff
	Handles legislation for higher-emission-standard fuels
Local Government	Approves legislation that mandates local governments perform certain tasks to protect environment within their areas
	Handles all local government regulatory requests
Finance	Handles tax incentives (important way to promote renewable energy)
	Analyzes economic impact (fiscal notes) of new environmental or energy-related legislation
Similar House and Senate Appropriation Subcommittees	
Health and Human Services	Determines where resources are needed to address environmental problems that impact health of N.C. citizens
	Handles septic system and hog farm issues
Natural and Environmental Resources	Allocates resources to protect or conserve environmental and natural areas
	Allocates resources to promote environmental programs within state government, which, in turn, impacts areas throughout state and its citizens
Similar House and Senate Commissions	
Environmental Review Commission	Includes chairs and cochairs of environmental committees in N.C. General Assembly
	Serves as forum for more thorough and detailed analysis of many environmental issues

TABLE 10.2. (*continued*)

Unique Senate Committee

Agriculture, Environment, and Natural Resources	Holds original jurisdiction over all environmental legislation in Senate
Commerce	Holds original jurisdiction over issues that impact electric utilities in Senate

Unique House Committee

Wildlife Resources	Handles legislation dealing with rules and regulations for wildlife and natural resources that impact citizens
Public Utilities	Holds jurisdiction over legislation addressing public utilities interests or rates in House
Environment and Natural Resources	Holds original jurisdiction over legislation that addresses environmental concerns and issues within state in House
	Addresses legislation pertaining to renewable energy or energy efficiency

Source: N.C. General Assembly (2006).

unusual for three or four committees or subcommittees to have an opportunity to derail or significantly alter a proenvironmental bill. Therefore, proenvironmental forces occupy a position in which a victory won in one venue could be overturned in another with little warning or logic.

As in all legislative chambers, leaders are responsible for appointing the chairs and members of each committee. By chamber rules, the leadership reserves for itself the right to serve on all committees and to appoint "roving" members to represent the leaders' preferred position on any specific issue before a committee. Another tool available to the chambers' leadership is the Rules Committee. Characterized by some observers as legislative leaders' ace in the hole, these two committees essentially determine whether environmental bills reach the floor for a vote. Conservation policy analyst Grady McCallie (2005a) described the Senate as a much more disciplined body in which leaders have more control over the process. The House, with a larger body, a smaller majority, and more fractious splinter groups, is less predictable from committee to committee. According to McCallie, "If Senate president pro tempore [Marc] Basnight wants a bill passed, it happens. Speaker of the House Black cannot make that happen so easily." Along the same lines, Environmental Review Commission staffer George Givens (2006) referred half-jokingly to the Senate as an autocracy while describing the decision process in the House as more anarchical.

One commonality between the chambers is the central role of staff in the policy development process. Givens has staffed both House and Senate environmental committees for more than two decades and is recognized as a key player in the policy process (Holman 2005). His expertise is recognized by committee members of both chambers, so he carries tremendous influence in the policy area. According to Givens (2006), almost all environmental issues engage four groups—environmental advocacy groups, the regulated community (including business interests), state agencies, and local governments. In terms of agenda setting, many environmental issues arise in the Environmental Review Commission while the legislature is in recess between sessions. (The N.C. General Assembly has its "long" session during odd-numbered years and its "short" session during even-numbered years). The Environmental Review Commission was created during reorganization battles in the mid-1980s as DENR evolved through its various stages. The commission includes the chairs and cochairs of the relevant environmental committees of the House and Senate and provides a forum in which many issues can receive more detailed analysis and attention.

Over the years, an informal process, known as the 605 process and orchestrated by Givens, has emerged in the development of potentially contentious legislation. The process is named for the room in the legislative building where the contending sides of the issue at hand engage in discussions. According to McCallie (2005a), the process is not a negotiation but rather a session during which the "losing side gets input into the bill but will not change its ultimate outcome." In essence, the legislature is attempting to maintain a sense of comity among regular, repeat players wherein one side might lose on this particular issue today only to win on another next week.

REGULATORY BODIES

In addition to the statutes emanating from the General Assembly, North Carolina also promulgates rules and regulations that directly affect the quality of the state's environment (see table 10.3). Four major independent regulatory bodies are heavily involved in the detailed oversight of the environmental regulatory arena—the Environmental Management Commission, the Wildlife Resources Commission, the Utilities Commission, and the Rules Review Commission. In addition, a number of specialized boards and commissions have narrower responsibilities that will be reviewed briefly.

The Environmental Management Commission (EMC) is a nineteen-member commission appointed by the governor, the Senate president pro tempore, and the speaker of the House. The commission bears responsibility for adopting rules for the protection, preservation, and enhancement of the North Carolina's air and water resources. Commission members are chosen to represent various interests, including the medical profession, agriculture, engineering, fish and wildlife, groundwater, air and water pollution control, municipal or county government, and the public at large. The commission oversees and adopts rules for several DENR divisions, including the Divisions of Air Quality, Land Resources, Water Quality, and Water Resources. The EMC has five committees: Steering, National Pollution Discharge Elimination System, Air Quality, Groundwater, and Water Quality. The relevant DENR divisions staff these committees. The commission also sits as a quasi-judicial body that hears cases on violations of commission rules and regulations and has the power to impose penalties when violations are found. The EMC meets monthly to approve recommended rules promulgated by its five committees.

In addition to the EMC, a handful of more targeted boards also serve DENR. The Clean Water Management Trust Fund was created in 1996 and provides grants to local governments, state agencies, and nonprofit agencies to acquire land that protects threatened watersheds. The Coastal Resources Commission was created in 1974 as part of the Coastal Zone Management Act and bears responsibility for adopting rules for coastal development, approves coastal county land-use plans, and designates areas of environmental concern. The Marine Fisheries Commission has roots back to 1822, when the General Assembly established the first rules on oyster harvesting; however, the commission did not become a formal regulatory body until well into the twentieth century. It has evolved into the main regulatory agency for recreational fishing in the state's estuaries and oceans.

The Wildlife Resources Commission, created in 1947, is a twenty-member body appointed for indefinite terms by the governor, speaker, and Senate president pro tempore. It is dedicated to the wise use, conservation, and management of the state's fish and wildlife resources. The Wildlife Resources Commission consists of wildlife and fisheries biologists, wildlife enforcement officers, educators, engineers, and administrative staff in nine districts across the state. It is organized into six divisions: Inland Fisheries, Conservation Education, Wildlife Management, Engineering Services, Law Enforcement, and Administrative Services. Each of these divisions, in turn, manages a specialized area of fish and game resources.

The N.C. Utilities Commission, the oldest formal regulatory body in the state, was created in 1891 to regulate railroads. The commission has seven members who serve eight-year terms. The governor appoints members, subject to confirmation by the General Assembly by joint resolution. The governor also designates a chair to serve a four-year term.

TABLE 10.3. Other Environmental Agencies in North Carolina

Agency	Issue Focus
Separate Regulatory Bodies	
N.C. Utilities Commission	Created by General Assembly to regulate rates and services for all public utilities within state
	Consists of seven members who serve eight-year terms
	Appointments made by governor, with confirmation from General Assembly
	Proscribes rules and regulations that impact renewable energy use within state
Environmental Management Commission	Consists of nineteen members appointed by governor, speaker of House, and Senate president pro tem
	Adopts rules and regulations for protection of environment—specifically, air and water resources
	Adopts rules and regulations for several divisions of DENR
Coastal Resources Commission	Provides policies for N.C. Coastal Management Program
	Designates areas of concern and adopts rule and policies for those areas
Department of Administration	
Energy Policy Council	Advises General Assembly and governor's office on energy policy issues
	Provides advice and guidance to N.C. State Energy Office
DENR Special Agencies and Programs	
Wildlife Commission	Enforces rules and regulations established by General Assembly and Wildlife Commission
	Enforces game, fish, and boating laws for protection of wildlife resources and state citizens
N.C. Ecosystem Enhancement Program	Created in 2003 through a memorandum of understanding between DENR, Department of Transportation, and U.S. Army Corps of Engineers
	Merges N.C. Wetlands Restoration program with resources from the Department of Transportation Office of Natural Environment
	Restores and protects North Carolina's wetlands and riparian areas

TABLE 10.3. (*continued*)

Stormwater Management Program	Created in late 1980s by Environmental Management Commission
	Requires developers to protect sensitive areas (designated as twenty coastal counties or areas that drain to outstanding resource waters or high-quality waters) through use of vegetative buffers, low use of impervious surfaces, and transportation of runoff through vegetation

Department of Transportation Special Programs

Office of Environmental Quality	Concerned with delivering quality transportation program that preserves and protects natural environment
	Coordinates, facilitates, and promotes environmental stewardship and streamlining within department
Highway Stormwater Program	Ensures that department provides effective transportation in North Carolina but does so in manner that protects and improves water quality
	Manages and reduces stormwater pollutants from roadways
3R Program	Ensures that environmental principle of "reduce, reuse, and recycle" is heeded throughout department
	Employs these principles from construction sites to office work

Sources: N.C. Coastal Resources Commission (2005); N.C. Department of Environment and Natural Resources (2005); N.C. Ecosystem Enhancement Program (2005); N.C. Environmental Management Commission (2005); N.C. Highway Stormwater Program (2005); N.C. Office of Environmental Quality (2005); N.C. Public Utilities Commission (2007); N.C. State Energy Office (2007); N.C. Stormwater Management Program (2005); N.C. 3R Program (2005).

The commission is an administrative agency of the General Assembly created for the principal purpose of carrying out the administration and enforcement of the Public Utilities Act and is subject to legislative oversight by the Joint Legislative Utility Review Committee. The commission is authorized to promulgate rules and regulations and to fix utility rates. For the purpose of conducting hearings, making decisions, issuing orders, and informal investigations where a record is made of testimony under oath, the commission has all the powers of a court of general jurisdiction.

As of 2005, the commission regulated more than 1,800 utility companies throughout the state with combined revenues of more than $10 billion per year

(N.C. Public Utilities Commission 2005). These utilities include electric companies, local and long-distance telephone companies, natural gas companies, household goods motor freight carriers, motor passenger carriers, companies providing private pay phone service, water and wastewater companies (traditional and resale, consisting of approximately 2,154 systems), and ferryboat operators. Because these utilities provide part of the infrastructure necessary for all commerce and industry in the state, they have an enormous impact on North Carolina's economy and environment.

Of major concern to the environmental community are the rules and regulations related to electricity generation, especially nuclear and renewable electricity generation. Because approximately half of the state's air pollution comes from burning coal to produce electricity (N.C. State Energy Office 2005), the Utilities Commission determines issues related to clean smokestacks (discussed later), renewable energy sources, and consumer costs for green energy. And while the federal Nuclear Regulatory Commission is responsible for standards for nuclear power safety, the N.C. Utilities Commission is responsible for issuing and renewing permits for nuclear power facilities.

The Rules Review Commission (RRC) is perhaps the most controversial entity of the group. Residing in the obscure Office of Administrative Hearings, the RRC possesses veto authority over the full range of environmental regulations coming from DENR and its various commissions. Created in the early 1990s, the RRC has ten members appointed by the speaker of the House and Senate president pro tempore. There are no specific qualifications for membership. Following the Republican ascendancy in the House during the 1995–99 sessions, the RRC's powers were expanded beyond simple procedural review of proposed rules (Grady and Simon 2002).

By statute, the RRC assess whether a rule (1) falls within the statutory authority of the agency proposing the rule; (2) is clear and unambiguous; and (3) is reasonably necessary to fulfill a duty delegated to the agency. However over the years, the RRC has denied rules in areas such as stormwater regulation that clearly fell within the criteria established by statute. Such actions have caused both the EMC and environmental lobbyists to file court briefs challenging the RRC's authority and constitutional status (Strom 2005).

According to one critique, "But since an industry friendly legislature gave the board veto power 10 years ago and appoints all the members, policymakers charged with protecting citizens' interests and public advocacy leaders say the commission has become yet one more political battlefield where private interests rule—particularly those whose profit margins are adversely affected by environmental regulations on development" (Strom 2005). The same analysis quotes Holman as calling the RRC "a wholly owned subsidiary of the North Carolina Home Builders Association" (Strom 2005). McCallie (2006) is less pointedly critical and points out that "the RRC isn't so much directly beholden to the home builders as it is a body with an inherently flawed mission—any group of people trying to carry out the RRC's mission is likely to become obsessed with form, because there's no way they can absorb and process all the substance."

Interest groups play a central role in the environmental policy process (Layzer 2006; Rosenbaum 2005; Vig and Kraft 2006). Scholars looking at the array of interests surrounding environmental concerns have divided this world into two camps—environmentalists and cornucopians (Dryzek and Schlosberg 1998). According to Judith A. Layzer (2006), the differences between these two camps center on values and worldview. Environmentalists essentially see a world of limits, where one generation bears responsibility for ensuring that future generations have a safe, clean, and sustainable life. Cornucopians, conversely, see the world as possessing boundless opportunities and virtually limitless resources that only await humans' creative ingenuity to unleash. Because these views are so diametrically opposed to one another and because values and worldviews are essentially nondebatable, the two sides battle over less predetermined positions. The debates regularly center on the scope of the state's environmental agenda, determining which scientific facts are valid and reliable, and the economic/environmental consequences of taking action or failing to do so. In the political arena, the two sides are hardly of equivalent strength. The cornucopians generally represent the viewpoint of state and national economic interests. Identified earlier by Givens as the "regulated" interests, this group possesses formidable resources.

An analysis by the progressive think tank Democracy South (1996) that focused on campaign contributions in North Carolina by the "pollution lobby" versus the environmental lobby reported,

On disclosure reports filed with the Secretary of State, 56 companies and trade groups in the pollution lobby said they paid 143 registered lobbyists $1.4 million during 1995 to promote—and often write—favorable legislation. They reported $226,000 in other expenses, although 28 reported no other expenses and a few failed to disclose any compensation.

By contrast, nine conservation groups reported spending a total of $92,100 for lobbying, including the lobbying time of several staff members and payments for two "full time" lobbyists (Bill Holman of the Sierra Club and Conservation Council of N.C. and Tom Bean of the N.C. Wildlife Federation). . . .

TABLE 10.4. Organizations under Regulated Lobby Category That Regularly Appear in N.C. Environmental Causes

Organization	Issue Focus
N.C. Citizens for Business and Industry (Formed in 1942)	North Carolina's chamber of commerce Represents business interests in North Carolina; generally resists regulations that might negatively impact business profits
N.C. Agribusiness Council (Formed in 1969)	Raises awareness of agribusiness in state and advances interests and programs
N.C. Home Builders Association (Formed in 1962)	Coalition of developer and real estate interests Focuses on pooling efforts and resources to provide clout and muscle that housing industry needs
Manufacturers and Chemical Industry Council (Formed in 1988)	Works with state and local governments to develop new policies and legislation that might impact their industries Consists mostly of representatives of chemical and drug organizations
Investor-Owned Utilities	Major members are Duke Energy and Progress Energy Opposes many environment-friendly energy policies (net metering, RPS) Opposes most new regulation on utilities industries
N.C. Pork Council	Promotes pork industry and advocates for needs of hog farmers
Farmers for Fairness (Formed in 1996)	Formed, in part, by hog farm equipment manufacturer Serves interests of farmers in North Carolina, with major focus on hog farmers and their needs
N.C. League of Municipalities (Formed in 1908)	Represents and lobbies for municipalities at federal and state levels Nonpartisan group of 530 towns, cities, and villages in North Carolina
N.C. Association of County Commissioners (Formed in 1908)	Serves an advocate for N.C. counties at state level

Sources: Manufacturers and Chemistry Industry Council (2006); Miller (1998); N.C. Agribusiness Council (2006); N.C. Association of County Commissioners (2007); N.C. Citizens for Business and Industry (2006); N.C. Home Builders Association (2006); N.C. League of Municipalities (2007); N.C. Pork Council (2007).

From January 1993 to April 1996, thirty-six political action committees affiliated with the pollution lobby spent $2,078,749, mostly in contributions to state legislative campaigns. That doesn't include donations from individual executives associated with these same firms, which easily exceeds the $2 million figure, or the money spent by bankers, retailers and other business interests that often oppose environmental regulations but are not included in the pollution lobby.

By contrast, the two environmental PACs (Sierra Club PAC and the NC League of Conservation Voters) spent $21,165 during the same period—about one percent of the pollution lobby's PAC money.

From the perspective of economic resources, there should be little competition between two such unevenly matched contestants. Nonetheless, such competition certainly exists, and it is a tribute to the environmental community that it has asserted itself as effectively as it has over the past three decades.

Table 10.4 lists the organizations in the "regulated lobby" category that regularly appear in environmental causes. As can be seen, this potent set of interests always appears at the top of lists specifying powerful influences in the General Assembly (N.C. Center for Public Policy Research 2005).

Table 10.5 lists the environmental organizations characterized as "Raleigh" groups, indicating that they regularly appear in the General Assembly as broad-based advocacy groups, frequently with paid lobbyists. Initially begun during the 1973–74 session when lone lobbyist Holman took a part-time position with the Sierra Club to monitor the beginning of the environmental policy process, the movement has now grown considerably both in size and influence.

In addition to the legislatively focused environmental advocacy groups, a number of more issue-specific groups have evolved over the past three decades. These groups typically focus on one environmental issue (for example, birds and the Audubon Society) or a geographic area of the state. Within their specific policy interests, these groups can bring substantial political clout to the table concerning matters that affect their interests. However, unlike the broad-based Raleigh groups, their involvement is episodic and more grassroots in nature. Table 10.6 lists these groups and their issue areas. The table also includes the funds that represent bodies with either appropriated or donated monies to purchase land or development rights for specific environmental purposes. Through these funds, the legislature allocates state appropriations for specific environmental enhancement projects. For example, during the 2005 legislative session, the Clean Water Management Trust Fund received $100 million from the state to provide grants to local governments and nonprofit conservation groups to protect clean water sources across the state.

TABLE 10.5. Broad-Based Advocacy Groups in North Carolina

Organization	Issue Focus
Conservation Council of North Carolina (Formed in 1970s)	Promotes positive environmental policies
	Supports full-time lobbyist in General Assembly
	Publishes legislative scorecard; holds legislators accountable for environmental legislation
	Represents environmental community before state agencies and commissions
Environmental Defense of North Carolina (Opened N.C. office in 1988)	Established North Carolina Action Network with two other environmental groups
	Coauthored North Carolina's Clean Smokestacks Act
	Organizes projects to protect and restore marine, coastal, and mountain ecosystems
	Emphasizes environmental justice
	Monitors hog-waste problems
North Carolina Conservation Network (Formed in 1998)	Umbrella network of more than 120 environmental and community groups
	Trains activists to become more involved and knowledgeable on environmental issues
	Provides updates and news to environmental groups
	Organizes meetings for specific issues that need to be addressed
N.C. Public Interest Research Group (Formed in 1973)	Clean water efforts focus on lakes and rivers that supply drinking water
	Addresses concerns of stormwater runoff
	Cleans up hog farms
	Advocates for cleaner energy sources to stop global warming
	Enforces and advocates for N.C. Clean Smokestacks Act
	Advocates for more protection of open space in North Carolina and protection of forests, farmlands, and wetlands
Sierra Club of North Carolina (N.C. chapter formed in 1979)	Protects N.C. coast through advocacy of clean waters and healthy fisheries regulations
	Cleans up stormwater runoff
	Protects air and water near hog farms
	Protects public lands from overdevelopment

TABLE 10.5. (*continued*)

Organization	Issue Focus
Southern Environmental Law Center (Founded in 1986)	Serves as prime legal advocate for environmental causes
	Sued U.S. Navy to halt OLF in eastern North Carolina
	Member of Clean Air Coalition that helped pass Clean Smokestacks Act
	Advocates strong stormwater runoff regulations

Sources: Conservation Council of North Carolina (2005); Environmental Defense of North Carolina (2005); N.C. Conservation Network (2005); N.C. Public Interest Research Group (2005); Sierra Club of North Carolina (2005); Southern Environmental Law Center (2007).

❖ North Carolina in Comparison with Other States

Looking at North Carolina from a comparative environmental perspective poses a challenge because very little work has been done on the topic. The most useful tool currently available is the Eric Siy, Leo Koziol, and Darcy Rollins's 2001 *State of the States* report, published by the Resource Renewal Institute (RRI), which builds on 1999 efforts by the Sierra Club (Sierra Club 1999) and a 2000 report from the Institute for Southern Studies (Institute for Southern Studies 2000) (see table 10.7). RRI, a nonprofit California-based environmental research and advocacy organization, developed the Green Plan Capacity Index to determine the "relative ability of states to pursue sustainable development using established principals of green planning as its basis" (Siy, Koziol, and Rollins 2001, 2) The index includes sixty-five measures divided into four major categories: administrative framework, innovation, resource commitment, and effective governance.

North Carolina places twentieth overall in the RRI rankings, between Utah at nineteen and the Wisconsin at twenty-one. In developing this index, the RRI evaluated the states on a scale with an upper range of 100. As the table shows, states ranged from a high of 73 for Oregon to a low of 8 for Alabama. North Carolina's overall score of 38 places it above most of the other southern states—the exceptions are Florida with 43, Georgia with 42, and Texas with 40. Contributing to North Carolina's relative ranking is its strength in state environmental management, the presence of green procurement plans, and its per-capita spending on environmental protection and on preserving open space (Siy, Koziol, and Rollins 2001, vi–x). RRI's environmental management subindex includes such factors as Web sites, state planning offices focused on land use or other environmentally

TABLE 10.6. Issue-Specific Environmental Groups in North Carolina

Organization	Issue Focus
Southern Alliance for Clean Energy (Formed in 1985)	Promotes clean air in southern Appalachians
	Promotes energy efficiency and green power to reduce global warming
Canary Coalition (Formed in 2000)	Broad-based grassroots network
	Focuses on air pollution in Smoky Mountains and Appalachian region
	Supports reduction of coal-burning power plants and greater use of clean energy transportation and planning
N.C. Coastal Federation (Formed in 1982)	Promotes greater land-use planning and development of blueprint for environmental protection
	Implements design standards for stormwater runoff and pollution
N.C. Audubon Society (Formed in 1902)	Promotes conservation and restoration of bird habitats
	Designates important bird areas that become focal point of all policy and lobbying initiatives (e.g., Pocosin Lake site)
Sustainable Energy Association (Formed in 1978)	Promotes renewable energy and energy-efficient technologies such as solar power, wind power, and biofuels
N.C. Wildlife Federation (Formed in 1945)	Promotes and advocates habitat conservation for all wildlife
	Promotes education on wildlife resources and importance of wildlife to all
Nature Conservancy (National organization founded in 1951)	International organization dedicated to protection of natural habitats and ecosystems
	Protects more than 105 sites across North Carolina
Trusts	
Farmland Preservation Trust Fund (Established in 1998 by General Assembly)	Provides grants to local governments and nonprofit organizations to purchase agricultural land and easements
Natural Heritage Trust Fund (Established in 1987 by General Assembly)	Serves as supplemental funding source for state agencies to protect ecosystems in North Carolina
	Acquires forest and natural lands for protection through state agencies

TABLE 10.6. (*continued*)

Organization	Issue Focus
Parks and Recreation Trust Fund (Established in 1994 by General Assembly)	Funds improvements in state park system
	Provides grants to local governments
	Serves as primary source of funding for new and existing state parks
Conservation Trust for North Carolina (Formed in 1992)	Umbrella organization of state's twenty-two land trust organizations
	Nonprofit committed to protection of statewide land and water
	Works directly with local conservation trusts, landowners, and local governments
Clean Water Management Trust Fund (Established in 1996 by General Assembly)	Provides grants to local governments and state agencies for projects that protect water areas and specifically address water pollution

Sources: Canary Coalition (2005); Clean Water Management Trust Fund (2005); Conservation Trust for North Carolina (2005); Farmland Preservation Trust Fund (2005); Natural Heritage Trust Fund (2005); Nature Conservancy (2005); N.C. Audubon Society (2007); N.C. Coastal Federation (2005); N.C. Sustainable Energy Association (2007); N.C. Wildlife Federation (2007); Parks and Recreation Trust Fund (2005); Southern Alliance for Clean Energy (2005).

sustainable issues, and state of the environment reports (Siy, Koziol, and Rollins 2001, vi). North Carolina finished tenth overall in this category.

North Carolina did not perform as well in the other subindexes. In the environmental innovation policy subindex, North Carolina ranked thirty-eighth, with only three policies rated above average. In the fiscal and program commitment subindex, North Carolina finished thirty-second, with only one above average program.

This comparative analysis clearly demonstrates North Carolina's ambiguous environmental legacy. In some respects, the state is well regarded and maintains a fair overall rating. However, North Carolina must do considerable work to make up ground relative to the leading environmental policy states.

❖ Case Studies

We now turn our attention to three case studies in which these environmental actors have squared off in the public arena, attracting significant public attention. For

TABLE 10.7. Resource Renewal Institute Rankings

Ranking	State	Framework (Out of 35 Points)	Innovation (Out of 40 Points)	Commitment (Out of 10 Points)	Governance (Out of 15 Points)	Green Plan Capacity Index
1	Oregon	33	24	7	8	73
2	New Jersey	31	26	7	8	71
3	Minnesota	26	23	4	9	64
4	Maine	23	29	4	3	59
5	Washington	26	18	5	8	57
6	Massachusetts	17	30	5	5	57
7	Vermont	22	23	5	5	55
8	Connecticut	19	20	5	2	45
9	Illinois	18	16	6	5	45
10	Florida	25	10	5	4	43
11	Maryland	19	13	5	6	43
12	California	9	26	5	2	42
13	Georgia	18	16	4	4	42
14	Pennsylvania	20	7	5	9	42
15	Indiana	16	15	2	7	41
16	Delaware	19	12	4	6	40
17	Texas	13	17	4	6	40
18	New York	5	27	5	2	39
19	Utah	21	7	3	8	39
20	North Carolina	19	7	3	9	38
21	Wisconsin	15	14	2	6	37
22	South Carolina	18	10	3	6	37
23	Kentucky	19	9	2	6	36
24	Missouri	15	10	4	8	36
25	Michigan	13	12	3	7	36
26	Iowa	12	13	2	6	34
27	Idaho	19	8	2	3	31
28	New Hampshire	12	11	4	4	31
29	Montana	10	12	3	5	30
30	Virginia	14	5	3	8	29
31	Arizona	6	17	3	3	29
32	Rhode Island	7	15	4	2	28
33	Tennessee	13	7	3	5	28
34	Hawaii	15	7	4	2	28
35	Ohio	7	9	3	6	26
36	Colorado	4	13	4	4	25
37	Kansas	12	6	1	5	24
38	Mississippi	4	14	2	4	23
39	South Dakota	4	10	3	5	22
40	Louisiana	5	9	2	5	22

TABLE 10.7. (*continued*)

Ranking	State	Frame-work (Out of 35 Points)	Innovation (Out of 40 Points)	Commit-ment (Out of 10 Points)	Governance (Out of 15 Points)	Green Plan Capacity Index
41	Nebraska	5	6	2	6	20
42	Nevada	5	6	3	4	19
43	Alaska	3	8	3	3	17
44	West Virginia	6	3	4	4	17
45	North Dakota	3	6	2	5	17
46	Oklahoma	3	8	1	3	15
47	Arkansas	4	7	2	2	15
48	New Mexico	2	5	2	2	11
49	Wyoming	2	4	0	3	10
50	Alabama	3	2	2	1	8

Source: Siy, Koziol, and Rollins (2001).

the sake of brevity, we have tried to focus on the essential political dynamics that played out as decisions were (or are being) reached over contentious environmental issues. In the clean smokestacks case, the environmental community achieved its goal. In the stormwater case, the opposite is true. In the final case, the naval landing field, the jury is still out.

CASE 1: CLEAN SMOKESTACKS ACT—
NORTH CAROLINA TAKES THE LEAD IN CLEANING UP ITS AIR

The Air Quality/Electric Utilities Act (often called the Clean Smokestacks Act) targeted North Carolina's fourteen coal-fired power plants specifically because of their environmentally detrimental nitrogen oxide and sulfur dioxide emissions. These pollutants have a negative impact on the ecosystem and result in decreased visibility in the mountains, decreased economic profits, and public health concerns.

In 2000, the EMC proposed a rule to comply with the federal Clean Air Act. In February 2001, the interest group Environmental Defense called for legislation addressing the Clean Air Act. The initial bill took shape in March during meetings and compromises between environmentalists and the utility companies that owned the coal-fired plants. The clean air issue arose in part because of a series of DENR public hearings on meeting EPA nitrogen oxide standards. The hearings were the venue to mobilize the environmental community and in March 2001, the "People's Plan for Clean Air" was published. This report focused on nitrogen oxide, sulfur dioxide, and carbon dioxide emissions and demonstrated the urgency, statewide relevance, and benefits of cleaner air.

A Democratic senator and a Democratic House member from Buncombe, in the mountain west, sponsored the Clean Smokestacks Act. The bill passed the Senate in May 2001 but stalled in the House because of business and industry opposition. Over the next year, proponents of the legislation waged an aggressive public education campaign. The timing was important because it coincided with the release of numerous reports and studies urging strong action on the problem of air pollution. In addition, daily television warnings about air quality during one of the hottest and driest summers on record made the public more conscious of the dangers posed by poor air quality.

The involvement of local advocates and public health officials proved important, making the issue salient for residents (McCallie 2005b). The issue became one of public health as daily radio alerts warned residents about hazardous ozone levels. Opponents of the bill believed it to constitute unwarranted and unnecessary regulation that would lead to higher energy prices. The opposition was less organized and did not receive widespread public support. The issue became framed as a question of profits for a few versus health for all. The bill also became caught up in a failed push to deregulate North Carolina's electric utilities. Had deregulation passed, the investor-owned utilities (Duke Energy and Progress Energy) would have had to open their books for a rate evaluation case. Their rates covered loan payments for nuclear plants built in the early to mid-1970s, costs that would soon be retired, thereby triggering a rate reduction. In March 2002, as the bill languished in the House Public Utilities Committee, Governor Easley stepped in to negotiate a settlement to the controversy. Instead of lowering their rates, the electric utilities agreed to use their surplus income to purchase emissions-reducing scrubbing equipment for the coal power plants. The clean smokestacks legislation required Duke and Progress's fourteen coal-burning plants to cut nitrous oxide and sulfur dioxide emissions by 70 percent before 2015. A key environmental provision in the bill disallowed emissions trading to ensure that benefits from cleaner air were not traded away but would be experienced directly by the state. The bill passed both chambers on June 12, 2002, and was signed in a rare public ceremony by the governor. Today, it is one of the most stringent clean air regulations on the books of any state, has served as an impetus for North Carolina officials to push neighboring states to lower their air emissions, and was used by the EPA as the model for its 2005 Clean Air Interstate Rule requiring twenty-eight downwind states to reduce sulfur dioxide and nitrogen oxide emissions.

In 1999, the EPA implemented Phase II Stormwater, a follow-up to the successful Phase I initiative, to reduce point-source water pollution. In North Carolina, the EMC is responsible for creating clean water rules. However, on the stormwater issue, the EMC ran afoul of the RRC. Clashes often arise between regulatory bodies such as the EMC, which is designed to create regulations, and the RRC, which is designed to make sure agencies do not overstep their bounds.

Stormwater refers to the runoff created when rains or water pour over an impervious surface. Water is absorbed or evaporates when it runs over natural surfaces, but paved surfaces, such as roads and parking lots, pose a problem because water runs off rapidly and in high volume. These impervious surfaces do not let the water run into the ground. Stormwater runoff creates two problems. First, it picks up pollution in the form of sediments and chemicals and washes it into rivers. This negatively affects drinking water, some of which can be treated, but only at a high cost. This runoff results in sick rivers and estuaries and inedible shellfish along the North Carolina coast. Second, the increased volume and speed of runoff causes downstream erosion and flooding. Several remedies are available, including runoff basins, porous pavement, and grassy ditches in residential areas.

In 1987, the federal Clean Water Act identified stormwater runoff as point-source pollution. Five North Carolina cities and one North Carolina county began Phase I Stormwater in 1990 when rules were issued by the EPA. Three years later, these Phase I communities implemented their programs. In 1999, because of the success of Phase I, the EPA issued national Phase II Stormwater rules, with a March 2003 implementation deadline. In North Carolina, the EMC began facilitating discussion regarding concerns and priorities among interested parties. Local government officials who would be responsible for enforcement found the Phase II rules confusing, in need of clarification. The EMC issued a temporary rule in October 2002 and a permanent rule the following July. The N.C. Home Builders Association immediately blasted the permanent rule, drawing the RRC's attention.

When a permanent rule is submitted to the RRC, it is either accepted or rejected. RRC staff members often look through recent rules and reject anything that is ambiguous or difficult to understand (McCallie 2005b). Regulatory bodies often will leave aspects of rules to future discretion because not all eventualities can necessarily be foreseen; in these cases, the RRC explores the risk that the agency will move beyond statutory authority. The RRC rejected the Phase II Stormwater rules on the grounds that they fell outside statutory authority, even though Phase II was a federal regulation. In the fall of 2003, the RRC sent the rule back three times, giving the EMC new complaints and opportunities to revise. By December 2003, the EMC made what it believed were the final changes. However, in January 2004, the

RRC vetoed the rule, and the EMC sued the RRC for acting "arbitrarily and capriciously" in its decisions.

In May 2004, the N.C. General Assembly passed a session law regarding Phase II (S.L. 2004-163). This measure expires in 2011 and is not as strict as many had hoped. It does not, however, prevent the EMC from making the regulations more stringent in the future. From the developers' perspective, this session law provides enough regulation without any further, permanent legislation. In June 2005, a state superior court ruled in favor of the EMC and against the RRC. The court remanded the rules back to the RRC and allowed grounds to object if specific problems to the Phase II rules were articulated. On November 18, 2005, the RRC unexpectedly approved the Phase II Stormwater rules. The permanent rules are stronger than the session law in two ways: (1) they cover all thirty-three counties potentially affected by urban runoff; and (2) they offer better protection for sensitive shellfish waters on the coast. A 605 process has been convened to hammer out a compromise between the environmental community and a coalition of local government officials and developers. Observers perceive that these permanent rules will be less stringent after the 605 process is completed (McCallie 2006).

CASE 3: NAVAL OUTLYING LANDING FIELD—
BEING A GOOD HOST TO A FIVE-HUNDRED-POUND GORILLA

An outlying landing field (OLF) provides the U.S. Navy with the ability to train pilots in a simulated flight and landing situation. In June 2000, the navy announced plans to bring a fleet of F/A-18 Super Hornets to the East Coast. Shortly thereafter, the navy announced the development of a new OLF "to mitigate noise complaints from residents in Chesapeake and Hampton, VA" ("Navy's Outlying Landing Field" 2007). The Audubon Society and other environmental groups first became involved in the OLF situation by preparing comments on one of the proposed sites, the Mattamuskeet National Wildlife Refuge in Craven County. However, the focus soon shifted to the Pocosin Lake site after the navy completed a draft environmental impact statement (EIS). At this time, Audubon leaders believed that the navy would not seriously consider either site because of the high risk of bird strikes (Canfield 2005).

After realizing that the navy was serious about the Pocosin Lake site, environmental groups began to educate residents and naval officials about the threat to the refuge area. Environmentalists traveled to the proposed site and made presentations to navy officials showing not only the impact on birds and wildlife but also how a potential OLF would endanger navy personnel. In July 2003, the navy released its final EIS; two months later, officials announced that the OLF would be situated on thirty thousand acres at the Pocosin Lake site. Soon thereafter, the

Audubon Society hired the Southern Environmental Law Center, which sued the navy. Federal district court judge Terrence Boyle granted a request for a preliminary injunction against the construction of the OLF.

In February 2005, Judge Boyle granted "a permanent injunction against the OLF saying the Navy failed to make an objective determination of the impact on the surrounding environment of an OLF and that it took the 'uninformed action' that the National Environmental Policy Act specifically prohibits" ("Navy's Outlying Landing Field" 2007). This injunction specifically banned the navy from building and/or planning for the OLF until it complied with the regulations of the National Environmental Policy Act. The Fourth Circuit Court of Appeals agreed to an expedited hearing and on September 7, 2005, ruled that the navy had failed to complete the initial EIS. The court ordered naval officials to complete a supplemental environmental impact statement (SEIS) before moving forward with the Pocosin Lake site. However, the Fourth Circuit ruling weakened Judge Boyle's injunction and allowed specific work on the site, including the purchase of land from potential sellers (Canfield 2005). Chris Canfield (2005), executive director of the N.C. Audubon Society, believes that the naval officials have now become more attached to the idea of an OLF at the Pocosin Lake site.

Environmental groups such as the Audubon Society, Defenders of Wildlife, and the N.C. Wildlife Federation have worked to oppose the proposed OLF, but individuals and small groups have also had an important effect. Joe Albea and Tom Earnhardt, two conservationists, have drawn attention to the OLF project. Perhaps most significant, however, have been efforts by grassroots organizations such as North Carolinians Opposing the Outlying Landing Field (NO-OLF), formed by residents in the affected communities. Many area residents have also lobbied General Assembly representatives and other lawmakers on the issue (Canfield 2005).

Perhaps the most intriguing issue is the breadth of the coalition opposed to the OLF. The anti-OLF forces comprise not only environmentalists but also states' rights advocates, private property supporters, and even the National Rifle Association—what Canfield (2005) calls the "widest and most diverse" coalition he has ever seen. This impact is important. With a wide range of opposition voices, political leaders have been forced to take a hard look at the issue. Canfield admits that if it were solely an environmental effort, the campaign against the OLF would be much less effective. This broad coalition has profoundly affected the OLF negotiations.

North Carolina's political leaders have been conflicted about the proposed OLF, but most welcomed the prospect of a new squadron of fighter jets in North Carolina. Democratic congressman G. K. Butterfield of North Carolina's First Congressional District (the affected region), asked Congress to remove money set aside for the project while the lawsuits were being decided. Although he opposed the proposed OLF site, Butterfield still wanted the Super Hornet squadron based in eastern North Carolina (Butterfield 2005).

Republican Elizabeth Dole, North Carolina's senior senator, has had a vocal role in negotiations regarding the OLF. She listened to community groups and activists and developed specific questions for the navy to answer. Many observers questioned whether Senator Dole received appropriate responses, and some expressed concerns that the navy's response was inappropriate and perhaps disrespectful to a senator on the Armed Services Committee (Canfield 2005). However, although she has not fully supported the OLF, Senator Dole has given the navy greater deference on the issue and, in the opinion of Canfield (2005), "has not done enough to solve the problem."

Republican Richard Burr (2005), North Carolina's junior senator, has stated that he will "support the Navy's decision regarding placement of an OLF in Eastern North Carolina if, and only if, the Navy has followed all rules and regulations governing its decision making process." He further notes that the Super Hornet squadron could bring approximately $40 million per year to the state.

Similarly, Governor Easley has agreed that an OLF would be good for the state but reiterated that all considerations and assessments must be made before a decision is reached. The governor's staff members negotiated with the navy, but as Canfield (2005) notes, the staff was "guided by a principle in the state that any push against the military, even for good reasons, is political suicide.... [T]he threat that bases would be closed in retaliation for more than symbolic resistance to the OLF ... came to rule in months leading up to those deliberations." This is an important note. The navy's proposed siting of the OLF in eastern North Carolina came at approximately the same time that the Department of Defense held base realignment and closure proceedings. With the North Carolina economy heavily reliant on military bases, many would-be objections to the OLF could easily fall by the wayside.

Another member of North Carolina's congressional delegation has acted strongly against the OLF. Congressman David Price of North Carolina's Fourth District was named to a committee on the military quality of life and veterans affairs. From this position, he has actively questioned navy officials about the proposed location of the OLF and has introduced language in certain bills that would encourage alternative sites (Canfield 2005).

The N.C. General Assembly has repealed a 1907 legislative act that waived North Carolina's right to approve federal acquisition of large tracts of land. The repeal had mostly symbolic value: the state cannot stop the navy from purchasing land, but the General Assembly must provide some approval (Canfield 2005).

However, the measure demonstrates that the General Assembly has reservations about the Pocosin Lake site.

The Fourth Circuit Court of Appeals's actions have two potential effects on the proposed OLF. On one hand, by ordering an SEIS, the court is chiding the navy for the poor quality of the initial EIS report. However, by narrowing the injunction, the court granted the navy leeway to perform additional work on the site. The navy could "sink more money and more institutional commitment to that specific site [and] no matter what the SEIS work shows, they will be wed more and more to ending up at the same place" (Canfield 2005).

The navy has now begun fieldwork for environmental impact assessments on five sites in eastern North Carolina, including the Pocosin Lake site (Allegood 2005). The five sites are located in a total of six counties, of which only one has expressed support for hosting the OLF. The investigation into additional potential sites seems to have led to greater resident opposition throughout the entire region. In fact, 225 residents turned out for an information session in Perquimans County to "express their concern" regarding the OLF. The navy has estimated that data collection would be finished in March 2006 and expected to deliver a new EIS in 2007 (Allegood 2005). For now, the issue of an OLF in eastern North Carolina appears to be in a holding pattern.

❖ Conclusion

North Carolina's political leadership has been involved in environmental politics for more than three decades, compiling a mixed record. The policy area engages a wide variety of political actors in a complex set of structural arrangements. Dozens of actors can be engaged in environmental policymaking at any particular point, and the policy terrain can shift quickly depending on the interests being challenged. As the case studies illustrate, when state leaders unite with a broad coalition of environmental interests and the issue can be framed in an understandable context such as health, the results can be very progressive. The clean smokestacks legislation is an example. However, when a narrower set of experts promotes policies that the public at large does not understand or appreciate and when that policy innovation ignites opposition among well-organized and resource-rich interests such as home builders, the policy will fail. The OLF controversy illustrates the collision of two major state interests, the military and wildlife and hunting groups. In this situation, the political establishment is essentially torn between groups it typically serves. Given this tension, the battle elevates to the federal court system so that state leaders are not forced to make a lose-lose choice.

As far back as V. O. Key's seminal 1949 study of southern politics, the Tar Heel State has generally been recognized as progressive—"progressive plutocracy" was Key's term. More than half a century later, this claim still holds true. As the comparative assessment of the state in terms of green planning illustrates, North Carolina stands in the top tier of southern states and securely in the top half of all states. Progressive policies are welcome as long as they do not disrupt the traditional interests of the economic elite, especially if the progressive policy can galvanize a broad coalition of grassroots activists. As Holman (2005) summarized environmental politics in his native state, "We've come a long way and we've got a long way to go."

❖ Note

The authors thank Cora McCold and Jonathan Kaepler for assistance in preparing the case studies in this essay.

❖ References

Allegood, Jerry. 2005. "Navy Continues Quest for Outlying Landing Field." *Raleigh News and Observer*, November 9. <http://www.newsobserver.com/159/story/363498.html>. Accessed September 23, 2007.

Audubon Society of North Carolina. 2005. "Proposed Outlying Landing Field: Threatening Wildlife and Our National Wildlife Refuges." <http://nc.audubon.org/>. Accessed October 20, 2005.

Burr, Richard. 2005. Personal communication, October 17. In possession of the authors.

Butterfield, G. K. 2005. "Butterfield Seeks Support of N.C. Delegation on OLF." Press Release. March 3. <http://www.house.gov/list/press/nc01_butterfield/03022005butterfieldseekssupportonolf.html>. Accessed October 1, 2007.

Canary Coalition. 2005. <http://www.canarycoalition.org/>. Accessed October 13, 2005.

Canfield, Chris. 2005. Personal communication, October 28. In possession of the authors.

Clean Water Management Trust Fund. 2005. <http://www.cwmtf.net/>. Accessed November 30, 2005.

Conservation Council of North Carolina. 2005. <http://ncconservationnetwork.org/>. Accessed November 30, 2005.

Conservation Trust for North Carolina. 2005. <http://www.ctnc.org>. Accessed November 29, 2005.

Democracy South. 1996. "The Pollution Lobby." <http://www.democracysouth.org/nc/ResearchPapers/1996/Pollution%20Lobby/pollutionlobby96.htm>. Accessed September 23, 2007.

Dryzek, John S., and David Schlosberg, eds. 1998. *Debating the Earth: The Environmental Politics Reader*. New York: Oxford University Press.

Environmental Defense of North Carolina. 2005. <http://www.environmentaldefense.org/aboutus.cfm?subnav=office_northcarolina>. Accessed November 29, 2005.

Erickson, Robert S., John P. McIver, and Gerald C. Wright Jr. 1987. "State Political Culture and Public Opinion." *American Political Science Review* 81:797–814.

Farmland Preservation Trust Fund. 2005. <http://www.farmland.org/southeast/nc_h067.htm>. Accessed November 30, 2005.

Givens, George E. 2006. Interview by author. Raleigh, N.C., February 2.

Grady, Dennis O., and Kathleen M. Simon. 2002. "Political Restraints and Bureaucratic Discretion: The Case of State Government Rule Making." *Politics and Policy* 30:646–79.

Holman, Bill. 2005. Interview by author. Raleigh, N.C., December 1.

Institute for Southern Studies. 2000. *Gold and Green 2000*. Durham, N.C.: Institute for Southern Studies.

Key, V. O., Jr. 1949. *Southern Politics in State and Nation*. New York: Knopf.

Layzer, Judith A. 2002. *The Environmental Case: Translating Values into Policy*. Washington, D.C.: CQ Press.

———. 2006. *The Environmental Case: Translating Values into Policy*. 2nd ed. Washington, D.C.: CQ Press.

Manufacturers and Chemical Industry Council. 2006. <http://www.mcicnc.org/>. Accessed January 17, 2006.

McCallie, Grady. 2005a. Interview by author. Raleigh, N.C., October 19.

———. 2005b. Interview by Cora McCold. Raleigh, N.C., November 2.

———. 2006. Personal communication, March 14. In possession of the authors.

Miller, Dale. 1998. "Farmers for Fairness." *National Hog Farmer*, May 1. <http://nationalhogfarmer.com/mag/farming_farmers_fairness/index.html>. Accessed January 12, 2005.

Natural Heritage Trust Fund. 2005. <http://www.ncnhtf.org/>. Accessed November 30, 2005.

Nature Conservancy. 2005. <http://www.nature.org/wherewework/northamerica/states/northcarolina/>. Accessed November 30, 2005.

"Navy's Outlying Landing Field (NC)." 2007. <http://www.southernenvironment.org/cases/navy_olf/timeline.htm>. Accessed September 23, 2007.

N.C. Agribusiness Council. 2006. <http://www.ncagribusiness.com>. Accessed January 17, 2006.

N.C. Association of County Commissioners. 2007. <http://www.ncacc.org>. Accessed October 26, 2007.

N.C. Audubon Society. 2007. <http://www.ncaudubon.org/>. Accessed October 26, 2007.

N.C. Center for Public Policy Research. 2006. "Most Influential Lobbyists in the N.C. General Assembly." Press Release. November 15.

N.C. Citizens for Business and Industry. 2006. <http://www.nccbi.org>. Accessed January 17, 2006.

N.C. Coastal Federation. 2005. <http://www.nccoast.org/>. Accessed November 30, 2005.

N.C. Coastal Resources Commission. 2005. <http://www.dem2.enr.state.nc.us/CRC/crc.htm>. Accessed November 28, 2005.

N.C. Conservation Network. 2005. <http://www.ncconservationnetwork.org/>. Accessed November 29, 2005.

N.C. Department of Environment and Natural Resources. 2005. <http://www.enr.state.nc.us>. Accessed November 28, 2005.

N.C. Ecosystem Enhancement Program. 2005. <http://www.nceep.net>. Accessed November 29, 2005.

N.C. Environmental Management Commission. 2005. <http://www.h2o.enr.state.nc.us/admin/emc/>. Accessed November 28, 2005.

N.C. General Assembly. 2006. <http://www.ncga.state.nc.us/CommitteeInfo/CommitteeInfo.html>. Accessed February 21, 2006.

N.C. Highway Stormwater Program. 2005. <http://www.ncdot.org/environment/stormwater/>. Accessed November 29, 2005.

N.C. Home Builders Association. 2006. <http://www.nchba.com/>. Accessed January 17, 2006.

N.C. League of Municipalities. 2007. <http://www.nclm.org>. Accessed October 26, 2007.

N.C. Office of Environmental Quality. 2005. <http://www.ncdot.org/environment>. Accessed November 29, 2005.

N.C. Office of Management and Budget. 2005. <http://www.osbm.state.nc.us/osbm/index.html>. Accessed February 16, 2006.

N.C. Pork Council. 2007. <http://www.ncpork.org>. Accessed November 4, 2007.

N.C. Public Interest Research Group. 2005. <http://www.ncpirg.org/>. Accessed November 30, 2005.

N.C. Public Utilities Commission. 2005. "History and Description of N.C. Public Utilities Commission." <http://www.ncuc.commerce.state.nc.us/index.htm>. Accessed November 28, 2005.

———. 2007. <http://www.ncuc.commerce.state.nc.us/>. Accessed October 26, 2007.

N.C. Rules Review Commission. 2006. <http://www.ncoah.com/rules/>. Accessed February 16, 2006.

N.C. State Energy Office. 2005. "North Carolina State Energy Plan: Prepared for the N.C. Energy Policy Council, June 2003; Revised January 2005." <//www.energync.net/epc/docs/Energy%20plan%202005.pdf>. Accessed October 1, 2007.

———. 2007. <http://www.energync.net>. Accessed October 26, 2007.

N.C. Stormwater Management Program. 2005. <http://www.ncstormwater.org>. Accessed November 29, 2005.

N.C. Sustainable Energy Association. 2007. <http://energync.org>. Accessed October 26, 2007.

N.C. 3R Program. 2005. <http://www.ncdot.org/environment/3R>. Accessed November 29, 2005.

N.C. Wildlife Federation. 2007. <http://www.ncwildlifefederation.org>. Accessed October 26, 2007.

N.C. Wildlife Resources Commission. 2005. <http://www.ncwildlife.org>. Accessed November 28, 2005.

Parks and Recreation Trust Fund. 2005. <http://www.partf.net/>. Accessed November 30, 2005.

Rabe, Barry G. 2006. "Power to the States: The Promise and Pitfalls of Decentralization." In *Environmental Policy: New Directions for the 21st Century*, edited by Norman J. Vig and Michael E. Kraft, 33–56. Washington, D.C.: CQ Press.

Rosenbaum, Walter A. 2005. *Environmental Politics and Policy*. 6th ed. Washington, D.C.: CQ Press.

Sierra Club. 1999. *Solving Sprawl: The Sierra Club Rates the States*. Washington, D.C.: Sierra Club.

Sierra Club of North Carolina. 2005. <http://www.nc.sierraclub.org/>. Accessed November 30, 2005.

Siy, Eric, Leo Koziol, and Darcy Rollins. 2001. "The State of the States: Assessing the Capacity of States to Achieve Sustainable Development through Green Planning." <http://greenplans.rri.org/pdf/sos.pdf>. Accessed September 23, 2007.

Southern Alliance for Clean Energy. 2005. <http://www.cleanenergy.org>. Accessed November 30, 2005.

Southern Environmental Law Center. 2007. <http://www.southernenvironment.org>. Accessed October 26, 2007.

Strom, Jennifer. 2005. "Growth Rules: Business Trumps the Public Interest on an Obscure Board That Has the Last Word on State Regulations." *Indy: The Independent Weekly*, July 6. <http://www.indyweek.com/gyrobase/Content?oid=oid%3A24666>. Accessed November 4, 2007.

Vig, Norman J., and Michael E. Kraft, eds. 2006. *Environmental Policy: New Directions for the 21st Century*. Washington, D.C.: CQ Press.

❖ 11. Education in the Tar Heel State
Public Elementary, Secondary, and Higher Education in North Carolina

HUNTER BACOT

North Carolina has long been praised as a leader in public education. Governor Charles Aycock, the first of many education governors, led the state toward public funding of education and progressive education policies (Key 1949). During the early 1960s, Governor Terry Sanford advocated a 3 percent tax on groceries, with the proceeds to go to education, and in the early 1990s, Governor Jim Hunt initiated the state's Smart Start program to prepare students for kindergarten (Luebke 1998). North Carolina has also been commended for its commitment to higher education (Christensen and Fleer 1999).

Despite these accolades, public education in North Carolina is at a crossroads. Responsibility for public education has meandered between the governor and the legislature as each promoted improved education for political and practical reasons. The judiciary recently has become involved, serving as a referee in battles over the course of public education. As a result, this pivotal point in North Carolina education is marked by the challenges of accountability, funding, enrollment growth, and educational equity. This essay focuses on these challenges and assesses the contemporary status of education in North Carolina through a comparative state perspective.

The essay begins by discussing the organization and background of elementary and secondary education.[1] Next, the essay turns to an examination of the contemporary condition of elementary and secondary education, focusing specifically on accountability and funding. The essay then considers inequities among public schools, profiling several notable court cases. The essay turns to educational achievement by comparing North Carolina's performance to that of other states and analyzing the growing achievement gaps within the Tar Heel State. The discussion then moves to current issues confronting higher education before offering some conclusions about the current status of public education in North Carolina.

❖ Organization and Background of Elementary and Secondary Education

While many functions involving elementary and secondary education in North Carolina are shared between the state and local governments, the state's system, like most educational systems in the United States, is organized from the top down. North Carolina's public elementary and secondary schools fall under the direction of the State Board of Education (SBOE), but local boards of education also share in the responsibility for directing educational affairs.[2]

The SBOE oversees public education in North Carolina and is responsible for setting statewide education priorities. Moreover, the SBOE must ensure that the General Assembly's legislative directives are implemented. Implementation of priorities and legislative initiatives also is the responsibility of an elected state superintendent of public instruction, who sits on the SBOE. The state superintendent is the public official responsible for elementary and secondary public education. The state superintendent must also see that the policy wishes of the members of the SBOE and the state legislature are implemented. Nationwide, only eight superintendents are elected in statewide, partisan elections; most state superintendents are appointed by the state's board of education (Wong 2004).

Elected officials who serve on the SBOE include the lieutenant governor and the state treasurer. The governor selects the eleven appointed members, who must be confirmed by a joint session of the General Assembly. Eight of these eleven appointees represent districts, while three are appointed at large. The superintendent of public instruction is the secretary and chief administrative officer of the SBOE (North Carolina Constitution, Article 9).

Local boards of education in North Carolina comprise elected officials who represent districtwide constituencies. These local boards of education develop education policies and typically depend on a professional superintendent of public schools to manage day-to-day affairs, provide budget direction, and recommend policy priorities. Local boards of education are responsible for adhering to state and federal regulations and guidelines, although some local discretion exists. For example, local boards determine their own personnel standards and curriculum offerings as well as decide on infrastructure needs, improvements, and maintenance.

Unlike many of their counterparts in other states, North Carolina's local boards of education generally do not have revenue-raising authority. While local education boards devise school budgets, these budgets are presented to the local commissions for consideration and funding. With the exception of those counties that have a special tax earmarked to support the local school systems, local school systems nationwide often rely on separate boards for revenues. The arrangement that permits one elected board to dictate the overall appropriations for another elected board can create fractious relationships between boards. As discussed in Sean Hildebrand and James H. Svara's essay in this volume, North Carolina counties have other service demands, many of which are mandated by the state, including hospitals, courts, and social services. Further complicating the relations between these boards is the fact that county commissions are reluctant to increase spending and prefer a tax rate amenable to residents.

Another organizational feature of North Carolina's educational system is countywide or consolidated school systems. Spurred by activities of the state legislature as well as federal government initiatives, many city and county school systems consolidated, reducing the number of local school systems in North Carolina from 174 in 1958 to 117 in 2006 (Peek 2006). Observers cite efficiency and financial capacity as reasons for consolidating school systems. In addition, national civil rights legislation, the creation of the SBOE in 1942, and North Carolina's $100 million bond package for public schools in 1963 contributed to consolidation (Peek 2006).

As figure 11.1 shows, 100 of North Carolina's 117 school systems are countywide systems, while the remainder are city- and community-based districts (N.C. Public Schools 2006a).[3] Residents of cities with citywide school districts are assessed an additional property tax levy beyond the combined city and county property tax to pay for these schools. For example, in 2006, Randolph County levied an additional school rate of $.1385 per $1,000 assessed value on property located in the city of Asheboro to support the city's public schools. This school rate is in addition to the county property tax rate of $.525 and the city of Asheboro's property tax rate of $.55, creating a total rate of $1.2135. In comparison, residents in neighboring Randleman, whose children attend Randolph County schools, pay a total of $1.035 per $1,000 assessed value—the combined Randolph County tax rate of $.525 and the city of Randleman tax rate of $.51 ("Randolph County Tax Rates" 2006).

Elementary and secondary education in North Carolina represents a concerted effort among agencies at both the state and local government levels. While this arrangement has proven sufficient and has offered many innovations, North Carolina's elementary and secondary educational system faces challenges in matching improvements in other states. As the next section shows, North Carolina has accomplished much in meeting the challenges confronting elementary and secondary education, but most other states have kept pace with the Tar Heel State's improvements. Therefore, as much as the state has accomplished, North Carolina remains in the lowest quartiles of national education ratings and rankings, particularly in areas related to spending or funding for elementary and secondary education.

FIGURE 11.1. School Systems in North Carolina, 2006

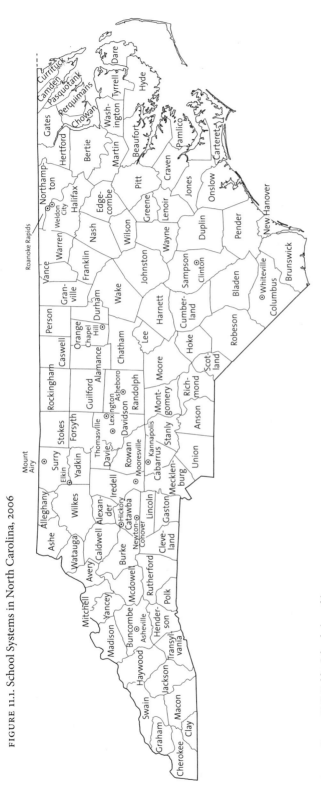

Source: N.C. Public Schools (2006b).

❖ Contemporary Education Policy in North Carolina: Accountability and Funding

North Carolina is a national leader in mandating accountability across its public schools. Since the 1970s, the state has made tremendous strides in holding local school boards accountable for student progress and performance ("History of Education in North Carolina" 2001; "History of the North Carolina State Board of Education" 2001). In fact, North Carolina has done so well that other states and the national government have adapted its ideas. Beginning with state legislative actions in the early 1970s, including the solving of some personnel issues and the passage of a $300 million school construction bond, North Carolina headed into the final twenty years of the twentieth century by initiating school reforms. Led by Governor Hunt and the state legislature, these reforms had significant positive consequences for North Carolina's elementary and secondary schools ("History of the North Carolina State Board of Education" 2001; Lyons and Calhoun 2000). Such activity bodes well for the state, as North Carolina currently ranks among the nation's elite in established testing and school standards policies (Wong 2004).

Many of the reforms promoted by Hunt and eventually approved by the state legislature were aimed at improving student performance. From the Basic Education Program in 1985 to the reauthorization of the School Improvement and Accountability Act in 1992, the common theme of these efforts was developing a means for assessing the performance of both the student and the system ("History of Education in North Carolina" 2001; Lyons and Calhoun 2000; Peek 2006). Efforts to assess student performance evolved into standardized end-of-grade tests for reading and math administered in the fourth and eighth grades. In addition, high schools were required to provide end-of-course tests for ninth through twelfth grades ("History of Education in North Carolina" 2001). Performance initiatives also extend to entire systems, which receive report cards on whether they meet state-mandated goals ("History of Education in North Carolina" 2001; "History of the North Carolina State Board of Education" 2001).

Other reform efforts—primarily the ABCs of Public Education (1995), the Excellent Schools Act (1997), and the Student Accountability Standards—sought to ensure that elementary and secondary students make proper progress and achievement. The ABCs of Public Education raised the ante on accountability by tying performance to remuneration. For example, teachers at schools that registered significant test score achievements and improvements received pay bonuses tied to the school's performance. Extending this accountability into the community, these data are available for review by parents and residents.

The Excellent Schools Act furthered this focus on enhanced instruction by ac-

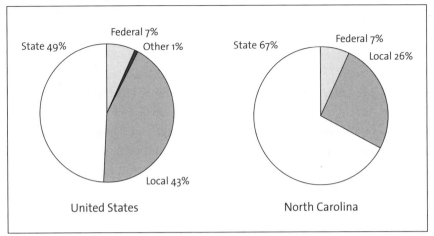

Source: Williams et al. (2005).

centuating the importance of qualified staff. Local school systems sought to attract better teachers by increasing pay and providing other financial incentives to
increase professional credentials and improve classroom performance. Not over-
looking Student Accountability Standards, the SBOE established performance requirements on end-of-grade tests for students in third, fifth, and eighth grades and
in high school and required successful completion of these tests for promotion to
the next grade.

With the advent of accountability measures, North Carolina has incurred additional costs for educating its children.[4] The Excellent Schools Act and the passage
of bond packages have increased the state's financial obligations for administrative
personnel, infrastructure, and teacher pay. Already considered a high-responsibility state with regard to funding elementary and secondary education, the state
assumed a dominant role in public education (Wong 2004, 366). State initiatives to
improve education introduced significant financial responsibility for school funding at the state level: the state finances about 66 percent of elementary and secondary education costs, while local school boards generally assume 26 percent of
these costs (see figure 11.2). The national average for dividing the financial burden
of elementary and secondary education between state and local governments is 50
percent/43 percent.

North Carolina receives laudable marks for the financial support it provides
to the many constituent parts of the state's accountability programs. In the aggregate, the state's support of public schools is high relative to other states (Zinth

2005). Considering that North Carolina ranks sixth in the number of large school districts in the country and has 5 of the 100 largest school districts in the United States, this support is even more impressive (Zinth 2005). The financial responsibility of providing nearly 70 percent of the support for public education, however, challenges the state to ensure equitable and adequate funding for all school systems. Thus, while North Carolina ranks high in its financial support of elementary and secondary education, this support is diluted among 115 school systems.

The state's contribution to education funding has also lost ground over time. Figure 11.3 shows education funding as a percentage of the state's general operating fund and the declining support for elementary and secondary education in the state since the 1970s.

Reviewing total per-student funding across a variety of indicators demonstrates the financial challenges North Carolina faces in sustaining reform efforts. In 2001, North Carolina's total per-pupil expenditures ranked fortieth among the states. North Carolina spent an average of $6,495 per student, compared with $7,727 nationally (see U.S. Department of Education, National Center for Education Statistics 2004). Yet data for revenues directed to North Carolina elementary and secondary schools for the same year show the state at thirteenth in gross revenues (see U.S. Department of Education, National Center for Education Statistics 2004).[5] As a result, a disparity exists between revenues raised for public education at the state level only and what is appropriated based on both state and local contributions. This disparity is explained somewhat by the state's low ranking relative to revenue and expenditures as a function of personal income. In 2004, North Carolina's median household income stood at $39,000, fortieth among the states and nearly 10 percent below the U.S. median of $44,473. Because personal income in the state is comparatively low, the ratio of revenues and spending per $1,000 of personal income is also low. This situation likely impedes per-pupil progress in elementary and secondary education relative to national standings (U.S. Census Bureau 2005).

North Carolina has accomplished much in promoting education since the 1970s, but other states have also made substantial progress. If North Carolina is to continue to improve its national education standing, dramatic changes in the allocation of revenue and expenditure are required. To move per-pupil expenditures past the national average reported above will require an average increase of $2,000 per pupil—nearly $3 billion annually, based on 2002 enrollment numbers. By accepting a dominant policy role in public education, the state also assumes a pronounced financial role and therefore obligates itself to ensure that elementary and secondary students are funded on an equitable per-pupil basis across the state, a topic discussed later in this essay.

FIGURE 11.3. Education Budget as Percentage of N.C. General Fund, 1970–2002

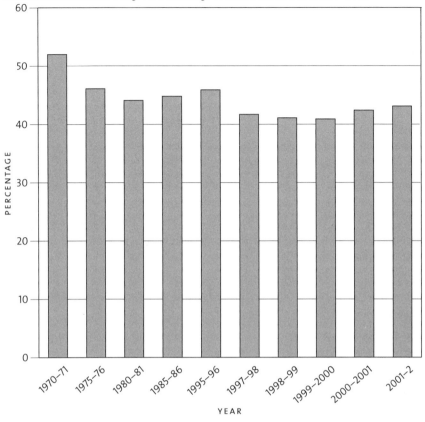

Source: School Forum of North Carolina (2006).

Overall, the fiscal status of public education in North Carolina continues to improve in some areas but remains distressed in others and cannot begin to compete
nationally. Lawmakers and public officials are attempting to address some of these
financing challenges by advancing new revenue sources such as the state lottery,
but these leaders still must contend with other issues that adversely affect state resources. Consequently, the fiscal situation of education funding in North Carolina
represents a moving target, as changing economic and social dynamics continually
complicate the state's ability to close in on national averages.

One of the foremost challenges affecting state appropriations is enrollment
growth. Total enrollment in the state has increased slightly more than 15 percent
from 1994 to 2004, an annual average increase of 1.25 percent (N.C. Public Schools
2004, 18).[6] Though not remarkable when viewed over time, the total enrollment
growth has implications for school funding. Increased enrollments demand additional classroom and overall facility space. Capital outlays for construction and

related costs across all school systems in North Carolina amounted to nearly $1 billion in 2002–3 (N.C. Public Schools 2004, 59).[7] Particularly problematic among the construction costs is the fiscal pressure exerted on local governments, which absorb 94 percent of construction costs (N.C. Public Schools 2004, 59).

Fortunately, the North Carolina lottery will provide relief: the current formula directs approximately 14 percent of lottery revenues for school construction (North Carolina General Statutes n.d., chapter 115c). However, lottery revenue distribution tends to favor larger, urban counties. Lottery funding is allocated for school construction based on a county's financial capacity. Eight local school systems, all in metropolitan areas, were projected to receive the bulk of lottery proceeds for school construction. For the 2006–7 fiscal year, metropolitan systems were estimated to receive between $4 million and $18 million each, while the remaining 107 systems were projected to receive between $200,000 and $3.5 million each. Mecklenburg County, for example, spent $7,231 per student, ranking fortieth among the one hundred fifteen districts in per-student funding, but was projected to receive $18 million. Similarly, Cumberland County ranked ninety-fourth at $6,384 per student and was projected to receive $7.5 million. Despite spending slightly more per student ($6,616), McDowell County ranked seventy-eighth and was projected to receive less than $500,000 (N.C. Department of Public Instruction, Financial and Business Services 2005).

As most of North Carolina's counties are growing, not all counties can fiscally accommodate this increased growth and therefore cannot pay for school construction projects that accompany growth. And, in a high-responsibility state, increased state responsibility is likely unless steps are taken to equalize fiscal responsibility across counties in North Carolina. Doing so, however, will require local governments substantially to raise taxes, a step that lies beyond the fiscal capacity and political will of most counties.

❖ Funding and Performance (In)Equity in North Carolina School Systems

Because the state must contend with increased costs for elementary and secondary education on a variety of fronts, equity issues will likely continue to complicate the fiscal situation at both the state and county levels. With policies such as the federal No Child Left Behind initiative, the state and local school systems must address additional costs associated with educational equity.

The accountability requirements of North Carolina's initiatives and No Child Left Behind do not carry significant fiscal consequences. In fact, many of the accountability requirements for reforming North Carolina education were already in place before passage of the federal legislation. State and federal reform efforts during the 1990s and early 2000s had the unintended consequence of permitting the identification of achievement gaps in North Carolina's reform efforts, as the following section discusses. These gaps pose fiscal burdens, particularly in areas with a large number of households at or near the poverty level or in areas with a significant number of households of children with disabilities. As the state addresses accountability in education, equity concerns based on funding and performance require both policy and financial attention.

❖ The *Leandro* Right

In North Carolina, the issue of equity moved into the courtroom as counties sought to redress unequal education funding. In a state with a comparatively high poverty rate, counties vary in their ability to raise revenues for education. Moreover, poverty in North Carolina follows distinct geographic patterns: the eastern coastal plains and westernmost mountain counties contain higher concentrations of poverty than do other areas. Mirroring the geography of poverty in these counties are concentrations of racial minorities, primarily blacks and Hispanics. Consequently, when inequities in education exist in these less densely populated counties, poverty and racial disparities are magnified (Stuart 2000). Racial and economic disparities are important for understanding disputes arising between the state and several rural counties that sought redress in state court to combat inequitable funding.

The *Leandro* case, discussed briefly in Ruth Ann Strickland's essay in this volume, is the most recent and highly publicized foray into education, race, and income politics in the Tar Heel State. The lawsuit against the state originated with a few poor, rural school systems and was eventually joined by many other counties that contended that the state provided insufficient funds to meeting the needs of at-risk and exceptional children (*Leandro v. State* 2004). The primary issue contested in the *Leandro* case concerned whether students in poor counties received an education similar to that provided to their counterparts in other areas of the state based on fairness in education funding.

The *Leandro* case traversed the state's court system, reaching the Supreme Court in 1997. The justices concluded that responsibility for a "sound basic education," as stated in the North Carolina Constitution, rests with the state. After an appeal, the Court affirmed lower court rulings in 2004 and declared that the state's school-aged children have an "individual right of an opportunity to a sound basic education" as provided in the North Carolina Constitution. The court also ruled that North Carolina had violated that right for children and established a standard for determining "a sound basic education" to be the Level III proficiency (*Hoke Board of Education et al.* 2004). In essence, the courts supported the idea that all children have a "*Leandro* right" and provided policymakers with a definition of a "basic education." As a consequence of the decision, the state now must work to equalize educational opportunities across all counties. The initial efforts to redress equitable deficiencies resulted in additional monies directed to counties not capable of funding their schools at the state average (Logan et al. 2006).

After the N.C. Supreme Court's final ruling in July 2004, the SBOE immediately addressed the funding issues through the Disadvantaged Student Supplemental Funding (DSSF). The SBOE also received significantly increased funding for Low-Wealth Supplemental Funding (Logan et al. 2006; N.C. Department of Public Instruction, Division of School Business 2006). Both the Low-Wealth Supplemental Funding (see figure 11.4) and the DSSF seek to alleviate inequities among disadvantage schoolchildren in underperforming and poor school systems. For example, DSSF funds are allocated based on each school system's assessments based on several criteria:

- percentage of students Level III and above
- percentage of public school students living in single-parent families
- percentage of population age five to seventeen below the poverty line
- percentage of public school students with at least one parent with less than high school degree
- index value (percentage or relative number of disadvantaged with regard to the state mean)
- percentage of average daily membership used for disadvantaged funding (24.13 percent plus index value). (N.C. Department of Public Instruction, Financial and Business Services 2004)

The *Leandro* court battle demonstrated to local school districts that gross disparities existed between North Carolina's haves and have-nots. The irony of the *Leandro* case, however, is that the measures used to evaluate system and student performance permitted plaintiffs to prevail in their case against the state. This case shows that these policies help to hold the state accountable for its actions as well as ensure that each public school student receives an equitable and standard education.

RESEGREGATION

The dispiriting aspects of the *Leandro* case, in which parents, students, and school systems had to battle the state to ensure that their students received an equal education, are not without precedent. In the 1970s, a similar landmark case involved

FIGURE 11.4. Low-Wealth Supplemental Funding in North Carolina, 2005–2006

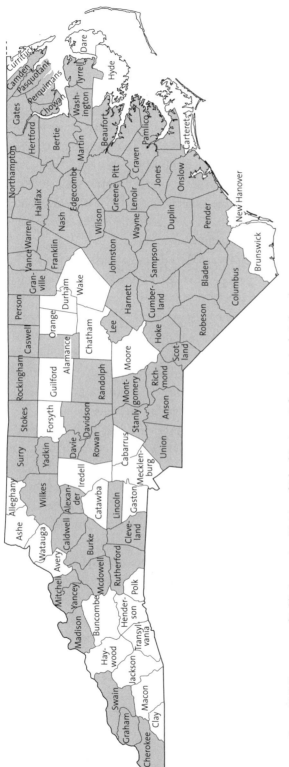

Source: N.C. Department of Public Instruction, Division of School Business, Information Analysis (2006), 19.

remedies to educational inequity based on race in the Charlotte-Mecklenburg school system. In *Swann v. Charlotte-Mecklenburg* (1969), the federal district court ordered the use of busing to achieve school desegregation. In fact, the *Swann* case was revisited in the late 1990s. According to the rulings in these cases, racial and economic diversity are requisite conditions of public education. Yet the means for achieving diversity in public schools and the extent to which diversity can coexist with overall educational goals require difficult decisions that do not please everyone. In the Charlotte-Mecklenburg schools, the later decision, *Capacchione v. Charlotte-Mecklenburg Schools* (1999), involved whether the school system remained under federal court order to ensure racial diversity through forced busing of schoolchildren. The court decision resulted in the local board of education abandoning busing as a means to achieve racial diversity in its schools, which has led to the resegregation of many of the system's schools.

Resegregation in North Carolina appears not to be a deliberate act on behalf of local education boards to separate whites, blacks, and Hispanics but an outcome of social and economic differences resulting from changing growth and development patterns. Though a phenomenon reserved for larger metropolitan areas in the state, the intersection of growth, development, and diversity is catalyzing introspection among the affected local school systems (Smith 2004).

By the late 1980s, Charlotte had established a reputation as a "junior Wall Street," home to numerous national banking and financial corporations. The city's population increased more than 25 percent during this time.[8] Residents and local civic and political leaders grew weary of busing to achieve desegregation, and this practice was reformed in the early 1990s and was formally challenged in court in 1997 (Smith 2004). Deciding the case two years later, the court declared that the school system had satisfied all requirements for achieving unitary system status and was therefore excused from all injunctions or court oversight. The court also permitted the formal dismantling of desegregation as practiced in Charlotte. However, the court stopped short of directing the school system to abandon race as a prescription for student assignment or resource allocation decisions (*Capacchione v. Charlotte-Mecklenburg Schools* 1999).[9] The removal of court oversight from the school system effectively resegregated the Charlotte-Mecklenburg schools (Smith 2004, 203–5, appendix). In the 2002–3 school year, 48 percent of blacks attended "black schools," and in 1999–2000, nearly 30 percent of white students attended "white schools" (Smith 2004, 73–74, 203). Yet the measures used in court by attorneys on behalf of Charlotte-Mecklenburg schools closely resemble those indicators used in the *Leandro* decision. Time will tell if schools in the Charlotte-Mecklenburg will meet the *Leandro* standards for receiving additional appropriations to counter elements of inequitable education.

❖ North Carolina's Educational Performance and the Achievement Gap

Given the reforms instituted during the final quarter of the past century, what is the current status of public elementary and secondary education in North Carolina? The state remains among the bottom half of states in student achievement and performance measures despite rating in the top half of states in aggregate spending and total number of students. While policy and legislative initiatives are well received, they do not always translate into high test scores. According to the U.S. Department of Education (National Center for Education Statistics, National Assessment of Educational Progress 2003), in 2003, North Carolina's eighth-graders barely exceeded the national average in reading, scoring 262 out of 500 and ranking thirty-second among all states.[10] Although the reading score remained the same as in 1998 (both nationally and in North Carolina), math scores during this period showed improvement. From 1996 to 2003, the average eighth-grade math scores in North Carolina improved 31 points, to 281, ranking the state twentieth nationwide (U.S. Department of Education, National Center for Education Statistics, National Assessment of Educational Progress 2003). North Carolina scored among the top seven states in number of students achieving proficient or advanced aptitude, demonstrating "competency over challenging subject matter" or "superior performance," respectively (U.S. Department of Education, National Center for Education Statistics, National Assessment of Educational Progress 2003).

North Carolina students' performance on standardized achievement tests also places them higher than students in most of the states in the immediate region. In reading proficiency for fourth- and eighth-graders, North Carolina trailed Virginia but scored better than Florida, Georgia, and South Carolina (Standard and Poor's 2006). North Carolina scored first among these states in fourth-grade math proficiency and second to Virginia in eighth-grade math proficiency (Standard and Poor's 2006). North Carolina's investment in performance accountability appears to pay some dividends for its students.

However, the events surrounding pivotal state and local legal battles over education in North Carolina point to unequal educational environments within school systems. The evidence of inequity in education lies in the achievement gaps—differences across student populations based on race and economics. School reforms are needed to enable the collection, measurement, and comparison of data. Regardless of the impetus surrounding legislation or initiatives directing acquisition of educational benchmarks, the state must now pay attention to what these data indicate about the status of public education. In fact, as executive and legislative leaders have learned, avoiding complete responsibility for education, for whatever reasons, surrenders such decisions to the judicial branch for remedy. And judicial policymaking leaves these leaders with no choice but to comply.

Courts have found educational inequities among schools and districts and have used these achievement gaps to justify policymaking by decree. These inequalities in education, though resulting largely from intrasystem dysfunction, are confirmed by achievement gaps across various groupings of students. Looking at state school systems according to race and poverty offers evidence of systemic or chronic problems in achievement and performance in our schools. In fact, the judiciary has chastised both the executive and legislative branches for failing students, particularly at the high school level, and is providing policy action from the bench aimed at addressing these inequities (*Hoke County Board of Education et al.* 2005).

Because the state and local governments remained in noncompliance with the court's direction in the initial *Hoke County* case, Judge Howard Manning addressed achievement gaps in a report to the SBOE. Manning's report included provisions for correcting these discrepancies and definitive consequences—closure of all underperforming schools—for those schools that failed to achieve at levels deemed acceptable by the court (Manning 2006). The achievement gaps in North Carolina's public high schools may stem from multiple sources, but these outcomes distinguish, via benchmarks and standards, among schools that do and do not achieve at specified levels. With a definite problem and no apparent meaningful action being taken toward progress, the courts are forcing the state to take action. Such court action may be the only politically viable way to direct resources to these schools. Politicians can blame the judiciary for forcing them to act and can hide behind the judge's order to avoid criticism for increased taxing and spending.

The collection and analysis of data ultimately tells a story, either positive or negative. When that story is positive, leaders can praise the results; when it is negative, as in some school systems and many high schools in North Carolina, civic and political leaders must address shortcomings. To their credit, North Carolina's leaders have investigated the achievement gap and have taken action at the elementary and kindergarten levels—for example, Governor Mike Easley's More at Four initiative—but have neglected to address chronic problems at the secondary level (Thompson 2002). Moreover, the legislation directing the research into the achievement gap called for the committee to look into the groups not achieving at grade level and to identify the most cost-effective methods for addressing the gaps (Thompson 2002). The legislation specified that the "Research Council and the Education Cabinet shall make recommendations to the Joint Legislative Education Oversight Committee by March 15, 2002, on the most cost-effective methods of improving student achievement among the targeted groups" (N.C. General Assembly 1999, 45). Mustering the public courage to act on these recommendations in a contentious political environment is challenging, but even more challenging is paying for the implementation of legislative initiatives. In the past, legislators have simply passed legislation but not provided funding for implementation.

❖ Higher Education in North Carolina

In keeping with the practice of state government control and centralized operations in North Carolina, higher education in the state is organized by the University of North Carolina (UNC), which oversees a university system comprised of sixteen constituent universities, and the North Carolina Community College System (NCCCS), which directs nearly sixty community colleges throughout the state. The UNC system is led by a board of governors whose thirty-two members are appointed to four-year terms by the governor and General Assembly, and the NCCCS is led similarly by the State Board of Community Colleges, whose twenty-one members also are appointed by the governor and General Assembly. Each of these boards selects a president to administer the relevant system. While the boards direct the overall efforts of their respective organizations, individual colleges and universities enjoy some autonomy. Each constituent institution has its own governing board (typically called a board of trustees), but as in most of North Carolina's government agencies, power is centralized.

Twelve of the thirteen members of each UNC system institution's board of trustees are selected by the UNC Board of Governors (eight selections) and the governor (four selections) based on recommendations from the constituent. The president of the student government serves as the thirteenth member (North Carolina General Statutes n.d., chapter 116, section 31). In the community college system, each institution's board of trustees also includes thirteen members: four appointed by the governor, four appointed by the local board of county commissioners, four appointed by the local board of education, and the president of the student government association. In both the UNC system and the NCCCS, each institution's board of trustees recommends a chancellor or president, whose appointment is subject to approval by the board of governors or by the State Board of Community Colleges.

Changes in the UNC system and the NCCCS have benefited North Carolina's institutions of higher education. Both systems received praise for their organizational innovations in the late 1970s and early 1980s. Both have systems flourished structurally and financially, embracing centralized administration and planning and responding to changing demographics. For example, the umbrella administrative structure has enabled system-level administrators to accommodate growing enrollment and changing programmatic needs by redirecting enrollment across institutions. Yet despite progress recent progress, two issues—financing and enrollment growth—continue to challenge these systems, particularly during the economic downturns encountered across the United States in the late 1990s and early 2000s.

Across the country, state funding for higher education continues to decline, while enrollments grow (Gianneschi and Yanagiura 2006). As figure 11.5 shows, North Carolina's higher education system has fared better financially than the national averages. However, North Carolina's postsecondary schools have much higher enrollments than the national averages. In fact, since the early 2000s, "total UNC state funding per full-time equivalent [FTE] student has dropped. . . . Overall funding per FTE has declined from $9,535 in 2000–2001 to $8,708 in 2003–2004 before rising to $9,172 in 2004–05. Adjusting for inflation, the real value of state appropriation per FTE in 2004 has declined to approximately $8,361 in 2000 dollars or a reduction of 12 percent" (Brown and Clark 2005, 8). As Clifford P. Harbour (2002, 33) notes, "Appropriations for community colleges (including funding from NCCCS administration) declined as a share of the overall state budget from FY 1989–90 to FY 1998–99." Despite these reductions, the UNC system has weathered the financial storm fairly well: according to Betsy E. Brown and Robert L. Clark (2005, 9), "While reductions in state funding have had a serious impact on University budgets, by this measure and others, UNC has fared better than its counterparts in many other states." Nevertheless, officials are exploring means to remedy the countervailing forces of declining funding and growing enrollments, including raising tuition and passing bond packages.

The North Carolina Constitution requires that education be as free as is practicable (Article 9, Section 9). Consequently, when the governing boards of the UNC System and the NCCCS began to consider raising tuition, vehement opposition arose. However, as state funding waned during the early 2000s, tuition had to increase to keep pace with the demand for higher education. As Brown and Clark (2005, 11) note, the resultant "rate of increase has been much higher than the average for similar institutions around the country"—almost 75 percent between 1998–99 and 2002–3, nearly triple the national average of just over 25 percent. By 2006, tuition provided approximately 32 percent of institutional revenue across the country, up from 26 percent in 2002; similarly, state funding for higher education across the country decreased from 68 percent to 62 percent over that span (Gianneschi and Yanagiura 2006, 19, table 2). Though specific figures are not available for North Carolina, this trend likely is present in the state as well. Responding to rising enrollments and stagnant state fiscal support for the UNC system and the NCCCS, North Carolina voters in 2000 passed an unprecedented bond package for higher

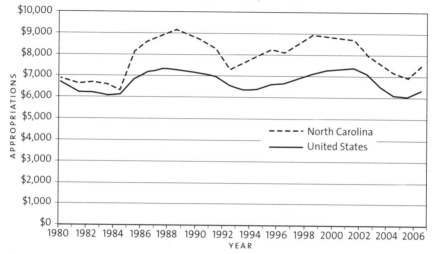

FIGURE 11.5. Comparing Educational Appropriations per Full-Time Equivalent in North Carolina and the United States, 1980–2006

Source: State Higher Education Executive Officers, Boulder, Colorado, "Public Postsecondary Enrollment, Educational Appropriations per FTE, and Total Educational Revenue per FTE, 1980–2006," <http://www.sheeo.org/finance/shef/shef_data.htm>, accessed September 17, 2007.

education. Nearly three-quarters of those who voted supported a bond package totaling $2.5 billion for the UNC System and $600 million for the NCCCS (Selingo 2000). With a predicted one-third increase in student enrollment for both systems, current state funding levels could not provide the necessary infrastructure. The bond package provided a substantial financial infusion for both systems, yet tuition continues to escalate.

The UNC and community college systems and their constituent institutions have made tough financial choices, adopted strategic plans to accommodate increased enrollments, and appear more cooperative in many ways. While higher education in the United States has faced tremendous challenges over the past two decades, North Carolina's 1960s commitment to a consolidated higher education system appears to have paid dividends decades later. As other state systems of higher education faced draconian cuts in the face of increasing enrollments, North Carolina institutions of higher education faced the situation collectively, an approach that has likely helped higher education persevere during these times.

❖ Conclusion

Most areas of elementary, secondary, and higher education in North Carolina have improved over the past quarter century. Civic and political leaders must make tough decisions that carry significant consequences. In fact, change is guaranteed as we move forward into the twenty-first century. North Carolina continues to place among the lower half of states in education rankings, but it does possess tools that identify education problems and provide direction for addressing them. In higher education, North Carolina may no longer achieve at the highest levels for which it has been renowned, but in many areas, the state continues to perform well. The judicial branch has accepted responsibility for ensuring adequate and equitable public education. Now the legislature must embrace its responsibility and fund public education at a level that will engage these prevailing issues, and the executive branch must lead in all efforts to equalize educational opportunities throughout North Carolina.

State and local civic and elected officials must make difficult choices and develop creative solutions. While many observers clamor that North Carolina is already doing enough (or sometimes that it is doing a bit too much), the results tell a different story. To restore the state's reputation as a national educational leader, officials must fund education at significantly greater levels—several billion dollars more per year. Addressing the situation intermittently and insufficiently only works to impede North Carolina's most valued resource—its children. In education, one decade of neglect leads to a generation of failure.

❖ Notes

1. The state of North Carolina enjoys highly respected community college and university systems not discussed at length in this essay. While higher education has received attention in the past decades, elementary and secondary education is the focus of much policy attention because of recent innovations, spending issues, and court cases. Consequently, we focus primarily on elementary and secondary education in this essay.

2. Local boards of education are commonly referred to as school boards. The SBOE refers to these local boards as local education agencies. This essay refers interchangeably to the local boards as "local boards of education" or "school boards."

3. The fifteen city districts include Asheboro, Asheville, Chapel Hill–Carrboro, Clinton, Elkin, Hickory, Kannapolis, Lexington, Mooresville, Mount Airy, Newton Conover, Roanoke Rapids, Thomasville, Weldon, and Whiteville.

4. National figures are used when comparing North Carolina to other states to ensure comparability. When discussing intrastate education issues, North Carolina education figures are used.

5. These figures are totals and do not dissociate revenues based on special provisions, personnel, and any earmarking requirements (funds dedicated based on regulation, matching, or mandate). Regardless, the state raises substantial funds for public schools.

6. Between 1993–94 and 2003–4, the African American share of the total enrollment in-

creased 1.1 percent, while Hispanic enrollment increased 5.3 percent. White enrollment, however, dropped 7.2 percent (N.C. Public Schools 2004, 18).

7. Using the SBOE definition, construction costs include "Capital I Projects: Acquisition of real property and construction; acquisition, reconstruction, enlargement, renovation or replacement of buildings and other structures. Capital II Projects: Acquisition or replacement of furnishings and equipment" (N.C. Public Schools 2004, 59, table 29).

8. This growth continued during the following decade (1990–2000), increasing another 26.7 percent (U.S. Census Bureau 2000).

9. For details of the case, see an excellent synopsis by Smith (2004, 159–68); for a summary of the decision, see Smith (2004, 168–71, 198–99).

10. The 2003 score represents the second iteration of testing. Eighth-graders were tested for the second time and the first time as third-graders in 1998. The first end-of-grade reading tests were administered in 1993.

❖ References

Brown, Betsy E., and Robert L. Clark. 2005. "North Carolina's Commitment to Higher Education: Access and Affordability." Paper presented at the conference on Assessing Public Higher Education at the Start of the Twenty-first Century, Ithaca, N.Y.

Capacchione v. Charlotte-Mecklenburg Schools. 1999. 57 F. Supp. 2d 228, 294, WDNC.

Christensen, Rob, and Jack D. Fleer. 1999. "North Carolina: Between Helms and Hunt No Majority Emerges." In *Southern Politics in the 1990s,* edited by Alexander P. Lamis, 81–106. Baton Rouge: Louisiana State University Press.

Gianneschi, Matt, and Takeshi Yanagiura. 2006. *State Higher Education Finance.* Boulder, Colo.: State Higher Education Executive Officers. <http://www.sheeo.org/finance/shef_fy06.pdf>. Accessed September 14, 2007.

Harbour, Clifford P. 2002. "The Legislative Evolution of Performance Funding in the North Carolina Community College System." *Community College Review* 29:28–49.

"The History of Education in North Carolina: An Addendum." 2001. <http://www.ncpublicschools.org/students/HistoryEd_Addendum.pdf> Accessed September 14, 2007.

"History of the North Carolina State Board of Education." 2001. <http://dpi.state.nc.us/state_board/SBE_history/>. Accessed September 14, 2007.*Hoke Board of Education et al. v. State of North Carolina and the State Board of Education.* 2004. N.C. Sup. Ct. 2004. 358 NC 605 530 PA 02.

Hoke County Board of Education et al. and Asheville City Board of Education et al. v. State of North Carolina State Board of Education. 2005. 95 CVS 1158, *Report from the Court: The High School Problem.* Judge Howard E. Manning Jr., May 24.

Key, V. O., Jr. 1949. *Southern Politics in State and Nation.* New York: Knopf.

Leandro v. State of North Carolina. 1997. 346 NC 336 179 PA 96.

———. 2004. 122 N.C. App. 1, 11, 468 S.E.2d. 543, 550.

Logan, Robert, Cliff Dodson, Ann Denlinger, William McNeal, and Don Martin. 2006.

"Memorandum to Honorable Howard Manning Jr. Re: *Leandro v. State*," May 4. <http://www.ncforum.org/resources/collateral/050406_Leandro-Letter%20to%20Manning%20re%20dismissal%20%20case.pdf>. Accessed October 2, 2007.

Luebke, Paul. 1998. *Tar Heel Politics 2000*. Chapel Hill: University of North Carolina Press.

Lyons, James E., and Mary Lynne Calhoun. 2000. "Public Education." In *The North Carolina Atlas: Portrait for a New Century*, edited by Alfred W. Stuart and James E. Lyons. Chapel Hill: University of North Carolina Press, 2000. <http://www.ncatlasrevisited.org/homefrm.html>. Accessed May 31, 2006.

Manning, Howard E., Jr. 2006. Memorandum to June St. Clair Atkinson and Howard N. Lee, March 3.

North Carolina Constitution. 1971. <http://www.ncga.state.nc.us/Legislation/constitution/ncconstitution.html>. Accessed September 24, 2007.

N.C. Department of Public Instruction. Division of School Business. Information Analysis. 2006. "Highlights of the N.C. Public School Budget." <http://www.ncpublicschools.org/docs/fbs/resources/data/highlights/2006highlights.pdf>. Accessed September 14, 2007.

N.C. Department of Public Instruction. Financial and Business Services. 2004. "Disadvantaged Student Supplemental Funding Data." <http://www.ncpublicschools.org/fbs/resources/data/disadvantaged/>. Accessed September 14, 2007.

———. 2005. "Estimated Lottery Distribution." <http://www.ncpublicschools.org/fbs/>. Accessed September 14, 2007.

N.C. Public Schools. 2004. *Statistical Profile, 2004*. Raleigh: N.C. State Board of Education. <http://www.ncpublicschools.org/docs/fbs/resources/data/statisticalprofile/2004profile.pdf>. Accessed November 4, 2007.

———. 2006a. "N.C. Local Education Agencies." <http://www.ncpublicschools.org/fbs/personnel/contacts/>. Accessed September 24, 2007.

———. 2006b. "North Carolina Map." <https://schooljobs.dpi.state.nc.us/hrms/HRMSHome.nsf/statemap?openform>. Accessed November 4, 2007.

N.C. School Boards Association. 2006. "History of NCSBA." <http://www.ncsba.org/about/history.htm>. Accessed November 4, 2007.

N.C. General Assembly. 1999. HB 1840, sec. 8.28, pp. 43–45.

North Carolina General Statutes. N.d.

Peek, William W. 2006. "History of Public Education in North Carolina." <http://www.ncpublicschools.org/students/history_of_ed.pdf>. Accessed September 14, 2007.

"Randolph County Tax Rates." 2006. <http://www.co.randolph.nc.us/tax/2005Rates.htm>. Accessed September 14, 2007.

School Forum of North Carolina. 2006. "National School Finance Overview." <http://www.ncforum.org/doclib/presentations/>. Accessed September 14, 2007.

Selingo, Jeffrey. 2000. "N.C. Passes Huge Bond Measure: Other States Vote on Education Referendums." *Chronicle of Higher Education*, November 17, 47, 12, A32.

Smith, Stephen S. 2004. *Boom for Whom?: Education, Desegregation, and Development in Charlotte*. Albany: State University of New York Press.

Standard and Poor's. 2006. "School Matters." <http://www.schoolmatters.com>. Accessed September 14, 2007.

Stuart, Alfred W. 2000. "Population." < http://www.ncatlasrevisited.org/homefrm.html>. Accessed September 14, 2007.

Swann v. Charlotte-Mecklenburg Board of Education. 1969. 300 F. Supp. 1358, 1360, WDNC.

Thompson, Charles L. 2002. *Research-Based Review of Reports on Closing Achievement Gaps.* Chapel Hill: N.C. Education Research Council.

U.S. Census Bureau. 2000. *North Carolina Census, 2000 Summary File 4.* Washington, D.C.: U.S. Department of Commerce.

———. 2003. *Current Population Survey, 2003.* Washington, D.C.: U.S. Government Printing Office.

———. 2004. *Current Population Survey, 2004.* Washington, D.C.: U.S. Government Printing Office.

———. 2005. *2005 Annual Social and Economic Supplements.* Washington, D.C.: U.S. Government Printing Office.

U.S. Department of Education. National Center for Education Statistics. 2004. "Documentation for the Common Core of Data, National Public Education Financial Survey (NPEFS): School Year 2000–01, Fiscal Year 2001." <http://nces.ed.gov/ccd/pdf/stfis01genr.pdf>. Accessed September 14, 2007.

U.S. Department of Education. National Center for Education Statistics. National Assessment of Educational Progress. 2002. *NAEP Reading Report Card for the Nation and States, 2002.* <http://nces.ed.gov/pubsearch/pubsinfo.asp?pubid=2003521>. Accessed September 14, 2007.

———. 2003. *NAEP Reading Report Card for the Nation and States, 2003.* <http://nces.ed.gov/pubsearch/pubsinfo.asp?pubid=20054537>. Accessed September 14, 2007.

Williams, Andra, Rolf K. Blank, Lori Cavell, and Carla Toye. 2005. *State Education Indicators with a Focus on Title I, 2001–02.* Washington, D.C.: U.S. Department of Education, Council of Chief State School Officers and Office of Planning, Evaluation, and Policy Development.

Wong, Kenneth K. 2004. "The Politics of Education." In *Politics in the American States,* edited by Virginia Gray and Russell L. Hanson, 357–88. Washington, D.C.: CQ Press.

Zinth, Kyle. 2005. *What Governors Need to Know: Highlights of State Education Systems.* Denver: Education Commission of the States.

❖ Conclusion

Rethinking Progressivism and Governance in North Carolina

CHRISTOPHER A. COOPER AND H. GIBBS KNOTTS

V. O. Key Jr.'s *Southern Politics in State and Nation* (1949) revolutionized political science. Nearly all work on southern politics or the politics of a southern state now begins with Key's seminal study. According to Key, North Carolina had more advanced industrial development, friendlier race relations, and a better educational system than its southern neighbors. Jack Bass and Walter DeVries (1995 [1976], 218) challenged this positive picture of North Carolina, labeling the state's reputation a "progressive myth."

In the introduction we reassessed Key's measures of progressivism using updated data and concluded that North Carolina is less progressive than previously appeared to be the case. North Carolina remains a regional leader in education, but the state lags behind in important measures of industrial development and race relations.

In this conclusion, we rethink what it means to be a progressive state in the twenty-first century and pull together the book's common themes. We discuss the historical forces that have shaped progressivism in North Carolina and evaluate that progressivism on six key dimensions. We then turn our attention to governance in North Carolina, focusing on both governmental performance and the state's capacity to govern. In the final section, we summarize our findings and highlight the states that have moved past North Carolina on our measures of progressivism.

❖ Rethinking Progressivism

In the first half of the twentieth century, an economy marked by agriculture and manufacturing was a sign of progress. Today, a state economy based solely on these sectors would be a sign of a traditional rather than progressive economy. Given these changes, we augment Key's definition of progressivism to meet today's economic and political realities.

In addition to Key's measures of progressivism discussed in the introduction, we evaluate the concept on six additional dimensions: party competition, racial and gender diversity, media quality, public opinion, policy outcomes, and governmental reform. A progressive state has healthy and active party competition, a vigorous and watchful media, progressive public opinion, diversity of officeholders, progressive policy outcomes, and innovative governmental reform efforts.

We also augment Key's conclusions by comparing North Carolina to all states as well as to its southern neighbors. In Key's time, the South was truly exceptional—different from the rest of the country in almost every way. Although the South remains unique (Black and Black 1987, 2007), regional economies have become increasingly interdependent. For example, North Carolina's prowess in the banking industry means that it competes with New York as much as with South Carolina. Similarly, businesses considering relocating to North Carolina can compare the suite of services and benefits the state offers to those in Oregon, Idaho, and Arizona as easily as those offered in Alabama.

❖ Evaluating Progressivism in the Twenty-first Century

North Carolina has long been known as a progressive force in southern political history. Thomas F. Eamon's essay largely supports this view of North Carolina, profiling important politicians who upheld and championed progressive traditions. He cites Governor Charles Aycock's commitment to education, Governor W. Kerr Scott's advocacy for roads and schools, and Governor Terry Sanford's willingness to increase taxes to support school programs. Eamon compares North Carolina's relatively enlightened reaction to the *Brown* school desegregation decision to the massive resistance undertaken in Virginia and the Deep South states.

Although he finds much reason to agree with Key, Eamon also emphasizes the conservative and traditionalistic elements that have long existed in North Carolina. He discusses Aycock's commitment to white supremacy and notes that Governor Cameron Morrison and Governor Melville Broughton were racially progressive but nevertheless supported segregation. Eamon also profiles two "apostles of social conservatism," Senator Furnifold Simmons and Senator Jesse Helms. Helms, one of the most nationally recognizable conservatives, championed traditional values and worked tirelessly to block the holiday honoring Dr. Martin Luther King Jr.

An evaluation of these historical forces supports the notion of a somewhat progressive North Carolina, particularly when compared to other southern states. The picture is less clear when North Carolina is compared to the rest of the country. States in most other regions of the country undoubtedly have much more progressive histories than North Carolina.

Healthy party competition can foster new ideas, enhance debate, and lead to innovative policy solutions. By and large, a progressive state is a two-party state. As Eamon notes, Republicans have always had a presence in North Carolina, even when other southern states had very little GOP activity. The Democratic stranglehold finally began to weaken with support for Republican presidential candidates and eventually James Holshouser's victory in the 1972 gubernatorial election. As highlighted in the introduction as well as in Charles Prysby's essay on political parties, North Carolina's electorate is currently split between those who identify themselves as Democrats and Republicans.

At the local level, Democrats maintain a slight numerical advantage. In chapter 9, Sean Hildebrand and James H. Svara report that Democrats have control of fifty-seven of North Carolina's one hundred county commissions. An analysis of local Republicanism during the 1990s found more Republican commissioners in areas with support for the Republican presidential candidate in 1988 as well as in western Piedmont counties, metropolitan counties, and counties with lower percentages of African American citizens (Knotts 2005).

Republicans have experienced moderate success at the state level in North Carolina. Several of the book's authors highlight the elections of Republican governors Holshouser and Jim Martin. Although the state has elected only two Republican governors since Reconstruction, Jack D. Fleer notes that since 1972, primary competition has become much more frequent in the Republican Party. Christopher A. Cooper emphasizes Democrats' dominant position in the state legislature but points out that the state House has recently fluctuated between Democratic and Republican control.

North Carolina has also enjoyed healthy two-party competition for national-level offices. In 2006, the state's U.S. House delegation included seven Democrats and six Republicans. Although both U.S. senators are Republican, Democrats have been competitive and have often occupied one of the two Senate seats. At the presidential level, much less competition exists between Democrats and Republicans. As several of this volume's authors note, Republican presidential candidates have received all of North Carolina's electoral votes since 1980.

Reflecting on these partisan realities, Charles Prysby argues that partisan realignment has led to clearer ideological differences between the parties. While many of North Carolina's conservatives formerly resided in the Democratic Party, Democratic officeholders and voters today are by and large more liberal than their Republican counterparts. Prysby also highlights the increased strength of both the Democratic and Republican organizations in North Carolina. Judging from these examples of healthy two-party competition, North Carolina appears fairly progressive.

RACIAL AND GENDER DIVERSITY

In addition to vigorous party competition, progressive states have a diverse group of political participants and officeholders. Racial and gender diversity has the potential to lead to innovative policies and provides a voice for groups traditionally left out of the political process.

As discussed in the introduction, African Americans make up the largest minority group in North Carolina, accounting for nearly 22 percent of the state's population. Hispanics comprise just over 6 percent. The introduction also presents data showing that African Americans hold just 8.5 percent of elected offices in the Tar Heel State. No southern states have equal percentages of minorities in office and in the electorate; North Carolina's officeholding diversity falls near the middle of that group. Moreover, neither major party has nominated an African American candidate for governor, and the lone African American candidate for U.S. Senate, Democrat Harvey Gantt, lost twice to Helms in racially charged campaigns. In addition to diversity in the legislative and executive branches, a diverse court system is also a sign of a progressive state. According to Ruth Ann Strickland, North Carolina has comparatively few African Americans on the bench.

In some areas, women officeholders fare better in North Carolina than elsewhere in the South. Cooper notes that the percentage of women in the General Assembly is consistent with national averages. Although North Carolina has not had a female governor, Elizabeth Dole represents the Tar Heel State in the U.S. Senate. However, Strickland reports that North Carolina ranks well below the national mean in the presence of women in the judiciary.

North Carolina's political record on racial and gender diversity is mixed. Racially, the state lags behind both nationally and in the South. However, aside from the judiciary, North Carolina has higher numbers of women in office than do its southern neighbors.

MEDIA QUALITY

Most people lack the time, ability, or inclination to monitor government directly and therefore rely on the media to keep a watchful eye on the political process. Of course, the media do not always adequately perform this function. Many observers argue that journalists are too Democratic, too Republican, too critical, or too soft to effectively monitor government and keep citizens informed. Politicians have also developed well-crafted strategies to spin journalists and favorably affect the news, making it even more difficult for average Americans to get an unfiltered and relatively unbiased view of what their government is doing.

A progressive state should have not only progressive governmental institutions and progressive policies but also a progressive press corps. This does not mean a press corps that tends toward the Democratic Party but rather a press corps that accurately, fairly, and consistently monitors state government. Ferrel Guillory, a former journalist, argues in chapter 5 of this book that although the teeth of the media watchdog may not be as sharp as was formerly the case, it still barks. North Carolina is blessed with a number of excellent newspapers and a long tradition of outstanding journalism. Most southern states are home to one or perhaps two major newspapers that can be counted on for quality coverage—North Carolina has many more. Some of these papers are national leaders. The *Charlotte Observer*, for example, was an early pioneer in the public journalism movement. Guillory's essay also points out the state's long tradition of winners of the Pulitzer Prize. Few states nationwide and even fewer in the South can boast as progressive a press corps as North Carolina.

PUBLIC OPINION

Signs of a progressive state are found not just in the government but also with the people. While Key made a number of observations about citizen opinions throughout the South, he was unable to systematically test them. Large-scale public opinion surveys—the kind that are common today—were not available during the first half of the twentieth century.

In chapter 2, Timothy Vercellotti compares national public opinion data to data from the Elon Poll, the most systematic survey of statewide attitudes in North Carolina, to analyze public opinion. Vercellotti concludes that North Carolina appears fairly progressive when compared to the rest of the South. North Carolinians are more likely to favor an active government and less likely to express attitudes of individualism than their southern neighbors. Vercellotti attributes these more progressive attitudes to the relatively large number of nonsoutherners who have immigrated to the state.

Examining additional data also casts North Carolina's public opinion as relatively progressive and introduces a potential difference between policy types. In economic policies, North Carolina appears fairly progressive. The Tar Heel State ranks seventh nationally and third in the South in support for higher levels of school funding (Norrander 2001). Similarly, North Carolina ranks twenty-fifth nationally and sixth in the South on support for spending on the environment (Brace et al. 2002).

When examining social policy opinions, the state appears more traditional.

North Carolina ranks fortieth out of the forty-five states for which data are available and ninth in the South on measures of public opinion on racial integration and on feminism (Brace et al. 2002). The opinions of North Carolinians on homosexuality are also fairly traditional—the state ranks thirty-ninth out of forty-five states on acceptance of homosexuality (Brace et al. 2002). As with other indicators of progressivism, we cannot conclude that public opinion in North Carolina is entirely traditional or entirely progressive. Public opinion in North Carolina falls in the middle nationally, although this relationship is mediated to some extent by the type of issue addressed. North Carolinians are much more progressive on economic issues than on social issues.

POLICY OUTCOMES

Policy outputs also serve as important indicators of progressivism. An analysis of policy outcomes presents a complicated state, one that certainly is not progressive but also is not completely traditional. Two informative contributions to this volume analyze environmental and education policy in North Carolina. Hunter Bacot reports that North Carolina has innovative state educational policies and encouraging outcomes related to eighth-grade testing. However, he also describes an educational system that is drastically underfinanced.

In chapter 11, Dennis O. Grady and Jonathan Kanipe present North Carolina's "ambivalent legacy" on the environment. In a comparative assessment of green planning, North Carolina ranks in the top tier of southern states and in the top half of all states. Grady and Kanipe also report on the progressive and successful Clean Smokestacks Act and the less progressive outcomes surrounding the naval outlying landing field.

Of course, a variety of other important policy issues go beyond education and the environment. As with public opinion, progressive policy outcomes are best explained by the type of issue addressed. In the economic sphere, North Carolina's policies appear fairly progressive. The state ranks sixteenth nationally in share of total personal income allocated to education spending and twenty-fourth nationally in the share of total personal income allocated to highway spending (Garand and Baudoin 2004, 295). Among southern states, North Carolina ranks fourth in per-capita education spending (trailing Arkansas, Alabama, and Mississippi) and fourth in per-capita highway spending (behind Mississippi, Arkansas, and South Carolina). The Tar Heel State also ranks twenty-sixth in entrepreneurial economic development policy (sixth in the South, behind Florida, Tennessee, Texas, Arkansas, and Louisiana) (Saiz and Clarke 2004, 436). On issues of economic policy, North Carolina falls in the middle both nationally and among its southern neighbors.

The state's social policies appear significantly more traditional than its economic policies. For example, the state ranks forty-fifth out of fifty on policies supporting gay civil rights (Eshbaugh-Soha and Meier 2004, 413). Within the South, North Carolina ranks eighth out of eleven states, ahead of only Alabama, Virginia, and Mississippi.

GOVERNMENTAL REFORM

A final component of progressivism in the twenty-first century is governmental reform. Although politicians have always had ethical problems ranging from improper influence to vote buying, North Carolina enjoyed a relatively clean reputation until the first decade of the twenty-first century. Since 2000, a number of high-profile politicians, including agricultural commissioner Meg Scott Phipps and speaker of the North Carolina House Jim Black, have pleaded guilty to corruption charges. Black provided or promised campaign contributions to Michael Decker in exchange for Decker's agreement to switch from the Republican to the Democratic Party in 2003, a move that created a 60–60 split in the House and eventually led to a co-speakership arrangement between Black and Richard Morgan.

In light of increasingly negative perceptions of government, many states have embraced governmental reform to create institutions that promote ethical behavior and punish unethical behavior. For example, states have strengthened campaign finance laws and restrictions on lobbyist behavior. We consider these reforms explicitly progressive. As Adam J. Newmark points out in his essay on interest groups, North Carolina is traditionally considered one of the least regulated states when it comes to lobbying, ranking low in the South and even lower nationally. This lack of regulation may be changing, however. As a result of recent scandals, the General Assembly passed the State Government Ethics Act in 2006. Sponsored by Democratic representative Joe Hackney and Democratic senator Tony Rand, the legislation authorizes an independent State Ethics Commission to oversee the legislative, executive, and judicial branches of government and bans gifts to public officials.

❖ Evaluating Governance

Whether Democrat or Republican, liberal or conservative, progressive or traditional, quality governance is one of the fundamental challenges facing states. How does North Carolina rank in terms of quality of governance? Academics working with the Government Performance Project (2005) have provided annual "Grading the States" reports that evaluate the quality of governance on several key dimensions. Funded by the Pew Charitable Trust, the Government Performance Project provides an independent and nonpartisan ranking of government performance. The results for North Carolina are underwhelming. The state received a C+ in overall performance, and although a number of states were tied with North Carolina, only five states ranked lower. The overall score was based on grades in four areas: money, people, infrastructure, and information. North Carolina received a B- in the money category and a C+ in the other three areas.

North Carolina ranks much better on a second component of quality governance, e-government, that describes the use of information technology to redefine and expand the relationships between citizens and government. In the 2006 e-government rankings, North Carolina appeared precisely in the middle at twenty-fifth nationwide. North Carolina was fourth in the South, after Texas (first overall), Tennessee (eleventh), and South Carolina (seventeenth). A year earlier, North Carolina ranked fourth nationally (West 2006).

Although not definitive, these two measures of governmental performance present a mixed review for North Carolina. The grades from the Government Performance Project suggest room for improvement, while the e-governance ranking provides some encouraging signs for the state's commitment to innovation and technology.

❖ Capacity to Govern

What will improve the quality of governance and the level of progress in North Carolina? As a result of devolution, state governments have greatly expanded their functions over the past half century. Residents in many states responded to this movement by granting power and resources to state governments. Others have been less willing to cede this capacity to govern.

Almost every state has increased the professionalism of the legislature—granting legislators more staff, increasing session lengths, and raising legislative salaries (King 2000). Professionalism rankings for all fifty states have the North Carolina legislature occupying a comparatively low position, particularly given the size and complexity of its operations. While good reasons may exist for having a less professional state legislature—keeping the legislators closer to the people, for one—the lack of professionalism has important implications for governance. Legislators have great difficulty finding the time and resources to govern effectively if they are trying to balance a second job and have little staff assistance. The compensation package and demands of the North Carolina legislature also limit the pool of potential General Assembly candidates.

Governors have also taken on increasing responsibility in the federal system. As Fleer's essay in this volume recounts, many states have given their governors powers resembling those held by the president of the United States—veto power, power over the budget, and the power of appointment. Although North Carolina has increased the institutional powers of its governor modestly over the past half century, the institution remains comparatively weak.

While the U.S. Supreme Court receives most of the headlines, state courts decide the vast majority of cases. As the number of cases has increased, however, many states have not responded by giving their courts more resources. Strickland's essay suggests that North Carolina has been a leader in judicial reform, particularly in the areas of business courts, drug treatment, and public financing of appellate court judicial campaigns. However, the General Assembly's unwillingness to provide adequate financing for the judiciary has limited the courts.

In sum, North Carolina falls near the middle of southern states in its capacity to govern. North Carolina ranks low among the fifty states, particularly given its size and complexity. Political leaders in the Tar Heel State should continue to provide government with the tools needed to accomplish its objectives.

❖ Traditionalism and Progressivism in the Twenty-first Century

This volume presents a dynamic and complex state that appears both progressive and traditional. North Carolina is more progressive than many of its southern neighbors, including Alabama, Arkansas, Mississippi, and South Carolina. However, North Carolina is no longer the regional leader, losing ground to peripheral South states such as Florida, Texas, and Virginia. Georgia, North Carolina's Deep South neighbor, can also legitimately claim to have surpassed North Carolina in terms of progressivism.

Comparisons to the South tell only part of the story, however. Given the rise of interregional economies and declining regional distinctiveness, it is important to evaluate where North Carolina ranks nationwide. Economically, the state continues to display signs of progressivism, ranking near the middle of all fifty states. However, with regard to social policies, the state is among the most traditional in the country.

Not surprisingly, the new politics of North Carolina differ substantially from politics during Key's time. Two-party competition is alive and well, and increasing numbers of African American and women officeholders have changed the ways the state is governed. New voters are pouring into the state in record numbers, and these voters do not look like the old ones—they are more likely to be Hispanic, less likely to be African American, more likely to have grown up in the Northeast, less likely to be born-again Christians, and more likely to have graduated from college (Quinterno 2004, 2). In addition, the emergence of new and different policy areas has provided opportunities for innovative Tar Heel politicians. At the same time, remnants of the old politics remain. Traditionalistic strands still exert influence, particularly in the realm of social issues and policy outcomes. Therefore, the new politics of North Carolina represents a combination of new and old. New opportunities and challenges have forced the state to change, but the old culture remains a powerful force.

❖ References

Bass, Jack, and Walter DeVries. 1995 [1976]. *The Transformation of Southern Politics: Social Change and Political Consequences since 1945*. Athens: University of Georgia Press.

Black, Earl, and Merle Black. 1987. *Politics and Society in the South*. Cambridge: Harvard University Press.

———. 2007. *Divided America: The Ferocious Power Struggle in American Politics*. New York: Simon and Schuster.

Brace, Paul, Kellie Sims-Butler, Kevin Arceneaux, and Martin Johnson. 2002. "Public Opinion in the American States: New Perspectives Using National Survey Data." *American Journal of Political Science* 46:173–89.

Eshbaugh-Soha, Matthew, and Kenneth J. Meier. 2004. "Economic and Social Regulation." In *Politics in the American States: A Comparative Analysis*, edited by Virginia Gray and Russell L. Hanson, 389–417. Washington, D.C.: CQ Press.

Garand, James C., and Kyle Baudoin. 2004. "Fiscal Policy in the American States." In *Politics in the American States: A Comparative Analysis*, edited by Virginia Gray and Russell L. Hanson, 290–317. Washington, D.C.: CQ Press.

Government Performance Project. 2005. "Grading the States '05." *Governing Magazine*, February. <http://www.governing.com/gpp/2005/intro.htm>. Accessed December 15, 2006.

Key, V. O., Jr. 1949. *Southern Politics in State and Nation*. New York: Knopf.

King, James D. 2000. "Changes in Professionalism in U.S. State Legislatures." *Legislative Studies Quarterly* 25:327–43.

Knotts, H. Gibbs. 2005. "Grassroots Republicanism: Evaluating the Trickle Down Realignment Theory in North Carolina." *Politics and Policy* 33:1–17.

Norrander, Barbara. 2001. "Measuring State Public Opinion with the Senate National Election Study." *State Politics and Policy Quarterly* 1:111–24.

Quinterno, John. 2004. "New Voters Altering Political Landscape." *North Carolina DataNet* 36:2–3.

Saiz, Martin, and Susan E. Clarke. 2004. "Economic Development and Infrastructure Policy." In *Politics in the American States: A Comparative Analysis*, edited by Virginia Gray and Russell L. Hanson, 418–47. Washington D.C.: CQ Press.

West, Darrell M. 2006. "State and Federal E-Government in the United States, 2006." <http://www.insidepolitics.org>. Accessed December 15, 2006.

❖ Contributors

Hunter Bacot is director of the Center for Public Opinion Polling, which conducts the Elon University Poll, and is an associate professor of political science and public administration at Elon, where he specializes in public opinion and public policy. His research has appeared in *American Review of Public Administration, Public Administration Review, Legislative Studies Quarterly, Policy Studies Journal*, and a variety of other journals and edited volumes. He holds a bachelor's degree in political science from the University of North Carolina at Chapel Hill and a doctorate from the University of Tennessee.

Christopher A. Cooper is director of the master of public affairs program and assistant professor of political science and public affairs at Western Carolina University. He holds a bachelor's degree in political science and sociology from Winthrop University and a doctorate from the University of Tennessee. His research on state politics, media and politics, and political behavior has appeared in a number of journals, including *American Politics Research, Policy Studies Journal, Political Research Quarterly, Public Administration Review, Social Science Quarterly*, and *State Politics and Policy Quarterly*.

Thomas F. Eamon teaches political science at East Carolina University. His work on southern politics, North Carolina politics, and the politics of race has appeared in *Social Science Quarterly* and *Southeastern Political Review* as well as other journals. He has also contributed to edited collections and is currently working on a book on North Carolina's political history. He holds a bachelor's degree in political science from the University of the South and a doctorate from the University of North Carolina at Chapel Hill.

Jack D. Fleer is a professor emeritus of political science at Wake Forest University. He has published books, essays, and articles on southern and North Carolina politics over the past half century and has provided frequent commentary for regional, national, and international media. His books include *North Carolina Government and Politics* (University of Nebraska Press) and *Governors Speak* (University Press of America). He holds a bachelor's degree in government from Oklahoma Baptist University and a doctorate from the University of North Carolina at Chapel Hill.

Dennis O. Grady is a professor of political science and director of the Energy Center at Appalachian State University. He holds a bachelor's degree in economics from the University of North Carolina at Chapel Hill and a doctorate from Emory University.

His research on state politics and policy has appeared in a number of journals and research outlets, including *Political Research Quarterly, State and Local Government Review, Review of Public Personnel Administration, Policy Studies Review, Journal of Politics and Policy,* and *The Book of the States.*

Ferrel Guillory is founding director of the Program on Public Life at the University of North Carolina at Chapel Hill, an interdisciplinary project that brings university scholarship to bear on the agenda and leadership in North Carolina and the South. He holds a bachelor's degree in journalism from Loyola University New Orleans and a master's degree from the Columbia University Graduate School of Journalism. Guillory is a lecturer in the UNC School of Journalism and Mass Communication, an adjunct faculty member in public policy, and a senior fellow at MDC, a nonprofit regional research firm in Chapel Hill. Before entering academia, Guillory spent more than twenty years as a reporter, editor, and columnist for the *Raleigh News and Observer*. He has coauthored *The Carolinas: Yesterday, Today, Tomorrow: An Exploration of Social and Economic Trends, 1924–1999* (Duke University Press) and has contributed essays to books on David Duke and the politics of race, on the transition in tobacco regions, and on North Carolina's politics and government. He was inducted into the North Carolina Journalism Hall of Fame in 2007.

Sean Hildebrand is a visiting assistant professor of political science and public affairs at Western Carolina University. He holds a bachelor's degree in political science and a master's degree in public administration from the University of Delaware and is currently completing a doctorate in public administration at North Carolina State University. His primary areas of interest include state and local politics, budgeting, and public policy formation, particularly in the areas of emergency management and homeland security. His dissertation focuses on local jurisdictions and the factors affecting their formation of emergency management policy and counterterrorism preparation.

Jonathan Kanipe holds a bachelor's degree in political science from the University of North Carolina at Chapel Hill and a master of public administration degree from Appalachian State University. He presented a paper at the American Political Science Association's 2005 annual conference on the politics of electricity deregulation and completed his capstone project at Appalachian State on the impact of wind farms on local property values. He currently serves as the town manager of Catawba, North Carolina.

H. Gibbs Knotts is an associate professor and department head of political science and public affairs at Western Carolina University. He holds a bachelor's degree in political science from the University of North Carolina at Chapel Hill and a doctorate from Emory University. His research interests include southern politics, political behavior, public policy, and community development. His work has appeared in *Journal of Politics, Public Administration Review, Social Science Quarterly*, and a variety of other journals and edited collections.

Adam J. Newmark is an assistant professor and director of the Department of Political Science and Criminal Justice's honors program at Appalachian State University. His teaching and research interests include state and local politics, political parties and interest groups, public opinion, and public policy. He has authored or coauthored articles appearing in the *Journal of Politics, State Politics and Policy Quarterly, Social Science Quarterly, Legislative Studies Quarterly*, and *Review of Policy Research*. He holds a bachelor's degree in political science from the University of Florida and a doctorate from the University of North Carolina at Chapel Hill.

Charles Prysby is a professor of political science at the University of North Carolina at Greensboro. He has coauthored *Political Choices: A Study of Elections and Voters* (Holt, Rinehart, and Winston) and *Political Behavior and the Local Context* (Praeger) and coedited *Southern Political Party Activists: Patterns of Conflict and Change, 1991–2001* (University Press of Kentucky). He has also produced a series of computer-based instructional packages on voting behavior in presidential elections (part of the American Political Science Association's SETUPS series). He has also authored or coauthored numerous articles on elections, voting behavior, and political parties. He holds a bachelor's degree in political science from Illinois Institute of Technology and a doctorate from Michigan State University.

Ruth Ann Strickland is a professor of political science at Appalachian State University. She holds a bachelor's degree in political science from Campbell University and a doctorate from the University of South Carolina. She became a member of the College of Arts and Sciences' Academy of Outstanding Teachers in 1998. Since coming to Appalachian State in 1987, she has published more than twenty peer-reviewed academic journal articles on a variety of topics, including cameras in the courtroom, abortion politics, sexual harassment, judicial federalism, mandated drug treatment, fetal abuse, and the U.S. constitutional amendment process. She has also published eight essays and four books, the latest of which is *Restorative Justice* (Lang).

James H. Svara is a professor in the School of Public Affairs and director of the Center for Urban Innovation at Arizona State University. He holds a bachelor's degree in history from the University of Kentucky and a doctorate from Yale University. His research and teaching focus on local government politics, management, and ethics. He has written numerous journal articles and essays, and his books include *Official Leadership in the City: Patterns of Conflict and Cooperation* (Oxford University Press) and *Two Decades of Continuity and Change in American City Councils* (National League of Cities). He previously served on the faculty of the University of North Carolina at Greensboro, where he directed the public administration program, and at North Carolina State University, where he served as director of the public administration program from 1990 to 1998 and as head of the department from 1998 to 2005. He was a visiting scholar at Southern Denmark University in 1998 and 2006.

Timothy Vercellotti is assistant director of the Center for Public Interest Polling at Rutgers University. He previously served as an assistant professor of political science and director of the Elon University Poll. Before entering academia, Vercellotti covered local and state government and politics as a reporter for the *Pittsburgh Press* and the *Raleigh News and Observer*. Vercellotti holds a master's degree in journalism from Columbia University and a doctorate in political science from the University of North Carolina at Chapel Hill.

❖ Index